AMERICAN LABOR

A PICTORIAL SOCIAL HISTORY

By M. B. Schnapper

Public Affairs Press, Washington, D. C.

TO HENRY C. FLEISHER
*whose devotion to and knowledge about the
American labor movement has enriched
almost every page in this book*

Published by Public Affairs Press
419 New Jersey Ave., S.E., Washington, D. C. 20003

Copyright, 1972, by M. B. Schnapper
Printed in the United States of America

Library of Congress Catalog Card No. 72-87531

Introduction

There are many books which celebrate the glories of our Presidents, our generals, our inventive geniuses, and our industrial leaders. This is a book of a different sort. It is a tribute to the working men and women of our nation.

This timely book reminds us of a much neglected aspect of American history—the role of the working people who for 200 years have toiled anonymously in factories and fields, who have furnished the skills and strength that created a thriving nation out of an untamed wilderness, and who have been the backbone of our democratic society.

To a far greater degree than is generally realized, most of the high living standards and cherished rights we now enjoy arose largely out of the struggles and triumphs of the American labor movement depicted so vividly in these pages. Free public education, the 8-hour-work-day, and statutory protection from economic insecurity, for example, did not just fall into our laps. It took many years of persistent struggle by workers, their unions, and their allies to make the gains and lay the foundations for the American way of life that is ours today.

This is not to say that all of the labor movement has invariably been on the side of the angels. What we must not forget, however, is that the nation as a whole has immensely benefited from the solidarity of the brave and simple men and women who fought long and hard for human rights above property rights.

No book of this type can possibly be a completely comprehensive and wholly unbiased history. Its great merit is that it sheds much new light on the trials, tribulations, and aspirations of the American worker throughout the nation's development. It is a genuinely authentic story because it is based primarily on contemporary material with a memorable "you are there" quality. Moreover, the text has the virtue of being highly relevent to the illustrations; perhaps Mr. Schnapper has leaned too heavily on eye-witness accounts and the opinions of historians but they fill out the story with authoritativeness and objectivity.

If, as the saying goes, a picture is worth a thousand words, Mr. Schnapper has brought to life in these pages a story far more informative than a whole shelf of books on the subject. *American Labor* is an outstanding contribution to our historical annals.

Mr. Schnapper has provided us with a graphic social record of the country's progress and problems. He rightly focuses our attention on the working people. He shows us how they lived, how they worked, how they fought for themselves, for their children, and for the realization of the American dream. It is an inspiring story every American should know and one in which we can all take pride.

There are many surprising, even startling, things in this book. Especially arresting are its revelations about the manner and extent to which the once powerful but short-lived Knights of Labor resorted to elaborate secrecy in order to avoid repression. The documents on pages 135-38 are made public for the first time.

Almost equally interesting are other unique documents and pictures that deserve special mention:

• A cogent broadside about the need for work relief in 1768.

• President Washington's precisely phrased "help wanted" ad for servants.

• Illustrations concerning the rise of local workingmen's parties during the 1820's.

• The offer of a $10 reward for the return of a runaway apprentice who later became the nation's President (Andrew Johnson).

• Rare Mathew Brady photographs of artisans employed by the Army's Quartermaster Corps during the Civil War.

• A blatant blacklisting letter Cyrus McCormick received from another employer in 1872.

• Crude anti-Chinese propaganda of the 1870's.

• John Barrymore's forceful drawings about exploitation of workers.

• Haunting photographs showing children working in unsafe mines and unsanitary canneries.

• Shocking pictures about the incredible Ludlow massacre of 1913.

• A candid camera photo of Samuel Gompers taken by a company detective assigned to shadow him.

• Surveillance reports about the private lives of workers during the 1920's.

• Searing pictures of jobless victims of the depression Thirties.

• A photo of factory workers grieving over the assassination of President Kennedy.

These are but a few of the many extraordinary illustrations Mr. Schnapper has brought together after ten years of intensive research in the archives of historical societies, libraries and trade unions throughout the country. His was clearly a labor of love and the end result is a book that greatly enhances our knowledge and understanding of a rich but too long neglected aspect of American history.

HARRISON WILLIAMS
Chairman of the U. S. Senate
Committee on Labor and Public Welfare

Acknowledgments

In the course of preparing this book, my research was greatly facilitated by the generous cooperation of the following organizations and individuals:

American Federation of Labor and Congress of Industrial Organizations—Saul Miller, Jean Weber, Mary Carr, and Stuart Brock.

U. S. Department of Labor—Joseph Loftus, Jonathan Grossman, Lillian Hamrick, Margaret Brickett, Sidney Kasper, Patrick Gannon, John Leslie, and Bert Sisson.

Labor History Archives of Wayne State University—Philip Mason and Warner Pflug.

International Ladies Garment Workers Union—Leon Stein.

Amalgamated Clothing Workers—Connie Kopelov.

Tamiment Library of New York University—Dorothy Swanson.

State Historical Society of Wisconsin—Paul Vanderbilt and Marsha Peters.

Smithsonian Institution—Philip Bishop, John Hoffman, Robert Vogel, Herbert Collins, and Melvin Jackson.

Library of Congress—Alan Fern, Virginia Daiker, and Milton Kaplan.

It was also my good fortune to benefit from cordial cooperation extended by:

New York Historical Society—James Heslin.

New York Public Library—Lenore Cowan.

Museum of the City of New York—Charlotte La Rue.

New York Department of Labor—Gloria Weinrich.

National Labor Relations Board—Lempi Wickline and Sam Zagoria.

California Historical Society—Lee Burtis.

Massachusetts Historical Society—Malcolm Freiberg.

Illinois Labor History Society—Leslie Orear.

University of Michigan Library—Edward Weber.

United Auto Workers—Frank Wallick, Gary Busch, and Leo Goodman.

International Association of Machinists and Aerospace Workers—Gordon Cole and Robert Rodden.

United Brotherhood of Carpenters—P. E. Terzick.

Boot and Shoe Workers Union—William Scanlon.

National Maritime Union—Bernard Raskin.

Textile Workers Union—Irving Kahan.

United Steelworkers of America—Raymond Pasnick.

Culver Pictures—Roberts Jackson.

Brown Brothers—Thomas Collins.

Bettman Archives—Otto Bettman

For editorial assistance I am exceedingly grateful to Theodore Watts, Kenneth Fiester, and Robert Cooney.

Very special thanks go to Thomas Morley, Strod Bock, and Thomas Curtis for their artistic contributions.

Edgar Morgan and Harold Griffin were most helpful in making available their files of Harpers Weekly, Judge, Puck, and other nineteenth century magazines.

Among those who were generous in their advice and assistance in a variety of ways were Wilbur Cohen, Oliver and Esther Peterson, Ruben Levin, Arch Mercey, Ernest Doerfler, Joseph Glazer, Eugene Berlin, Louis Segadelli, David J. Saposs, Wesley McCune, Jack Barbash, Harry Douty, Frank Palmer, Derek Fox, Joseph Cooper, Harry Barnard, Frank Cormier, Charles R. Baker, and Siert Riepma.

Throughout the book's gestation period Walter B. Wheeler and E. William Marclay were invaluable aides.

Of the scores of works about the labor movement I have consulted, the following were especially valuable: *Labor in America* by Foster Rhea Dulles (Crowell, 1966), *Organized Labor in American History* by Philip Taft (Harper & Row, 1960), *Toil and Trouble* by Thomas R. Brooks (Delacorte Press, 1964), and *A History of American Labor* by Joseph G. Rayback (Free Press, 1966).

M. B. SCHNAPPER

"All that serves labor serves the nation." —Abraham Lincoln

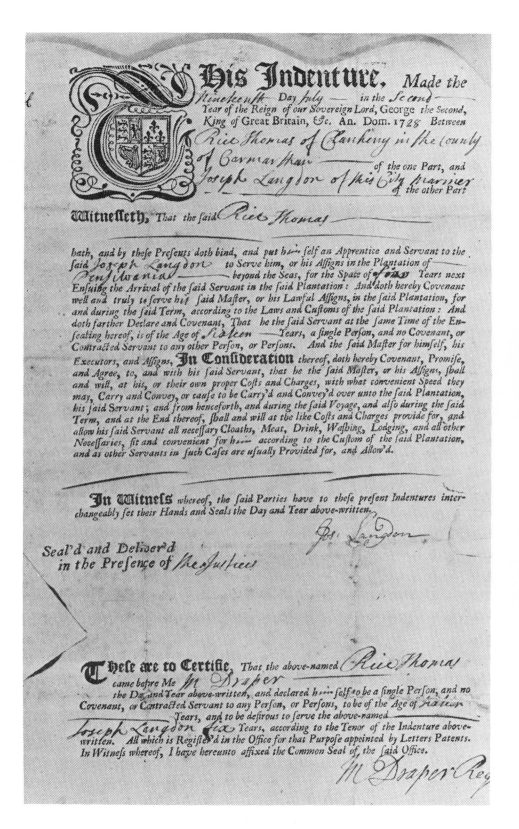

**HUMAN
BONDAGE**

Apart from Negro slaves, many (perhaps most) of the working people of colonial America were indentured servants who bound themselves to employment for three to seven years in return for their passage across the Atlantic. Under the terms of this typical indenture contract of 1726, Rice Thomas was required to serve as a farm laborer for six years.

THE INDENTURE SYSTEM

For all its evils, the indenture system was a necessity from Britain's viewpoint because manpower was in extremely short supply throughout the colonies. The hardships experienced by the earliest settlers of Jamestown, Virginia, were due in large part, as Captain John Smith complained, to the presence of too many "gents" unable or unwilling to do hard work. He so despaired of establishing a stable colony that he advised his London Company backers: "When you send again, I entreat you rather send but thirty carpenters, husbandmen, gardners, fishermen, masons and diggers of trees' roots . . . than a thousand such as we have."

To provide the labor urgently needed by the colonies, England sanctioned arrangements under which workingmen placed themselves in bondage until they had paid off the cost of their transportation. Many, however, were duped by extravagant promises and claims made by recruiters unpopularly nicknamed "crimps". The unemployed, the poor, and the credulous were easily led to believe that America was a place "where food shall drop into their mouthes," where they would be paid high wages after serving out their indentures, and where free land was to be had for the taking. Women and children were often kidnapped or hustled aboard ships against their will and sold into bondage. And a countless number of vagrants, debtors or petty criminals were sentenced to involuntary servitude.

Indentured servants, both voluntary and involuntary, led a hard life. For legal purposes their status was little different from that of slaves who were treated with greater consideration because, as permanent property, they were more valuable.

"None," according to historian John McMaster, "could marry without the consent of the master or mistress under penalty of an addition of one year's service to the time set forth in the indenture. They were worked hard, were dressed in the cast-off clothes of their owners, and might be flogged as often as the master or mistress thought necessary. If they ran away, at least two days might be added to their time of service for each day

they were absent. Father, mother and children could be sold to different buyers . . . [some] were bought in lots of 50 or more by a class of speculators known as 'soul drivers,' who drove them through the country like so many cattle and sold them for what they would bring."

The cheap labor provided by the slaves and indentured servants operated to the disadvantage of the worker who could choose his own job. "Competition of this sort," McMaster emphasized, "made the lot of the free laborer hard indeed, but it was made harder still by the usages of the time. He worked from sunrise to sunset, earned less wages in winter than in summer, was paid at irregular intervals, and if not paid at all had no lien on the product of his labor. If he were so unfortunate as to fall into debt, though it were for but a sixpence or penny, he might at the will of his creditor be torn from his family and cast into jail, there to remain until the debt and the prison charges were paid or he died of hunger or disease."

Advertisements about the arrival and escape of indentured servants frequently competed for attention in colonial newspapers. At the left is an announcement in the Virginia Gazette, March 28, 1771. At the top are extracts from the Pennsylvania Packet and General Advertiser, February 10, 1772.

The highly profitable tobacco trade fastened slavery on the colonies. The first Negroes brought to Virginia were treated as though they were indentured servants but slavery was recognized by law in 1670. "All servants not being Christians imported into this colony by shipping" were declared to be "slaves for their lives." Notwithstanding this qualified phrasing, the descendants of slaves inherited the same status. The above wharf scene is an illustration from a map drawn by Thomas Jefferson's father, Peter. The varied labors required by the processing of tobacco were quite similar to those shown below in a seventeenth century print depicting the chores performed in a typical plantation "factory-yard" in the West Indies.

1. Petum [Tobacco]-house.	4. Negro who rolls it.	8. The Press.	12. The kitchen
2. Negro who tears the tobacco apart.	5. Negro who scrapes the manioc [cassava]	**FACTORY-YARD** 9. Negress sifting the flour.	13. Cassava drying.
3. Negro who twists it.	6. Mill to grind the manioc.	10. Negress who cooks the cassava.	14. Corozo-tree.
	7. Ancient method of grinding the manioc.	11. The house of the master.	

The Earliest Known Illustration Showing An American Tobacco-Factory. From the HISTOIRE GENERALE DES ANTILLES, by Father Jean Baptiste Du Tertre, Paris, 1667-1671.

ARTICLES AND REGULATIONS

OF

FRIENDLY SOCIETY

HOUSE CARPENTERS,

THE

OF TRADESMEN,

In the City of *New-York*,

Made and agreed upon the 10th Day of *March*, in the Year of our LORD, 1767,

For the USES and CONSIDERATIONS herein after mentioned.

WE whose Names are hereunto subscribed, in the Book of Proceedings of this our Society, DO, out of christian Love and true Friendship, promise to assist each other as far as in us lies, and keep a strict Observance of the following RULES and ORDERS of this our SOCIETY, so that they may prove as beneficial and useful as possible.

I.

EVERY Person that desires Admittance into this Society, must profess himself a House-Carpenter, free from all bodily Distempers, and between the Age of Forty and Twenty-one Years.

II.

THERE shall be one President, one Secretary, and one Clerk, who shall be appointed and elected annually, on the first *Tuesday* in *January*, by a Majority of Voices of this Society, or the old Ones confirmed in their respective Offices for one Year longer ; also two Stewards, who shall act as such for one Month, to take their Turns alternately, as their Names are subscribed in the List of Members of this our Society. As also there shall be belonging to this Society, one Chest or Box, with three different Locks and Keys, which shall be disposed of in Manner following, viz. The President shall have one Key, and the two Stewards shall each have one Key, and the Chest or Box shall be kept in the House where the Society meets, the Landlord giving good and sufficient Security for the said Chest or Box, with the Money and Bonds therein contained, from whence it shall not be removed without some satisfactory Reason, and by and with the Concurrence of a Majority of this Society.

III.

ALL the Affairs relative to this Society, shall be registered in our Book of Transactions, by our Secretary or Clerk, who shall keep our Accounts in a fair and concise Manner, so as to render a true State thereof when required ; and all the Members shall have an indubitable Right to inspect the same as often as they shall see fit.

IV.

ANY Person desirous of becoming a Member of this Society, shall first give in his Name to the President, Secretary, Clerk, or either of the Stewards, who shall examine into his Character, and report the same to the Secretary the next monthly Meeting, when they shall all canvas the Matter of Report. and object or vote his Admittance, by Majority of Voices ; if in the Affirmative, he shall be admitted as a Member of this Society, subscribing his Name, and paying to the common Stock, the Sum of Four Shillings, of which Benefit he is not to be entitled until he has been a Member of this Society for one Year.

V.

ON the first *Tuesday* in every Month, there shall be held a monthly Meeting of this Society, when each Member (excepting the Secretary and Clerk) shall pay into the common Stock, One Shilling ; besides which, every Person then present, without Exception, shall pay for the Expence of the Night, during Club Hours, Six-pence: And any Member neglecting to give his Attendance at these our monthly Meetings, and paying the aforesaid Sums of Money, shall forfeit for every such Default to the common Stock, Six-pence ; and if any neglect or refuse the Payment of the aforesaid Fines, after three succeeding Meetings, he shall be expelled this Society : Nevertheless, if he will again return, and deposite in our common Fund, the Sum of Eight Shillings, with all his Arrearages, he shall be re-admitted a Member of this Society.

VI.

THE President, Secretary, Clerk, and two Stewards, shall duly attend our monthly Meetings and annual Feasts ; but if they should be sick, or have some special Reason whereby they are necessarily detained, then they (the President and two Stewards) shall send their Keys by some one or other of the Members, or a good and sufficient Hand ; if the Presidents Key, it shall be delivered into the Hands of one of the then present Members, who shall be appointed a Deputy President by a Majority of Voices for the Night being ; and should it be either or both of the Stewards Keys, they shall be delivered into the Hands of the Person or Persons who are to succeed to that Office, agreeable to Article the Second, in order that the Chest or Box may be opened in proper Time, without any Let, Hindrance, or Interruption of this Society : But should any or either of the before-mentioned Officers neglect to give their Attendance, or refuse to act in their respective Offices, agreeable to any or either of these our Rules and Articles, he shall, for every such Default, be fined and pay into the common Stock, the Sum of Four Shillings, or be expelled this Society.

VII.

IF any of our Members fall sick, or through Age or Accidents are rendered incapable of getting his Livelihood, he shall, after Six Days Illness, give proper Notice to the President, or either of the Stewards, and the Stewards shall visit the sick Member twice in the Week, and by Order of the President, shall pay unto the impotent Member, the Sum of Ten Shillings, at the End of every seven Days, after due Application having been made ; and if the said Stewards shall neglect or refuse to do as aforesaid, they shall respectively be fined and deposite in the common Stock, for every such Default, the Sum of Four Shillings, or expelled this Society : But if any Members Sickness exceed the Term of three Months, then he shall receive such a continual Allowance as shall be judged proper by a Committee of Six Members, appointed by Majority of Voices for that Purpose ; which Allowance shall be administered to the infirm Member by the Stewards, as is before directed.

VIII.

ANY Member receiving the Benefits allowed in the preceeding Article, that shall begin to work and carry on Business before he hath given due Notice of his Recovery to one of the Stewards, shall be expelled this Society.

IX.

IF any of our Members should go in the Country and fall sick, or be by any other unforeseen Accident rendered incapable of supporting himself, he shall transmit to some one of the Members of this Society, a Certificate, signed by two or more credible Witnesses, before a Justice of the Peace, or the Parson of the Parish where he then resides, before he shall be entitled to the Benefits resulting to him as a Member of this Society.

X.

ON the Death of any of our Members, there shall be allowed for his funeral Expence, the Sum of Four Pounds, to be taken out of the principal Stock ; and in order to supply that Deficiency, each Member, at the next Meeting, shall pay One Shilling extraordinary : But should any die without the District of this City and County, there shall be transmitted to this Society, a Certificate of his Death, as prescribed in the preceeding Ninth Article, in order to their receiving the Benefits before-mentioned.

XI.

WHEN any of our Members die within this City, Information thereof shall be brought to the two Stewards, and the said Stewards shall give proper Notice to as many Members of this Society as they can, to attend the Funeral of the deceased Member, for which the said Stewards shall receive the Sum of Four Shillings each ; and if any Member, that is duly warned as aforesaid, shall neglect to attend, they shall forfeit Six-pence to the common Stock.

XII.

IF any Member calls for Liquor without the Approbation of the Stewards, he shall pay for the same himself ; and if the Stewards call for more than what each Mans allotted Quota will pay, they shall make good the Deficiency.

XIII.

IF any of our Members bring an Accusation against another Member, that might indanger or cause him to be expelled, if he that brings the Accusation cannot, or does not make good his Assertion, he shall forfeit Eight Shillings to the Box.

XIV.

IF any Member presume to curse or swear, or cometh disguised in Liquor and breed Disturbance, or if any be absent half an Hour after Time affixed for Meeting, or refuse Silence when commanded three Times by the Steward, or interrupteth a Member in his Discourse at a publick Meeting, or promoteth Gaming at Club Hours, he or they so offending, shall pay to the common Stock, for every such Default, Six-pence ; and for actual Gaming, shall forfeit Two Shillings.

XV.

THE appointed Times of monthly Meetings of this Society, shall be in Manner following, viz.

March,	Half an Hour after 6 o'Clock,
April,	7 o'Clock,
May,	Half an Hour after 7 o'Clock,
June, July, and *August*,	8 o'Clock,
September,	Half an Hour after 7 o'Clock,
October,	7 o'Clock,
November,	Half an Hour after 6 o'Clock,
December, January and *February*	6 o'Clock.

XVI.

ANY Member that shall be fined, or shall be in Arrears agreeable to any of the within mentioned Articles, and does not pay them in three succeeding Meetings from the Time the said Forfeitures commenced, such Member shall be totally excluded.

XVII.

NO Person that hath any Distemper wherewith he hath been afflicted from his Infancy, or any Disease or Sickness he hath brought on himself by a loose and disorderly Life, shall be entitled to the Benefits resulting to him as a Member of this Society : Any Disputes that shall happen relative to this or any the Affairs of this Society, shall be finally determined and ended by a Majority of Voices of the then present Members.

XVIII.

THE several Members of this Society shall, as much as in them lies, endeavour to establish and make permanent the same, and shall not be dissolved but by and with the Consent and Concurrence of at least Eight to One of a full Meeting of all the Members thereof.

XIX.

IT is agreed upon by the Members of this Society, that once in a Year there shall be made ready a Supper for an annual Feast, which shall be on the 10th Day of *March* ; and to defray the Expence thereof, each Member of this Society, shall deposite One Shilling extraordinary at their preceeding monthly Meeting.

XX.

LASTLY, If any Articles or Regulations should hereafter be made, that should be thought requisite, and prove more binding than the foregoing, such Articles and Regulations shall be ingrossed in our Book of Transactions, and shall be as binding on each of us as these our printed Articles.

New York carpenters agreed to these rules for their mutual benefit in 1767.

BRITISH RESTRAINTS

In spite of British efforts to discourage the colonies from becoming self-sufficient, many small industries were thriving. When the above drawing was made in 1766 Boston was already a bustling commercial center in which artisans found a ready market for their skills.

As far as England was concerned, the colonies existed primarily for the advancement of its interests rather than their own—a policy bitterly resented by merchants, farmers, and workers.

The chief means by which Britain carried out her restrictive economic policy were the Navigation Acts placing control over all goods exported from or imported into the colonies. Thus England could to a large degree exercise a monopoly on commerce, collect high duties, and impose restraints on American growth. However, production of commodities needed or desired by Britain was encouraged. While the making of pig iron was sanctioned, for example, the erection of mills for the rolling of iron was forbidden—as indicated in the proclamation at the side.

Products such as woolen goods and beaver hats could not be exported to England or even shipped from one colony to another.

British restrictions were not always enforced and were frequently evaded, but the net effect was friction that contributed to the American Revolution.

By the HONOURABLE
JAMES HAMILTON, Esq;

Lieutenant Governor, and Commander in Chief, of the Province of *Pennsylvania*, and Counties of *Newcastle*, *Kent* and *Sussex*, on *Delaware*,

A PROCLAMATION.

WHEREAS by an Act of Parliament, passed in the Twenty-third Year of His Majesty's Reign, entituled, *An Act to encourage the Importation of Pig and Bar Iron from His Majesty's Colonies in America, and to prevent the Erection of any Mill, or other Engine, for slitting or rolling of Iron, or any plating Forge to work with a Tilt Hammer, or any Furnace for making Steel, in any of the said Colonies*; it is enacted, " That from and after the Twenty-fourth Day of " *June*, in the Year of our Lord One Thousand Seven Hundred and Fifty, every Go- " vernor, Lieutenant Governor, and Commander in Chief, of any of His Majesty's " Colonies in *America*, shall forthwith transmit to the Commissioners for Trade and " Plantations, a Certificate under his Hand and Seal of Office, containing a particular " Account of every Mill or Engine for slitting and rolling of Iron, and every plating " Forge to work with a Tilt Hammer, and every Furnace for making Steel, at the " Time of the Commencement of this Act, erected in his Colony; expressing also " in the said Certificate such of them as are used, and the Name or Names of the " Proprietor or Proprietors of each such Mill, Engine, Forge and Furnace, and the " Place where each such Mill, Engine, Forge and Furnace, is erected, and the Num- " ber of Engines, Forges and Furnaces, in the said Colony." To the End therefore

GIVEN under my Hand, and the Great Seal of the Province of Pennsylvania, *at* Philadelphia, *this Sixteenth Day of* August, *in the Twenty-fourth Year of the Reign of our Sovereign Lord* GEORGE *the Second, King of Great-Britain, France and* Ireland, &c. *and in the Year of our Lord,* 1750.

By His HONOUR's Command,
RICHARD PETERS, *Secretary*

JAMES HAMILTON.

GOD Save the KING.

PHILADELPHIA: Printed by B. FRANKLIN, Printer to the Province. MDCCL.

11

Proposals for carrying on a Manufacture in the Town of BOSTON, for Employing the Poor of said Town.

WHEREAS for many Years past, there have been, and still are great Numbers of the Inhabitants of Boston, very poor, and altho' in Health, are unable to support themselves for want of Employ, and these so daily increasing, that the Expence and Charge of the Town for their Maintenance is almost insupportable, the same being the last Year near *Nineteen Thousand Pounds* Old Tenor ; and the Town having at their general Meetings several Times taken this Affair into their serious Consideration, did on the 28th of October last, appoint a Committee " to consider of some Mea-" sures for employing the Poor, by reviving the " Linen Manufacture, or in any other Ways that " should be thought beneficial". And the said Committee on the 28th of December last, reported to the Town, their Sentiments as to the carrying on the Linen Manufacture, and that such Difficulties must necessarily attend it, as it could not be undertaken at present in a Factory, without incurring a great Loss, and the good Intention of the Town, viz. employing the Poor, be defeated ; but that upon an Alteration of some Circumstances relating to that Manufacture, they were in hopes, it might be carried on to Advantage. The said Committee in a second Report on the 13th of January last, recommended to the Town the carrying on a Manufacture for making of Duck or Sail Cloth, which might be done with less Expence, would be a more constant Employ for the Poor, and they judged more beneficial to the Publick, than the Linen, provided suitable Encouragement was given to such Persons as should appear to undertake the same on their own Account and Risque, viz.

First, That the Government grant the Use of the Manufactory-House in Boston, to the Undertakers, for a certain Term, or so long as they may continue to carry on the Manufacture of Duck, Check, or Plain Linen.

Secondly, That a Sum be immediately raised by Subscription, to be given to the Undertakers, for purchasing Looms, Wheels, and other Utensils, necessary for carrying on said Manufacture, learning of Spinners, repairing the House, and such other incidental Charges as may arise.

Thirdly, That as the Prospect of Advantage to the Undertakers, is not sufficient to induce any to engage in it, without some Assistance from such as are of Ability to afford it ; and as it will be necessary for them to hire a considerable Sum of Money, for a Stock to carry on this Manufacture, for which they must give their own personal Security, and pay the Interest thereof : The Committee proposed, that a Subscription should be opened, for the annual Payment of such a Sum, as each Person should incline to give, for the Space of five Years at least ; and this to be given to the Undertakers, to enable them to pay the Interest of the Money they may borrow for this Purpose.

Which Report after the most mature Consideration, was unanimously accepted by the Town, and thereupon it was then

Voted, That the Committee be desired to procure Undertakers for the Execution of the Scheme ; and when Undertakers shall appear, " the Town recom-" mend to the Inhabitants, a Subscription for the " Purposes aforesaid". Also,

Voted, " That the Gentlemen who Represent the " Town in General Assembly, be desired to counte-" nance and forward all in their Power, any Appli-" cation that may be made to the Court, by the " Undertakers, for their Assistance in said Under-" taking".

And no Persons having as yet appeared to undertake this Business, although Application has been made to several. And We the SUBSCRIBERS, who were part of the said Committee, being sensible of the Advantages that will arise to the Town, from such an Undertaking, in case it is pursued with Resolution, and can be established ; informed the Gentlemen the Select-Men, that rather than the good End intended by the Town should be frustrated, We would undertake the carrying on said Manufacture, upon the Encouragement mentioned in the Committee's Report ; and the Select-Men having expressed their great Satisfaction upon our engaging in it :

We would now inform the Publick, that we have procured the Manufactory-House in the Common for seven Years, for that Purpose, on keeping the same in Repair at our Expence. This House will contain about twenty-five Looms, in which 1400 or 1500 Pieces of Duck may be made in a Year ; and that we hope to make that Quantity every Year, unless we shall find, that Check or Plain Linen, can be made to equal Advantage : And should this be the Case, we shall with Pleasure improve Part of the Stock in that Manufacture, provided the late Society will grant us the Looms, and other Utensils for that Purpose, now in the Factory.

We are well informed Duck has been made here of a superiour Quality to any Imported from Russia, and for about the same Price, as that Sort of Duck costs

A 1768 appeal for community support of work relief for the needy.

THE SONS OF LIBERTY FIGHT
FOR THEIR INALIENABLE RIGHTS

In the forefront of the fight against Britain's unpopular measures were the Sons of Liberty, composed chiefly of workingmen. Led by merchants and professional men, they conducted boycott campaigns against goods made in England and organized protest demonstrations in Boston, New York, Philadelphia, and Charleston.

Historians credit the militancy of small tradesmen, artisans, and mechanics—derided as the "Mobility" by Tories—with keeping the revolutionary movement alive when cautiously inclined merchants faltered.

"The popular party in Boston so astutely led by Samuel Adams," Foster Dulles points out, "was in large part made up of wharfingers, shipwrights, bricklayers, weavers and tanners who were equally opposed to rule by British officials or colonial aristocrats. The Sons of Liberty, and later the local Committees of Correspondence, were generally recruited from workers from the docks, shipyards and ropewalks."

Hostility between workers and British troops precipitated the Boston Massacre of 1770 that contributed to the outbreak of the Revolutionary War. Since the Red Coats quartered in the city were allowed to accept private employment when they were not on duty, their competition was strongly resented, all the more so because the troops were willing to accept less compensation than prevailing wage rates.

In his authoritative book, "Government and Labor in Early America," Prof. Richard B. Morris of Columbia University tells what happened:

"On the second of March 1770, three British privates in the 29th Regiment went to the ropewalk belonging to John Gray looking for work. A journeyman by the name of William Green insulted one of them, and the soldiers challenged him to a fight. After being worsted in fisticuffs, the soldiers ran back to the barracks in the immediate neighborhood and returned with several companions, who were driven off. The Red Coats then reappeared, reinforced to the number of some thirty or forty, armed with clubs and cutlasses, but the thirteen or fourteen hands of Gray's ropewalk were joined by fellow workers from neighboring ropewalks to the number of perhaps nine or ten, and the assault was again beaten off. Gray, the master, alarmed at the turn of events, made a personal complaint to Colonel Dalrymple, warning him that his soldiers were determined to even their score with the ropewalk workers. When Dalrymple placed the blame for instigating the riot upon Gray's journeyman, Gray discharged the accused on Monday morning, March 5th.

"Testimony is virtually unanimous that the soldiers nursed their humiliation at the hands of the ropewalks journeymen and were making rash threats of avenging the insult promptly. On the evening of the fifth some British soldiers sallied out of Smith's barracks, beat up a number of persons, and were finally driven back to their barracks. Actually the incident followed the taunt of an apprentice boy hurled at a soldier, charging him with not paying a barber's bill to the lad's master. The soldier struck the apprentice, a general altercation ensued, and the exasperated soldiery fired, killing a number of persons, including Sam Gray, who had actively participated in the affray at the ropewalk on the preceding Friday. As to whether Gray was recognized and deliberately shot, or hit without special design, there was a conflict of testimony. Killroy, one of the soldiers positively identified as firing at the crowd, was known to have participated in the fight at the ropewalks, as was Warren, another soldier."

The Boston Council's account of these events placed blame on the Red Coats. According to the Council "the affair which more immediately was introductory to the said Massacre was a quarrell between some Soldiers of the 29th Regiment and certain Rope-makers at the Ropewalk of one Mr. Gray. In the contest the Soldiers were worsted: and this reflecting, as they thought, on the honour of the Regiment there was a Combination among them to take vengeance on the Town indiscriminately. Of such a combination there is satisfactory proof."

A DEMOCRATIC NATION EMERGES

What had begun as a war in behalf of the "rights of Englishmen" and the redress of grievances soon became a truly Revolutionary War in which men fought and died to throw off the yoke of British monarchy and control their own destiny.

The new nation faced many trying problems. For all the lofty sentiments in the Declaration of Independence there were, to be sure, many inequalities throughout the thirteen states—the inequality of rich and poor, of black and white, of men and women. Yet less than a year after Cornwallis' surrender a Frenchman turned American citizen could offer this glowing, if somewhat exaggerated, account of life in America:

"He [the immigrant] does not find, as in Europe, a crowded society, where every place is overstocked; he does not feel that perpetual collision of parties, that difficulty of beginning, that contention which oversets so many. There is room for everybody in America. Has he any particular talent or industry? He exerts it in order to procure a livelihood, and it succeeds. Is he a merchant? The avenues of trade are infinite. Is he eminent in any respect? He will be employed and respected. Does he love a country life? Pleasant farms present themselves; he may purchase what he wants, and thereby become an American farmer. Is he a laborer, sober and industrious? He need not go many miles, nor receive many informations before he will be hired, well fed at the table of his employer, and paid four or five times more than he can get in Europe. Does he want uncultivated lands? Thousands of acres present themselves, which he may purchase cheap. Whatever be his talents or inclinations, if they are moderate, he may . . . satisfy them."

When at last the Constitution became the law of the land there were celebrations up and down the eastern seaboard. In Philadelphia, where the document was drawn up, a grand parade took place on July 4, 1788. Katherine Shippen has provided a vivid description of the procession.

"Behind the military, behind the bands and the allegory, behind the handsome copy of the Constitution, came the real life of the procession, and the cries of the spectators mounted to a roar as they saw workers and journeymen of every trade, craft, and profession go swinging by. Here walked the architects and house carpenters (four hundred and fifty of them). Then came the Manufacturing Society. They had a carriage thirty feet long on which were a carding machine worked by two persons, a spinning machine of eighty spindles worked by a woman, a lace loom on which a man was weaving a kind of cotton cloth with a fly shuttle. On the cart behind these the people could see . . . the latest devices in the textile industry.

"Behind the textile exhibit marched the shipmasters. They carried quadrants, trumpets, spyglasses, charts—all the tools of their trade. And they pulled along a model of the ship Constitution, decorated lavishly with emblems and beautifully painted."

A program about Philadelphia's celebration includes these notations about participants in the parade:

"Cordwainers (6 men actually making shoes, 300 marching) . . . Coach Painters (10 with palettes and pencils in their hands) . . . Cabinet and Chair Makers (a moving workshop with a master, journeyman, and apprentices at work) . . . Brick Makers (over a hundred, with a motto: 'It was found hard in Egypt, but this prospect'—the new government—'makes it easy') . . . Drayman with five barrels of 'Federal Flour' which was afterward delivered to the overseers for the use of the poor . . . Bricklayers (masters and workmen with aprons and trowels) . . . Blacksmiths, Whitesmiths and Nailers (over 200, several of them at work on a moving forge) . . . Potters (a potter's wheel and men at work turning out cups, mugs, and bowls) . . . Breeches Makers and Glovers (58 in buckskin breeches and gloves)."

(At top is a help wanted ad President Washington placed in Dunlop's American Daily Advertiser in 1791.)

14

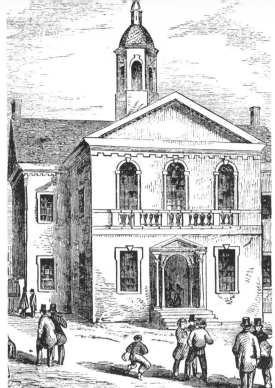

HISTORIC HALL

Selection of Carpenter's Hall in Philadelphia for the meetings of the First Continental Congress in 1774 served as a tacit reminder that the concerns of the nation's founding fathers touched those who worked with their hands.

In Boston, Revolutionary shipyard workers who held secret meetings in Caulkers Hall came to be known as the "caucus"; hence the origin of this political term.

The seal of the Carpenters Company of Philadelphia founded in 1724.

15

IT is agreed between the Maſer, Seamen or Mariners of the *Sloop George of Boston, John Choate* Maſter, now bound from the Port of *Boston, to one or more of the Southern States, and to the West Indies and back again to some Port or Ports, in the United States – Boston being her Port of disch.*

THAT in Conſideration of the monthly or other Wages againſt each reſpective Seaman or Mariner's Name hereunder ſet, they ſeverally ſhall and will perform the above-mentioned Voyage; and the ſaid Maſter doth hereby agree with, and hire the ſaid Seamen or Mariners for the ſaid Voyage, at ſuch monthly Wages, or Prices, to be paid purſuant to this Agreement, and the Laws of the Congreſs of the United States of America, and the Cuſtom and Uſage in the Port of *Boston* And they the ſaid Seamen or Mariners do hereby promiſe and oblige themſelves to do their Duty, and obey the lawful Commands of their Officers on board the ſaid Veſſel, or the Boats thereunto belonging, as become good and faithful Seamen or Mariners; and at all Places where the ſaid Veſſel ſhall put in, or anchor at, during the ſaid Voyage, to do their beſt Endeavours for the Preſervation of the ſaid Veſſel and Cargo, and not to neglect or refuſe doing their Duty by Day or Night, nor ſhall go out of the ſaid Veſſel on board any other Veſſel, or be on Shore, under any Pretence whatſoever, until the abovesaid Voyage be ended, and the Veſſel diſcharged of her Loading, without Leave firſt obtained of the Captain, or commanding Officer on board; that in Default thereof, they will be liable to all the Penalties and Forfeitures mentioned in the Marine Law, enacted for the Government and Regulation of Seamen in the Merchants' Service, in which it is enacted, "That if any Seaman or Mariner ſhall abſent himſelf from on board the Ship or Veſſel without Leave of the Maſter, or Officer commanding on board; and the Mate, or other Officer having Charge of the Log-Book, ſhall make an Entry therein, of the Name of ſuch Seaman or Mariner, on the Day on which he ſhall ſo abſent himſelf; and if ſuch Seaman or Mariner ſhall return to his Duty within forty-eight Hours, ſuch Seaman or Mariner ſhall forfeit three Day's Pay, for every Day which he ſhall ſo abſent himſelf, to be deducted out of his Wages; but if any Seaman or Mariner ſhall abſent himſelf for more than forty-eight Hours at one Time, he ſhall forfeit all the Wages due to him, and all his Goods and Chattels which were on board the ſaid Ship or Veſſel, or in any Store where they may have been lodged, at the Time of his Deſertion, to the Uſe of the Owners of the Ship or Veſſel; and moreover ſhall be liable to pay to him or them, all Damages which he or they may ſuſtain, by being obliged to hire other Seamen or Mariners in his or their Place."——And it is further agreed, by both Parties, that each and every lawful Command which the ſaid Maſter ſhall think neceſſary hereafter to iſſue for the effectual Government of the ſaid Veſſel, ſuppreſſing Immorality and Vice of all Kinds, be ſtrictly complied with, under the Penalty of the Perſon or Perſons' diſobeying, forfeiting his or their whole Wages, or Hire, together with every Thing belonging to him or them, on board ſaid Veſſel. And it is further agreed on, that no Officer or Seaman, belonging to the ſaid Veſſel, ſhall demand, or be intitled to his Wages, or any Part thereof, until the Arrival of the ſaid Veſſel at the above-mentioned Port of Diſcharge, and her Cargo delivered. And it is hereby further agreed between the Maſter and Officers of the ſaid Veſſel, that whatever Apparel, Furniture and Stores each of them may receive into their Charge belonging to the ſaid Veſſel, ſhall be accounted for on her Return; and in Caſe any Thing ſhall be loſt or damaged, through their Careleſſneſs or Inſufficiency, it ſhall be made good by ſuch Officer or Seamen, by whoſe Means it may happen, to the Maſter and Owners of the ſaid Veſſel. And whereas it is cuſtomary for the Officers and Seamen, on the Veſſel's Return Home, in the Harbour, and whilſt her Cargo is delivering, to go on Shore each Night to ſleep, greatly to the Prejudice of ſuch Veſſel and Freighters; Be it further agreed by the ſaid Parties, that neither Officer or Seaman ſhall, on any Pretence whatſoever, be intitled to ſuch Indulgence, but ſhall do their Duty by Day in Diſcharge of the Cargo, and keep ſuch Watch by Night as the Maſter ſhall think neceſſary to order for the Preſervation of the above. And whereas it often happens that Part of the Cargo is embezzled after being ſafely delivered into Lighters; and as ſuch Loſſes are made good by the Owners of the Veſſel; Be it therefore agreed by theſe Preſents, that whatever Officer or Seaman the Maſter ſhall think proper to appoint, ſhall take Charge of her Cargo in the Lighters, and go with it to the lawful Key, and there deliver his Charge to the Veſſel's Huſband, or his Repreſentative, or ſee the ſame ſafely landed. That each Seaman or Mariner who ſhall well and truly perform the above-mentioned Voyage, provided always that there be no Plunderage, Embezzlement, or other unlawful Acts committed on the ſaid Veſſel's Cargo or Stores, ſhall be entitled to the Payment of the Wages, or Hire, that may become due to him, purſuant to this Agreement, as to their Names is ſeverally affixed and ſet forth. That for the due Performance of each and every of the above-mentioned Articles and Agreements, and Acknowledgement of their being voluntary, and without Compulſion, or any other clandeſtine Means being uſed, agreed to and ſigned by us; in Teſtimony whereof, we have each and every of us under affixed our Hands, the Month and Day againſt our Names as here under-written. *Decem 9th 1804*

NAMES.	Stations.	Time of Entry.	Time of Diſcharge.	Time of Service.	Monthly Wages.	Advanced before ſailing.	Advanced abroad.	Whole Amount of Wages.	Due.	Witneſſes.
...n Choate	*Master*	*Decem 9th 1804*			*40*	*40*				*Dan'l Big...*
...orge Frowell	*Mate*	*Do*	*March 20 1805*		*27*	*27*				*N Whitt...*
...Burgess	*Seaman*	*Decem 17th 1804*	*March 20 1805*		*23*	*20*				
					18	*18*				
...ath Rand	*Do*	*Decem 9 1804*			*14*	*14*				

Earliest evidence of governmental concern about the unfair treatment of workers, these documents specify the rights of merchant seamen and the responsibilities of their employers. At the top is an agreement of the type required by the 1790 statute reproduced in part below. Congress later enacted other legislation.

CONGRESS OF THE UNITED STATES.

AT E SECOND SESSION,

Begun and held at the City NEW-YORK, *on Monday the 4th of January,* 1790.

AN ACT

For the Government and egulation of Seamen in the Merchants' Service.

BE *it enacted by the* SENATE *and* HOUSE OF REPRESENTATIVES *of the United States of America, in* CONGRESS *aſſembled*, That from and after the firſt day of December next, every maſter or commander of any ſhip or veſſel bound from a port in the United States to any foreign port, or of any ſhip or veſſel of the burthen of fifty tons or upwards, bound from a port in one State, to a port in any other than an adjoining State, ſhall, before he proceed on ſuch voyage, make an agreement in writing, or in print, with every ſeaman or mariner on board ſuch ſhip or veſſel (except ſuch as ſhall be apprentice or ſervant to himſelf or owners) declaring the voyage or voyages, term or terms of time, for which ſuch ſeaman or mariner ſhall be ſhipped. And if any maſter or commander of ſuch ſhip or veſſel ſhall carry out any ſeaman or mariner (except apprentices or ſervants as aforeſaid) without ſuch contract or agreement being firſt made and ſigned by the ſeamen and mariners, ſuch maſter or commander ſhall pay to every ſuch ſeaman or mariner, the higheſt price or wages, which ſhall have been given at the port or place where ſuch ſeaman or mariner ſhall have been ſhipped for a ſimilar voyage, within three months next before the time of ſuch ſhipping: *Provided* ſuch ſeaman or mariner ſhall perform ſuch voyage; or if not, then for ſuch time as he ſhall continue to do duty on board ſuch ſhip or veſſel; and ſhall moreover forfeit twenty dollars for every ſuch ſeaman or mariner, one half to the uſe of the perſon proſecuting for the ſame, the other half to the uſe of the United States: And ſuch ſeaman or mariner, not having ſigned ſuch contract, ſhall not be bound by the regulations, nor ſubject to the penalties and forfeitures contained in this Act.

And be it enacted, That at the foot of every ſuch contract, there ſhall be a memorandum in writing of the day and the hour, on which ſuch ſeaman or mariner, who ſhall ſo ſhip and ſubſcribe, ſhall render themſelves on board to begin the voyage agreed upon. And if any ſuch ſeamen or mariner ſhall neglect to render himſelf on board the ſhip or veſſel, for which he has ſhipped, at the time mentioned in ſuch memorandum, and if the maſter, commander, or other officer of the ſhip or veſſel ſhall, on the day on which ſuch neglect happened, make an entry in the log-book of ſuch ſhip or veſſel, of the name of ſuch ſeaman or mariner, and ſhall in like manner, note the time that he ſo neglected to render himſelf (after the time appointed); every ſuch ſeaman or mariner ſhall forfeit for every hour which he ſhall ſo neglect to render himſelf, one day's pay, according to the rate of

maſter or commander ſhall, in the firſt inſtance, pay all the coſts of ſuch view, report, and judgment, to be taxed and allowed on a fair copy thereof certified by the ſaid judge or juſtice. But if the complaint of the ſaid crew ſhall appear upon the ſaid report and judgment, to have been without foundation, then the ſaid maſter, or the owner, or conſignee of ſuch ſhip or veſſel, ſhall deduct the amount thereof, and of reaſonable damages for the detention (to be aſcertained by the ſaid judge or juſtice), out of the wages growing due to the complaining ſeamen or mariners. And if after ſuch judgment, ſuch ſhip or veſſel is fit to proceed on her intended voyage, or after procuring ſuch men, proviſions, ſtores, repairs or alterations as may be directed, the ſaid ſeamen or mariners, or either of them, ſhall refuſe to proceed on the voyage, it ſhall and may be lawful for any juſtice of the peace to commit by warrant under his hand and ſeal, every ſuch ſeaman or mariner (who ſhall ſo refuſe) to the common gaol of the county, there to remain without bail or mainprize, until he ſhall have paid double the ſum, advanced to him, at the time of ſubſcribing the contract for the voyage, together with ſuch reaſonable coſts as ſhall be allowed by the ſaid juſtice, and inſerted in the ſaid warrant, and the ſurety or ſureties of ſuch ſeaman or mariner (in caſe he or they ſhall have given any), ſhall remain liable for ſuch payment, nor ſhall any ſuch ſeaman or mariner be diſcharged upon any writ of habeas corpus, or otherwiſe, until ſuch ſum be paid by him or them, or his or their ſurety or ſureties, for want of any form of commitment, or other previous proceedings: *Provided*, That ſufficient matter ſhall be made to appear, upon the return of ſuch habeas corpus, and an examination then to be had, to detain him for the cauſes herein before aſſigned.

And be it enacted, That if any perſon ſhall harbour or ſecrete any ſeaman or mariner belonging to any ſhip or veſſel, knowing them to belong thereto, every ſuch perſon, on conviction thereof, before any court in the city, town or county, where he, ſhe or they may reſide, ſhall forfeit and pay ten dollars for every day which he, ſhe or they ſhall continue ſo to harbour or ſecrete ſuch ſeaman or mariner, one half to the uſe of the perſon proſecuting for the ſame, the other half to the uſe of the United States; and no ſum exceeding one dollar, ſhall be recoverable from any ſeaman or mariner by any one perſon, for any debt, contracted during the time ſuch ſeaman or mariner ſhall actually belong to any ſhip or veſſel, until the voyage, for which ſuch ſeaman or mariner, engaged, ſhall be ended.

clerk of ſuch court ſhall iſſue proceſs againſt the ſaid ſhip or v and the ſuit ſhall be proceeded on in the ſaid court, and final j ment be given, according to the courſe of admiralty courts in caſes uſed, and in ſuch ſuit, all the ſeamen or mariners (having of complaint of the like kind, againſt the ſame ſhip or veſſel) ſha joined as complainants, and it ſhall be incumbent on the maſt commander to produce the contract, and log-book, if require aſcertain any matters in diſpute, otherwiſe the complainants ſha permitted to ſtate the contents thereof, and the proof of the con ſhall lie on the maſter or commander; but nothing herein conti ſhall prevent any ſeamen or mariner from having or maintaining action at common law, for the recovery of his wages, or from i diate proceſs out of any court having admiralty juriſdiction, w ever any ſhip or veſſel may be found, in caſe ſhe ſhall have lef port of delivery, where her voyage ended, before payment o wages, or, in caſe ſhe ſhall be about to proceed to ſea before th of the ten days, next after the delivery of her cargo or ballaſt.

And be it enacted, That if any ſeaman or mariner, who ſhall ſigned a contract to perform a voyage, ſhall, at any port or p deſert, or ſhall abſent himſelf from ſuch ſhip or veſſel without of the maſter, or officer commanding in the abſence of the maſt ſhall be lawful for any juſtice of the peace within the United S (upon the complaint of the maſter) to iſſue his warrant to appre ſuch deſerter, and bring him before ſuch juſtice; and if it ſhall appear by due proof, that he has ſigned a contract within the i and meaning of this act, and that the voyage agreed for is not fi ed, altered, or the contract otherwiſe diſſolved, and that ſuch ſe or mariner has deſerted the ſhip or veſſel, or abſented himſelf out leave, the ſaid juſtice ſhall commit him to the houſe of co tion, or common gaol of the city, town or place, there to re until the ſaid ſhip or veſſel ſhall be ready to proceed on her vo or till the maſter ſhall require his diſcharge, and then to be deli to the ſaid maſter, he paying all the coſt of ſuch commitment deducting the ſame out of the wages due to ſuch ſeaman or ma

And be it enacted, That every ſhip or veſſel belonging to a ci or citizens of the United States, of the burthen of one hundred fifty tons, or upwards, navigated by ten or more perſons in whole, and bound on a voyage without the limits of the United S ſhall be provided with a cheſt of medicines, put up by ſome ap cary of known reputation, and accompanied by directions fo

HARMONIOUS ALLIANCE OF MASTERS AND JOURNEYMEN

Composed of master craftsmen and journeymen who were jacks-of-many trades, the Massachusetts Mechanic Association had much in common with a score of similar groups organized during the early 1800's. Masters employed journeymen but their economic and social interests were fairly similar. Masters usually worked side by side with journeymen, lived in much the same way, and held almost identical political views. As differences arose, however, master artisans and journeymen gradually parted company. In 1817, for example, a New York printers' society decided that "since the interests of the journeymen are separate and in some respects opposite to those of employers, we deem it improper that they [masters] should have any voice or influence in our deliberations."

Membership certificates of the New York Mechanick Society (1791) and the Society of Master Sailmakers (1795).

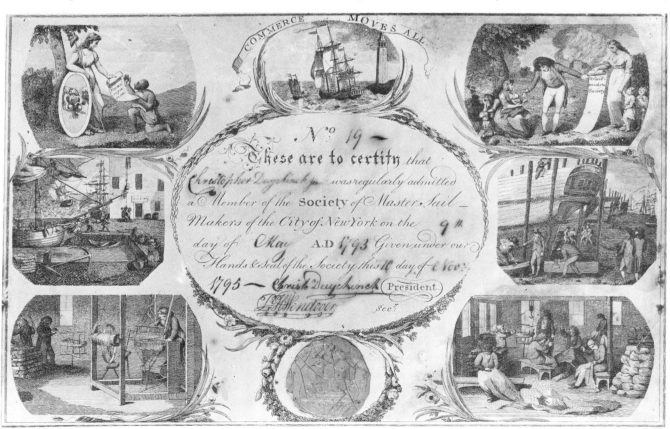

INDUSTRIAL BEGINNINGS SPURRED BY THE WAR OF 1812

The growth of manufacturing in general and of the textile industry in particular was in large part a consequence of the embargoes placed on foreign goods during the War of 1812. Drastic curtailment of imports from England and Europe encouraged American merchants to turn their attention to the development of domestic industries. Hundreds of small factories of the most diverse kind were started up along the eastern seaboard. By the end of the war the textile industry alone employed 100,000 workers.

Like other textile mills, those of the Union Manufactories of Maryland (above) erected at Patapsco Falls near Baltimore, relied almost wholly on child labor. Of its 184 employees in 1822, only six were men; the remainder were 120 girls and 58 boys between the ages of seven and eighteen years. A journalist who visited the mills wrote a glowing account of what he saw:

"The girls and boys live with their parents on the ground, where there is now a population exceeding six hundred people, living in the dwellings of the factory village, for which they pay rent. There is a school-house under good supervision, which is also used as a house of worship, is well attended to by ministers of various denominations, and where all employed by the company have free access . . . An extensive store is kept by the company, affording every article of provision and clothing sufficient for those employed in the neighborhood for many miles around."

The employment practices of the Union Manufactories were in line with recommendations made by Secretary of the Treasury Alexander Hamilton in 1791: "It is worthy of particular remark that in general women and children are rendered more useful, and the latter more easily useful, by manufacturing establishments than they otherwise would be."

(Below is an 1814 banknote showing glass factory buildings in which workers both toiled and lived.)

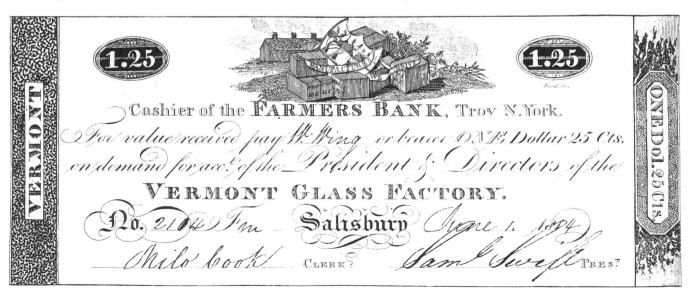

HANDPOWER OCCUPATIONS
OF COTTAGE INDUSTRIES

These drawings from Edward Hazen's "Popular Technology" depict the occupations of cooper, saddler, dyer, distiller, and wood turner early in the nineteenth century. The shops in which the men worked were usually attached to the owners' homes.

The crude beginnings of technology are evident in the wood turner's shop (bottom right) in which the motion of a hand-propelled wheel is transferred to a shaft by means of a rope or belt. Under the bench may be seen a wheel moved by a foot treadle that set a shaft in motion.

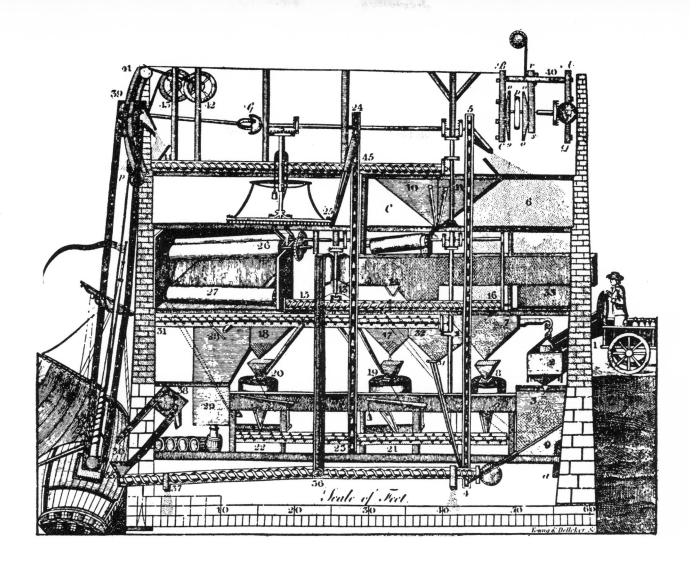

UNTOUCHED BY HUMAN HANDS

In the very year that Alexander Hamilton wrote his famous report about the potentialities of American industry, Oliver Evans, a former apprentice to a Delaware wagon maker, laid the basis for mass production by patenting his invention of the world's first automatic factory—a mechanical flour mill.

The water-powered machinery Evans devised made it possible for a mill to take in grain, weigh it, raise it to the top of the building, drop it into hoppers where it passed between millstones and was ground, elevate the meal, cool it, drop it again, bolt it, and then barrel it without intervention by a single manual operation. Here for the first time was an uninterrupted process of mechanical manufacture from raw material to finished product.

Like Robert Fulton's steamboat "folly," Evans' invention was derided. An observer of its operations reported that "the whole contrivance is a set of rattle traps unworthy the attention of common sense." Nevertheless, many similar mills were built without regard to

the patent Evans obtained over a protest by Thomas Jefferson, who felt the inventor had merely adapted existing knowledge. What Evans' contemporaries could not appreciate was that he had launched the revolutionary continuous process system which the twentieth century would associate with the name of Henry Ford.

Initially, Evans' invention cut labor requirements of a flour mill by half. Where the work of one man was formerly required for every ten barrels of flour, one man was now sufficient for twenty barrels. Six men, mostly employed in closing barrels, could convert annually about 100,000 bushels of grain into flour.

Of no importance to future generations but immensely useful when England cut off supplies from the embattled colonies was Evans' earlier invention of an automatic machine for making the metal teeth used to comb raw wool and cotton before spinning into yarn. He thought up the machine while doing menial work in a factory. His device even fed materials into itself so that all a worker had to do was turn a crank.

21

SHIPBUILDING BOOM

Vital to the commerce of the new nation, shipbuilding became a major east coast industry. By 1802 Boston alone had two dozen shipyards. Below is a scene in Joshua Humphrey's shipyard near Southark, Delaware, shortly before the War of 1812 broke out.

Shipbuilding was one of the few colonial industries England had actively encouraged. By the time of the Revolution about one third of all British vessels were American built. With the outbreak of war, New England shipyards turned to the construction of hundreds of fast privateers that easily outran the British blockade of Atlantic coast ports. The skill thus acquired was later to shape the great Yankee clippers.

THE ERIE CANAL STIMULUS

Construction of the Erie Canal, the world's longest artificial waterway, gave a tremendous impetus to the development of the young nation. Begun in 1817 under the supervision of amateur engineers, it was built by an army of laborers from Ireland (average wage was $7 a month) who encountered many difficulties as they hacked and dug their way through virgin forests.

When the canal was completed in 1825, it became a great spur to new farms, industries, and cities between the Hudson River and the Great Lakes. Everywhere along the waterway towns sprang up to tap the exchange of western products for eastern manufactures. The canal's magic touch especially benefited the growth of Syracuse, Buffalo, Cleveland, Detroit, and Chicago.

BRANCH OF THE GENERAL TRADES UNION.

N.YORK, 1833.

Combin'd to Protect but not to Injure.

UNION SOCIETY OF JOURNEYMEN HOUSE CARPENTERS

THE BIRTH OF TRADE UNIONS

Few of the characteristics of modern trade unionism existed during the early days of the republic. At that time and for some years to come guildlike organizations composed of masters and journeymen were primarily concerned with craftsmanship standards and competition considered injurious to their trade.

For all practical purposes American trade unionism was born when Philadelphia journeymen began to engage in activities specifically designed to improve their lot. In 1786 the city's printers established an historic precedent when they went on strike for a minimum wage of a $1 a day. (Before they took this action they sensibly set up a special fund to take care of their families' needs during the strike). Five years later Philadelphia's carpenters "turned out" to persuade their employers to limit the work day to ten hours. And in 1792 the city's shoemakers organized what can be considered the nation's first full fledged trade union—with a constitution, dues, a treasury, and regular meetings.

Workingmen in other cities gradually followed suit. The carpenters and cordwainers (leather workers) of Boston organized in 1793, the printers of New York in 1794, and the shoemakers of Pittsburgh in 1809. There were others but information about them is scanty.

Only some of the unions lasted more than a few years. Some disbanded after specific demands were won or lost. Some couldn't enlist enough members to keep going. Most couldn't survive because of employer opposition.

The first known strike in the building trades occurred in 1791 when the "Journeymen Carpenters of the City and Liberties of Philadelphia" struck against master carpenters who "meanly attempted" to reduce wages "by every means within the power of avarice to invent." In justifying their strike the journeymen complained that they had "heretofore been obliged to toil through the whole course of the longest summer's day, and that too, in many instances, without even the consolation of having our labour sweetened by the reviving hope of an immediate reward." They "bound" themselves, therefore, "by the sacred ties of honour" to abide by the following resolution: "That, in future, a Day's Work, amongst us, shall be deemed to commence at six o'clock in the morning, and terminate at six in the . . . evening of each day."

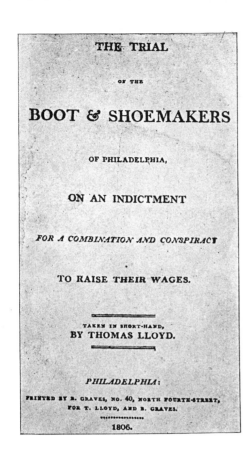

THE TRIAL

OF THE

BOOT & SHOEMAKERS

OF PHILADELPHIA,

ON AN INDICTMENT

FOR A COMBINATION AND CONSPIRACY

TO RAISE THEIR WAGES.

TAKEN IN SHORT-HAND,
BY THOMAS LLOYD.

PHILADELPHIA:

PRINTED BY B. GRAVES, NO. 40, NORTH FOURTH-STREET,
FOR T. LLOYD, AND B. GRAVES.

1806.

PERSECUTION OF UNIONS AS "CONSPIRACIES"

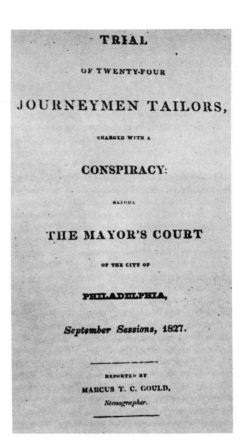

TRIAL

OF TWENTY-FOUR

JOURNEYMEN TAILORS,

CHARGED WITH A

CONSPIRACY:

BEFORE

THE MAYOR'S COURT

OF THE CITY OF

PHILADELPHIA,

September Sessions, 1827.

REPORTED BY

MARCUS T. C. GOULD,
Stenographer.

Persecution of unions as "conspiracies" in restraint of trade," a doctrine based on English common law, placed labor at an enormous disadvantage.

Typical of many similar actions was the trial in 1806 against eight members of the Journeymen Boot and Shoemakers of Philadelphia who were the leaders of a fruitless strike for higher wages. They were indicted for combining and conspiring to "prevent by threats, menaces and other unlawful means, other artificers, workmen, and journeymen in the said art and occupation, but at certain large prices [wages] and rates which they . . . then and there fixed."

The issues involved sharpened differences between Hamiltonian Federalists and Jeffersonian Republicans. The latter championed the right of workers to organize and strike while the former took an opposite stance. The Philadelphia Aurora, the nation's leading Jeffersonian newspaper, opened its columns to a bitter protest by the indicted bootmakers:

"In the constitution of [Pennsylvania] it is declared . . . 'that the citizens have a right in a peaceable manner to assemble together for the common good.' For fifteen years and upwards we have assembled together in a peaceable manner and for our common good, and to guard against the accidents to which industrious men are exposed to promote the happiness of the individuals of which our little community is composed, and to render service to those whom age or infirmity may have rendered incapable of labor . . .

"The master shoemakers, as they are called after the slavish style of Europe, but who are only the retailers of our labor, and who in truth live upon the work of our hands, are generally men of large property, to whom the suspension of business, though it is a loss, it is not so great a loss as the total suspension of the means of subsistence is to us who obtain our income from week to week. These masters as they are called, and who would be masters and tyrants if they could, or the law would allow them, have their associations, their meetings, and they pass their resolutions; but they are rich and we are poor—they seem to think that we are not protected by the constitution in meeting peaceably together and pursuing our own happiness. They suppose that they have a right to limit us at all times, and whatever may be the misfortune of society, the changes in the value of necessaries, the encrease or the decrease of trade, they think they have the right to determine for us the value of our labor; but that we have no right to determine for ourselves, what we will or what we will not take in exchange for our labor. . . .

"If the association of men to regulate the price of their own labor is to be converted into a crime, and libeled with the same reproachful terms as a design against the freedom of the nation, the prospect is a very sad one . . . What we have here said will . . . shew that under whatever pretences the thing is done, the name of freedom is but a shadow, if for doing what the laws of our country authorize we are to have taskmasters to measure out our subsistence pittance—if we are to be torn from our fireside for endeavoring to obtain a fair and just support for our families, and if we are to be treated as felons and murderers only for asserting the right to take or refuse what we deem an adequate reward for our labor."

The fate of the strikers was sealed when a Federalist judge bluntly instructed the jury: "A combination of workmen to raise their wages may be considered from a twofold point of view; one is to benefit themselves . . . the other is to injure those who do not join their society. The role of law condemns both."

The jury accepted the judge's interpretation of the law and found the journeymen "guilty of a combination to raise wages," but the decision evoked attacks from Jeffersonians who considered it contrary to the basic principles of the Constitution. They contended that it was "tyrannical" to deny workmen the right to combine in order to protect their interests:

"Shall all others, except only the industrious mechanics, be allowed to meet and plot; merchants to determine their prices current, or settle the markets, politicians to electioneer, sportsmen for horse-racing and games, ladies and gentlemen for balls, parties and bouquets; and yet these poor men be indicted for combining against starvation . . .?" Such a policy, it was asserted, was "incompatible with the existence of freedom, and prostrates every right which distinguishes the citizen from the slave."

Similar arguments were made in behalf of 25 journeymen tailors of Philadelphia who were indicted in 1827 "for conspiring to raise their wages to exact and exert from . . . master tailors higher wages than were usually paid."

A Pittsburgh judge held that trade union activities of shoemakers in that city also constituted a "conspiracy." While he conceded that "the human mind spontaneously revolts at the idea of oppression" of the type described by the workers in their defense, he ruled it was illegal for "divers persons [to] confederate together by indirect means to impoverish or prejudice a third person, or to do acts unlawful or prejudicial to the community."

In almost all of the conspiracy trials between 1806 and 1842 the charge remained essentially the same: workers who banded together for the purpose of securing higher wages were guilty of "conspiracy." It was not until 1842 that this concept finally became subject to juridical challenge. In that year Massachusetts Supreme Court Chief Justice Lemuel Shaw held that it was "not unlawful" for workers to peacefully engage in union activity for the purpose of improving their lot.

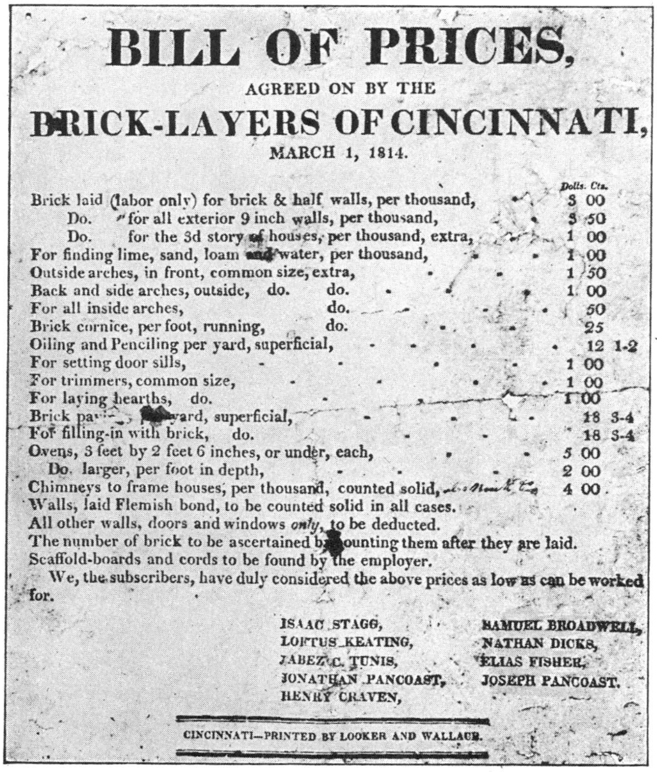

BILL OF PRICES,

AGREED ON BY THE

BRICK-LAYERS OF CINCINNATI,

MARCH 1, 1814.

	Dolls. Cts.
Brick laid (labor only) for brick & half walls, per thousand,	3 00
Do. for all exterior 9 inch walls, per thousand,	3 50
Do. for the 3d story of houses, per thousand, extra,	1 00
For finding lime, sand, loam and water, per thousand,	1 00
Outside arches, in front, common size, extra,	1 50
Back and side arches, outside, do. do.	1 00
For all inside arches, do.	50
Brick cornice, per foot, running, do.	25
Oiling and Penciling per yard, superficial,	12 1-2
For setting door sills,	1 00
For trimmers, common size,	1 00
For laying hearths, do.	1 00
Brick paving, per yard, superficial,	18 3-4
For filling-in with brick, do.	18 3-4
Ovens, 3 feet by 2 feet 6 inches, or under, each,	5 00
Do. larger, per foot in depth,	2 00
Chimneys to frame houses, per thousand, counted solid,	4 00

Walls, laid Flemish bond, to be counted solid in all cases.
All other walls, doors and windows only, to be deducted.
The number of brick to be ascertained by counting them after they are laid.
Scaffold-boards and cords to be found by the employer.
We, the subscribers, have duly considered the above prices as low as can be worked for.

ISAAC STAGG,   SAMUEL BROADWELL,
LOFTUS KEATING,   NATHAN DICKS,
JABEZ C. TUNIS,   ELIAS FISHER,
JONATHAN PANCOAST,   JOSEPH PANCOAST,
HENRY CRAVEN,

CINCINNATI—PRINTED BY LOOKER AND WALLACE.

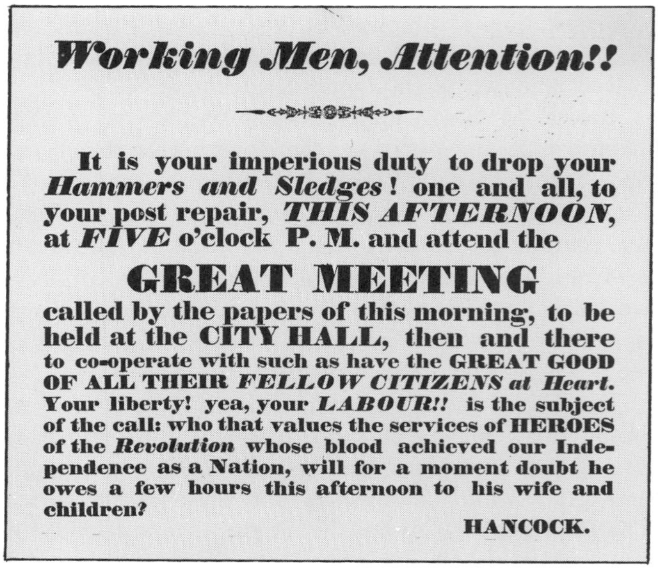

Working Men, Attention!!

It is your imperious duty to drop your Hammers and Sledges! one and all, to your post repair, THIS AFTERNOON, at FIVE o'clock P. M. and attend the

GREAT MEETING

called by the papers of this morning, to be held at the CITY HALL, then and there to co-operate with such as have the GREAT GOOD OF ALL THEIR FELLOW CITIZENS at Heart. Your liberty! yea, your LABOUR!! is the subject of the call: who that values the services of HEROES of the Revolution whose blood achieved our Independence as a Nation, will for a moment doubt he owes a few hours this afternoon to his wife and children?

HANCOCK.

Above is a broadside relating to labor troubles in New York City in 1837. At the side is a notice indicating that Cincinnati bricklayers held out for relatively high wages ("prices") but such action ran the risk of being considered conspiratorial.

JACKSONIAN DEMOCRACY: ERA OF THE COMMON MAN

Swept into office as the champion of the the humble members of society, President Andrew Jackson gave bold expression to popular hopes previously frustrated by Federalist policies.

Now at last "a man of the people" was the nation's chief executive. Cheered on by western backwoodsmen and eastern workers who idolized him, Jackson took up the cudgels in behalf of their interests.

"Jacksonian democracy," as Foster Dulles has pointed out, "had a broader basis than Jeffersonian democracy . . . [because it was] compounded of both the individualistic spirit of the frontier and the equalitarianism of eastern workingmen." Fellow historian Harold Faulkner offers this explanation:

"While Jacksonian democracy accepted the Jeffersonian principles, it was none the less a different brand of democracy. Jefferson had aimed at strong state democracies; Jackson probably had in mind a national democracy. Jefferson had believed in as little central government as possible; Jackson believed that the people ought to govern themselves as much as possible. Jackson represented a new time, a new section and a newly class-conscious group, and he belonged to each.

"Jefferson was a Virginia aristocrat, one of the dynasty, who had a tender feeling for the masses and believed in and championed them; but he did not intend that they should be the political masters. One able writer has even suggested that 1828 [the year in which Jackson was elected to his first term as president] is a more important date in the history of American democracy than 1776. Although Jefferson's Declaration of Independence gave us a new political dream, it remained for Jacksonian democracy to give real form in government to Jefferson's ideals. At best Jeffersonianism was a government of the people and for the people. Jacksonianism created a government of the people, for the people, and *by* the people."

While historians disagree somewhat about the extent to which Jackson was influenced by pressures from workingmen, it is generally agreed that the concept of "Jacksonian democracy" encompasses the movements, events, and policies between 1827 and 1840 that reflected or expressed the upsurge of the common people during those years—i.e., the rise of trade unions, the proliferation of local Workingmen's parties, the elimination of property requirements restricting who could vote and hold office, the beginning of free public education, and abolition of imprisonment for debt.

In spite of gloom and doom predictions of what would happen during Jackson's administration, the country enjoyed a substantial period of growth.

"On a general survey," exulted Senator Henry Clay in a peroration on February 2, 1832, "we behold culti-

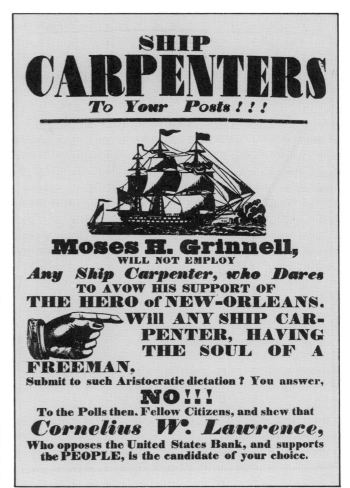

vation extended, the arts flourishing, the face of the country improved, our people fully and profitably employed, and the public countenance exhibiting tranquility, contentment and happiness. And if we descend into particulars we have the agreeable contemplation of a people out of debt; land slowly rising in value, but in a secure and salutary degree; a ready though not extravagant market for all the surplus productions of our industry; innumerable flocks and herds browsing on ten thousand hills and plains covered with rich and verdant grasses; our cities expanded and whole villages springing up as it were by enchantment; our exports and imports increased and increasing; our tonnage, foreign and coastwise, swelling and fully occupied; the rivers of our interior animated by the perpetual thunder and lightning of countless steamboats; the currency sound and abundant; the public debt of two wars nearly redeemed; and, to crown all, the public treasury overflowing, embarrassing Congress, not to find subjects of taxation, but to select the objects which shall be liberated from the impost."

Allowing for some exaggeration, these words were a fairly accurate description of the state of the nation during the early 1830's.

NEW VOICES, NEW CHOICES

Launched at almost the same time that small but exceedingly articulate Workingmen's parties were coming into existence, the "Working Man's Advocate" gave them much needed support. In its first issue it endorsed the New York party's candidates for the state legislature. The paper's primary purpose was to assist "the useful and industrial classes of this populous city . . . in ascertaining the best and most effectual remedies for the evils and deprivations under which they are suffering . . ."

Some of the candidates of the New York party weren't active journeymen. Alexander Ming, for example, ran his own print shop; Thomas Skidmore was an ex-machinist turned inventor and reformer. Ebenezer Ford, a carpenter, was one of the few candidates elected. However, the party rolled up such a sizeable number of votes that many of the reforms it espoused were subsequently backed by Tammany Hall.

RISE OF THE WORKINGMEN'S PARTIES

Crude cartoons characterized the propaganda of the Workingmen's parties that began to spring up almost simultaneously with the removal in the late 1820's of the property requirements for voters and office holders. The above drawing shows a merchant conspiring with the devil to buy an election while an honest artisan offers his vote to the candidates listed on the banner of the New York Workingmen's Party.

The first of such parties was established in 1828 by the Mechanics' Union of Trade Associations in Philadelphia. The objects of the organization, the nation's first city-wide union of unions, were "to avert, if possible, the desolating evils which must inevitably arise from a deprivation of the intrinsic value of human labor; to raise the mechanical and productive classes . . . to true independence and equality . . . [and] to aid in conferring a . . . full proportion of that invaluable promoter of happiness, leisure, upon all its useful members."

The example set by the Philadelphia Workingmen's Party was soon followed in New York, Boston, Albany, and other leading industrial cities. A meeting of New York mechanics, called to support the ten-hour day, became the germ of a local party organization that succeeded in securing the election of several candidates to the state legislature.

It was partially a result of the efforts of these groups that electoral reforms were effected, free public schools were established, imprisonment for debt was abolished, compulsory military service was curtailed, wages became subject to protection by lien laws, and monopolistic practices of banks were brought under control.

Since most of these reforms were achieved under the banner of the Democratic Party during the administrations of Presidents Andrew Jackson and Martin Van Buren, the Workingmen's parties lost their appeal and gradually disappeared.

SPECIAL PLEADING

Derision of "Matty" Van Buren in Whig campaign broadsides helped elect William Henry Harrison ("Tip") and John Tyler ("Ty") in 1840.

It was a strange contest. Harrison, the wealthy son of an ex-governor of Virginia, was transformed into a humble backwoodsman while Van Buren, a true-blue Jacksonian, was denounced as an elegant epicure who sneered at common folk and consorted with monied men. While President, Van Buren had established ten hours as the maximum work day on government projects.

Below is a Whig lithograph showing Van Buren being battered by labor.

TIP. TY. TOM. & NAT.

Our Country is safe, in such Hands.

Matty's policy, 12½ cts. a day and French soup.

Our policy, 2 Dolls. a day and Roast Beef.

Directed against continuation of Jackson's policies by Martin Van Buren, his successor, these lithographs depict demoralizing effects of the 1837 depression. Be-

low a jobless workman bemoans his fate as he is about to be served with an eviction notice. Sabotage of Jackson's policies by bankers contributed to the depression.

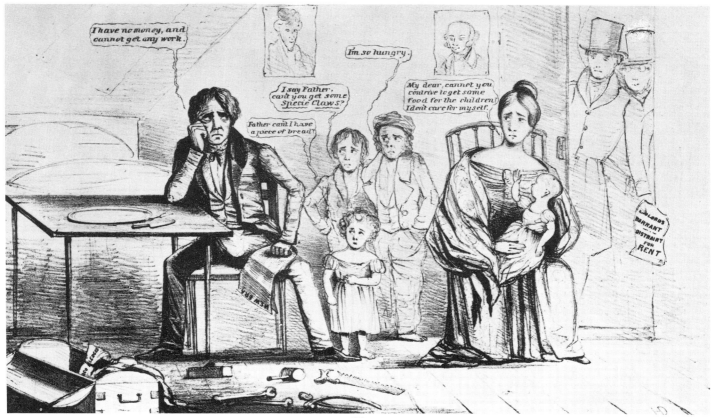

WHIG EXHORTATIONS

　These contrasting scenes are examples of Whig propaganda that contributed to the defeat of Martin Van Buren in his bid for reelection as President in 1840. Voters decided they preferred "Harrison and Prosperity," as envisioned above, to "Van Buren and Ruin" as shown below, although bankers opposed to Van Buren's continuation of Jacksonian policies were considered responsible for the economic downtrend during his administration. At the side are extracts from a contemporary poem written in Van Buren's support.

　"The Whigs were the party of property and talents," according to historians Samuel Morison and Henry Steele Commager. "In the North . . . they carried on the nationalist and paternal tradition of Alexander Hamilton. The manufacturing interests which wanted protection, the merchants and bankers who suffered from Jackson's financial vagaries, went Whig. The Anti-Masons, the nativists, and the anti-slavery followers of J. Q. Adams were also absorbed. A large number of Westerners were attracted by . . . the hope of getting something done about the public lands. In the South the Whigs were the party of gentility and property. Sugar planters who wanted protection against Cuba; big cotton planters who regretted [Jackson's] veto of the United States Bank . . . antique Republicans of Virginia and North Carolina . . . all went Whig. Nowhere but in America could a political party have been formed from such heterogeneous elements."

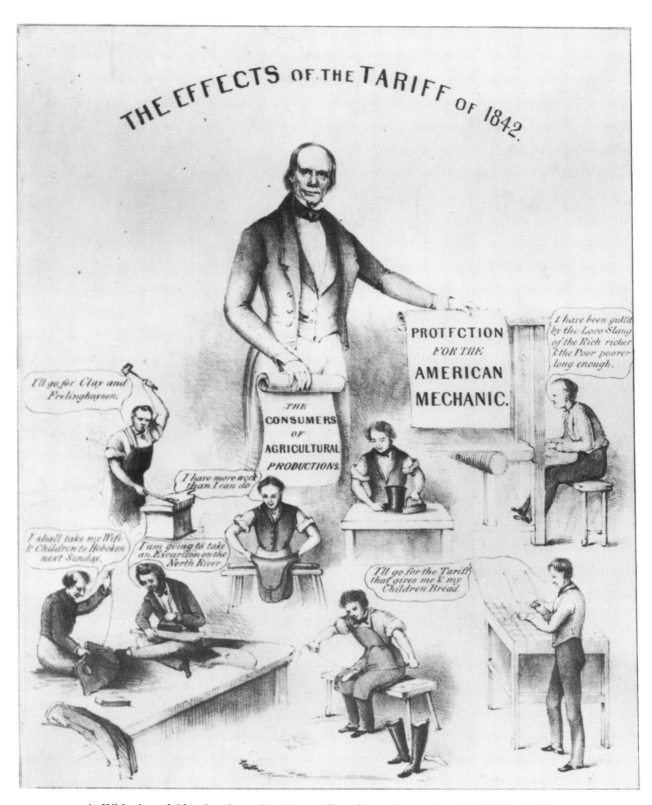

A Whig broadside showing why Henry Clay favored enactment of high tariffs.

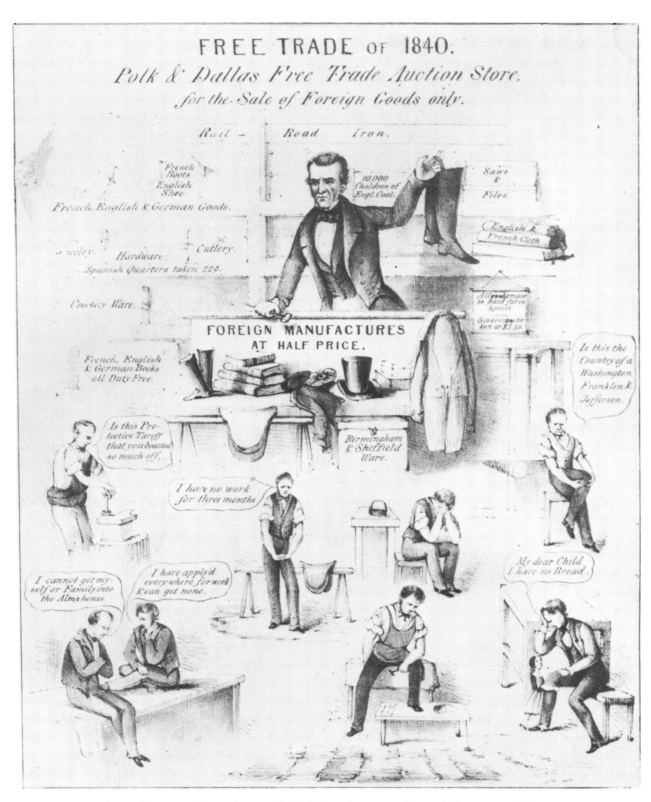

A partisan attack on James K. Polk's advocacy of restrictions on tariff rates.

LOCOFOCO LABORITES

Election of James K. Polk as President in 1844 was attributed to outright   purchase of votes from workingmen in New York and other cities.

During the same period the Democratic Party was split apart by sharp differences between Tammany Hall and "Locofoco" dissidents with reform notions substantially supported by workingmen. (The dissidents got their nickname from their use of large locofoco matches to light candles during meetings at Tammany headquarters deprived of gas lamp illumination.) Subsequently the "locos" organized the Equal Rights Party, a short-lived but potent force favoring labor's struggles and opposing monied interests. By the late 1840's most leaders of the party had returned to the Democratic fold.

FACES OF THE FORTIES

These rare photographs were probably taken during the late 1840's. They include gold miners in California, two New Orleans bakers, a "woodsawyer" and his youthful apprentice, and a New England toleware maker. Photography was in its infancy at the time.

Ten Dollars Reward.

RAN AWAY from the Subscriber, on the night of the 15th instant, two apprentice boys, legally bound, named WILLIAM and AN DREW JOHNSON The former is of a dark complexion, black hair, eyes, and habits. They are much of a height, about 5 feet 4 or 5 inches The latter is very fleshy freckled face, light hair, and fair complexion. They went off with two other apprentices, advertised by Messrs Wm. & Chas. Fowler When they went away, they were well clad—blue cloth coats, light colored homespun coats, and new hats, the maker's name in the crown of the hats, is Theodore Clark. I will pay the above Reward to any person who will deliver said apprentices to me in Raleigh, or I will give the above Reward for Andrew Johnson alone.

All persons are cautioned against harboring or employing said apprentices, on pain of being prosecuted.

JAMES J. SELBY, Tailor.

Raleigh, N. C. June 24, 1824.   26 3t

APPRENTICESHIP WOES

A carry-over from colonial times, the indentured apprenticeship arrangement remained in effect for a good many years. Above is an 1824 advertisement about a runaway apprentice who became the nation's President.

Bereft of his father, a tavern handyman, Andrew Johnson was bound out at 14 to tailor James Selby for six years, but he ran away after serving only a third of this period. With the help of brother William, a fellow runaway, he set up his own tailor shop after a fruitless attempt to reach an agreement with his former master.

During Johnson's apprenticeship he benefited from the custom of tailors to permit newspapers to be read to the workmen as they sat cross-legged on their tables while stitching clothes. His interest in political questions was stimulated by lively discussions that annoyed his employer. Later his education was broadened by the conscientiousness of his wife in teaching him to write. In time his tailorshop in Greenville, Tennessee, became a meeting place of townsmen who promoted his election to mayor on a Workingmen's Party ticket.

Under the indenture system, the apprentice typically was bound to his master for a period of seven years or until he reached the age of 21. He usually did not receive even token wages. It was his master's duty to teach him the trade and provide him with food, lodging, and clothing.

In effect this system constituted limited involuntary serviture. Its chief advantage was that it provided a means by which a boy could learn a skilled trade, but it was subject to much misuse.

Although never legally abolished, the indentured form of apprenticeship was modified and eventually discarded as the century progressed. In some trades, however, employers drew so heavily on voluntary apprentices as a source of cheap labor that unions insisted upon regulations to prevent abuses. After a while the unions placed so many restrictions on the apprentice system that it became a device resented by employers because it circumscribed their ability to train young workers.

37

THE PERILOUS HAZARDS OF WHALING

Whaling crews were paid by shares in the profits from a voyage but many of the men didn't last out voyages that extended over several years. Brutal skippers gave their crew such a rough time that men frequently deserted ship at intermediate ports, thus forfeiting their shares. Even those who returned home as crew members found themselves so much in debt for advances of pay and credit that their wages were negligible. Men who sustained injuries seldom received any extra compensation.

Capturing whales was an exciting but dangerous occupation of New England seamen. Harpooning the huge animals involved contests that were frequently prolonged for hours while the wounded creatures whipped the sea with their powerful tails. Oil from the blubber of whales was needed for lamp fuel.

38

ABUSE OF SEAMEN

For relatively minor infractions of discipline, merchant seamen were flogged in full-view of almost indifferent passengers.

Shipboard life was extraordinarily crude and hard. A "scramble for the salt junk" invariably took place when the cook placed a bucket of meat on the deck. In the fight for the biggest pieces many a seaman suffered bodily injury.

Publication of Richard Henry Dana's "Two Years Before the Mast" in 1840 shocked middle class sensibilities. Based on his experiences while serving aboard the "Pilgrim" for two years, the book revealed astonishing details about brutal treatment of seamen and led to some reforms. In the opinion of Van Wyck Brooks, the book did "as much for sailors as Dickens had done for the debtors and orphans of England and 'Uncle Tom's Cabin' for the slaves." A later book, "The Seamen's Friend," was a useful guide to legal rights that were often flagrantly breached.

Dana's sympathy with the common tar broadened into concern about the welfare of workers in general.

Beating, wounding, imprisonment, withholding of food, and other punishments continued to be inflicted by masters permitted to exercise their discretion in maintaining discipline. Such treatment was sanctioned by a Massachusetts judge who held:

"The simple and somewhat rude character of seamen . . . renders a prompt and energetic government indispensably necessary to good discipline . . . There is a good sense in the remark of one of the latest French writers on maritime law on this subject. 'It is impossible to hasten a manoeuvre if the command may not be accompanied with coercive means. Here neither gentleness nor politeness are in place; the punishment of the moment is necessary to quicken the caviller and and the lazy.' . . . When it is apparent that punishment is merited . . . [the court cannot] adjust very accurately the balance between the magnitude of the fault and the quantum of punishment."

Lured to America by exaggerated reports of high wages, many young women wound up working in New England textile mills under conditions little different from those prevailing in England, except that opportunities for improved standards of living were greater. The above woodcut shows John Bull trying to hold back workers who continued to leave Britain in large numbers until the Civil War years.

PATERNALISM IN THE TEXTILE FACTORIES OF NEW ENGLAND

Probably the first American example of a company house organ, the "Lowell Offering" created the impression that working in Massachusetts textile mills was an idyllic experience.

Daniel Webster and Edward Everett, avid New England boosters, went about saying that its factories were wonderful places to work in and that the girls employed by them were the luckiest of women. A contemporary pastoral ditty ran as follows:

> *O sing me a song of the Factory Girl*
> *So merry and glad and free—*
> *The bloom on her cheeks, of health it speaks!—*
> *O a happy creature is she!*

Henry Clay, high priest of the American System, returned from a trip through Massachusetts factories with the feeling that they were run humanely, but Seth Luther inveighed against their working conditions.

Clay wasn't aware of the grim realities Luther described:

> *The widow's grief, the orphan's nakedness,*
> *The poor man's woe,*
> *These [visitors] can never see.*
> *And their dull ear*
> *Can never catch the wailing wretchedness*
> *Wrung from the lowly lived.*
> *The bitter tears that sickness or misfortune*
> *Cause to flow, ne'er warmed the ice*
> *Of their obdurate hearts.*

As more factories sprang up, manufacturers sent agents into rural areas to round up farm girls to work in the mill towns. The "slavers" used by the agents evoked this complaint by a writer in the "Voice of Industry" (Lowell) of January 2, 1846:

"Observing a singular-looking, 'long, low, black' wagon passing along the street, we made inquiries respecting it, and were informed that it was what we term a 'slaver.' She makes regular trips to the north of the state, cruising around in Vermont and New Hampshire, with a 'commander' whose heart must be as black as his craft, who is paid a dollar a head for all he brings to the market, and more in proportion to the distance—if they bring them from such distance that they cannot easily get back. This is done by 'hoisting false colors,' and representing to the girls, that they can tend more machinery than is possible, and that the work is so very neat, and the wages such, that they can dress in silks and spend half their time in reading. Now is this true? Let those girls who have been thus grossly . . . deceived answer."

The best aspects of mill-town life described by British visitors and played up in publications like the "Lowell Offering" didn't jibe with growing complaints about low wages and paternalistic domination. And when the "slavers" ran out of susceptible maidens in New England, "baggage wagons" were sent to Quebec to bring in peasant girls who neutralized militancy among native workers.

(Below is a retouched drawing of the much hated "slaver" carriage.)

Although inaccurate in some respects, these prints from the "Memoirs of Samuel Slater," published in 1836, depict methods similar to those used in his New England mills. Production of cotton textiles was made more efficient by the use of power loom weaving (top), calico printing equipment (center), and mechanized carding, drawing, and spinning (bottom).

In describing Massachusetts cotton mills of the 1830's, an English observer reported that they produced more yarn and cloth from each spindle and loom in a given time than was produced in any European factory. Another visitor of the period commented: "There are no people more ingenious in the use and invention of machinery, no country more prolific in patents. . ."

Rules & Regulations

TO BE OBSERVED BY ALL PERSONS EMPLOYED IN THE FACTORY OF

AMASA WHITNEY.

RULE 1. The Mill will be put in operation 10 minutes before sun-rise at all seasons of the year. The gate will be shut 10 minutes past sun-set, from the 20th of March to the 20th of September; at 30 minutes past 8, from the 20th of Sept. to the 20th of March. Saturdays, at sun-set.

2d. It will be required of every person employed, that they be in the room in which they are employed, at the time mentioned above for the mill to be in operation.

3d. Hands are not allowed to leave the factory in working hours, without the consent of their Overseer; if they do, they will be liable to have their time set off.

4th. Any one who by negligence or misconduct causes damage to the machinery, or impedes the progress of the work, will be liable to make good the damage for the same.

5th. Any one employed for a certain length of time, will be expected to make up their lost time, if required, before they will be entitled to their pay.

6th. Any person employed for no certain length of time, will be required to give at least 4 weeks notice of their intention to leave, (sickness excepted) or forfeit 4 weeks' pay, unless by particular agreement.

7th. Any one wishing to be absent any length of time, must get permission of the Overseer.

8th. All who have leave of absence for any length of time, will be expected to return in that time; and in case they do not return in that time, and do not give satisfactory reason, they will be liable to forfeit one week's work or less, if they commence work again. If they do not, they will be considered as one who leaves without giving any notice.

9th. Any thing tending to impede the progress of manufacturing in working hours, such as unnecessary conversation, reading, eating fruit, &c. &c., must be avoided.

10th. While I shall endeavor to employ a judicious overseer, the help will follow his directions in all cases.

11th. No smoking will be allowed in the Factory, as it is considered very unsafe, and particularly specified in the Insurance.

12th. In order to forward the work, job hands will follow the above regulations as well as those otherwise employed.

13th. It is intended that the bell be rung 5 minutes before the gate is hoisted, so that all persons may be ready to start their machinery precisely at the time mentioned.

14th. All persons who cause damage to the machinery, break glass out of the windows, &c., will immediately inform the overseer of the same.

15th. The hands will take breakfast, from the 1st of November till the 1st of March, before going to work—they will take supper from the 1st of May till the last of August, 30 minutes past 5 o'clock, P. M.—from the 20th of September till the 20th of March, between sun-down and dark—25 minutes will be allowed for breakfast, 30 minutes for dinner, and 25 minutes for supper, and no more from the time the gate is shut till started again.

16th. The hands will leave the Factory so that the doors may be fastened within 10 minutes from the time of leaving off work.

Winchendon, (Mass.) July 5, 1830.

AMASA WHITNEY.

Sun rises as early as 4:27 in summer.

Sun sets as late as 7:41 P.M. (in June)

4 Weeks pay held back apparently

4 Weeks pay lost probably

No time to wash up, or change clothes

Sluice gate for water power

Four hours after sunset (in December)

No appeal

Breakfast in mill other 8 months

Supper in mill all year round apparently

HARSH WORKING AND LIVING CONDITIONS

Time Table of the Holyoke Mills,

To take effect on and after Jan. 3d, 1853.

The standard being that of the Western Rail Road, which is the Meridian time at Cambridge.

MORNING BELLS.

First Bell ring at 4.40, A. M. Second Bell ring in at 5, A. M.

YARD GATES

Will be opened at ringing of Morning Bells, of Meal Bells, and of Evening Bells, and kept open ten minutes.

WORK COMMENCES

At ten minutes after last Morning Bell, and ten minutes after Bell which "rings in" from Meals.

BREAKFAST BELLS.

October 1st, to March 31st, inclusive, ring out at 7, A. M.; ring in at 7.30, A. M.
April 1st, to Sept. 30th, inclusive, ring out at 6.30, A. M.; ring in at 7, A. M.

DINNER BELLS.

Ring out at 12.30, P. M.; ring in at 1, P. M.

EVENING BELLS.

Ring out at 6.30,* P. M.

* Excepting on Saturdays when the Sun sets previous to 6.30. At such times, ring out at Sunset.

In all cases, the *first* stroke of the Bell is considered as marking the time.

Strict rules like these were rigorously enforced by northern textile mill owners prior to the 1860's.

Contemporary living conditions, according to historian John B. McMaster, were "almost execrable" in factory towns:

"Sand sprinkled on the floor did duty as a carpet. There was no glass on his table, there was no china in his cupboard, there were no prints on his wall. What a stove was he did not know, coal he had never seen, matches he had never heard of . . . He rarely tasted fresh meat as often as once in a week, and paid for it a much higher price than his posterity . . .

"If the food of an artisan would now be thought coarse, his clothes would be thought abominable. A pair of yellow buckskin or leathern breeches, a checked shirt, a red flannel jacket, shoes of meat-skin . . . and a leathern apron comprised his scanty wardrobe."

(The handwritten comments about the Whitney factory were evidently made much later.)

Assembly-line techniques were introduced by Isaac Singer in his first sewing machine factory (above) during the late 1850's. (Walter Hunt, an earlier inventor of the machine, never applied for a patent because he felt that too many seamstresses would be thrown out of work.) Most shoe manufacturers, however, continued to rely heavily on low-paid child labor. The wood engraving below appeared in the National Magazine in 1854.

INDUSTRIAL PROGRESS

The changing nature of American industry was clearly evident in the huge factories that were springing up in the north. Demand for Cyrus McCormick's ingenious reaping machine was so great that he kept his Chicago factory (below) operating both night and day. Above is an 1854 sketch of the Appleton Mills in Massachusetts; dormitory buildings that housed workers, mostly women and children, can be seen in the background at the left side.

Mining of the anthracite coal deposits on the surface of Pennsylvania's Mauch Chunk Mountain, seen above in an 1831 lithograph, marked the beginning of a new industry. Digging usually started at sunrise and continued until sundown.

Unlike bituminous coal, anthracite was considered unsuitable as a fuel until an American manufacturer of iron products learned by accident how it could be burned. Below is a busy canal scene near coal-rich Pottsville, Pennsylvania, as depicted in the 1840's.

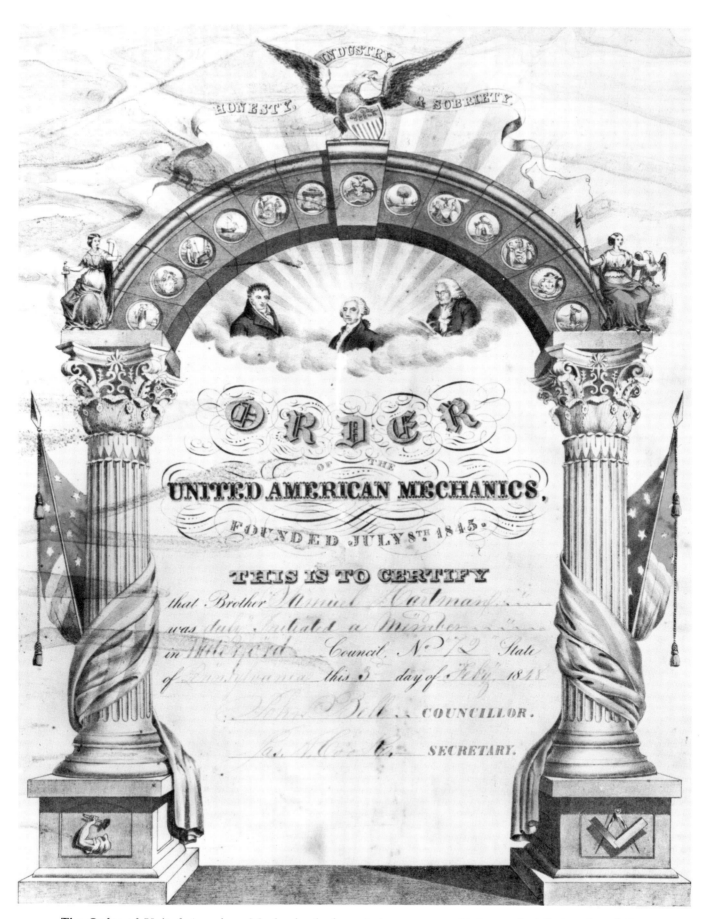

The Order of United American Mechanics had much in common with benevolent fraternal societies.

LEADERS AND DREAMERS

They served labor's cause in varied ways during the 1830's and 40's. Left to right (top to bottom): Ely Moore, president of the General Trades Union of New York and the National Trades Union, became labor's first Congressman in 1834; Mathew Carey, a Philadelphia businessman who had struggled upward from poverty, wrote books about the wretched plight of the poor; Robert Dale Owen, eldest son of British reformer Robert Owen, was an influential advocate of changes beneficial to labor; William H. Channing, a Boston Brahmin, supported the efforts of the New England Working Men's Association to raise wages and improve social conditions.

JOURNALS OF SOCIAL FERMENT

Born out of the workingmen's need for publications of their own, a score of newspapers and magazines devoted to the interests of labor and social reform appeared during the 1840's. Most were destined for an early death; only Horace Greeley's New York Daily Tribune survived the decade.

The original purpose of the Tribune, according to Greeley, was to promote "the elevation of the masses through the diffusion and inculcation of intelligence, freedom, industry, skill, virtue, and the subsequent abolition of ignorance, slavery, idleness, pauperism, and vice." He opened the columns of his paper not only to general news of interest to the common people but also to articles and editorials friendly toward unions, improvement of labor conditions, Fourierism, homestead legislation, and other reforms.

Greeley came by his pro-labor sympathies naturally. During the hard times of 1807-1809 his father had to flee New Hampshire in order to avoid debtor's jail. After four years of apprenticeship in a print shop, Greeley worked as a compositor on several New England newspapers, helped a New York printer's union survive during the depression of 1837, became a successful job printer, and ventured into daily journalism.

In time Greeley became so intensely active in Republican politics that the Tribune devoted less and less space to matters of special interest to workingmen, but it remained for many years one of the few daily newspapers generally sympathetic toward labor's cause. John R. Commons has credited the Tribune with being "the first . . . great vehicle this country has known for the idea and experiment of constructive democracy."

(Below is a printing union membership card authorized by Greeley.)

JUSTICE SHAW'S
LANDMARK DECISION

Rugged Lemuel Shaw, Chief Justice of the Massachusetts Supreme Court, handed down an historic decision when he ruled in 1842 that unions had a legal right to exist and did not constitute conspiracies, as previous judges had held. The purpose of the Journeymen Bootmakers Society of Boston, he declared in the case of Commonwealth vs. Hunt, was to persuade workers engaged in the same occupation to become members and this could not be treated as unlawful. Agreement for common action to achieve a lawful purpose was, he held, perfectly proper. Moreover, he did not consider refusal of the bootmakers to work for an employer who hired a non-member a criminal act.

"Inducing all those engaged in the same occupation to become members of [a union] . . . is not unlawful," he declared. "It would give them [the members] a power which might be used for useful and honorable purposes, or for dangerous and pernicious ones . . . But in order to charge all those who become members of an asso-

ciation with the guilt of a criminal conspiracy, it must be averred and proved that the actual, if not the avowed object of the association was criminal . . . When an association is formed for purposes actually innocent, and afterwards its powers are abused by those who have the control and management of it to purposes of oppression and injustice, it will be criminal in those who misuse it, or give consent thereto, but not in the other members of the assocation . . . In this state of things, we cannot perceive that it is criminal for men to agree to serve together to exercise their own acknowledged rights in such a manner as best to subserve their own interests."

Impressed by Justice Shaw's landmark decision, the courts of other states gradually became disinclined to invoke the "conspiracy" doctrine as a means of repressing unions although it continued to crop up. A major roadblock to union organizing was gradually removed but the thorny thickets of injunctions, lockouts, and strikebreaking still lay ahead for many years.

LADY SHOEMAKERS GO ON STRIKE

Unfazed by snow and taunts from onlookers, the women employed at shoe factories in Lynn, Massachusetts, turned out in an impressive strike parade in March, 1860. A week after they stopped working, according to historian Roger Butterfield, "the ladies all went to an outdoor chowder party, which was followed by dancing and kissing games. A riot almost occurred when a boss machinist named Piper boasted that he had persuaded two girls to go back to work. A committee of strikers escorted Piper off the grounds while the band played the 'Rogue's March' . . . At Lowell [the mill girls] captured their superintendent . . . and ducked him under a pump." Lynn's lady shoe workers later established the Daughters of St. Crispin, an offshoot of the short-lived, semi-secret Knights of St. Crispin. (In 1873 the Knights reportedly had about 50,000 members "determined to resist wage cuts by shoe manufacturers who are installing machinery.")

The decorum of the lady shoemakers is not evident in these drawings of scenes during the Lynn walkout. For weeks the city was in turmoil. Indignation reached a fever pitch when it was discovered that scab-made boots were being shipped to Boston. When huge crowds of angry workers and citizens blocked further movement of goods, the factory owners finally made concessions that brought the strike to an end.

TURMOIL IN LYNN

As these Winslow Homer drawings indicate, women and children constituted a substantial part of New England's factory labor during the late 1860's. In the sketch at the top workers are streaming out of the textile mills of Lawrence, Massachusetts. Below is an engraving entitled "The Morning Bell." Daybreak and nightfall marked the beginning and end of the typical working day. During 1860-1870 about 58% of northern cotton mill hands were women and approximately 7% were children under 12.

RULES

FOR

GRANITEVILLE.

RULE 1. Persons employed by the Company, or who occupy their Houses, will not be permitted to bring into the place any intoxicating liquors; and persons will not be continued in the service of the Company, who lend their aid directly or indirectly to the encouragement of those who may vend liquors in the vicinity.

RULE 2. It is considered a part of this contract, and indispensable to the occupancy of a house, and employment by the Company, that parents and heads of families, shall send all their children to the Graniteville public school, whose ages will permit, and who are under 12 years of age, who will be required to pay 5 cents a day to the School Fund for each absentee from school without a good and sufficient excuse. All excuses to be rendered to the President of the Company for his decision, which I agree to abide by.

RULE 3. The above exaction of 5 cents a day for absentees is not levied as a fine, but is exacted as a contribution to make good to the School Fund the 5 cents a day which the State pays for indigent children in attendance at school. Parents will be held responsible for the orderly behavior of children. All *males* over 12 years of age, and not at school, must be engaged in some useful employment, as they will not be permitted to remain in idleness about the Village.

RULE 4. Tenants of Boarding Houses, are not allowed to receive into their houses, as Boarders, any persons not in the employment of the Company, except by special permission. Buildings, yards and fences must be kept clean and in good order; and if injured otherwise than by ordinary wear, repairs will be charged to the occupant.

RULE 5. Dwelling Houses will be let from month to month, and the rent paid accordingly. Occupants, after four weeks' notice to that effect, will consider themselves bound to yield up their houses at the end of any one month, the Company may require them so to do.

RULE 6. All those occupying the Company's houses, who keep hogs, must have a convenient place for them in the back yard, and not allow them to run about the Village of Graniteville.

RULE 7. Tenants or occupants of houses and stores, upon leaving the Village, or moving from one house to another, shall not be allowed to remove or injure any improvements they may have made upon either the house or house lot, and this rule must apply to ornamental shrubbery and fruit as well as buildings.

RULE 8. As the Sabbath is a day of rest and peace, no street sports, or disorderly conduct, either in the Village or neighborhood, will be permitted on that day.

RULE 9. The above regulations, are to be considered a part of the contract, entered into by all those employed by the Graniteville Manufacturing Company, or occupying their houses.

I further agree to deliver up the house I occupy at whatever time the Graniteville Company may desire me so to do

WITNESS: *By James Montgomery*
Sept 5 1861

Elizabeth X *Vaughen*
her
Mark

THE GREGG SYSTEM OF CONFORMITY

Strict compliance with these paternalistic rules was required by the Graniteville Manufacturing Company of South Carolina. Its cotton mill, one of the largest in the South, employed about 300 persons. Owner William Gregg, "the father of Southern cotton manufacturing," ran his village-factory with as lively an interest in the proper behavior of his workers as in the profits he derived from efficient production. He considered it his "moral" duty to help alleviate the plight of "the thousands of poor, ignorant, degraded white people among us, who, in this land of plenty, live in comparative nakedness and starvation."

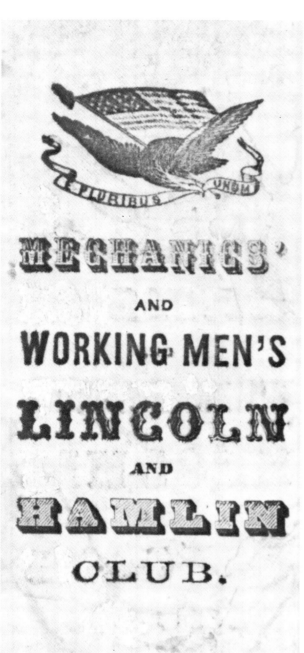

"FREE SOIL, FREE SPEECH, FREE LABOR, AND FREE MEN"

Although slavery was the main issue during the 1860 presidential campaign, the Republican Party placed the issue in a broader context expressed by slogans such as "Free Soil, Free Speech, Free Labor, and Free Men."

Lincoln enjoyed a preponderance of support among workingmen despite their mixed feelings about the abolition of slavery. Fearful of competition from liberated Negroes willing to accept low wages, some trade union leaders favored the Crittenden Compromise permitting the continuance of slavery in the South but prohibiting its existence in new territories.

When Lincoln ran for reelection in 1864, his friendliness toward labor's interests was played up in handbills depicting him as a supporter of free schools for both white and black children.

55

AMBIVALENT FEELINGS ABOUT SOUTHERN SLAVERY

Generally speaking, Northern labor attitudes toward slavery were somewhat ambivalent. Prior to the Civil War many, perhaps most, low paid unskilled workers felt that their conditions were only marginally better than those of slaves below the Mason-Dixon line. Among skilled workers there was relatively little disposition to **allow** sympathy for the Negro to distract them from concentrating their efforts on unionization.

But in New England there was considerable abolitionist sentiment, especially among cotton mill workers. As far back as 1846, when insurrections among slaves were alarming the South, a convention of Massachusetts workers adopted the following resolution:

"Whereas there are at the present time 3,000,000 of our brothers and sisters groaning in chains on southern plantations; and whereas we wish not only to be consistent but to secure to all others those rights and privileges for which we are contending ourselves; therefore be it

"Resolved that while we honor and respect our forefathers for the noble manner in which they resisted British oppression, we, their descendants, will never be guilty of the glaring inconsistency of taking up arms to shoot and stab those who use the same means to accomplish the same objects.

"Resolved that while we are willing to pledge ourselves to use all the means in our power, consistent with our principles, to put down wars, insurrections, and mobs, and to protect all men from the evils of the same, we will not take up arms to sustain the southern slaveholder in robbing one-fifth of our countrymen of labor.

"Resolved, that we recommend our brethren to speak in thundered tones, both as associations and as individuals, and to let it no longer be said that northern laborers, while they are contending for their rights, are a standing army to keep three millions of their brethren and sisters in bondage . . . at the point of the bayonet."

A period of severe unemployment that followed Lincoln's election left labor apprehensive as the prospect of war loomed ahead. At a mass meeting held in Louisville, Kentucky, on December 28, 1860, workingmen pledged allegiance to the Union and the Constitution, but urged avoidance of military conflict. At similar meetings in the North labor groups endorsed the Crittenden Compromise prohibiting slavery in new territories while permitting its continuance in the South, but when the first gun was fired on Fort Sumter on April 12, 1861, Northern workers abandoned their peace agitations and vied with farmers in furnishing volunteers. Entire local unions enlisted at President Lincoln's call to arms and leaders who had supported the Crittenden Compromise helped recruit troops.

Backbreaking toil, from dawn to dusk, was the unremitting lot of Southern slaves.

DENUNCIATION OF WAGE SLAVERY IN THE NORTH

Southerners coupled their defense of slavery with attacks on Northern factory conditions. The latter, they claimed, had more evil consequences for the working-man than slavery.

"Whilst labor saving processes have probably lessened by one half . . . the amount of work needed for comfortable support," George Fitzhugh declared in a blatantly prejudiced tract on the subject, "the free laborer [in the North] is compelled by capital and competition to work more than he ever did before, and is less comfortable. The organization of society cheats him of his earnings, and those earnings go to swell the vulgar pomp and pageantry of ignorant millionaires."

Compared to Northern production methods, Fitzhugh asserted, the Southern system of slavery was much more humane:

"The division of labor [in the North] is a curse to the laborer . . . Division makes labor ten times more efficient, but by confining each workman to some simple, monotonous employment, it makes him a mere automaton, and an easy prey to the capitalist. The association of labor, like all associations, requires a head . . . and that head . . . will become a cheat and a tyrant, unless his interests are identified with the interests of the laborer. In a large factory, in free society, there is division of labor, and association too, but association and division [are] for the benefit of the employer and to the detriment of the laborer. On a large farm, whatever advances the health, happiness and morals of the Negroes renders them more prolific and valuable to their master. It is in his interest to pay them high wages by way of support and he can afford to do so, because association renders the labor of each slave five times as productive and efficient as it would be, were the slaves working separately . . .

"We have endeavored to show . . . that the Negro slave, considering his indolence and unskillfulness, often gets his fair share, and sometimes more than his share, of the profits of the farm, and is exempted, besides, from the harassing cares and anxieties of the free laborer. Grant, however, that the Negro does not receive adequate wages from his master, yet all admit that in the aggregate the Negroes get better wages than free laborers. Therefore, it follows that, with all its imperfections, slave society is the best form of society yet devised for the masses. When Socialists and Abolitionists, by full and fair experiments, exhibit a better [form of society] it will [then] be time to agitate the subject of abolition.

"The industrial products of black slave labor have been far greater and more useful to mankind, than those of the same amount of any other labor."

Southern plantation owners insisted that their slaves were far better off than Northern and British workers exploited by industrial plutocrats.

An ex-slave who became a firebrand abolitionist, Frederick Douglass (above) was the vice president of the American League of Colored Laborers (1850) and a co-founder, with Isaac Myers, of the Colored National Labor Union (1869). He served as president of the latter organization during the early 1870's. In his famous autobiography he recounts his experiences as a slave and his later efforts to organize Negroes into segregated unions because of unwillingness of white workers to grant them equal status.

(Adjoining photos were taken during the 1860's).

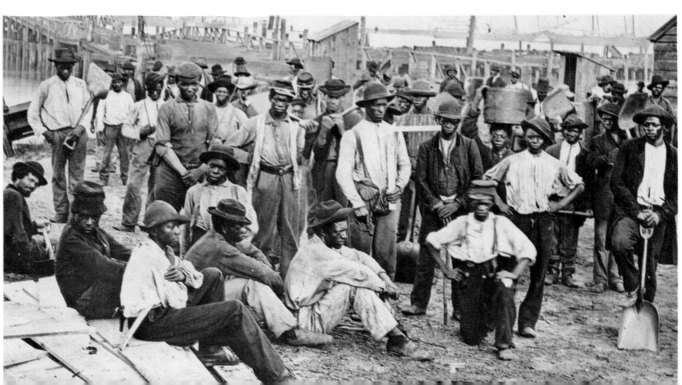

CONSCRIPTION RIOTS

Antagonized by the Conscription Act of 1863 sanctioning evasion of military service by northerners who could afford to pay a $300 commutation fee, large numbers of workers rioted in New York and other cities. Trouble-making Copperhead elements charged the war was being waged "to enable abolitionist Capitalists to transport Negroes into the northern cities to replace...striking workers."

Alienation from the Union cause was strengthened by a persuasive Copperhead argument emphasizing that conditions of laborers in the north were only slightly different from those of slaves in the south: "Where a man is compelled to labor at the will of another and to give him much the greater portion of the product of his labor, there slavery exists, and it is immaterial by what sort of compulsion the will of the laborer is subdued..." Copies of the adjoining broadsides, attributed to "A Democratic Workingman", were distributed during the New York conscription riots.

LABORING MEN
OF NEW YORK.

COMRADES :---Do you want to pay heavy taxes ? Do you want to suffer loss and ruin ? Do you want to be trampled under foot by ambitious demagogues ? Do you want to have your homes filled with sorrow, and your eyes run over with tears ? If not, then

STOP AND THINK!

The property destroyed by a riot must be paid for by the city, and in this way every act of disorder, violence and house-burning, is only laying heavier taxes on your own shoulders. Every disorderly act that is done only calls for greater expenses on the part of the city government. The United States does not pay the damages, but the City of New York alone. Of course, all the disturbances, losses and damages, only

FALL UPON OUR OWN HEADS.
COMRADES,
STAND BY THE LAW !

Stand by good order and good sense, and you will find it good policy. If any law is bad, let it be settled by the courts in a proper form. Do not listen to bad men who are only leading you to your ruin.

The politicians and business men of New York must stand by the law and the Constitution.

It is cheaper and better to Stand by the Law !

For when the law is broken and property destroyed, and lives lost, we all suffer more or less by the injury. Comrades! In the name of God---in the name of our wives and children---in the name of every thing that is dear to us---

STOP and THINK !

Stand up as Democratic Workingmen should stand up before the world, and show the traitors of the South, and the friends of tyranny all over the world, that

The Workingmen of New York are able to govern themselves !

Stand by the Union, the Constitution and the Laws ! Then peace, freedom and prosperity will be secure to you and to your children after you.

KEEP HONESTLY AT YOUR WORK !
GIVE NO HEED TO BAD ADVICE !

Any man that advises you to break the law is your enemy, and the enemy of your wives and children. These troubles will make the times only the worse for us all. High prices, heavy rents, and heavier taxes. Comrades! Keep the peace and all will be well.

WHITE SLAVES.

It is of the greatest importance to the workingmen of the United States to understand the true sentiments and objects of the leading traitors of the South. Their opinions of workingmen---who earn their support by their daily labor---are clearly set forth in the following extract from the speech of Mr. Hammond, of South Carolina, in the Senate of the United States, on the 4th of March, 1858.

"In all social systems there must be a class to do the mean duties, to perform the drudgery of life---that is, a class requiring but a low order of intellect, and but little skill. Its requisites are vigor, docility, fidelity. . . . . It constitutes the very mud-sills of society and of political government ; and you might as well attempt to build a house in the air, as to build either one or the other except on the mud-sills. Fortunately for the South, she found a race adapted to that purpose to her hand. . . . We use them for the purpose, and call them slaves.

The man who lives by daily labor, and scarcely lives at that, and who has to put out his labor in the market, and take the best he can get for it---in short, your whole class of manual laborers and operatives, as you call them, are SLAVES. The difference between us is, that our slaves are hired for life, and well compensated ; there is no starvation, no begging, no want of employment among our people, and not too much employment either. Yours are hired by the day. . . . YOUR SLAVES ARE WHITE, OF YOUR OWN RACE---you are brothers, of one blood. Our slaves do not vote. We give them no political power. Yours do vote ; and, being the majority, they are the depositories of all your political power. If they knew the tremendous secret, that the ballot-box is stronger than an army with bayonets, where would you be ?---Your society would be reconstructed. . . . Not by meetings in parks, with arms in their hands, but by the peaceful process of the ballot-box."

The law-abiding and union-loving workingmen of the Union---whom the Senator denounces as "White Slaves," went to the ballot-box, according to the Constitution, and effected "a peaceful revolution." But the "gentlemen" traitors of the South, less loyal and less honest, went "with arms in their hands," and treason in their hearts, and have compelled the workingmen of the South to rise against their brothers of the North, in order to make "white slaves" of them all.

There are many other advocates of the doctrine of Senator Hammond who can be produced.

These things being true, I charge,

1st. That the rebellion of the South Carolina traitors is an attempt to destroy the interests of the democratic working classes of the Union.

2d. That it is an effort to build up forever a system by which *"Capital shall own Labor."*

3d. That it is an attempt to make slavery---and property in slaves---the controlling interest of the Union.

4th. That Slavery is, and from its nature must be, the deadly enemy of Free Labor.

5th. That the success of the traitors will be a death-blow to the interests of Free Workingmen, North and South.

6th. That self-interest and patriotism both call upon Workingmen to stand by the government firm as a rock till the rebellion is put down, and peace restored by the constitutional authorities.

I challenge Hon. Fernando Wood, Hon. Benjamin Wood, C. Godfrey Gunther, Esq., and Prof. Mason, of New York ; F. W. Hughes, Esq. and Hon.

Conscription didn't apply to skilled shipyard artisans needed for the construction of Union naval vessels. Above are workers laying iron plates at a San Francisco drydock in 1863. Below is a scene at a Delaware shipyard during construction of an enormous battleship. The know-how acquired during this period greatly encouraged the expansion of the American shipbuilding industry after the war.

Rare Mathew Brady photos of workers employed by the
Union Army's Quartermaster Corps during the Civil War.

EXPANSION OF COMMERCE AND AGRICULTURE

Sparked by inventions that increased both agricultural and industrial production, the economy underwent a tremendous upsurge after the Civil War. "The decade following the war," wrote exuberant Joshua Lippincott "marks the beginning of one of the very greatest industrial eras of all times. Even the most enthusiastic word painters of former times failed to foresee the rapid growth of population, the opening of many new resources, the appearance of hundreds of new industries, the unusual development of business enterprise, and the great increase of wealth."

"Along the Docks, New York City" (above) appeared in Harper's Weekly, September 4, 1869. Underneath is an agricultural scene of about the same period.

LINKING THE EAST AND WEST

There was ample reason for boisterous celebration when the labor gangs of the Union Pacific and Central Pacific railroad lines met at Promontory, Utah, on May 10, 1869. They had performed an extraordinary feat in laying tracks across 1,775 miles of plains, mountains, and ravines. Most of the Union Pacific laborers were burly, hard-drinking Irishmen who were contemptuous of the little Chinese employed by the Central Pacific. (Below is a typical work camp site. Supervisory personnel was housed in the outfit cars; the trackmen lived in tents).

Completion of the first transcontinental railroad linking the east with the west set in motion forces that were to have a marked influence on the economic growth of the nation. Rapid railway expansion not only opened up enormous markets for manufactures and farm products, but also greatly facilitated access to vast mineral and other natural resources.

Despite obstacles and hardships, construction gangs built thousands of miles of railroad tracks. At the left is a work train inching its way across California's Sierra Mountains. On the right are Central Pacific laborers who reached Utah on April 28, 1869. Below is a track laying scene in a Nevada desert.

Still wearing their native hats, Chinese laborers employed by the Central Pacific did most of the backbreaking roadbed work in the western states. Construction superintendent J. H. Strobridge was initially averse to hiring them but he soon came to the conclusion that they were "the best [laborers] in the world. They learn quickly, do not fight, have no strikes that amount to anything, and are very cleanly in their habits."

For similar reasons railroad tycoon Leland Stanford was also highly appreciative of the Chinese who helped build the Central Pacific. "As a class," he advised President Andrew Johnson, "they are quiet, peaceable, patient, industrious and economical. Ready and apt to learn all the different kinds of work required in railroad building, they soon became as efficient as white laborers. More prudent and economical, they are content with less wages . . . No system similar to slavery, serfdom or peonage prevails among these laborers. Their wages, which are always paid in coin each month, are divided among them by their agents who attend to their business according to the labor done by each person. These agents are generally American or Chinese merchants who furnish them their supplies of food, the value of which they deduct from their monthly pay."

The grim, tired faces of men who worked on the railroads suggest the effects of long hours and wearisome toil. The youngster at the extreme left in the picture below, taken in 1870, is future labor leader Eugene V. Debs. He is seen with fellow shopyard workers of the Terre Haute and Indianapolis Railroad.

At Norwalk, Ohio, wood-burning locomotives, circa early 1870's, were serviced around the clock before heading west.

Some track-laying crews lived in three-story cars providing protection from hostile Indians and inclement weather.

Spurred by railroad expansion, steel manufacture was rapidly becoming a major industry dependent largely on semi-skilled workers. Later use of Bessemer converters of the type seen above was to greatly facil- itate production at reduced cost. As of 1868 steel rails sold for $168 a ton; by 1884 the cost was only $31. Simultaneously profits kept rising steadily but wages generally lagged behind.

Hazardous manual operations prevailed in glassworks employing a large number of youngsters. Above is a drawing of a Pittsburgh factory published in the March 18, 1871, issue of "Every Saturday." Below is a lithograph depicting the interior of the modernized Hobbs glassworks in Wheeling, West Virginia, in 1877.

It took plenty of muscle, daring, and ingenuity to build the Brooklyn Bridge.

CONSTANT DANGER

The hazards of erecting the Brooklyn Bridge were faced daily by the men who built it. Twenty-four lost their lives and scores were injured during the 13 years (1869-1883) it took to complete construction of the bridge.

Working in the caissons eighty feet below the water's surface was especially dangerous. Sandhogs were repeatedly incapacitated by air pressure resulting in the "bends." They were paid at the unheard of rate of $2 a day, but they went on strike and won a 25c raise.

New Yorkers marveled at the coolness with which bridge workers crossed the catwalk.

The crudity of iron ore mining in northern Michigan and oil well drilling at Titusville, Pennsylvania, during the late 1860's (when these photos were taken) persisted throughout most of the 1870's.

Slaughtering and Dressing Hogs

Drying and Trimming Hogs

The Curing Cellar

The Lard-Rendering Room

Production line techniques were extensively used in meat plants by the 1870's, but conditions were hardly as neat and tidy as the above drawings suggest. Meat processing was emerging as a great national industry. Railroad transportation made it possible to move livestock across vast distances to big city slaughterhouses from which meat was distributed over wide areas. Large scale packing plants sprang up soon after Chicago's massive Union Stockyards opened their doors in 1866. Below is an illustration drawn during the late 1850's.

FACTORY PRODUCTION

For all its benefits, industrialization was a mixed blessing. Previously, an artisan with a pair of able hands and a set of good tools was on fairly even terms with his employer. Usually he produced directly for purposes of consumption, took considerable pride in what he did, and had a reasonable degree of independence.

Under the impact of large scale production, the worker lost his sense of status. Too often his manpower was treated like a commodity not unlike the materials fed into the machine he served. He labored not directly to produce but to keep the machines going for an employer he rarely knew, and his conditions of employment seldom took into account his personal well being or his needs as a family wage earner.

Not surprisingly, many workers resented the factory system and the changes that accompanied it. "To them," as Aleine Austin has observed, "industrialization did not represent progress—it represented degradation. Under the impact of large-scale production, they felt themselves sinking to a lower and lower social level; they saw their entire pattern of living shattered and uprooted."

(At the top is a sketch of workers in a type foundry. Below is a scene in a textile factory).

77

THE PRICE OF MECHANIZATION

As industry became bigger, more mechanized, more specialized, the skilled worker's pride of craftsmanship diminished. In testifying about the changes in his line of work, machinist John Morrison graphically told a U. S. Senate committee in 1883:

"The trade has been subdivided and those subdivisions have been again subdivided, so that a man never learns the machinist's trade now. Ten years ago he learned, not the whole of the trade, but a fair portion of it . . .

"In the case of making the sewing machine, for instance, you frequently find that the trade is so subdivided that a man is not considered a machinist at all. Hence, it is merely laborers' work and it is laborers that work at that branch of our trade.

"The different branches of the trade are divided and subdivided so that one man may make just a particular part of a machine and may not know anything whatever about another part of the same machine. In that way machinery is produced a great deal cheaper than it used to be formerly, and in fact, through this system of work, 100 men are able to do now what it took 300 or 400 men to do fifteen years ago. By the use of machinery and the subdivision of the trade they so simplify the work that it is made a great deal easier and put together a great deal faster. There is no system of apprenticeship . . . You simply go in and learn whatever branch you are put at, and you stay at that unless you are changed to another . . ."

One Senator questioned Morrison about the long-range opportunities for conscientious machinists. "What is the prospect," he asked, "for a man working in one of these machine shops, a man who is temperate and economical and thrifty to become a boss or a manufacturer of machinery himself from his own savings? Could a man do it without getting aid from some relative who might die and leave him a fortune, or without drawing a lottery prize, or something of that sort?"

"Well," Morrison replied, "speaking generally, there is no chance. They have lost all desire to become bosses . . . because the trade has become demoralized. First they earn so small wages; and, next, it takes so much capital to become a boss now that they cannot think of it, because it takes all they can earn to live."

Employers sometimes destroyed their old equipment as a means of getting rid of their skilled workers and making room for new machinery that could be tended by women paid lower wages. A cotton mill superintendent admitted such sabotage was practiced in connection with a new technique called ring-spinning that replaced mule-spinning, a highly skilled occupation. "The mule-spinners," he explained, "are a tough crowd to deal with. A few years ago they were giving trouble at this mill, so one Saturday afternoon, after they had gone home, we started right in and smashed up a room-full of mules with sledgehammers. When the men came back on Monday morning, they were astonished to find there was no work for them. That room is now full of ring frames run by girls."

GENTEEL TRADES

Women were turning their hands to a variety of occupations. These illustrations from Harper's Bazaar of 1868 show paper collar cutters, hoop skirt makers, photograph mounters, candle makers, silver burnishers, hat trimmers, type setters, and shoe fitters. These were considered "suitable genteel trades for unmarried women."

"WONDERFULLY NIMBLE AND CONSCIENTIOUS GIRLS"

Young women predominated in clothing and cigarette factories similar to those shown here. At the top is a loft in which garments were manufactured for New York's A. T. Stewart Department Store; at the bottom is a scene in the packaging room of a Richmond, Virginia, cigarette factory.

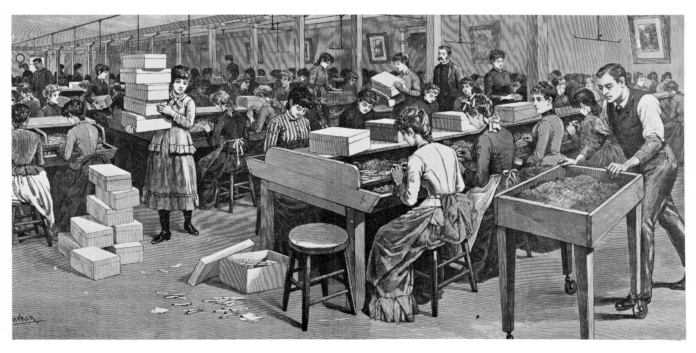

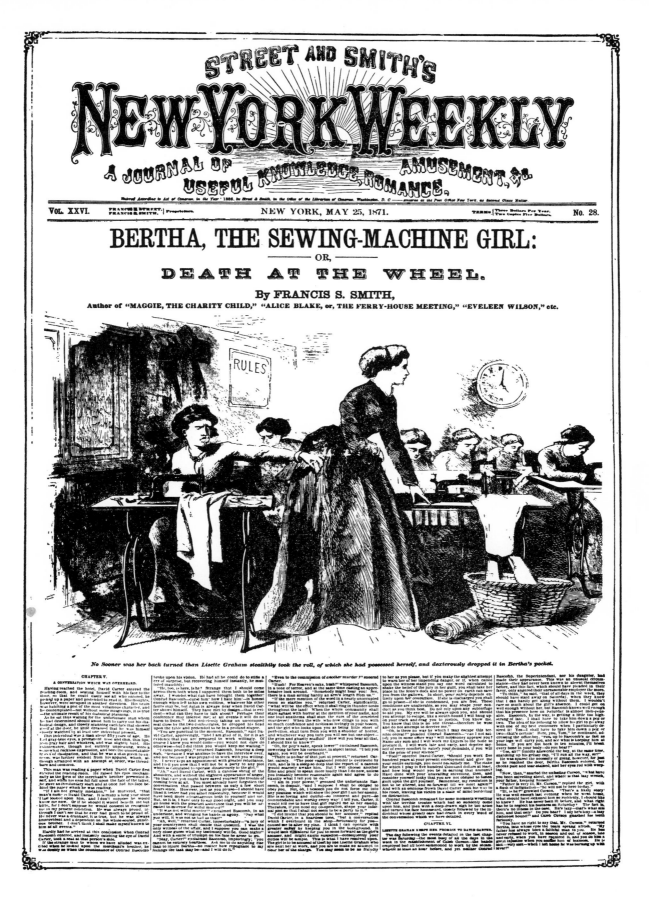

Working girl readers of the New York Weekly could readily identify with Bertha's trials and tribulations.

Indifference toward the plight of working women persisted despite occasionally fervent pleas in their behalf. Their exploitation went unchecked until they were unionized early in the twentieth century.

A Plea For Working Girls.

(Editorial by Anna Raymond published in Street & Smith's *New York Weekly*, August 31, 1871)

Do the rich and well-to-do think of the poor girls in their employ, and of their privations? Here and there a generous and noble-hearted individual remembers kindly those in his employ, but if the majority give a thought to them it is only to say mentally: "I pay the regular price, and that is all my duty."

But do you pay the girls in your employ within twenty per cent of the value of their work to you? Is the price you pay sufficient to support them honestly and respectably? Yet in most stores and shops the girls are required to dress neatly and well; if not, the penalty is dismissal. Can they do this, and purchase healthful food upon the paltry sum you pay for their services? No, no, and so half-fed upon cheap food they go to work day after day, the cheek growing thinner and paler; hope dying out of the eye, until an early death makes room for another martyr; or, wearying of this toiling life, they marry for a home and support, with little or no love for the husband, and enter upon new duties with a physical organization weakened by overwork and insufficient food, and with a hopeless heart. Is it strange that children given to that home die young, or grow up pale and delicate, fit subjects for that American epidemic, consumption?

Again, many of these girls have widowed and sick mothers, or young brothers and sisters to support, and beside being in the store all day, do plain sewing at home, working more than half the night. Yet these girls, so nobly, so heroically fighting the battles of life, are looked upon with scorn by many who are living in luxurious ease. There is one now, hurrying home from her daily toil, that she may care for a sick mother. How the crowd jostles her. She is "only a working girl;" and a richly dressed woman brushes against her, looking scornfully upon her faded dress in last year's style. Oh, woman of wealth and fashion, do you know that poor girl may be as much purer in heart and life than you are, as the beautiful snowflake floating in mid-air is cleaner and whiter than that trodden in the filthy street.

What working girls want is to be better paid, and according to the value of their work;—not pity, not the charity of the rich man or woman's purse, but the charity of the heart that thinketh kindly of the toiling. And one word to you who employ these girls, and have grown rich on their hard work, while you have starved them body and mind. Why is it that each year you pay a less price, for the same work? For instance, straw-sewers are this year paid more than one-third less than formerly, and so also in other branches of business. Do you wish to drive them to desperation or death, and have their sin or death registered against you in Heaven? Oh, ye employers, if you persist in longer crushing, and starving these noble, honest, but poor girls, you will be indirectly guilty of the evil consequences that, in some instances, may arise from it. As you measure to them, so will a just God mete it out to you in the life that is to come. Then will you not deal more kindly with them, and pay according to the value of their work?

"I cannot, because others do not," says one. Let one or more rich men try it, and so shut up the low shops where work is half done and half paid for, and let every man and woman, who is truly the friend of the poor, patronize such stores, and so bring about a reform that "woman's suffrage" never will, neither "women's parliaments" called to advertise one woman, or a club of women.

One word to you, my toiling sisters,—work on hopefully—perhaps a better day is dawning,—ever be honest to yourselves, and to the whole world. It may be that you will find rest and peace in a cheerful home, where you will be kindly shielded from toil;—or perchance the sky may brighten, and you make a home for yourself and those you love. Strive to do right, and though your hopes are not realized, you will have the consciousness of having done the best you could even in the darkest hour, and if your reward comes not to you here, it will come in the eternal hereafter.

Standing next to Jonathan Fincher is William H. Sylvis, president of the National Labor Union.

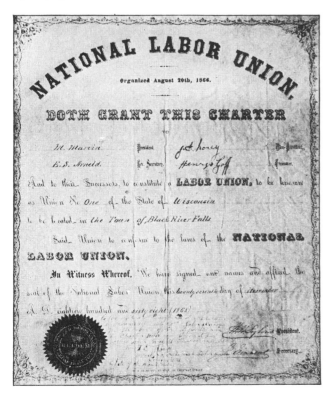

EMERGENCE OF THE NATIONAL LABOR UNION

The birth of the National Labor Union after the Civil War gave promise of a robust life.

Essentially a loosely-knit organization, it was composed chiefly of local unions and trades assemblies convinced that the future of labor depended upon fundamental reforms. No one felt this more strongly than president William H. Sylvis, the first truly outstanding figure in the American labor movement.

"Few labor leaders," historian Foster Dulles has said of Sylvis, "have been more devoted to the cause, more willing to sacrifice every personal consideration in working for labor's interests, or commanded more loyalty and affection on the part of his fellow workers. He was literally to wear himself out in their behalf."

Achieving an 8-hour day headed the agenda of the organization's first meeting. "The first and great necessity of the present," the delegates declared in a ringing resolution "is to free labor of this country from capitalistic slavery [by] . . . passing of a law by which eight hours shall be the normal working day in all states of the American Union." Agitation toward that end was led by Ira Steward, a self-educated Boston mechanic who popularized the slogan "Whether you work by the piece or work by the day, decreasing the hours increases the pay."

A direct result of such pressure was Congressional enactment in 1868 of a law establishing an 8-hour day for employees of the federal government.

At Sylvis' urging, the organization decided that political action was the best means of achieving its objectives. It hastily launched the National Reform and Labor Party as the elections of 1872 approached. In arguing for this action, Sylvis declared:

"We have tried the balance-power or make-weight expedient of questioning candidates, and throwing our votes in favor of such as endorsed or were pledged to our interests. How vain and futile this expedient has proven is known to all. It is but a history of broken promises and violated pledges and invariably ends in exposing our weakness; for say what you will, men of opposite opinions to the candidate's will not trust him in the face of such frequent deceptions . . . We must keep clear of entangling alliances. With a distinct workingmen's party in the field, there can be no distrust, no want of confidence."

Some elements in the National Labor Union weren't enthusiastic about the idea because they felt that labor was then far too weak to enter politics.

Confidence in the organization gradually diminished. Its interests became too diffuse for most of its members. Charles O'Conor, a New York lawyer nominated for President by the National Labor Reform Party in 1872, received only 30,000 votes.

(At the bottom is a charter the National Labor Union granted to an affiliate in Black River Falls, Wisconsin.)

In both appearance and fact, labor leaders of the late 1860's had an air of respectability that belied a contemporary charge that "ruffians . . . are stirring up trouble among workingmen." Ideas similar to those of the National Labor Union were espoused in 1865 by the above organizers of the short-lived Industrial Assembly of North America. Below are founders of the National Marine Engineers Beneficial Association.

MOUNTING PRESSURE FOR
THE SHORTER WORK DAY

All but a few delegates to the 1869 convention of the National Labor Union (held in Philadelphia) agreed that reduction of the work day should remain the organization's primary aim.

About 150 delegates represented the leading national unions of the time (molders, printers, machinists, blacksmiths, and carpenters), some state federations (Pennsylvania, Kansas, and California), several dozen local unions, and an assortment of reform groups. Women delegates included pioneer suffragist Susan B. Anthony, founder of the Working Women's Protective Association.

At the side is a contemporary drawing of an eight-hour-day parade near New York's Cooper Union building.

POWERFUL UNIONS

Primary backers of the National Labor Union, the iron molders' and machinists' unions took firm root during the Civil War years. By the 1870's both of these unions were so powerful that they encouraged their local affiliates to establish cooperative factories which competed with firms refusing to engage in collective bargaining. Eventually poor management and other difficulties forced most of the cooperatives out of business.

SIGNIFICANT MILESTONE

A direct result of pressure by the National Labor Union was the passage in 1868 of a law establishing an eight-hour day for "all laborers, workmen, and mechanics now employed or who may be employed by or on behalf of the Government of the United States." President Andrew Johnson, who owed his rise in Tennessee politics to Workingman's Party support, signed the measure shortly before he became the target of impeachment proceedings. His successor, Ulysses S. Grant, encountered difficulty in securing observance of the law. Non-compliance by government contractors was sanction-ed by a Supreme Court decision holding that the law did not apply to them.

Boston machinist Ira Steward, self-appointed high priest of the eight-hour movement, devoted most of his life to convincing unions and employers that a shorter work day was to their mutual benefit. In 1863 he prevailed upon the Machinists and Black-smiths Union to pass a resolution affirming that "From east to west, from north to south, the most important change to us as workingmen, to which all else is subordinate, is a permanent reduction to eight of the hours exacted for each day's work."

THE NECESSITY OF THE PERIOD—"EIGHT-HOUR MEN."

"Now, therefore, I, Ulysses S. Grant, President of the United States, do hereby direct that from and after this date no reduction shall be made in the wages paid by the Government by the day to such laborers, workmen, and mechanics, on account of such reduction of the hours of labor" to eight hours a day.

Derision accompanied President Grant's decision to pay government workers as much for an eight-hour day as they had received for ten hours. Similar conditions were demanded in banners borne by New York laborers (below) who marched in an 1872 parade for shorter hours. The average working day of most wage earners continued to range between ten and fourteen hours. Typically, employers inveighed against demands for a shorter day on the ground that it would encourage "folly and worse because idleness breeds sloth."

TRADE UNION NEWSPAPERS

Unlike previously published papers primarily concerned with social reforms, the publications that appeared in the late 1860's and 1870's were devoted to news about the progress of trade unionism.

In terms of authoritativeness and journalistic standards the most outstanding was Fincher's Trades Review— "one of the best labor papers ever published in the United States" in the opinion of John R. Commons. During its brief existence between 1863 and 1866 the Review gave organized labor not only solid support but also reliable, well-written reports about the activities of emerging unions. As secretary of the powerful Machinists and Blacksmiths Union, editor Jonathan Fincher kept in close touch with labor officers throughout the country, thus enabling him to make his paper "a truly national publication." Frequent contributors to its columns were leaders like William Sylvis, Richard Trevellick, and Ira Steward.

Since the Review did not accept commercial advertising, its existence depended on subscriptions from unions as well as paid notices about their activities but neither yielded adequate income. When the paper collapsed in August, 1866, it printed its own pathetic obituary: "Having donned our sackcloth and ashes, and humbled ourselves before the possessors of mammon . . . and completely exhausted our threadbare credit . . . the end of our tether has been reached."

The labor movement, still small, still unsteady, simply wasn't ready for Fincher's Review. Besides newly established unions with substantial memberships were launching their own organs. Those relating to trades employing large numbers of immigrants often contained special sections printed in foreign languages.

Sign This!

"You Slaves of the 19th Century."

Below is a copy of the agreement that is being circulated for signatures, and without signing which no person is allowed to work on the Wabash:

"I (giving name) do promise to leave the Knights of Labor, all Brotherhood organizations, all labor unions, etc., and also agree to willingly pay the hospital assessments, whatever it may amount to. EMPLOYE."

As unionization widened, employers resorted to blacklisting and other means of intimidation.

Workers even suspected of being union members were discharged as "undesirable." Their names were placed on confidential lists that were circulated among employers. Once a man's name appeared on such a list it became extremely difficult for him to get another job in the same trade.

Blatant blacklisting is spelled out in the above confidential letter the Vulcan Iron Works sent to Cyrus McCormick in March 1872. "The Moulders named below," the letter states, "discontinued work in our shop in consequence of our refusal to continue in our employ strikers from the shop of N. S. Benton & Co. who were inadvertently hired by us . . . Please keep names and act accordingly."

To prevent unionization employers often insisted that their workers sign the "iron clad," an oath by which they became subject to dismissal if they joined a union. (At the side is an 1885 broadside about the "iron clad.")

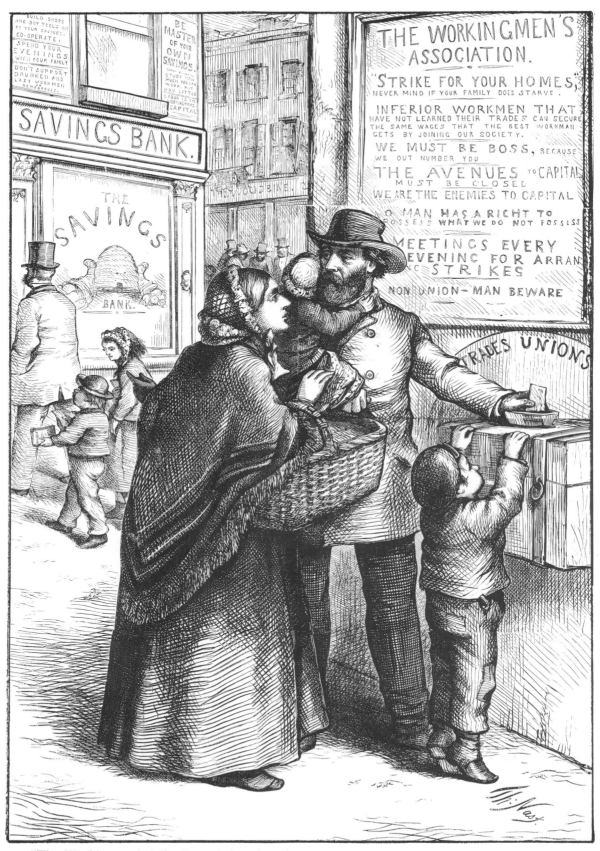

"The Workingman's Mite," a rebuke of trade unionism by famed cartoonist Thomas Nast.

Pity the poor employer. "Has Capital Any Rights That Labor Is Bound To Respect?" is the caption that accompanied the Keppler drawing at the left when it appeared in Puck's pages.

MISERY DURING THE 1870'S

Precipitated by reckless speculative sprees, the Panic of 1873 set in motion an era of misery. Millions of workers lost their jobs as thousands of businesses failed or cut production drastically. Suffering became so intense that a Harper's Weekly article about conditions in New York during the winter of 1873 stated that 900 persons had starved to death, 3,000 infants were abandoned on doorsteps, and more than 11,000 boys were left homeless. Countless numbers of men and women slept in hallways and the public parks.

At a meeting of the unemployed held in the Cooper Union auditorium placards told of their misery:

7,500 LODGED IN OVERCROWDED CHARNEL HOUSES
10,000 HOMELESS MEN AND WOMEN IN OUR STREETS
20,850 IDLE MEN FROM 11 TRADE UNIONS

Despite the clear evidence of widespread distress, some who were not hard hit by the depression berated the unemployed as "lazy, idle, worthless loafers, frauds, [and] blackguards." By way of refutation John Swinton, a New York journalist, pointed out:

"Take the records of but a single soup kitchen and free lodging house—that in Leonard Street, for the last month. In that month among the applicants registered you will find 398—what? Loafers? No! carpenters. And 383—what? Thieves? No! painters. And 234—what? Blackguards? No! printers . . .

"Are such men—and this report is a fair specimen of the reports—loafers, vermin, outlaws, or outcasts? We hear also that many of the recipients of relief were men who refused to work at fair wages. You must judge whether it be just to say such things of our mechanics and laborers, or whether such men actually prefer the humiliation of idle pauperism to the pride of industrious independence. It is false to them, to human nature, and to all our experience, to say that they do."

POVERTY AMID PLENTY DURING THE 1870'S

In his book "Progress and Poverty," published in 1879, Henry George focused attention on a question that especially perplexed labor; Why should the advance of the industrial revolution, with more and more machinery for producing wealth, result in greater poverty? Unlike trade unionists who felt that the main reason was the unwillingness of employers to raise wages, George blamed inequities of the time especially on the tendency of the wealthy to monopolize land and hold it out of use while waiting for value to rise. Since, he concluded, all wealth comes ultimately from the soil or under it, the degree to which land is not readily available to farmers and workers is also the degree to which society is poorer than it should be. Moreover, he contended, since land is a "limited commodity," monopolistic landlords could charge excessive rents and thereby drive down wages.

A firm believer in the private enterprise system, George did not propose socialism as a remedy. Instead he urged what he called the "single tax" on land values. The rate of this tax would be based not on the existing value of the land but on its real worth. By taxing land into maximum productivity, he argued, prosperity would result. His ideas had great appeal among labor leaders convinced of the need for basic land reforms.

The persistent evidence of poverty in the midst of plenty seemed intolerable to journalist Horace Greeley.

"I believe," he declared, "that there need be, and should be, no paupers . . . and that civilized society pays more for the support of able-bodied pauperism than the necessary cost of its extirpation.

"I believe that they babble idly and libel Providence who talk of surplus Labor, or the inadequacy of Capital to supply employment to all who need it . . . Where Labor stands idle, save in the presence of some great public calamity, there is demonstrated deficiency, not of Capital, but of brains.

"I believe that the efficiency of human effort is enormously, ruinously diminished by what I term Social Anarchy . . . It is quite within the truth to estimate the annual product of our National Industry at less than half what it might be if better applied and directed."

(Below is a wood engraving entitled "A Midnight Visit to One of the Cheap Lodging Houses." It accompanied an article about "Our Homeless Poor" published by Frank Leslie's Illustrated Newspaper in 1872.)

DEPRESSION GRIEVANCES

Mounted police ruthlessly clubbed down unemployed demonstrators who gathered in New York's Tompkins Square on January 13, 1874. Organized to call attention to the need for relief, the meeting had been sanctioned by local officials and Mayor Havemeyer himself promised to speak, but at the last minute the city's permit was withdrawn, ostensibly because radical leaders of the International Workingmen's Association participated in the arrangements.

Unaware of the permit's cancellation, hundreds of workers gathered in the square at the scheduled hour when a squadron of mounted police suddenly charged into the crowd, "indiscriminately swinging their clubs and hitting out at everyone within reach," including women and children who "were ridden down as they fled in panic . . . [while] scores of innocent bystanders were injured in trying to escape the police charge."

In its account of the incident the New York Times reported that the police applied their clubs with "reasonable but not excessive authority" and that "the scrambles of the mob as the officers advanced were not unamusing."

Young Sam Gompers, a cigar union organizer who barely managed to escape the police clubs, came away with misgivings about mass demonstrations.

At the side is a contemporary attack on Tammany Hall rule of New York by "Boss" William Marcy Tweed. Such cartoons plagued him until his downfall.

THE BED OF ROSES.

"THE RICH GROWING RICHER, THE POOR GROWING POORER."

"—WE DRINK, TO OUR CONSTITUENTS. MAY THEY LIVE LONG, SO THAT WE MAY PROSPER."

"—YES. THE RENT IS "PERHAPS EXORBITANT." BUT YOUR HUSBAND ALWAYS VOTES FOR THE VERY MEN WHO MAKE EVERY THING "PERHAPS EXORBITANT." BED OF THORNS.

BRINGING THE THING HOME.

Such scenes of squalid misery belied the boast that "ours is a land of plenty for all." Suffering during winter months was only partially alleviated by free coal dumped in the streets of New York City.

RADICAL RUMBLINGS

The hard times of the 1870's provided fertile ground for the radical ideas of the International Working-men's Association (the "First International") sired by Karl Marx with the help of British trade unions. Unsuccessful in its efforts to establish itself on American soil via the National Labor Union, the IWA wielded some influence on "sections" organized in the nation's larger industrial cities.

In 1870 three sections of the association (German, French, and Bohemian) created a tightly knit central committee in New York City and by 1871 there were eight sections in the U. S. Two additional groups were organized by William West, Victoria Woodhull, and Tennessee Claflin, but when their ideas were disowned in 1872 they created what they called an "American Confederation."

Indicative of activities of American sections of the IWA was a memorial demonstration (illustration at top) in honor of French revolutionaries executed by the Thiers government in 1871. In the procession was a funeral canopy drawn by six gray horses draped in black. Most of the marchers wore red ties.

Contrary to expectations, removal of the headquarters of the First International from London to New York contributed to its dissolution although agitation by American members continued to encourage radicalism among workers in New York, Chicago, and other industrial cities.

Below is a panel from a mural painted during the 1940's by famed Diego Rivera. Marx is seen holding a scroll bearing his forecast of class struggle in the U. S. Below him collaborator Friedrich Engels is facing Daniel De Leon, organizer of the Socialist Trade and Labor Alliance; Eugene V. Debs, founder of the American Railway Union who became the Socialist Party's candidate for President; William Haywood, leader of the Industrial Workers of the World; and other laborites and left wingers Rivera considered exponents of Marxism.

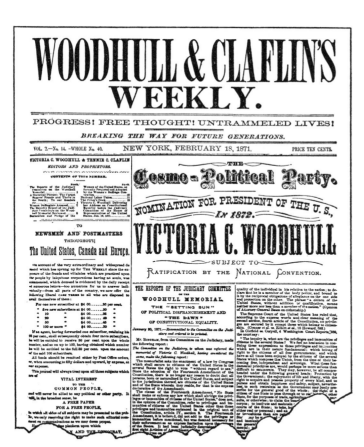

EQUAL RIGHTS COALITION

Formerly active in the International Workingmen's Association, flamboyant Victoria Woodhull ran for President in 1872; her Vice Presidential running mate was Frederick Douglass, the head of the Colored National Labor Union. Their miniscule Equal Rights Party (initially spawned as the "Cosmo-Political Party") promised Negroes and women redress of their grievances but the electorate at large remained massively indifferent. Only a year before Mrs. Woodhull and her sister, Tennessee Claflin, waged a widely publicized campaign against Wall Street speculators.

THE CHIMERA OF GREENBACKISM

Philanthropist-businessman Peter Cooper made a very poor showing as the presidential candidate of the Greenbackers in 1876.

An outgrowth of the depression of the 1870's, revolt by western farmers, and the political activities of the National Labor Union, the Greenback Labor Party demanded the issuance of government currency ("greenbacks") in place of bank notes and insisted on other reforms endorsed by union leaders who sought to break up the monopolistic power of banks, abolish the "robbery of interest rates," and liberate the public from dependence upon gold that required "the very heart's blood of the workingman [to be] mortgaged from the cradle to the grave."

Greenback currency reform, the National Labor Union contended, "would effect the equitable distribution of the products of labor between non-producing capital and labor, giving to laborers a fair compensation for their products, and to capital a just reward for its uses, remove the necessity for excessive toil and afford the industrial classes the time and means necessary for . . . culture."

National Labor Union president William Sylvis wielded considerable influence in behalf of Greenbackism. "There are," he said, "about three thousand trades unions in the United States . . . We must show them that when a just monetary system has been established there will no longer exist any necessity for trade unions."

DERISION OF THE "REGENERATED WORLD"

Despite such ridicule, fifteen candidates of the Greenback Labor Party were elected to Congress in 1878 and scores of others won state offices. Peter Cooper is seen upholding the "Regenerated World" he hatched as the party's presidential candidate two years earlier. Greenback syrup is being served by General Ben Butler, pro-labor Governor of Massachusetts who became the party's presidential nominee in 1884.

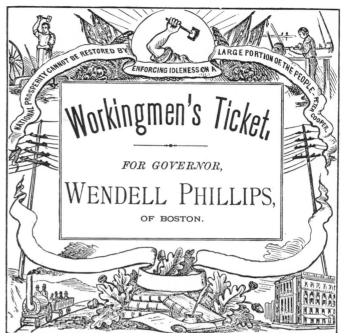

Hitch-hiker Ben Butler, a radical Reconstructionist abhorred in the South as "Beast Butler", sought the Presidency on the Greenback Labor ticket.

Wendell Phillips, a Boston Brahmin, made a poor showing when he ran for Governor of Massachusetts in 1870 but he remained a "truly loyal...and steadfast friend of New England workingmen".

The broadside at the bottom alludes to a Pennsylvania offshoot of the Greenback movement.

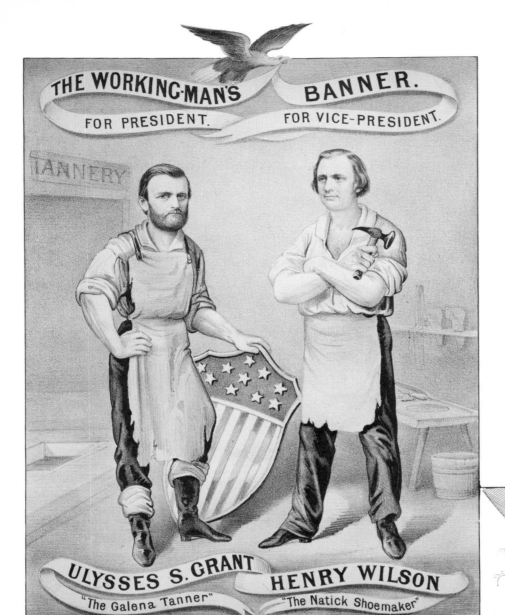

THE WORKING-MAN'S BANNER.

FOR PRESIDENT. FOR VICE-PRESIDENT.

TANNERY

ULYSSES S. GRANT
"The Galena Tanner"

HENRY WILSON
"The Natick Shoemaker"

BEFORE AND AFTER GRANT'S ELECTION

Republican Party exploitation of Grant's humble origins helped secure his reelection in 1872 but when the country went into an economic tailspin shortly after his inauguration he remained aloof to pleas for federal action to alleviate suffering.

Strictly speaking, Grant's ties to labor were somewhat tenuous. During his youth he had worked in his father's tannery for short periods. Vice President Henry Wilson was a rags-to-riches type who rose from shoe cobbler to shoe manufacturer.

Uncle Sam, a modern Noah, opened his arms wide to the peoples of Europe during the 1870's and 1880's. Drawn to America by the lure of freedom and reports of high wages, millions of immigrants came streaming into the country. About 85% were fugitives from poverty and oppression in the western and northern nations of Europe. Those with special skills as artisans readily found employment but others were less fortunate. For all, however, the Statute of Liberty, a gift from France commemorating the Declaration of Independence centenary in 1876, became an inspiring symbol at the entrance to New York's harbor.

ARRIVAL OF EMIGRANTS FROM CASTLE GARDEN TO TAKE THE PLACES OF THE STRIKERS — A SCENE IN WEST ST.

THE CONTRACT LABOR SYSTEM

Of all the moves to encourage immigration, none incensed workers more than a federal law permitting American employers to place liens on the labor and property of immigrants to whom they advanced passage money. In effect the odious indenture of colonial times was resurrected.

Under arrangements sanctioned by Congress in 1864 manufacturers were encouraged to obtain cheap foreign labor, thus enabling them to cut the wages of their regular workers and readily replace strikers. Small wonder that the hastily organized American Emigrant Company (an enterprise backed by businessmen as well as Chief Justice Salmon Chase, Senator Charles Sumner, and the Reverend Henry Ward Beecher) had no trouble raising more than half a million dollars worth of stock to finance its efforts as an "efficient channel of intercourse" between American employers and European workingmen.

"Northern manufacturers," Aleine Austin pointed out, "need no longer fear the competition of goods produced abroad . . . No longer need they worry about the comparatively high wages of American workers, either . . . Here was an ideal solution to the manufacturers' labor . . . problem. It means low wages—not only for the European immigrant, but also for native American workers who competed with the immigrants for factory jobs. The manufacturers, indeed, were in the saddle."

Alarmed trade unionists bitterly denounced the "nefarious machines" set up under the law. The situation became especially disturbing when it became evident that contract labor was facilitating the use of immigrants as scabs. During a strike of bituminous operators in Pennsylvania and West Virginia, for example, English miners were brought over to replace them.

Since it was difficult to stop such practices once the immigrants had arrived in the United States, some labor leaders urged British unions to block the European recruitment drives of the American Emigrant Company. Almost coincidentally, concern about the importation into England of strikebreakers from continental Europe persuaded British unions to participate in the creation of the International Workingmen's Association (the First International) inspired into existence by Karl Marx.

Because of the evils arising under the contract labor law, the National Labor Union sought restriction of immigration with the help of the IWA. Some Americans, however, feared that union hostility toward immigrants was fanning flames of prejudice that could backfire. This worried William Sylvis as president of the Iron Molders Union, an organization composed largely of workers who had migrated from Germany, England, and Ireland. "God in the amplitude of his omniscient wisdom," he reminded his union, "reserved this continent . . . as an asylum wherein the toil-worn sons of humanity may find an abiding place free from the curse of landless and homeless toil . . . here is the land which 'Heaven reserved in pity of the poor.'"

THE "YELLOW PERIL" RAISES ITS PIGTAILED HEAD

Prejudice against Chinese immigrants was whipped into unreasoning hatred by lurid cartoons like the above, but the facts hardly warranted the alarm that arose on the West Coast in the late 1870's.

As long as labor was in relatively short supply, the docile, squint-eyed Chinese who held menial jobs were regarded with amused tolerance. Animosity toward them began building up as employers found it expedient to hire them at low wages in preference to white workers who kept asking for more pay and causing trouble when they couldn't get it. And outright hostility broke loose as jobs became quite scarce after the Panic of 1873.

"Most of the [Chinese] immigrants," according to historian Allan Nevins, "were . . . honest, healthy, self-respecting, frugal. They did much to build the Far West, . . . their gentleness, patience and dignity did not compare unfavorably with the motley white stocks that flowed into early California. But as the population on the Pacific Coast increased, the rougher white element felt increasing jealousy of all alien breeds—'greasers' from Mexico, other Latin-Americans, and the Chinese."

105

Regular Workingmen's Ticket,

SANTA CRUZ COUNTY.

For

1. DELEGATE AT LARGE TO CONST'L CONVENTION, PAUL BONNET.
2. DELEGATE AT LARGE TO CONST'L CONVENTION, A. FISCHER.
3. DELEGATE AT LARGE TO CONST'L CONVENTION, J. W. JAMISON.
4. DELEGATE AT LARGE TO CONST'L CONVENTION, JAMES KIDNEY.
5. DELEGATE AT LARGE TO CONST'L CONVENTION, J. R. PICO.
6. DELEGATE AT LARGE TO CONST'L CONVENTION, J. R. SHARPSTEIN.
7. DELEGATE AT LARGE TO CONST'L CONVENTION, CHARLES TILLSON.
8. DELEGATE AT LARGE TO CONST'L CONVENTION, J. A. WHELAN.
9. DELEGATE AT LARGE TO CONST'L CONVENTION, P. S. DORNEY.
10. DELEGATE AT LARGE TO CONST'L CONVENTION, J. B. KELLY.
11. DELEGATE AT LARGE TO CONST'L CONVENTION, H. P. WILLIAMS.
12. DELEGATE AT LARGE TO CONST'L CONVENTION, H. L. McKELVEY.
13. DELEGATE AT LARGE TO CONST'L CONVENTION, JOHN GREENWELL.
14. DELEGATE AT LARGE TO CONST'L CONVENTION, L. J. MORROW.
15. DELEGATE AT LARGE TO CONST'L CONVENTION, G. THOM.
16. DELEGATE AT LARGE TO CONST'L CONVENTION, J. M. TODD.
17. DELEGATE AT LARGE TO CONST'L CONVENTION, W. F. STONE.
18. DELEGATE AT LARGE TO CONST'L CONVENTION, W. H. NORTHCUTT.

IMPACT OF RACIAL PREJUDICE

Antagonism toward "the coolies" by the Workingmen's Party had both overt and covert support from the business community.

As long as the Chinese were willing to work for low wages, their white employers saw no reason to be alarmed about the Yellow Peril. But it was a different story when the Chinese began to establish their own shops. Now their ex-employers became allies of labor.

Many businessmen weren't at all loathe to back boycotts of products made in Chinese-owned shops. Cigar manufacturers who recognized the International Cigar Makers Union readily agreed to use its distinctive label. Upon discovering that labels printed with water-resistant black ink were being soaked off empty boxes and pasted on boxes containing Chinese or non-union cigars, the union adopted a blue ink that deteriorated when placed in contact with water.

One of the most original devices of American trade unionism, the label came to be widely adopted as employers realized that the consuming power of union labor could be helpful in encouraging the purchase of union-made products.

SMOKERS! -- SEE THAT THIS LABEL (IN BLUE) IS ON EACH BOX, THE ONLY GUARANTY AGAINST CHINESE MANUFACTURED CIGARS — SMOKERS!

REMEMBER THE ONLY WAY THAT YOU CAN HELP THE WHITE CIGARMAKER, AND WITHOUT ANY EXPENSE TO YOURSELF, IS BY SMOKING ONLY SUCH CIGARS AS HAVE THE LABEL ATTACHED TO THE BOX.

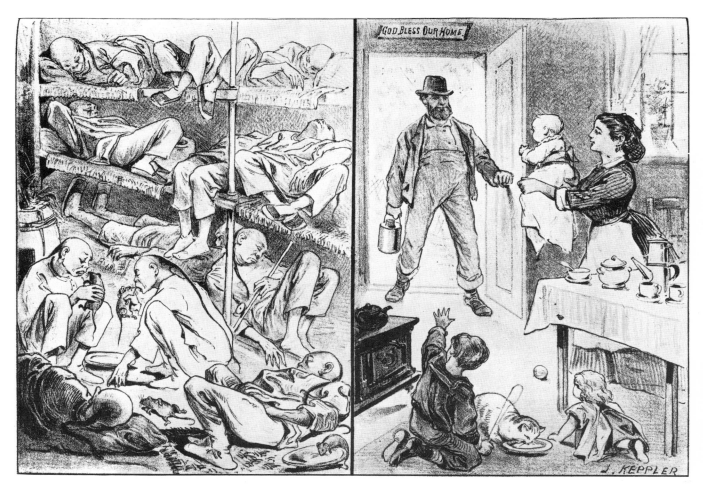

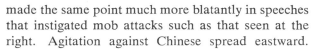

Comparisons like the above leave no room for doubt about why the Chinese were considered undesirable. Blustering Dennis Kearney (left below) made the same point much more blatantly in speeches that instigated mob attacks such as that seen at the right. Agitation against Chinese spread eastward.

107

SOCIAL SCIENCE SOLVED.

ANTI-CHINESE RIOTS

At sand lot meetings in San Francisco, anti-Oriental resolutions were passed by boisterous acclamation following inflammatory speeches by Dennis Kearney. Some employers hastily discharged their Chinese laborers but rehired them after troubles died down.

Kearney is seen being drawn proudly through the city when he was released from jail for inciting riots that resulted in attacks on Oriental laborers.

An offshoot of the anti-Chinese movement, the Workingmen's Party of California founded by Kearney became a powerful force throughout the state. To the surprise of oldline politicians, fifty of its candidates were elected delegates to the state's constitutional convention of 1878 and in the following year the party succeeded in placing twenty-eight supporters in the state legislature. In municipal elections Workingmen's candidates were chosen mayors of San Francisco, Oakland, and Sacramento.

Largely because of the party's influence, the state's constitution included provisions calling for improvement of working conditions, tighter control of corporations, and a more equitable system of taxation.

EXPANSION OF POLITICAL POWER

This contemporary lithograph, "Triumph of Labor," symbolizes the victories of the Workingmen's Party during California's constitutional convention of 1878. Chinese labor is depicted as the principal victim of revenging lightning, but politicians and greedy businessmen are also shown in agonizing defeat.

The credo of the party was a curious mixture of intolerance, idealism, and radicalism—as is evident in the platform it adopted in 1877:

"The object of this association is to unite all poor and working men and their friends into one political party, for the purpose of defending themselves against the dangerous encroachments of capital on the happiness of our people and the liberties of our country.

"We propose to wrest the government from the hands of the rich and place it in those of the people, where it properly belongs.

"We propose to rid the country of cheap Chinese labor as soon as possible, and by all the means in our power, because it tends still more to degrade labor and aggrandize capital.

"We propose to destroy land monopoly in our state by such laws as will make it impossible.

"We propose to destroy the great money power of the rich by a system of taxation that will make great wealth impossible in the future.

"We propose to provide decently for the poor and unfortunate, the weak, the helpless, and especially the young, because the country is rich enough to do so, and religion, humanity, and patriotism demand that we should do so.

"We propose to elect none but competent workingmen and their friends to any office whatever. The rich have ruled us until they have ruined us. We will now take our own affairs in our own hands. The republic must and shall be preserved, and only workingmen will do it. Our shoddy aristocrats want an emperor and a standing army to shoot down the people.

"For these purposes, we propose to organize ourselves into the Workingmen's Party of California, and to pledge and enroll therein all who are willing to join us in accomplishing these ends."

Ah Sin's Curiosity.

Far away from his country and kin
From Canton came the guileless Ah Sin.
  As he watched men make shoes,
  He exclaimed "What's the use.
They won't hire me," but still he stepped in.

Crispin Instructs Him.

But the foreman just wanted a hand,
Few white men were then in the land;
  And the placid Ah Sin
  Went to work with a grin,
And a smile that was childlike and bland.

His "Bludda" is Introduced.

Soon another Chinee comes along—
The humble and patient Ah Hong—
  With the awl and the last,
  He learns just as fast,
And his labor he gives for a song.

A White Minority.

And so they came in by the score,
While the white men went out at the door,
  While the Melicans napped,
  Their cheap pupils were apt;
And the foreman is left now—no more.

The Last of the Crispins.

For a while the white workman held on
To the bench, where he first had taught John,
  Till at last he is 'fired'
  By Ah Sin—whom he hired—
And the last of the Crispins is gone.

Master of the Situation.

Ah Sin has grown wealthy and great,
And he shipps boots all over the State,
  From the white man he learned,
  A pile he has earned.
And his teachers must now emigrate.

The competition of Chinese workers evoked these cartoons in an 1878 issue of the Wasp. The Knights of St. Crispin, originally a semi-secret organization of boot and shoe makers, was for a few years a powerful trade union with affiliates throughout the country.

110

THE MOLLY MAGUIRES
AND THE PINKERTONS

Collapse of miners' unions under the crushing weight of operators who forced their men to accept drastic wage cuts during the 1870's led to desperation that encouraged terrorism attributed to the Molly Maguires, a secret organization of workers charged with destruction of mine property and outright murder of foremen and superintendents in the Pennsylvania coalfields.

An offshoot of the Ancient Order of Hibernians, the Molly Maguires were so named because of their alleged similarity to rebels in Ireland who dressed up in women's clothing during raids on the homes of oppressive landlords. While hothead miners undoubtedly resorted to vengeful violence, it is by no means certain that the Mollies constituted, as employers claimed, a labor organization. Moreover, much of the evidence amassed against them by Pinkerton agents remains suspect in the judgement of historians because subsequent disclosures indicated that mine operators and Pinkertons deliberately instigated violence in order to discredit legitimate union activities. By way of substantiation Foster Dulles relates the following:

"The bitterly anti-labor head of the Philadelphia and Reading Railroad, which controlled many of the mines,

took the initiative in this campaign. He hired a Pinkerton detective, one James McParlan, to get proof of the criminal activity of the Molly Maguires at any cost. Posing as a fugitive from justice, McParlan won his way into their confidence, and under circumstances not entirely clear, finally succeeded in turning up evidence in the fall of 1875 that led the authorities to make a series of arrests. His testimony on the stand and that of other witnesses turning state's evidence was in many respects suspect, but the trials resulted in the wholesale conviction of twenty-four of the Molly Maguires. Ten of them were hanged for murder and the others sentenced to jail for terms from two to seven years.

"Peace and order were restored in the coal fields. Whatever the power and influence of the secret society had really been, it was shattered by this attack. But the operators had also succeeded in breaking the Miners' Benevolent Association and forcing the strikers back to work on their own terms. The long strike ended in complete failure for the workers and the virtual collapse of their union."

Labor leaders had no kind words for the Pinkertons. Said John McBride, president of the United Mine Workers in the 1890's: "They have awakened the hatred and detestation of the workingmen of the United States; and this hatred is due not only to the fact that they protect the men who are stealing the bread from the mouths of the families of strikers, but to the fact that as a class they seem rather to invite trouble than to allay it . . . They are employed to terrorize the workingmen, and to create in the minds of the public the idea that the miners are a dangerous class of citizens that have to be kept down by armed force. These men had an interest in keeping up and creating troubles which gave employers opportunity to demand protection from the state militia at the expense of the state, and which the state has too readily granted."

(Below is a warning received by a Molly victim.)

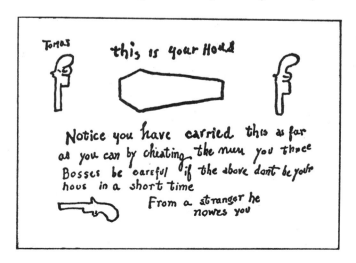

James McParlan, a Pinkerton agent who pretended to be a fugitive from justice, testified he had to remain on his knees during his initiation as a Molly.

Unexpectedly ambushed, mine superintendent John P. Jones was reportedly assassinated in full view of witnesses who were fearful of intervening.

Bare-armed McParlan is seen above during a brawl at a secret Molly meeting. These drawings are reprinted from Allan Pinkerton's highly sensational book "The Molly Maguires and the Detectives," published in 1877.

Private coal police are seen as they trained their guns at a demonstration by "rioters" outside the West Shenandoah Colliery. McParlan had tipped off the police about plans for the demonstration.

Above is a battle between Maguires and coal company guards at Raven Run on September 2, 1875.

Allegedly the Maguires sometimes capriciously shot and killed men they disliked for personal reasons.

Thanks to the reputation it acquired in the suppression of the Molly Maguires, the Pinkerton National Detective Agency found its resourceful services highly valued in the industrial world. Supplying spies and strikebreakers became a distinctly profitable business.

Founder Allan Pinkerton, a U. S. Secret Service agent during the Civil War, was not inclined to underestimate the seriousness of the labor menace. The Knights of Labor, he charged, "is probably an amalgamation of the Molly Maguires and the Paris Commune"—an assertion totally lacking in credibility.

For several decades there were persistent rumors that the Maguires remained secretly in existence and had infiltrated or seized control of unions.

Below at left is a courtroom scene at the trial of Thomas Mumley, a Molly accused of murder by Pinkerton spies. The adjoining drawing shows four convicted Mollies just before their execution.

In offering its espionage services to potential clients, the Pinkerton agency pointed out that "corporations and individuals desirous of ascertaining the feeling of their employees and whether they are likely to engage in strikes or are joining any secret labor organization with a view of compelling terms from corporations or employers, can obtain . . . a detective suitable to associate with their employees."

During large-scale conflicts, the Pinkerton agency frequently furnished private armies of strikebreakers who used brute force as a means of settling differences between workers and their employers.

TAUNTING THE "BLACKLEGS"

Irate wives of miners made life uncomfortable for Pinkerton guards and strikebreakers during coalfield troubles that persisted after suppression of the Molly Maguires. "The language these women use," a clergyman wrote, "is unprintable. I have rarely heard such profanity.... But it is not surprising. Their husbands have lost their jobs and their children are starving.... People in such dire circumstances lose their faith in God; they feel alienated from society."

THE GREAT UPHEAVAL OF 1877

As the country struggled through the prolonged depression that followed the Panic of 1873, the outlook for workingmen seemed bleak indeed. The number of the unemployed rose to a peak of about five million. Business conditions remained so stagnant that in June, 1877, the American Iron and Steel Association considered the possibility that within a few years the furnace stacks of the industry "would only be useful as observatories for the study of astronomy." The wages of those fortunate enough to hold jobs diminished steadily month by month.

As many as fifteen million persons were living close to the level of starvation and misery. Manifestations of pauperism and social unrest were everywhere evident. Viewed against this background the chaotic upheaval that accompanied the massive strike of railroad workers in 1877 was probably inevitable. And yet it was unpredictable.

"The Great Strike," as David Burbank has pointed out, "had, in fact, nothing in the nature of central leadership or direction. An entirely spontaneous outburst of labor discontent, it has never been paralleled on such a large scale in the United States. The railroad employees, subjected to special and galling pressures by their companies, were ready to strike in sheer desperation; the conservative leaders of the brotherhoods were in no position to get a hearing for their counsels of caution and moderation once the movement got under way. And the railroads served as a fuse, carrying the spark of rebellion to the unemployed multitudes in the major cities who were even less disposed than the railroad workers to pay attention to the advice of conservative labor leaders—whose organizations existed mostly on paper."

The strike began in Martinsburg, West Virginia and quickly spread to nearby states. In Baltimore (top) troops fired point-blank at approaching workers. Below is a sketch of Robert Ammon, leader of the strikers in Pittsburgh, as he telegraphed news to workers in other cities.

When the strike infected workers of the New York Central line, president William H. Vanderbilt haughtily adopted the stratagem of minimizing the possibility of any uprising. On being informed that employees of his line had decided to walk out if they were not granted an increase in their wages, he remained indifferent.

"There is a perfect understanding between the heads of departments and the employes," Vanderbilt told reporters, ". . . they appreciate, I think, so thoroughly the identity of interest between themselves and us that I cannot for a moment believe that they will have any part in this business. I am proud of the men of the Central and my great trust in them is founded on their intelligent appreciation of the business situation at the

present time. If they shall stand firm in the present crisis it will be a triumph of good sense over blind fury and fanaticism."

When the threatened strike began, Vanderbilt sent Central's workmen a suave telegram: "The public interests should not suffer from any differences between the road and its employes. Keep at work until the excitement is over, and a fair conference can be held."

Thereafter Vanderbilt blandly declared in an interview that his men were too sensible and grateful to strike of their own volition.

115

Firing indiscriminately, state militia mowed down both strikers and innocent bystanders in downtown Baltimore. Twelve persons were killed and scores wounded as the troops pushed their way toward the city's railroad station. Below is a scene near the New York Central Railroad depot in Albany.

During disturbances in Pittsburgh several million dollars worth of property was destroyed or damaged.

Above is a scene at the Union Depot. In the drawing below strikebreakers are being dragged from trains.

As rifles blazed away at workers in Chicago (above), strikes flared up like a prairie fire, reaching all the railroads except in New England and the South. In Pittsburgh Bishop Tuigg (below) risked his own life while performing last rites for dying militiamen and workers.

Although the strikers had a great deal of popular support, even among merchants, President Rutherford Hayes called out federal troops to prevent "national insurrection." When the strikes collapsed, the defeated workers had no choice but to accept the wage cuts that had precipitated the uprising.

Convinced that the strikes were the result of a foreign conspiracy associated with the Paris Commune of 1871, Congress hurriedly authorized funds for the construction of armories in leading cities.

THE RAILROAD WAR

Bloody Work Inaugurated at Baltimore.

SIXTH REGIMENT FIRE ON THE MOB

A NUMBER OF PERSONS KILLED AND WOUNDED,

THE CITY WILD WITH EXCITEMENT

The Torch Applied to the Depot at Camden Station.

BANKED FIRES

The Great Strike Spreading in Various Directions.

GROWING WARM AT BUFFALO

A Mob Disperses the Militia on Guard.

PRIVATE ESTABLISHMENTS RAIDED

Rolling Mills, Machine Shops and Factories Closed.

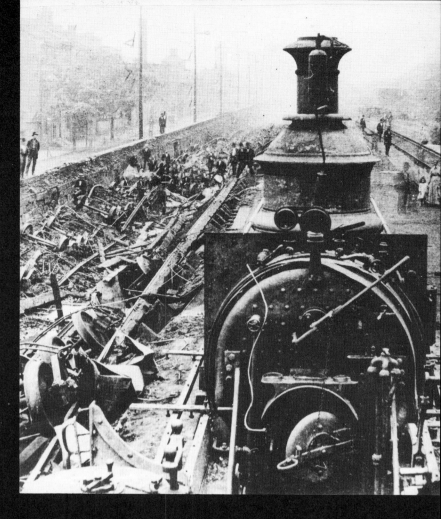

Destruction of railroad property was extensive. These photos show damage to Pennsylvania Railroad equipment in Pittsburgh.

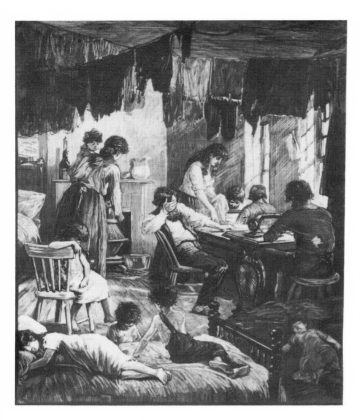

LIFE IN THE TENEMENT SLUMS

In his book "How the Other Half Lives," reporter Jacob Riis pried open to public view the dark corners of New York slum conditions similar to those festering in Chicago and Pittsburgh during the 1880's.

"Be a little careful . . . The hall is dark and you might stumble over the children pitching pennies back there. Not that it would hurt them; kicks and cuffs are their daily diet. They have little else. Here where the hall turns and dives into utter darkness is a step, and another and another. You can feel your way, if you cannot see it . . . All the fresh air that ever enters these stairs comes from the hall-door that is forever slamming, and from the windows of dark bedrooms that in turn receive from the stairs their sole supply of the elements God meant to be free, but man deals out with such niggardly hand.

"That was a woman filling her pail by the hydrant you just bumped against. The sinks are in the hallway [so that] all the tenants may have access—and all be poisoned alike by their summer stenches. Hear the pump squeak! It is the lullaby of tenement-house babies. In summer, when a thousand thirsty throats pant for a cooling drink in this block, it is worked in vain. But the saloon whose open door you passed . . . is always there. The smell of it has followed you up."

In his indictment of the conditions that produced "the evil offspring of public neglect and private greed," Riis placed primary blame on slum landlords who "saw in the homeless crowds from over the sea only a chance for business, and exploited them to the uttermost, making sometimes a hundred percent on the capital invested —always most out of the worst houses, from the tenants of which 'nothing was expected' save that they pay the usurious rents."

A Tenement House Commission that investigated the effects of slums on children was appalled by its discoveries. Approximately 20% of all babies born in East Side tenements died within the first few years of birth.

In 1885 a New York statute forbidding the making of cigars in tenements was overthrown by an appeals court decision which held that the law impaired the tenement owner's property, infringed the liberty of workers to earn their living in whatever way they chose, and threatened to undermine family life. "It cannot be perceived," sad the court, "how the cigarmaker is to be improved in his health or his morals by forcing him from his home and its hallowed associations and beneficent influences to ply his trade elsewhere."

A young legislator named Theodore Roosevelt had become an ardent champion of the statute as a result of his personal investigation of tenement conditions.

"In the overwhelming majority of cases," he wrote, "there were one-, two- or three-room apartments; the work of manufacturing the tobacco by men, women, and children went on day and night in the eating, living, and sleeping rooms—sometimes in one room. I have always remembered one room in which two families were living. On inquiry as to who the third adult male was I was told he was a boarder with one of the families. There were several children, three men, and two women in this room. The tobacco was stowed about everywhere, alongside the foul bedding, and in a corner where there were scraps of food. The men, women, and children in this room worked by day and far on into the evening, and they slept and ate there."

Roosevelt had reason to feel that the court was mistaken about the "beneficent influences" of the tenement homes he had visited. "The decision first waked me to a dim and partial understanding of the fact that the courts were not necessarily the best judges of what should be done to better social and industrial conditions. I grew to realize that all that Abraham Lincoln had said about the Dred Scott decision could be said with equal truth and justice about the numerous decisions which in our own day were erected as bars across the path of social reform."

Chicago's slum areas were no better than New York's. An 1884 report told of "the wretched condition of the tenements into which thousands of working-men are huddled, the wholesale violation of all rules for drainage, plumbing, light, ventilation and safety in case of fire or accident, the neglect of all laws of health, the horrible conditions of sewers and outhouses."

BASEMENT HOVELS

Exhausted and almost hopeless men lived under degrading conditions in tenement house basements that offered lodging at "Five Cents a Spot." These photos of New York's East Side hovels were taken by flashlight in the late 1880's by journalist Jacob Riis. Regarding a scene he encountered one night, he commented: "In a room not thirteen feet either way slept twelve men and women, two or three in bunks set in a sort of alcove, the rest on the floor. A kerosene lamp burned dimly in the fearful atmosphere, probably to guide later arrivals to their 'beds'." Similar conditions prevailed in lodging houses of other cities.

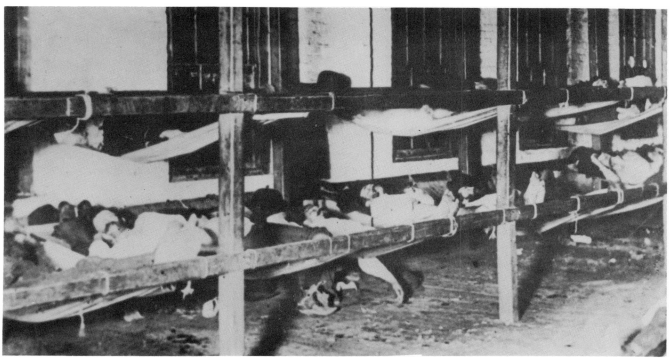

Desperate men resorted to scavenging in order to
keep alive. These pictures were taken by Jacob Riis
in New York City during the early 1880's.

WAIFS OF THE POOR

Homeless families were permitted to bed down in police stations and prisons during inclement weather.

More fortunate were the children of the tenements who received nursery care in settlement houses. "Prayer Hour in the Nursery of the Five Points House of Industry" is the title Jacob Riis gave to the photo at the bottom.

These pictures were taken by Riis in the late 1880's while he was waging a one-man campaign against East Side slums.

At garbage dumps on the outskirts of Chicago youngsters played games while searching for edible food and cast off clothes. Below is a Brooklyn dockworker who appears to be on the lookout for a "shape up."

Public concern about health hazards that festered in tenement house workshops was sparked by an intensive campaign launched by the Cigar Makers Union during the 1880's. Below is a sketch of tobacco stripping in a tenement bedroom; it appeared in Leslie's Illustrated Newspaper.

HAUNTS OF SQUALOR AND DISEASE

MY EXPERIENCE AS A "SWEATER."

PASS along any of our great commercial thoroughfares and you will see displayed in show-windows suits of clothes for sale at $5, $6, $7, $8, $9, and $10. You marvel. How can they do it?

I went through the "sweaters'" district on the East Side, where the streets are so narrow and the houses so high that it is only occasionally you catch more than a glimpse of the blue sky; where the tenements are filled like bee-hives, and filthy, half-clad little children, the majority of them deformed or diseased, tumble about on the dirty pavement or in the slime of the gutters, and in the pinched features, waxy complexions, stooping shoulders, and shrunken chests of the poor wretches who hive there I found my answer.

A sweater's shop is a place where clothing is made for the big dealers at the prices that enable them to undersell their rivals and offer gar-

ments so wonderfully cheap; and it is, in addition, a graveyard for youth and hope.

A sweater is a man who contracts to make the garments for a certain price—always a very small one—and he in turn hires the work done and makes a profit sufficient to support himself. The shops are run by foreigners, generally Russian or Polish Jews, and they employ, as far as possible, their own kind. From dawn till long after dark, if you pass through any of those wretched streets like Hester, Ludlow, Columbia, Cannon, Norfolk, Houston, Stanton, Delancey, or Essex, you can hear the hum and whirr of sewing machines overhead, and if you look up you can see at every window slovenly, half-clad men and women stitching away for dear life, while in low, damp basements they are huddled together in badly-lighted rooms, sewing by hand and machine, and so busy that you can stand and watch them for minutes without attracting their attention.

Putting on the most threadbare clothes I had I went among them asking for work. The first place I tried was 96 Cannon Street. I went through a dark, unclean passage-way for wagons, across a court as bad, and up rickety wooden stairs with foot-worn hollows, into a barn-like sort of place—room I suppose they call it—with half the window-panes broken, and the rest so grimy that only a dull, gray light sifted through them. Near the door was a stove nearly red-hot, with flat-irons covering its available surface. Men with nothing on but their undershirts, open over the breast, and trousers and shoes, were pressing seams at tables in the middle of the room; tired, disheveled women, with careworn faces, were working at the noisy machines near the windows, and groups of girls were sewing by hand, finishing the garments, while the perspiration dropped from their faces or washed the dust down in little streaks. I stumbled over rolls of cloth on the floor to where the

(Continued on page 534.)

Such sweatshops persisted until the needle trades were unionized in the early 1900's.

ABUSE
AND REPRISAL

Harrowing experiences of working girls were commonplace until they closed ranks, compelling their employers to treat them with greater consideration.

The plight of the virgin in industrial capitalism was bemoaned in "The Ballad of the Shop Girl":

The wolf of poverty follows me
on,
Through the dingy streets of the
town;
So near to my side that his
shaggy hide
Can almost touch my gown;
While after him the wolves of
lust
Are coming to drag me down.
And many and fast the days
whirl past
While early I work and late;
And along my path for the
aftermath
The basilisk watchers wait;
And civilization bids me choose
The grave or the harlot's fate.

In 1896 a group of laundresses organized a precedent-breaking sit-down strike (bottom illustration) that outraged their boss and bemused trade unionists.

GENERAL ASSEMBLY

OF THE
NOBLE AND HOLY ORDER
OF THE
Knights of Labor,

OF NORTH AMERICA.

Peace and Prosperity to the Faithful.

TO ALL WHOM IT MAY CONCERN:

WHEREAS, a petition in due form has been received from

Joseph Harry, Fred L. Winsurry, Charles F. Tidington, Joseph T. Patterson, E. Poot Kane, J.E. Brick, William C. Higgins, William Reed, N.J. Titeh W.D. Frank F. Howe, Fred M. Kelleher.

praying to be founded as an **Assembly** under the name of Bradford Assembly, No 2306 to be located at Bradford, McKean County, Pennsylvania.

Now Know Ye, that, acting under authority vested in us by the Laws and Usages of the

General Assembly of North America

of the N. and H. O. of the K. of L., we do direct this **Warrant** and **Charter** to be issued to the petitioners named above, and their associates and successors, under the title aforesaid, to bear date the Fifteenth day of October, 1882.

And by virtue of this **Warrant** and **Charter** the said **Assembly** is empowered to do and perform such acts and enjoy such privileges as are prescribed in the **Adelphon Kruptos** and in the **Laws** and **Usages** of the **Order** of K. of L., and the members thereof are strictly enjoined to bear constantly in mind and always practice the cardinal principles of the Order,

Secrecy, Obedience and Mutual Assistance.

The **General Assembly** reserves the right to suspend or reclaim this **Warrant** and **Charter**, and to annul the rights and privileges herein conferred, for any neglect or refusal to perform the duties required by the **Adelphon Kruptos** or by the Laws and Usages of the Order, as adopted and promulgated by the **General Assembly**, or by any of its **Officers** acting under legally invested authority.

In Witness Whereof, this **Warrant** and **Charter** has been signed by the **Grand Master Workman** and **Grand Secretary**, and the **Seal** of the **General Assembly** has been affixed this Second day of November, 1882.

T.V. Powderly *Grand Master Workman.*

Robt. D. Layton *Grand Secretary.*

THE KNIGHTS OF LABOR GO FORTH INTO BATTLE

Meteorlike, the Noble and Holy Order of the Knights of Labor blazed across the nation's industrial sky in the 1880's. Almost overnight its membership rocketed from 50,000 in 1884 to 750,000 in 1886 as workingmen swarmed into its ranks in the wake of impressive but short-lived strike victories. "Never in all history," exulted labor editor John Swinton, "has there been such a spectacle as the march of the Order of the Knights of Labor at the present time."

Here at long last was—or appeared to be—a dynamic and truly national organization of workingmen.

Several times in a row the organization had locked horns with the powerful railroads and each time it had won its demands. In the Knights' first great show of strength in 1884 they had shut down the Union Pacific Railroad so effectively that the railroad hurriedly agreed to restore wages to their previous level. A year later an even more sensational success climaxed a strike that threatened to tie up the entire Southern railway system controlled by Jay Gould. Caught unprepared to cope with a massive walkout at a time when he was experiencing financial difficulties, Gould capitulated. "No such victory," exclaimed the St. Louis Chronicle, "has ever been secured in this or any other country."

The successes provided a tremendous spur to the Knight's membership growth. But in March, 1886, Gould, now fully prepared for battle, forced the Knights into an ill-advised strike that ended in ignominious defeat of the organization.

The Knights' Holy Order was founded on December 28, 1869, at a meeting of seven tired tailors who talked long into the night at the threadbare Philadelphia home of Uriah Stephens, an unprepossessing but articulate garment worker who had been educated for the Baptist ministry.

Much was on the minds of these men. The benefit society to which they had belonged no longer served their needs. The standards of their trade, undermined by cheap work on army uniforms during the Civil War years, were rapidly disappearing. The conditions of their employment, like those of most wage earners of the time, were barely tolerable. Their work day usually began at sunrise and often continued beyond sunset. Their wages were hardly sufficient to meet the minimum needs of their families.

These men weren't bitter about their lot. They were proud of their skill as tailors. They enjoyed their fellowship. And they believed in the American dream.

By the time they had talked themselves out and wearily found their way home, they had set in motion forces that were to exert an enormous influence on the future of American labor. In establishing Assembly No. 1 of the Knights' Noble and Holy Order they had laid the basis for the modern labor movement.

Workers of the 1970's owe much to this extraordinary organization, especially its mistakes. In the course of its brief but spectacular history, the Noble Order paved the way to many of the economic, social, and political gains American wage earners enjoy today. It was a truly great failure.

That the Knights succeeded as much as they did is far more surprising than that they failed. When Assembly No. 1 was established, only a negligible number of wage earners were members of unions and these had little in common with each other except a desire to increase wages and shorten the work day. By 1886 about 750,000 workers affiliated with the Knights had a sense of unity that was soon to find permanent expression in the American Federation of Labor.

In 1869 employers could capriciously do as they chose in their relations with their workers. By 1885 some of the nation's largest corporations found they had to negotiate with the Knights to avoid becoming embroiled in costly strikes.

The voice of labor was rarely heard—or, for that matter, listened to— in the 1860's. By the 1880's the voice of the Knights had become a roar that could be heard across the length and breadth of the land. No legislator could afford to say he wasn't listening.

Clearly the Knights had a great deal going for them. Yet such were their weaknesses that their organization began sputtering out of existence at the very same time it appeared to be at the very zenith of its power. It wasn't quite equal to the tasks it had set for itself. Its interests were too diffuse and its structure had no firm foundation.

(Below is a lithograph showing Knights leaders grouped around a portrait of Uriah S. Stephens, founder of the organization. Left to right are William Cook, James Wright, Robert Maculey, James Hilsee, Robert Keen, and Joseph Kennedy.)

PREAMBLE AND DECLARATION OF PRINCIPLES OF THE KNIGHTS OF LABOR OF AMERICA.

TO THE PUBLIC:—The alarming development and aggressiveness of great capitalists and corporations, unless checked, will inevitably lead to pauperization and hopeless degration of the toiling masses.

It is imperative, if we desire to enjoy the full blessings of life, that a check be placed upon unjust accumulation, and the power for evil of aggregated wealth.

This much-desired object can be accomplished only by the united efforts of those who obey the Divine injunction, "In the sweat of thy face shalt thou eat bread."

Therefore, we have formed the Order of Knights of Labor, for the purpose of organizing and directing the power of the industrial masses, not as a political party, for it is more—in it are crystallized sentiments and measures for the benefit of the whole people, but it should be borne in mind, when exercising the right of suffrage, that most of the objects herein set forth can only be obtained through legislation, and that it is the duty of all to assist in nominating and supporting with their votes only such candidates as will pledge their support to these measures, regardless of party. But no one shall, however, be compelled to vote with the majority, and calling upon all who believe in securing "the greatest good to the greatest number," to join and assist us, we declare to the world that our aims are:

1. To make industrial and moral worth, not wealth, the true standard of individual and National greatness.

2. To secure to the workers the full enjoyment of the wealth they create, sufficient leisure in which to develop their intellectual, moral and social faculties; all of the benefits, recreation and pleasures of association; in a word, to enable them to share in the gains and honors of advancing civilization.

In order to secure these results, we demand at the hands of the State:

3. The establishment of Bureaus of Labor Statistics, that we may arrive at a correct knowledge of the educational, moral and financial condition of the laboring masses.

4. That the public lands, the heritage of the people, be reserved for actual settlers; not another acre for railroads or speculators; and that all lands now held for speculative purposes be taxed to their full value.

5. The abrogation of all laws that do not bear equally upon capital and labor, and the removal of unjust technicalities, delays and discriminations in the administration of justice.

6. The adoption of measures providing for the health and safety of those engaged in mining, manufacturing and building industries, and for indemnification to those engaged therein for injuries received through lack of necessary safeguards.

7. The recognition by incorporation of trades' unions, orders, and such other associations as may be organized by the working masses to improve their condition and protect their rights.

8. The enactment of laws to compel corporations to pay their employees weekly, in lawful money, for the labor of the preceding week, and giving mechanics and laborers a first lien upon the product of their labor to the extent of their full wages.

9. The abolition of the contract system on National, State and Municipal works.

10. The enactment of laws providing for arbitration between employers and employees, and to enforce the decisions of the arbitrators.

11. The prohibition, by law, of the employment of children under 15 years of age in workshops, mines and factories.

12. To prohibit the hiring out of convict labor.

13. That a graduated income tax be levied.

And we demand at the hands of Congress:

14. The establishment of a National monetary system, in which a circulating medium in necessary quantity shall issue direct to the people, without the intervention of banks; that all the national issue shall be full legal tender in payment of all debts, public and private; and that the Government shall not guarantee or recognize any private banks, or create any banking corporations.

15. That interest-bearing bonds, bills of credit or notes shall never be issued by the Government, but that, when need arises, the emergency shall be met by issue of legal tender non-interest-bearing money.

16. That the importation of foreign labor under contract be prohibited.

17. That, in connection with the post-office, the Government shall organize financial exchanges, safe deposits, and facilities for deposit of the savings of the people in small sums.

18. That the Government shall obtain possession, by purchase, under the right of eminent domain, of all telegraphs, telephones and railroads, and that hereafter no charter or license be issued to any corporations for construction or operation of any means of transporting intelligence, passengers or freight.

And while making the foregoing demands upon the State and National Government, we will endeavor to associate our own labors:

19. To establish co-operative institutions such as will tend to supersede the wage-system, by the introduction of a co-operative industrial system.

20. To secure for both sexes equal pay for equal work.

21. To shorten the hours of labor by a general refusal to work for more than eight hours.

22. To persuade employers to agree to arbitrate all differences which may arise between them and their employees, in order that the bonds of sympathy between them may be strengthened and that strikes may be rendered unnecessary.

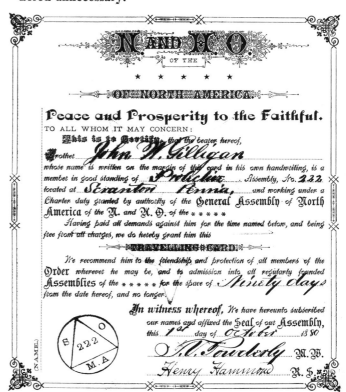

131

Women were welcomed into the Knights as members of separate assemblies. About 200 of these groups were affiliated when the adjoining picture was taken at a national meeting in 1886.

GROWING STRENGTH DURING POWDERLY'S REIGN

Exaggerated reports about the growing strength of the Knights alarmed public opinion into thinking the order constituted a threat to the nation.

"Five men in this country," the New York Sun warned its readers, "control the chief interests of 500,000 working men and can at any moment take the means of livelihood from 2,500,000 souls. These men compose the executive board of the Noble Order of the Knights of Labor of America. The ability of the President and cabinet to turn out all the men in the civil service, and to shift from one post to another the duties of the men in the army and navy, is a petty authority compared with that of these five Knights. The authority of the [church] is narrow and prescribed so far as material affairs are concerned in comparison with that of these five rulers.

"They can stay the nimble touch of almost every telegraph operator; can shut up most of the mills and factories, and can disable the railroads. They can issue an edict against any manufactured goods so as to make . . . tradesmen stop selling them.

"They can array labor against capital, putting labor on the offensive or defensive, for quiet and stubborn self-protection, or for angry organized assault . . ."

Clustered around Grand Master Workman Powderly in the lithograph on the facing page are less widely known labor leaders of his time—including Samuel Gompers, Adolph Strasser, Peter McGuire, George Mc-Neill, and others who were to attain fame as founders of the American Federation of Labor.

Ironically, Powderly not only did not look like a labor leader, he did not act like one. John Swinton, who knew him well, penned this vivid vignette:

"Powderly is a slender man, under average height with mild blue eyes behind glasses. A blonde mustache hides his mouth and bends down to below his chin. Light brown hair in curves that are neither waves nor curls rests on his coat collar, heavy behind but almost burned away at the top. Wears at conventions double-breasted, black, broadcloth coat, stand-up collar, plain tie, dark trousers and narrow small shoes. He looks like a man of good breeding, accustomed to the usages of society, but is unlike the average labor reformer in appearance . . . English novelists take men of Powderly's look for their poets, gondola scullers, philosophers and heroes crossed in love but no one ever drew such a looking man as the leader of a million of the horny-fisted sons of toil."

URIAH S. STEPHENS
FOUNDER OF THE KNIGHTS OF LABOR.

P. G. McGUIRE.
JOHN SWINTON.
RICHARD GRIFFITH.
P. M. ARTHUR.
ROBERT HOWARD.
J. R. BUCHANAN.
RICHD. F. TREVELLICK.
WM. WEIHE.
F. K. FOSTER.
CHAS. H. LITCHMAN.
ALBERT A. CARLTON.
FRANK JONES.
J. J. O'KEEFE.
D. J. O'DONOGHUE.
ADOLPH STRASSER.
ISAAC CLINE.
FREDERICK TURNER.
W. L. DOUGLAS.
ED. L. DAILEY.
JOHN McBRIDE.
JOSIAH DYER.
JOHN W. HAYES.
JAS. B. GRAHAM.
SAMUEL GOMPERS.
JOHN JARRETT.
THOS. B. BARRY.
JOHN M. FARQUHAR.
HENRY GEORGE.
W. H. BAILEY.
JOSEPH WILKINSON.
GEO. E. McNEILL, SEC'Y OF EX. COM.

T V Powderly
GEN'L MASTER WORKMAN.

By comparison with other labor leaders of the 1880's, Grand Master Powderly seemed "a veritable giant".

ADVOCACY OF SOCIAL JUSTICE

Unlike craft labor leaders, the Knights felt that unions were too narrow in their interests, too restrictive in their membership, and too limited in their objectives. The basic principles of the Knights called for far-reaching economic and political reforms.

"The reason why men are forced to work long hours today," Grand Master Powderly contended "is because machinery controls mankind. It guides our destinies, and its wonderful achievements make it possible for the man who controls machinery to control those who manage it as effectually as though the slave ship had dumped its load of human chattel on the floor of the factory. To talk of reducing the hours of labor without reducing the power of the machinery to oppress instead of to benefit is a waste of energy. What men gain through a reduction of hours will be taken from them in another way while the [age] of iron continues . . . [We] must labor for the establishment of a just and humane system of land ownership, control of machinery, railroads, and telegraphs as well as an equitable currency system before we will be able to retain the ground gained when the hours of labor are returned to eight per day."

(At the side is a photo of Grand Master Powderly standing next to Charles Lichtman, second in command until they parted company because of personal differences. Below is a group of Knights known as "The Blue and the Gray." These and other pictures were found in the Powderly Collection at Catholic University.)

ARBITRARY CYPHER WORDS

On and after November 1st, 1882, and until further notice, the following cypher will be used for all telegrams and other communications likely to fall into the hands of those not entitled to the information contained therein:

The number of words contained in any communication to be transmitted in this cypher *must be divisable by 4*, as 8, 12, 16, etc.; and where the message does not contain sufficient words to be so divisable by 4, enough *meaningless* words *must* be added to make it so.

In preparing a message for transmission in this cypher, first write it out *four words to the line*, as in the following example:

Corresponding	delegates	should	have
their	monthly	reports	in
the	hands	of	District
Secretary	by	second	or
third	of	the	month
so	that	he	may
be	able	to	compile
and	forward	to	each
Assembly	a	detailed	statement
of	the	condition	of
the	District	laughter	tears

(It will be seen that the last two words: "laughter, tears," are *meaningless*, and are merely added to make the number of words divisable by four.)

To reduce the foregoing message to cypher, proceed as follows:

Read the fourth column *down*.
" " first " "
" " third " "
" " second " "

After having been re-written according to these instructions, the message will read as follows:

"Have in District or month may compile each statement of tears, corresponding their the Secretary third so be and Assembly of the should reports of second the he to to detailed condition laughter delegates monthly hands by of that able forward a the district." (44 words.)

To translate the message as it stands in cypher, proceed as follows:

Make four ruled columns, *then take the first fourth of the whole number of words in the message*, (being 11 in this case) and, beginning at the *top* place them, one under another in the *fourth* column; next take the second eleven words, and, beginning at the *top* of the *first* column, write them one under another, commencencing with "Corresponding," then putting "their" under it, then "the," and so on; next take the *third* 11 words, commencing at "should" and write them one under another in the *third* column; next take the *fourth* and last 11 words, and, beginning at the top of the *second* column, write them one under the other.

When the operation is completed, it will be seen that the message stands just as it did when first placed in the ruled columns preparatory to being put in cypher.

By observing the foregoing rules it will be easy to prepare for transmission or translate any message, always remembering that "4" is the governing number.

COVERUP OPERATIONS

"Calling A Meeting" (above) shows a miner chalking out a triangle notice about a clandestine meeting. At the side are extracts from a Knights document explaining a cypher code devised "for all telegrams and other communications likely to fall into the hands of those not entitled to information contained therein."

SWORN TO SECRECY

Without secrecy the Knights could not have survived for very long but it became a handicap that seriously threatened their growth.

At the time the organization came into existence and for many years thereafter secrecy was necessary because, as one of its officers explained, "a great deal of bitterness was evinced against union organizations . . . men were blacklisted to an extent hardly ever equaled." Another reason was that mysterious rituals and customs appealed to workers unable to join Masonic and other fraternal groups that operated behind the cloak of mystic abracadabra.

Secrecy, in short, was initially both necessary and desirable in that it gave members the security of safety from informers and a sense of brotherhood.

For years the organization didn't use its name publicly. It simply referred to itself as ★★★★★. This gave rise to the nickname "The Five Star Society." Slogans prefaced by stars turned up on walls, fences, and sidewalks. Members were sworn to silence about whatever was said or done during their elaborately ritualistic assemblies.

Whoever was privileged to join the Knights prior to 1879 was required to take the following oath: "I . . . do truly and solemnly swear (or affirm) that I will never reveal by word, act or implication, positive or negative, to any person or persons whatsoever, the name or object of this Order, the name or person of anyone a member thereof, its signs, mysteries, arts, privileges or benefits, now or hereafter given to or conferred on me, any words spoken, acts done or objects intended; except in a legal or authorized manner specified by special permission of the Order granted to me."

The Knights couldn't, of course, operate in total secrecy. Inevitably their activities became the subject of disturbing rumors. Some employers spread word that the organization was engaging in clandestine actions similar to those of the Molly Maguires in the 1870's. Membership was expressly forbidden by Catholic pre-

W.A. (or M.W.) Venerable Sage, How can the **PIⱯOW** and **XIOZ IHⱯWH** of the **CPONXEL IM OVⱯIH** attain their objects.

V.S By ever standing **MIIE EL MIIE, XVPⱯ OP XVPⱯ,** and **BOPⱯ ⱢOLX BOPⱯ** an unbroken circle of HARMONY.

W.A. (or M.W.) Venerable Sage, How do the **PIⱯOW** and **XIOZ IHⱯWH** of the **CPONXEL IM OVⱯIH** receive others into fellowship?

V.S. By standing **MIIE EI MIIE,** etc. *(as above)*, an unbroken circle of HARMONY and FRIENDSHIP.

W.A. (or M.W.) Venerable Sage, how can the **PIⱯOW** and **XIOZ IHⱯWH** of the **CPONXEL IM OVⱯIH**

The W.A. (or M.W.) shall draft or describe the **NHWVE LWVO IM CPONXEXIIⱯ** at the centre, and when done resume his station, give **EXHWW HVFL,** form the members of the new Assembly in a chain around the centre (the other officers standing at their stations) and say: —

W.A. (or M.W.) Thus do I imprint the **NHWVE LWVO IM CPONXEXIIⱯ** on the centre of the Sanctuary, and thereby dedicate it to the service of God by serving Humanity. Brothers, look well upon that Sacred Symbol of "God and Humanity," and indelibly imprint it upon your memory.

lates who were convinced that the order was surreptitiously hostile to religion. And in the public mind there was growing suspicion that the organization was plotting against the republic.

In an effort to counteract the difficulties they were encountering, the Knights stripped away some of their secrecy. This put them in a better position to wage strikes and boycott campaigns but members continued to be enjoined against divulging details about rituals and other matters.

(Prior to their publication in this book, the accompanying documents about the Knights' secrecy remained buried away in the voluminous Powderly Collection at Catholic University).

THIS CARD MUST BE KEPT BY THE M. W.

PASS-WORD
FOR a LOCAL ASSEMBLY ATTACHED to the GENERAL ASSEMBLY,
Good until July 1, 1886.

PASS-WORD
TO BE GIVEN AT THE OUTER VEIL,
EXOPC

TO BE GIVEN AT THE INNER VEIL,
ⱯWMIHW VAEOPN
When a Local is transferred to a District Assembly, this Password must be no longer used.

SECRET WORK AND INSTRUCTIONS.

We give you herewith the official and correct secret work for Locals. If there is any sign or portion of a sign, grip or part of a grip, words or symbols, in use in your Local different from what you find laid down here, discard the same at once, no matter where or from whom received. It is not official or authorized. Give the secret work hereafter just as you find it here; give nothing that you do not find here, and there will be no trouble from lack of uniformity throughout the Order.

The work is here given, for the sake of convenience, in the order in which it occurs in the instructions of the Venerable Sage, as follows:

ENTERING SIGNAL—INNER VEIL.

Three raps, given in this peculiar manner: One, a short pause—then two in quick succession.

SIGN OF OBLITERATION.

Place the palm of the right hand ON the palm of the left hand—both hands in front of the body at the height of the elbow—elbows close to the body—right hand uppermost. Then separate the hands right and left, as if wiping something off the left hand with the right—elbows still touching the sides—right palm down—left palm up. Then drop both hands naturally at the sides.

SPECIAL INSTRUCTIONS.—Do not bring the hands together with a slap or noise. Do not hold the hands higher than the elbows. In separating the hands, do not throw them out sideways beyond a line with the body. This sign being used more than any other, strive to have your members make it in an easy and graceful manner.

ANSWER—SIGN OF DECORATION.

Place the index finger of the right hand on the left breast, back of hand to the front.

GRIP.

The grip is to be made as in ordinarily shaking of hands. The thumb to be placed over the fingers immediately back of the knuckles. Give one heavy pressure with the thumb, and, if returned, answer with two light pressures in quick succession without removing the hand.

The single asterisk or star stands for "thumb," thus: As the thumb distinguishes man, etc.

SIGN OF INTELLIGENCE.

The Sign of Intelligence is made by placing the index finger of the right hand in the centre of the forehead—the last three fingers of the hand closed over the thumb—back of hand to the front.

SIGN OF RECOGNITION.

Carelessly close the fingers over the thumb of the left hand and drop it to the side. The answer to be made with the right hand in the same manner. In case of doubt reverse the action.

VERBAL CHALLENGE.

The following words are to be used when a member is seeking work or information: "I AM HERE." A member replying to the challenge with: "YOU ARE WELCOME." Any other words may be used after the word "here," so as not to attract attention, as "I am here" on business, and the answer "You are welcome" to any assistance I can give you.

CRY OF DISTRESS.

To be used in the dark, or when the Sign of Recognition cannot be used. The words are: "I am a stranger," giving emphasis to the word stranger. Any member of the Order hearing this will answer: "A stranger should be assisted."

CAUTION.—As the value of the Cry of Distress, for practical use, depends entirely on accuracy of wording, great care should be exercised in instructing candidates, especially as great irregularity now exists. The words given above are all of the official work, although members are allowed to supplement the words given with others, so as not to attract undue attention from those not members, as, for instance: "I am a stranger, and need assistance." Answer—"A stranger should be assisted, and I for one am willing to help you." Any other similar additional words may be used, but when instructing candidates use care not to confound the official part with the unofficial.

SIGN OF CAUTION.

Close three fingers of the right hand, leaving the thumb and index finger parallel to each other and pressed together. Bend the first and second joints of the index finger over the end of the thumb, and with the hand thus closed place it under the chin, which will thus rest upon the thumb and index finger.

These signs should not be used except in cases of absolute necessity.

SPECIAL MEETING SIGN.

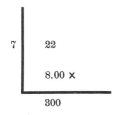

A perpendicular and horizontal line, meeting at right angles. The hour of meeting is placed over the *horizontal* line, the number of the Local under it. The month, designated by a figure, as 7 for July, is placed to the left of the *perpendicular* line; the day of the month to the right of it. The horizontal line may be placed either at the top or bottom of the perpendicular line, and may run either to the right or left of it. All that is required are two lines, one horizontal and the other perpendicular, meeting at right angles. When the hour of meeting is *before* noon, the sign X is placed *before* the hour of meeting. When it is *after* noon, then *after* the hour. The illustration given reads that a special session of Local Assembly No. 300 will be held July 22, at 8 o'clock, P. M.

NOTE.—This sign is to be used only in cases where Locals are working secretly.

THE TEST.

The Master Workman and Worthy Foreman are the only officers of a Local Assembly allowed to be instructed in the test, as the Worthy Foreman has to act in the absence of the Master Workman, and must be competent to examine a visiting member, or give the proper instructions to a member who has been granted a traveling card. It must never be given to candidates as part of the instructions of the Venerable Sage, nor to any member until a traveling card has been granted, except as hereafter provided. The

Master Workman of a Local is authorized to instruct in the test and communicate the annual traveling password to a visiting member of the Order upon the presentation of a traveling card and a written request, over the signatures of Master Workman, Recording Secretary and Financial Secretary of the Assembly to which the visitor belongs. (See No. 85, Decisions of the General Master Workman.)

The Master Workman of a Local may also instruct in the test and communicate the annual traveling password to any member of the Local who may have been elected as a Representative to the General Assembly, but only just previous to starting for the session. With these exceptions, neither the test nor the annual traveling password can be given except to a member who has been granted a traveling card. It is intended solely for the protection of Locals against the large number of expelled and suspended members who are roaming around the country, and, taken in connection with the annual traveling password and traveling card, is a sure protection, for if the laws are complied with by Local officers it will be an impossibility for a member not in good standing to get possession of all three.

The following instructions will insure both a proper examination of visitors and instruction of members who have been granted a traveling card:

A member of the Order visiting a Local on a traveling card will be admitted to the Vestibule, give the entering signal at the Inner Veil, and pass in the traveling card instead of the usual written slip. This will be announced in the usual manner by the Worthy Foreman. The Master Workman and Worthy Foreman will call some competent members to their chairs and proceed to the Vestibule and receive from the visitor the annual traveling password. It is not intended that the test shall be imperatively exacted from a visitor in every case. A traveling card, where the time written upon its face has not expired, is evidence of membership in good standing in the Order, and ordinarily is deemed sufficient, with the annual traveling password, to admit the visitor to the Assembly. The test is simply additional evidence of membership in good standing, and it is left optional with officers, to be guided by circumstances and their best judgment in the matter. Should there be anything in the appearance of the visitor or the card to warrant a reasonable suspicion that all was not right, the Master Workman will furnish the visitor with a piece of paper and pencil and request the test.

SYMBOL.

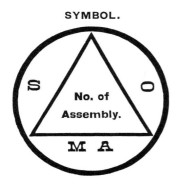

The visiting member must make the Symbol, as shown in the diagram, without hint or assistance. Place it on the triangular table, and place the *Master Workman* opposite the letters "M. A.;" the *Worthy Foreman* opposite the letter "O.;" and the visiting member opposite the letter "S." The words to be used are: "I am a member in good standing," the visitor beginning and ending, each saying one word at a time, in a double round, thus: *Visitor*, "I"—*W. F.*, "am"—*M. W.*, "a"—*Visitor*, "member"—*W. F.*, "in"—*M. W.*, "good"—*Visitor*, "standing."

Members who have been granted a traveling card must be thoroughly instructed in the *test*, so as to know what will be expected of them. The *Venerable Sage*, being a retired Master Workman, is always supposed to be in possession of the *test*, and can take the place of the Master Workman or Worthy Foreman in the examination of visitors, if desired. Organizers are also furnished with the *test*, and should thoroughly instruct the Master Workman or Worthy Foreman of new Locals. If there is a change in the office of Master Workman or Worthy Foreman, it is the duty of the retiring Master Workman to instruct the new officers in all the secret work, including the *test*.

The General Assembly, at the Philadelphia session, decided to return to the old form of initiation, and the A. K. is changed accordingly. The Unknown Knight administers the pledge, after which he proceeds with candidate to the Worthy Foreman for instructions, then to the Master Workman for the address, and finally to the Venerable Sage.

The password issued by District Master Workmen for the use of Local Assemblies attached to Districts is changed semi-annually, in January and July of each year.

The following instructions by the General Master Workman as to the proper manner of opening a Local Assembly are hereby officially promulgated:

"When the Master Workman takes his stand at the capital and says: 'All persons not entitled to sit,' etc., the Worthy Inspector takes the Globe and Lance and proceeds to mark the Outer and Inner Veils with them. Previous to that all persons were at liberty to enter the room, but the Veils are then closed and none can enter without giving the password. When the Worthy Inspector goes to the Outer Veil to put the Globe in its place the Outside Esquire takes his place in the ante-room, and when the Worthy Inspector enters the Inner Veil the Inside Esquire takes his place. The Worthy Foreman brings the Outside Esquire in with him when he returns after examining the Veils. A member of the Order is not required to give the password at the Veils until the proper symbols are in their places; and if these were not in place, while the Worthy Inspector was taking up the password a shrewd person could slip in without giving the password to either the Outside Esquire or Inside Esquire, and at the same time elude the vigilance of the Worthy Inspector."

Fraternally,

Jno. W. Hayes.

General Secretary-Treasurer.

From Local Assembly No._____   Recorded on page_____

Shinnying up a hole smeared with "monopoly grease," a participant at a Knights picnic struggles to reach food and higher wages for his family while capitalists Jay Gould, Russell Sage, Cyrus Field, William Vanderbilt, and John Roach look on with amusement.

Thin-skinned Grand Master Powderly had reason to be bitterly philosophical about criticism of his "pompous posturings." The above comments by him were found in his papers.

He was especially riled when he was castigated for setting up the Knights' headquarters in a Philadelphia mansion purchased at a cost of $50,000. An irate critic accused Powderly and other national officers with "enjoying the pleasures of Byzantine ease and grandeur, Roman feasts, and houris". Below is a caricature showing Powderly reading Henry George's "Progress and Poverty" in a sumptuous office while workers await an audience with him.

THE TROUBLESOME RACE QUESTION

Virginia Governor Fitzhugh Lee glowered when Frank M. Farrell, a Negro Knight, presented Grand Master Powderly to cheering delegates at the national assembly held in Richmond in 1886. Southern members of the organization resented such conspicuous black participation in the assembly's sessions. Trouble was avoided by the passage of a compromise resolution in which the Knights recognized "the civil and political equality of all men and women in the broad field of labor" but conceded there was "no purpose to interfere with or disrupt the social relations which may exist between different races in different portions of the country." This expedient phrasing succeeded in placating Southerners without alienating Negroes who constituted a sizeable portion of Knights membership in New York, Pennsylvania, and Illinois.

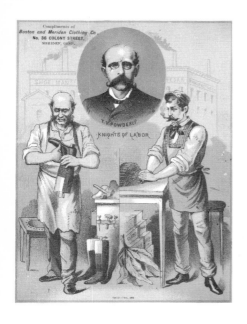

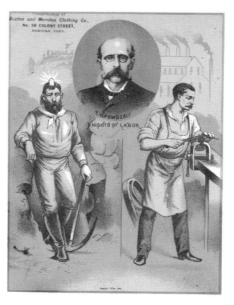

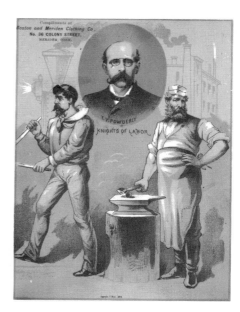

These picture cards were distributed by tobacconists and haberdashers who solicited trade from members of the Knights of Labor. Powderly raised no objection to "tasteful" use of his portrait in such advertising

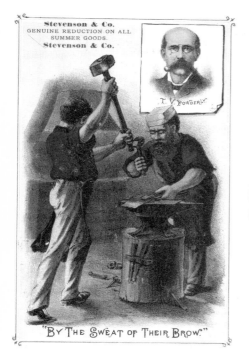

"By The Sweat of Their Brow."

"Worthy of Their Hire."

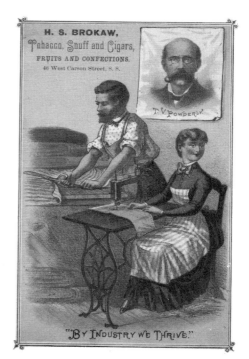

"By Industry We Thrive."

PRELUDE TO DEFEAT

For railroad workers the 1880's were turbulent years. Antagonized by wage cuts and spurred on by mounting Knights of Labor militancy, shopmen of the Union Pacific struck so effectively in 1884 that the railroad quickly agreed to restore wages to their earlier level. A year later an even more sensational success climaxed a strike that threatened the entire Southwest railroad system controlled by powerful Jay Gould. Caught unprepared to cope with a massive walkout at a time when he was experiencing financial difficulties, Gould capitulated. "No such victory," exclaimed the St. Louis Chronicle, "has ever been secured in this or any other country."

Workers throughout the country were so impressed that the membership of the Knights of Labor shot up spectacularly—rising from 50,000 to 750,000 between 1884 and 1886. Although national leaders of the Knights had very little to do with the strikes and had even discouraged such drastic action, the organization was generally credited with achieving the victories of 1884-1885. Subsequent defeats, however, showed that the Knights were far from invincible. Crafty Gould had retreated in 1885 only to gather strength for a devastating counter-attack in 1886 that set in motion forces which sent the Knights reeling into ignominy.

The ease with which railroad companies were able to smash strikes convinced Eugene Debs, secretary-treasurer of the Brotherhood of Locomotive Firemen, that a federation of railroad unions "is essential for purposes of strength when unity is required to secure a righteous settlement of controversies which relate to their welfare." As a result of his efforts the Supreme Council of the United Orders of Railway Employees was created in 1889 but its inability to eliminate jurisdictional quarrels led to Debs' establishment of the American Railway Union several years later. Entire lodges of firemen, conductors, and switchmen transferred their memberships to this industrial union but the failure of its Pullman strike in 1894 and imprisonment of its leaders were to undermine the ARU before it could lay a firm basis for permanence.

At the side are drawings by a participant in the strike against the Chicago, Burlington, and Quincy Railroad in 1888.

ATTACK AND COUNTERATTACK

Frequent clashes between private guards, vigilantes, and workers occurred during the railroad strikes of 1885-86. At left is a scene in Fort Worth, Texas. The adjoining drawing depicts trouble in the East St.. Louis yards. The illustration below accompanied a Harper's Weekly article about attacks on strikers in Illinois.

While masked workers sabotaged a Missouri Pacific engine, strikers openly attacked scab switchmen and brakemen of the Chicago, Burlington & Quincy Railroad. At the top is a freight yard scene.

THE RAILROAD BROTHERHOODS

In the tug-of-war with railroad tycoons like Jay Gould, William Vanderbilt, and Edward H. Harriman, the trainmen gradually won concessions. Their bargaining power was enhanced by general resentment of the railroads' high handedness. "The public be damned!" was Vanderbilt's blunt response to complaints about the rates he charged. Gould boasted: "I can hire one half of the working class to kill the other half."

Railroad workers emerged from the upheaval of 1877 with determination to shun violent means of achieving their ends. In the years that followed they generally remained aloof from the turbulent currents of the labor movement. From their viewpoint there was little to be gained and much risked by affiliation with the Knights of Labor or the American Federation of Labor.

Convinced that their members constituted the aristocracy of American labor because their jobs required a combination of skill, discipline, and responsibility not characteristic of other occupations, the brotherhoods found it inadvisable to become involved in sympathy strikes or share the burdens of weak unions. Moreover, their strategic importance in the nation's economy gave them a sense of power and independence they had no desire to dilute.

BETTER WAGES OR BIG STRIKE

Railway Trainmen of the Middle West are Preparing Demands on Railroads.

Better wages and better hours are to be demanded by the trainmen of the middle west. The Brotherhood of Railway Trainmen and the Order of Railway Conductors are behind the movement and have so far perfected their plans, according to authoritative statements, that a meeting of committees has been called to meet in Chicago the first week in October to formulate demands.

It is asserted with great positiveness that if the demands are not granted a strike tying up the train service of the entire north middlewest will follow.

The members of the grievance committees of the Brotherhood of Railway Trainmen and Order of Railway Conductors will meet in Chicago the first week in October to formulate demands upon the railroads between Chicago and the Missouri river and Chicago and the twin cities.

The demands have not yet been formulated, it having been left with the grievance committees to state them. In general, however, the railroads will be asked to place their employees on a par with the trainmen east of Chicago.

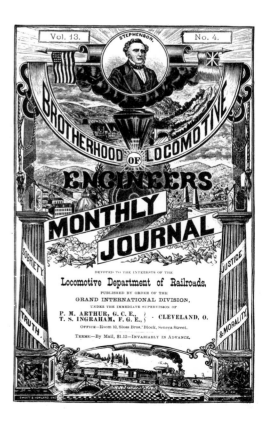

Benevolence, sobriety, and industry are stressed in this certificate of locomotive firemen.

Such membership certificates were hung on parlor walls by proud locomotive engineers.

STREETCAR STRIKES
IN NEW YORK CITY

Violent streetcar strikes were enflamed in 1886 by disclosure that New York's board of aldermen had approved franchises giving the rapid transit interests enormous profits while conductors worked 12, 14, and even 16 hours a day for meager wages.

Although relatively indifferent toward the franchise give-aways and the indictment of bribe-taking aldermen, the public was righteously indignant toward the strikers.

TRAGIC VIOLENCE:
THE HAYMARKET EXPLOSION

May 1, 1886, was a momentous day for the labor movement. In a score of cities thousands of workers (close to half a million in all) downed their tools and went on strike for an eight-hour day.

Unlike Chicago employers who were generally taken by surprise, the McCormick Harvester Company anticipated the strike and had locked out those of its workers who were known to be union members. On May 3rd several hundred of these workers clashed with scabs outside the McCormick factory. Sticks, stones, bricks, and some bullets flew through the air before police "restored order" by firing on the locked out men — killing several and wounding twenty.

On the following night several thousand angry workers, responding to the adjoining leaflets, gathered in Haymarket Square to protest the police brutalities. After listening to speeches in which Mayor Carter Harrison, Governor Richard Oglesby, and Chicago's police chief were vituperatively denounced, the crowd dwindled to a few hundred persons. For reasons that remain unclear the police decided to break up the gathering; suddenly, as they raised their clubs, a dynamite bomb exploded in their midst. In the affray that followed the police opened fire on the crowd and Haymarket became a battleground. By the time reinforcements arrived, seven policemen lay dead and scores were wounded. Four workers also lost their lives and fifty or more were injured but these casualties went almost unnoticed in hysterical accounts of the tragedy.

Blame for the bomb explosion was placed on eight "conspirators" who had openly espoused anarchism — Albert Parsons, August Spies, Adolph Fisher, George Engel, Louis Lingg, Samuel Fielden, Michael Schwab, and Oscar Neebe — although prosecutors did not produce any evidence directly connecting them with the crime.

According to historians, their trial was a travesty of justice. In the absence of clear proof of their guilt, Judge Joseph Gary advised a packed jury that it was sufficient to establish that the "conspirators" had "advocated the use of deadly missiles against the police." All but Neebe were promptly found guilty and sentenced to death; Neebe was given fifteen years in prison. Later Fielden and Schwab pleaded for executive clemency; their sentences were changed to life imprisonment.

Attention Workingmen!

GREAT
MASS-MEETING
TO-NIGHT, at 7.30 o'clock,
AT THE
HAYMARKET, Randolph St, Bet. Desplaines and Halsted.

Good Speakers will be present to denounce the latest atrocious act of the police, the shooting of our fellow-workmen yesterday afternoon.

Workingmen Arm Yourselves and Appear in Full Force!
THE EXECUTIVE COMMITTEE

Achtung, Arbeiter!

Große
Massen-Versammlung
Heute Abend, ½8 Uhr, auf dem
Heumarkt, Randolph-Straße, zwischen Desplaines- u. Halsted-Str.

☞ Gute Redner werden den neuesten Schurkenstreich der Polizei, indem sie gestern Nachmittag unsere Brüder erschoß, geißeln.

☞ Arbeiter, bewaffnet Euch und erscheint massenhaft!
Das Executip-Comite.

REVENGE!

Workingmen, to Arms!!!

Your masters sent out their bloodhounds — the police —; they killed six of your brothers at McCormicks this afternoon. They killed the poor wretches, because they, like you, had the courage to disobey the supreme will of your bosses. They killed them, because they dared ask for the shortening of the hours of toil. They killed them to show you, 'Free American Citizens!' that you must be satisfied and contended with whatever your bosses condescend to allow you, or you will get killed!

You have for years endured the most abject humiliations; you have for years suffered unmeasurable iniquities; you have worked yourself to death; you have endured the pangs of want and hunger; your Children you have sacrificed to the factory-lords — in short: You have been miserable and obedient slave all these years: Why? To satisfy the insatiable greed, to fill the coffers of your lazy thieving master? When you ask them now to lessen your burden, he sends his bloodhounds out to shoot you, kill you!

If you ar men, if you are the sons of your grand sires, who have shed their blood to free you, then you will rise l your might, Hercules, and destroy the hideous monster that seeks to destroy you. To arms we call you, to arms!

Your Brothers.

Rache! Rache!
Arbeiter, zu den Waffen!

"We are peaceable," Samuel Fielden reportedly told the police a few minutes before the Haymarket explosion. During his trial, however, it was asserted that he urged workers to attack the police. Last rites were given dying victims while other officers awaited treatment of their wounds in an emergency first-aid station.

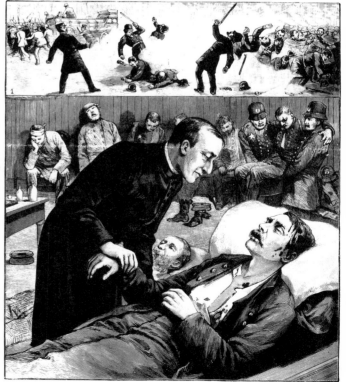

SMOLDERING RESENTMENT

In an officially published report dealing with industrial relations in Chicago shortly before the Haymarket incident, E. L. Bogart sheds some light on the tinderbox situation at the time:

"The police force of Chicago reflected the hostility of the employing class, regarding strikes per se as evidence that the men had placed themselves in opposition to law and order. During these months of unrest it became a pastime for a squad of mounted police, or a detachment in close formation, to disperse with the billy any gathering of workingmen. The billy was an impartial instrument: men, women, children, and shopkeeping bystanders alike composed its harvest. It was the police, aided by the 'Pinkertons,' who added the great leaven of bitterness to the contest. To the workingmen they furnished concrete and hateful examples of the autocracy against which they protested."

At the side are "typical banners" attributed to Chicago anarchists. Richard Oglesby was Illinois' Governor; Carter Harrison was Chicago's Mayor. Some of the banners were made of red and black material.

"A police patrol wagon attacked by a mob of 12,000 rioters, May 3rd" is the grossly inaccurate caption Leslie ran with the drawing below. According to reliable accounts less than five hundred workers were on hand when the police arrived.

1. "The greatest crime these days is Poverty."
3. "Millions work for the benefit of the few. Let us work for ourselves."
6. This is a bit of doggerel directed against the capitalistic press, and in advocacy of the

Arbeiter-Zeitung and of Johann Most's paper, *Die Freiheit.*
7. "Proletarians of all lands, unite."
8. This is a bit of Socialist "poetry" expatiating on the efficacy of the "boycott."

A. R. PARSONS.

SAMUEL FIELDEN.

LOUIS LINGG.

AUGUST SPIES.

MICHAEL SCHWAB.

GEORGE ENGEL.

ADOLPH FISCHER.

SCAPEGOATS?

Despite lack of evidence that these men had any direct connection with the bomb explosion, they were sentenced to death for the crime. Judge Joseph Gary ruled they could be convicted because testimony indicated they had "conspired to . . . excite the people . . . to sedition, tumult, and riot" that culminated in the Haymarket deaths. In the opinion of historian Roger Butterfield, "They were railroaded to the gallows . . . because they were labor agitators and outspoken enemies of the capitalist system."

During their trial much was made of the fact that most of them were foreign born, but the jury was surprised to learn that Albert Parson's ancestors fought in the American Revolution. A native of Alabama, he had been active in Chicago's printing union and had turned anarchist because his experience with blacklists and union-busting convinced him that American workers would remain repressed if they did not defend their rights through violent means.

Parsons was associated with August Spies and Michael Schwab in the publication of "Die Arbeiter Zeitung." Samuel Fielden was an ex-Methodist minister, Oscar Neebe an organizer of the Beer Wagon Drivers' Union, Adolph Fischer a printer, George Engel a toy maker, and Louis Lingg an officer of the Carpenters' Union.

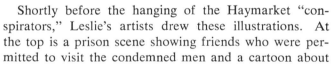

Shortly before the hanging of the Haymarket "conspirators," Leslie's artists drew these illustrations. At the top is a prison scene showing friends who were permitted to visit the condemned men and a cartoon about clemency appeals labor groups made in their behalf. Seen below are preparations for the execution that were under way when Louis Lingg escaped the gallows by exploding a dynamite tube in his mouth.

"The Law Vindicated—four of the Chicago anarchists pay the penalty of their crime."

**HAYMARKET
AFTERMATH**

While disreputable agitators representing "Anarchy" try to drag workers into the mire of "Disorder," Terence Powderly (Grand Master of the Knights of Labor) and P. M. Arthur (head of the Brotherhood of Locomotive Engineers) come to the rescue. Arthur is pointing the way to peaceful arbitration. Although Knights participated in the eight hour strike preceding the Haymarket explosion, Powderly insisted his organization was in no way to blame since the strike had been initiated by the Federation of Organized Trades and Labor Unions.

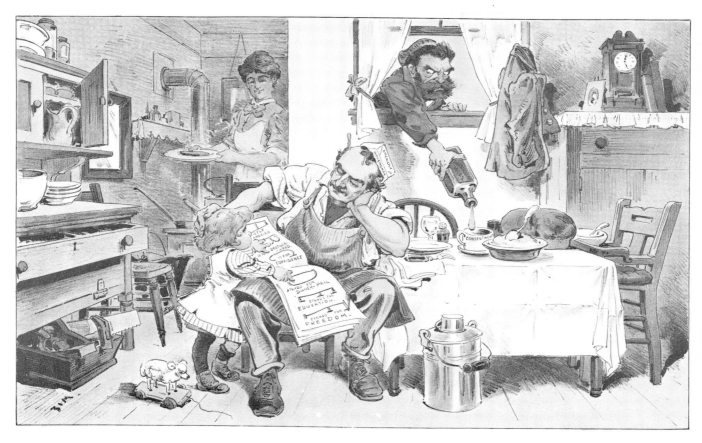

Seemingly labor was enjoying contentment until "Anarchism" came along and spoiled everything. Underneath the table in "The Suckers of the Workingman's Sustenance" (below) are an "Incendiary Editor," a "Walking Delegate," and a "Boycotter"—all "false friends of the laboring man . . ."

A lithograph depicting union officers as "merely puppets in the anarchist editor's hands."

The above cartoon shows a worker caught between the wolf of "Hunger" and the hell of "Union Tyranny." The sign at the entrance to hell says "All Independence Abandon Ye Who Enter Here." Below a worker and his family are depicted as "Slaves" being subjected to ruthless bullying by a malevolent "Labor Agitator."

"The Evolution of the Anarchist" (above) depicts the transformation of immigrants into trouble-making malcontents. "The Slave Market of Today" (below) shows intimidated labor being auctioned off on the block of monopolistic trade unionism by a high tariff pitchman serving the crass interests of big business.

The  World.

VOL. XXV., NO. 8,472. NEW YORK, THURSDAY, OCTOBER 30, 1884.—WITH SUPPLEMENT. PRICE TWO CENTS.

THE ROYAL FEAST OF BELSHAZZAR BLAINE AND THE MONEY KINGS.

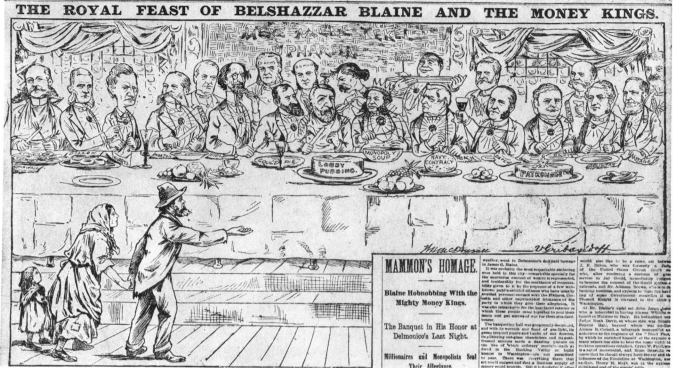

MAMMON'S HOMAGE.

Blaine Hobnobbing With the Mighty Money Kings.

The Banquet in His Honor at Delmonico's Last Night.

Millionaires and Monopolists Seal Their Allegiance.

Lavish banquets in behalf of James G. Blaine, Republican Presidential nominee in 1884, provided Democrats with an opportunity to attack him for masquerading as "a two-faced friend of the workingman who hobnobs with the rich." Below are cartoons that helped bring about his defeat by Grover Cleveland.

Singled out for derision as wild-eyed men of the 1880's are advocates of prohibition, socialism, abolition of poverty (Father Edward McGlynn), the single tax (Henry George), Greenbackism (Ben Butler), and anarchism. The scornful gentlemen in the foreground of the above caricature are Knights of Labor leader Terence Powderly, Carl Schurz, Senator John Sherman, Senator James G. Blaine, and banker Levi Morton. Below are shipwrecked Labor Party adherents awaiting rescue by a phantom ship offering promises of high wages, a six-hour work day, "equal division of wealth," low rents, and free trade.

Puzzled by solicitation when elections approached, the average workingman found it hard to draw sharp distinctions between Democratic and Republican promises, but he was practically indifferent to pleas from Belva Lockwood, a feminist who ran for President on the Equal Rights ticket in 1884.

As the elections of 1888 approached, Lady Labor found herself importuned by advance men for presidential aspirants James G. Blaine, David Hill, and General Ben Butler. Below Democratic managers are seen eyeing the Labor Party pitcher uneasily as he winds up to throw a curve toward Grover Cleveland.

Despite such ridicule, single-taxer Henry George came surprisingly close to being elected Mayor of New York as the candidate of the United Labor Party in 1886. Democrat Abram Hewitt won, but George got a larger vote than neophyte Theodore Roosevelt, the Republican nominee.

THE IMPACT OF
HENRY GEORGE AS
THE APOSTLE OF REFORM

THE LAND AND LABOR LIBRARY.

Published weekly, by Henry George, at the office of The Standard, 12 Union square, New York. Postoffice box 15, Station D. Annual Subscription, Two Dollars.

NO. 77.　　　　　NEW YORK, JUNE 30, 1888.　　　　　PRICE, ONE CENT.

Price of this tract in quantities.—25 copies, 10 cents; 100 copies, 25 cents; 1,000 copies, $2; 5,000 copies, $8.50.

TO WORKINGMEN.

BY HENRY GEORGE.

I am one of those who believe that it is possible for workingmen to raise wages by an intelligent use of their votes; that this is the only way in which wages can be generally and permanently raised—the only way labor can obtain that share of wealth which is justly its due. And I am one of those who believe that this is the supreme object that workingmen should seek in politics. In seeking to raise wages, to improve the conditions of labor, we are seeking, not the good of a class, but the good of the whole. The number of those who can live on the labor of others is and can be but small as compared with the number who must labor to live. And where labor yields the largest results *to the laborer,* where the production of wealth is greatest and its distribution most equitable, where the man who has nothing but his labor is surest of making the most comfortable living and best provide for those whom nature has made dependent upon him, there, I believe, will the general standard of intelligence and virtue be highest, and there will all that makes a nation truly great and strong and glorious most abound.

Believing this, I am glad that the presidential campaign this year is to turn, not upon sectional issues or matters of party or personal character, but upon a great question of national policy—the question of protection or free trade; and that this is to be discussed, as it is most important that it should be discussed, in its relation to wages. What is thus entering our politics is more than a question of higher or lower duties, or no duties at all—it is the most important of all questions, the great labor question. And what is really involved in the decision that will be asked of you as to whether protection or free trade is best for the interests of labor, is whether the emancipation of labor is to be sought by imposing restrictions or by securing freedom. Until the men who would raise wages and emancipate labor settle that for themselves, they cannot unite to carry out any large measure.

In the coming campaign the most frantic appeals will be made to workingmen to vote for protection. You will be told that "protection" means "protection to American labor;" that that is what it was instituted for, and that is why it is maintained; that it is protection that makes this country so prosperous and your wages so high, and that if it is abolished, or even interfered with, mills must close, mines shut down, and poor labor stand idle and starve until American workmen are forced to work for the lowest wages that are paid in Europe.

Don't accept what any one tells you—least of all what is told you by and on behalf of those who have an enormous pecuniary interest in maintaining what is styled "protection." Hear what they say, but make up your minds for yourselves. There is nothing in the tariff question that cannot readily be mastered by any one of ordinary intelligence, and the great question whether what is called "protection" does or does not benefit the laborer can be settled for himself by any one who will ask himself what protection really is, and *how* it benefits labor.

WHAT IS PROTECTION ?

Now what is "protection?" It is a system of taxes levied on imports for the purpose of increasing the price of certain commodities in our own country so that the home producers of such commodities can get higher prices for what they sell to their own fellow countrymen.

This is all there is to "protection." Protection can't enable any American producer to get higher prices for what he sells to people of other countries, and no duty is protective unless it so increases prices as to enable some one to get more from his fellow citizens than he could without protection. How "protection" may thus benefit some people is perfectly clear. But how can it benefit the whole people? That it may increase the profits of the manufacturer, or the income of the owner of timber or mineral land, is plain. But *how* can it increase wages! "Protection" raises the price of commodities. That may be to the advantage of those who buy labor and sell commodities. But *how* can it be to the advantage of those who sell labor and buy commodities?

Never mind the confused and confusing claims that are put forth for protection until you can see *how* it can do what is claimed for it.

Ask yourselves what protection is and how it operates, and you will see that the only way it can benefit any one, or by "encouraging" him give him power to encourage or benefit any one else, is by enabling him to get from his fellow citizens more than he could otherwise get. This is the essence of protection; and if it has any stimulating or beneficial effect it must be through this. The protective effect of any protective duty is precisely that of a subsidy paid by the government to some people out of taxes levied on the whole people. The only difference is, that in what is called the subsidy system the government tax gatherers would collect the tax from the whole people and pay it over to some people, while in what is called the protective system the government tax gatherers collect a tax on foreign goods so as to "protect" the favored people, while they for themselves collect taxes on their fellow citizens in increased prices.

Among those who campaigned in Henry George's behalf when he ran for Mayor of New York on the United Labor Party ticket were outspoken Father Edward McGlynn (seen above), Terence Powderly, Grand Master of the Knights of Labor, and Samuel Gompers, youthful president of a still obscure organization known as the American Federation of Labor.

George's spectacularly successful book, "Progress and Poverty," published in 1879, had made him an idol of the labor movement.

His book, based upon "burning personal knowledge of poverty" (forced to go to work at 14, George had frequently experienced unemployment as a seaman and printer) painted a searing portrait of the hard times millions of Americans were experiencing. His indignant contrast between "The House of Have" and "The House of Want" was a devastating indictment of economic forces that resulted in great wealth for the few and impoverishment for the many. This paradox, George contended, could best be met by a single tax on land that would eliminate large fortunes, ease the burdens of the poor, and bring an end to cyclical depressions. His solution had the characteristics of a panacea but his facts were irrefutable.

Catholic objections to Henry George's radical notions were ignored by workers who came under the spell of Father Edward McGlynn (below). Although considered a free-wheeling heretic, McGlynn had a large following among Catholics who backed his Anti-Poverty Society's efforts to achieve economic and social reforms espoused by George. Archbishop Corrigan warned Catholics against "being deluded by men who advocate revolutionary doctrines" of the type ascribed to George and McGlynn.

Union Labor National Platform

General discontent prevails on the part of the wealth-producer. Farmers are suffering from a poverty which has forced most of them to mortgage their estates, and the prices of products are so low as to offer no relief except through bankruptcy. Laborers are sinking into greater dependence. Strikes are resorted to without bringing relief, because of the inability of employers in many cases to pay living wages, while more and more are driven into the street. Business men find collections almost impossible, and meantime hundreds of millions of idle public money which is needed for relief is locked up in the United States treasury or placed without interest in favored banks in grim mockery of distress. Land monopoly flourishes as never before, and more owners of the soil are daily becoming tenants. Great transportation corporations still succeed in extorting their profits on watered stock through unjust charges. The United States senate has become an open scandal, its membership being purchased by the rich in open defiance of the popular will. Various efforts are made to squander the public money, which are designed to empty the treasury without paying the public debt. Under these and other alarming conditions we appeal to the people of our country to come out of old party organizations, whose indifference to the public welfare is responsible for this distress, and aid the Union Labor party to repeal existing class legislation and relieve the distress of our industries by establishing the following:

LAND.

While we believe that the proper solution of the financial distress will greatly relieve those now in danger of losing their homes by mortgage foreclosures, and enable all industrious persons to secure a home at the highest result of civilization, we oppose land monopoly in every form, demand the forfeiture of unearned grants, the limitation of land ownership and such other legislation as will stop speculation in lands and holding it unused from those whose necessities require it. We believe the earth was made for the people and not to make an idle aristocracy to subsist through rents upon the toils of the industrious, and that corners in land are as bad as corners in food, and that those who are not residents or citizens should not be allowed to own lands in the United States. A homestead should be exempt to a limited extent from execution or taxation.

TRANSPORTATION.

The means of communication and transportation shall be owned by the people as is the United States postal system.

MONEY.

The establishment of a national monetary system in the interest of the producer, instead of the speculator and usurer, by which the circulating medium in necessary quantity and full legal tender, shall be issued directly to the people without the intervention of banks and loaned to citizens upon land security at a low rate of interest so as to relieve them from the extortion of usury and enable them to control the money supply. Postal savings banks should be established, and while we have free coinage of gold we should have free coinage of silver. We demand the immediate application of all the money in the United States treasury to the payment of the bonded debt, and condemn the further issue of interest-bearing bonds, either by the national government or by states, territories or municipalities.

LABOR.

Arbitration should take the place of strikes and other injurious methods of settling labor disputes. The letting of convict labor to contractors should be prohibited, the contract system be abolished on public works, the hours of labor in industrial establishments be reduced commensurate with the increased production by labor saving machinery, employes protected from bodily injury, equal pay for equal work for both sexes, and labor, agricultural and co-operative associations be fostered and encouraged by law. The foundation of a republic is in the intelligence of its citizens, and children who are driven into work-shops, mines and factories, are deprived of the education which should be secured to all by proper legislation.

PENSIONS.

We demand the passage of a service pension bill to every honorably discharged soldier and sailor of the United States.

INCOME TAX.

A graduated income tax is the most equitable system of taxation, placing the burden of government on those who can best afford to pay, instead of laying it on the farmers and producers, and exempting millionaires, bondholders and corporations.

UNITED STATES SENATE.

We demand a constitutional amendment making United States senators elective by a direct vote of the people.

CONTRACT LABOR.

We demand the strict enforcement of laws prohibiting the importation of subjects of foreign countries under contracts.

CHINESE.

We demand the passage and enforcement of such legislation as will absolutely exclude the Chinese from the United States.

WOMAN SUFFRAGE.

The right to vote is inherent in citizenship irrespective of sex, and is properly within the province of state legislation.

PARAMOUNT ISSUES.

The paramount issues to be solved in the interests of humanity are the abolition of usury, monopoly and trusts, and we denounce the Democratic and Republican parties for creating and perpetuating these monstrous evils.

The Hercules of Labor saving his Country.

A Government of the People, by the People, and for the People, shall not perish from the Earth.—A. LINCOLN.

Slaying the Democratic and Republican parties was easier to depict than to accomplish. The Union Labor Party's Hercules barely pricked opponents in the 1888 election. Although the party failed to win substantial support among workingmen, some of its proposals were later endorsed by Populists and Democrats.

UNION LABOR CANDIDATES FOR PRESIDENT AND VICE PRESIDENT 1888

Although they ran on a platform nailed together with planks borrowed from the Knights of Labor and Henry George's mayoralty campaign, the Union Labor Party had more in common with farmers than with workers. In Kansas, where the party got its largest vote, not a single labor man was on the ticket.

Politics and Industry.

PLAIN TALK WITH WORKINGMEN.

Every Intelligent Workingman

Knows that wages are much better in this country than in Europe. Every one knows that the reason for this is that American labor is protected by a tariff which taxes foreign goods, and keeps foreigners from underselling our own manufacturers. The articles made by the cheap labor of Europe cannot come into our markets to compete with our own products without paying a tax at the custom house.

This is what is called the Protective System. Under it our manufactures have increased to an enormous extent during the last twenty years. Hundreds of thriving manufacturing villages have sprung up, and cities have doubled and quadrupled in size. Hundreds of thousands of industrious men and women are enabled to get employment and earn wages. All over the Northern States are scattered many thousands of happy homes, which could not exist if foreigners were allowed to undersell our manufacturers in our own markets. The maintenance of this Protective System is vital to the interests of American workingmen.

This is so well understood by the men who work in shops, factories, furnaces and mines, that it is not necessary to argue the question. No man wants to work for the wages paid in England, Belgium and Germany. No man can do it in this country and support a family decently.

We are in the midst of a political campaign. Tariffs are made by political parties through their representatives in Congress. Now it is for the interest of every workingman to know how the great political parties of the country stand on the question of keeping up the protective system. Let us inquire first,

What does the Democratic Party say?

Here is the clause in their platform relating to the tariff:

"A TARIFF FOR REVENUE ONLY."

This is all the party says. What is a tariff for revenue only? Why, a tariff got up with a view of yielding as much money as possible, without any regard to the effect on American industry. The more foreign goods imported the more revenue collected—that is plain. So there must be a low schedule of duties to encourage foreigners to send us their goods and pay the rates at our custom-houses. The more foreign goods imported the fewer American goods will be made and sold—that is plain, too. The fewer goods made in this country, the less demand for labor—another self-evident proposition. The less the demand for labor the lower will wages be, and the harder will it be to get work.

What does Gen. Hancock say about the Tariff?

He doesn't say a word in his letter of acceptance. He never once mentions the subject. Of course, he will carry out the Democratic platform, and help abolish the Protective System. If he did not approve the platform he would have said so in his letter. Let us ask now,

What does the Republican Party say?

Here is the declaration of the Republican platform on the subject: *We affirm the belief, avowed in 1876, that the duties levied for the purpose of revenue should so discriminate as to favor American labor.*

Mark the difference. Not a tariff *for revenue only,* but a tariff that shall *so discriminate as to favor American labor.* That's what the present tariff does. It was adopted by the Republicans in Congress, and has been sustained by them for twenty years against the attempts of the Democrats to repeal it.

What does Gen. Garfield say?

He was a workingman himself in his early days. He was a good carpenter and a good wood-chopper, and he once drove horses on a tow-path. He ought to sympathize with laboring men. He does. Read what he says in his letter of acceptance:

In reference to our custom laws a policy should be pursued which will bring revenues to the Treasury, and will enable the labor and capital employed in our great industries to compete fairly in our own markets with the labor and capital of foreign producers. We legislate for the people of the United States, and not for the whole world, and it is our glory that the American laborer is more intelligent and better paid than his foreign competitor. Our country cannot be independent unless its people with their abundant natural resources possess the requisite skill at any time to clothe, arm and equip themselves for war, and in time of peace to produce all the necessary implements of labor. It was the manifest intention of the founders of the Government to provide for the common defence, not by standing armies alone, but by raising among the people a greater army of artisans whose intelligence and skill should powerfully contribute to the safety and glory of the nation.

This has the right ring. Garfield is a man of the people, and will protect the interests of the people.

Why do the Democrats want to Break Down the Protective System?

Because their party is ruled by the South. The South has no manufactures. It wants to buy its goods in Europe at cheap prices and import them at low rates of duties. It despises Northern artisans and operatives. It used to call them "Northern Mudsills." It would not care if every furnace, machine-shop and factory in the North were closed.

Vote for Garfield and Protection to American Industry.

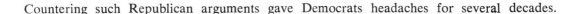

Countering such Republican arguments gave Democrats headaches for several decades.

THE FIRST LABOR DAY PARADE

On September 5, 1882, ten thousand workmen marched around Manhattan's Union Square in a procession that was, according to Leslie's Illustrated Newspaper, "in every way creditable to those engaged in it . . . their orderly appearance and sobriety of manner won hearty applause from the spectators who lined the sidewalks." The placards bore slogans such as "Labor Creates All Wealth," "The True Remedy Is Unionization and the Ballot," "8 Hours of Work, 8 Hours of Rest—8 Hours of What We Will!" and "Agitate, Educate, Organize."

Oregon was the first state to make the day a holiday, but it was not until 31 other states did the same that President Grover Cleveland made it a national holiday in 1894.

Peter J. McGuire, founder of the Brotherhood of Carpenters and Joiners and the first secretary of the American Federation of Labor, is generally recognized as the father of Labor Day. However, the International Association of Machinists insists that this credit belongs to Mathew Maguire, an early officer of that union.

By-products of Labor Day unity were strike parades. Sympathetic workers cheered New York freight handlers who walked off their jobs spontaneously when their demands for higher wages and fewer hours were rebuffed in 1882. In Pittsburgh thousands of workers joined in a parade (below) organized by steel strikers.

SOLIDARITY

While public sentiment was still smoldering over the Haymarket tragedy, trade unionists in Leadville, Colorado (above) and other cities paraded on Labor Day of 1886 with more solidarity than ever before. Below is a photo of a procession in New York City a year later.

Small town Labor Day festivities of the period were similar to those of July 4th. Almost everyone in Muncie, Indiana, turned out for that city's Labor Day celebration in 1891. Festivities began at 4 a.m. with an "artillery signal of 44 rounds" and proceeded throughout a crowded day with parading, band music, orations, greased pole climbing, bicycle races, pie-eating contests, reading of the Declaration of Independence, and baseball games. In the evening there was dancing and fireworks.

NATIONAL LABOR LEGISLATORS.

NEW YORK LABOR LEADERS.

IMPORTANT LEADERS OF THE 1880'S

Except for Henry George, these labor leaders of the 1880's were barely known to the public at large.

The men in the panel at the left constituted a "reliable labor bloc" in the U. S. House of Representatives. Prior to his election to Congress, Martin Foran was the head of the Coopers (barrelmakers) Union. James B. Weaver, founder of Iowa's Union Labor Industrial Party, won a million votes as the presidential candidate of the Populist Party in 1892.

Like George, John Swinton (the central figure in the right panel) had no formal status in the trade union movement but he devoted much of his life to writing and lecturing about labor, exerting "a profound . . . personal influence on public opinion." In the course of his varied journalistic career he was chief of the editorial staff of the New York Times.

Samuel Gompers, an ex-cigarmaker, was the president of the newly organized American Federation of Labor. John M. Farquhar, the president of the National Typographical Union, was active in Republican politics.

RISE OF THE AMERICAN FEDERATION OF LABOR

The trade unionists who formed the American Federation of Labor in 1886 had little use for the Holy Order of the Knights of Labor. Its aims, they felt, were too diffuse, too impractical, too ambivalent to effectively serve the cause of labor.

The nucleus of the AFL began to take shape in the Federation of Organized Trades and Labor Union established in 1881 by six of the leading craft unions—cigarmakers, carpenters, printers, iron and steel molders, and glassworkers. Overshadowed by the Knights, the FOTLU was a loosely knit and almost rudderless organization when it was absorbed by the newly founded federation.

While the Knights declined, the American Federation of Labor took firm root although the late 1880's and most of the 1890's were not auspicious years. Unlike the Knights, the federation devoted itself principally to "pure and simple unionism." Its primary objectives were higher wages, a shorter work day, and better working conditions. When its down-to-earth president, Samuel Gompers, was asked what the organization wanted, he replied, "More and more, here and now." Adolph Strasser, who helped Gompers found the federation, expressed the same idea this way: "We are fighting only for immediate ends—objects that can be realized in a few years."

Most of the organization's strength resided in constituent craft unions that enjoyed almost complete autonomy. In essence, as Gompers explained, the federation served as "a central body bearing the same relation to national unions that the federal government bears to the States of our Union." Its structure was somewhat similar to that of the British Trades Union Congress, which also allowed autonomy to its affiliates. And, like the British organization, its scope was largely restricted to craft unions.

At its first meeting the federation authorized a very limited budget and only one full-time officer—president Gompers. The dues paid by member unions were so low (a quarter of a cent per capita every month) that Gompers and the executive council were hard put to fulfill their responsibilities:

• Assist in the formation of central labor bodies in cities where such groups did not exist.

• Encourage the establishment of national unions in unorganized trades.

• Promote the passage of desirable legislation with the help of public opinion.

• Provide financial help for unions engaged in strikes or subjected to lockouts.

Since the executive council seldom met, the major burden of its early responsibilities fell on Gompers' broad shoulders.

These men were the executive council of the Federation of Organized Trades and Labor Unions, predecessor of the American Federation of Labor. Left to right are Charles Burgman, Samuel Gompers, Richard Powers, William H. Foster, and Alexander Rankin. Like Gompers, Burgman rose from the ranks of the Cigar Makers Union. Foster, secretary of the organization until its amalgamation with the AFL, was an officer of the Typographical Union. Powers represented the Lake Seamen's Union; Rankin was the president of the powerful Iron Molders Union.

Below at left is J. P. McDonnell, first editor of the American Federationist; W. D. Connelly (right) helped organize the American Federation of Labor.

FIGHTING FOR SUPREMACY

In the bitter conflicts between the Knights of Labor and the trade unions of the American Federation of Labor it seemed as if they might destroy each other.

"Two Roads For the Workingman: One Leads to Prosperity and the Other to Violence and Ruin" (the above cartoon by Joseph Keppler) shows members of the Brotherhood of Locomotive Engineers (a union that eschewed militancy under the leadership of P. M. Arthur) comfortably ensconced on the train of "Progress" while officers of the Knights of Labor and craft union leaders clobber away at each other with great zest.

The caption on the train quotes Arthur: "I believe that in these labor troubles the only true remedy is that suggested by St. Paul: 'Come, let us reason together.' I hold that capital has rights that labor is bound to respect . . . I am opposed, decidedly opposed, to the means of coercion and violence to which some labor organizations resort."

In the tilt depicted below, big business appears to be enjoying the spectacle.

A DISCORDANT ORCHESTRA WITHOUT A LEADER

The discord that beset the labor movement in the late 1880's is satirized in this Puck cartoon by Frederick Opper. "At left (physically but not politically)," Bernard Weisberger has pointed out in a commentary about the drawing, "sits Terence Powderly of the Knights of Labor, plucking the harp . . . [while] Heber Newton, a 'liberal, humanitarian' Episcopalian, tootles a flute in support of Henry George's bass viol (far right) . . . Sourly viewing the whole scene stands Father Edward McGlynn, a Roman Catholic priest who fiddles more or less in tune with George and Newton . . . Drowning out the oompahs from the walking delegate's tuba (right rear) is the blaring trombone of one anarchist, behind Newton, and the angry drumming of another next to the unconcerned Henry George . . . At center, Robert G. Ingersoll has ceased trumpeting and is covering an ear to the din . . . Only Gompers, among the players in this 'Benefit Concert', would learn the score well enough to assert needed leadership. . . . [and] rise to leader of the orchestra."

THE CASE
FOR ARBITRATION

Mounted atop a volume entitled "Common Sense," Puck replaces the pendulum of Monopoly with that of Arbitration while Management and Labor differ about the position of the clock hands.

An accompanying editorial blamed strikes on short-sightedness by both employers and unions: "Workers are not more wise, more temperate, more just than their employers. The employers, having power, have misused it . . .[workers] will likewise misuse power. Where they have the upper hand, they will tyrannize. They will strike and paralyze business, not only to enforce just demands, but to enforce unjust demands. Their employers will use the power of money to retaliate as best they may."

As the lithograph below suggests, Terence Powderly, Grand Master of the Knights of Labor, felt that business and labor should settle their disputes through arbitration.

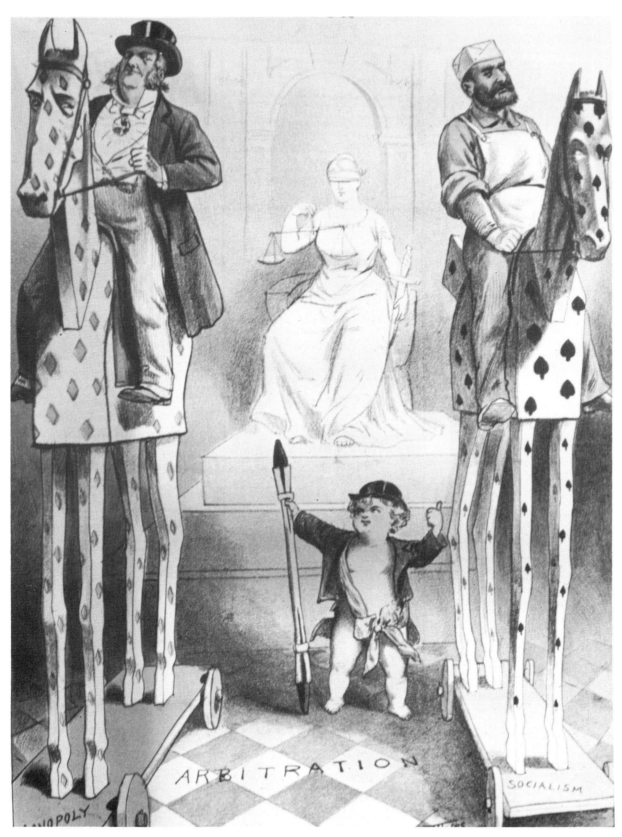

"The Proper Way" shows Puck pleading in behalf of arbitration: "Come down, both of you, off your high horses and meet on equal ground." Settlement of disputes through arbitration was generally favored by unions and even endorsed by some businessmen, but most employers were loathe to make any concessions that would limit their power to do as they chose.

THE BOOTSTRAP MYTH

A serious obstacle to unionization was the persistence of the myth, believed by many wage earners throughout the nineteenth century, that every American could by sheer willpower raise himself by his own bootstraps out of the working class. Some could and did, but they were very few of the many workers who were susceptible to Horatio Alger's formula for self-made success.

Refusal to even recognize the presence of a distinct laboring group was a persistent problem, as James Barnes has pointed out:

"Wage earners were merely individuals who were temporarily employed by others until they had set themselves up in businesses of their own. The belief that every deserving man had it within his power to become a property owner was universal; failure to do so was conclusive evidence of a lack of initiative. Hardships and problems were for the worthy only stepping-stones on the road to greatness. The laborer himself was first to deny that he was born to toil and die in poverty amid the whirling spindles and grinding wheels of the factories.

"There was some truth in this fiction that grew up in the early years of the nation. Before 1860—and even long afterward—the wage earner often labored alongside of the man for whom he worked, sharing in his economic troubles and sometimes falling heir to the establishment through marriage with the owner's daughter. Regardless of how seldom it occurred, acceptance of this happy ending as a social possibility was of immense importance."

THE COMPETITION OF CHEAP LABOR

The ready availability of immigrants was becoming an increasingly vexatious problem. Their willingness to work for low wages kept depressing the general pay scale and their frequent use as strikebreakers was a serious obstacle to trade unionism.

In this Judge cartoon of 1888 immigrants outweigh strikers to the distinct satisfaction of big business. "As long as I am plentifully supplied with immigrant labor," says the portly manufacturer, "I shall be deaf to the demands of the native workingmen."

During the 1880's the number of foreign born persons who entered the country—mostly from southeastern and central Europe—was twice that of the previous decade. Al-

though many of these immigrants were of peasant background, only a handful went into farming. Relatively few, according to J. C. Furnas, arrived "with even the meager cash they needed to begin homesteading . . . Basically it was not land-hunger but livelihood-hunger, the prospect of a wage-earning industrial job that brought them overseas—one reason why they were often in bad odor with union men as strikebreakers in mines and steel mills. They knew nothing of labor's struggles, had merely gone where the often predatory but helpful big-city labor agency had set up paying jobs."

In all, about eight million immigrants arrived between 1870 and 1890.

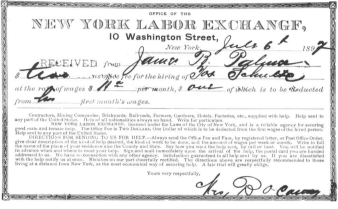

Hiring practices varied considerably. The prevalence of unscrupulous exploitation prompted social agencies to provide counselling services, but employers continued to prey on "greenhorns."

THE PERILS OF THE WORKING GIRL

Inspired by evidence indicating a close connection between low wages and prostitution, cartoons such as these highlighted a problem that troubled clergymen and civic leaders.

"Grinding poverty is a very general cause of prostitution," New York's Labor Commissioner reported in 1885. "The prominent fact is that a large number of female operatives and domestics earn such small wages that a temporary cessation of business or being a short time out of situation is sufficient to reduce them to absolute distress, and it becomes a literal battle for life."

Conflicting statements were made by witnesses who appeared before an Illinois legislative committee that investigated the problem in 1913. Social workers and shopgirls testified that low wages encouraged white slavery. Speaking in behalf of Sears Roebuck, Julius Rosenwald admitted that 1,465 of its women employees earned less than $8 a week, but he assured the committee that his company did not hire girls who did not live with their parents. An official report on Chicago vice conditions recommended that shopgirls be urged to practice self-restraint in their relations with men.

THE DOMESTICS ARE "GETTING OUT OF HAND"

Preference for factory jobs was creating "a very trying situation for mistresses fearful of losing servants who no longer appreciate their good fortune." Impertinent "domestics", complained a petulant matron, "will not call the lady of the house 'mistress' or drop a curtsey when honored with a command and if they do not happen to like the usage they receive they will be off in an instant. . . They are getting out of hand because they expect to be treated like equals."

To make matters worse, some maids were turning to unionization. "Even household servants are organizing," Harper's Weekly told its readers in 1903. "At its recent congress the American Federation of Labor granted a charter to the Household Employees' Union of Holyoke, Massachusetts . . . Their platform demands an eight-hour day, with one afternoon and evening and part of Sunday off each week; cooks to have $5, chambermaids $4, apprentices $3; cooks are not permitted to wash or iron. It is difficult to say how any possible act could make the domestic servant problem more serious than it already is."

184

It clearly wasn't easy to stay on good terms with the help.

THE CATHOLIC CHURCH
TAKES A CONTROVERSIAL STAND

Thanks in part to the influence of Cardinal James Gibbons, the first prominent American Catholic clergyman to speak out in behalf of workingmen, Pope Leo XIII issued in 1891 an historic encyclical calling for the application of Christian ethics to relations between capital and labor.

The document took into account relative rights and mutual duties of the rich and the poor, of Capital and of Labor. It deplored "the hard-heartedness of employers and the greed of unchecked competition," pointing out that "a small number of very rich men have been able to lay upon the teeming masses of the laboring poor a yoke little better than slavery itself."

While emphasizing that a constructive solution of social and economic problems must be based upon adherence to Christian tenets, the Pope decried the growth of Socialist ideas and advocacy of class warfare.

Prior to the encyclical, the Catholic hierarchy in the United States had tended to view trade unions with hostility. Membership in the Knights of Labor was inveighed against because of the order's secret and ritualistic customs. In Canada, where the Knights had many affiliates, Catholics were expressly forbidden to join them. These were important factors in the decision of the Knights to strip away much of their secrecy. At the urging of Grand Master Powderly, a Catholic, Cardinal Gibbons induced the Pope to disavow banning of membership in the Knights' organization.

ENCYCLICAL LETTER of OUR HOLY FATHER BY DIVINE PROVIDENCE

POPE LEO XIII

ON

THE CONDITION OF LABOR

OFFICIAL TRANSLATION

To Our Venerable Brethren, All Patriarchs, Primates, Archbishops and Bishops of the Catholic World,

In Grace and Communion with the Apostolic See, POPE LEO XIII.

Venerable Brethren,

Health and Apostolic Benediction

It is not surprising that the spirit of revolutionary change, which has long been predominant in the nations of the world, should have passed beyond politics and made its influence felt in the cognate field of practical economy. The elements of a conflict are unmistakable: the growth of industry, and the surprising discoveries of science; the changed relations of masters and workmen; the enormous fortunes of individuals and the poverty of the masses; the increased self-reliance and the closer mutual combination of the working population; and, finally, a general moral deterioration. The momentous seriousness of the present state of things just now fills every mind with painful apprehension; wise men discuss it; practical men propose schemes; popular meetings, legislatures, and sovereign princes, all are occupied with it—and there is nothing which has a deeper hold on public attention.

The State Must Protect the Laborers' Rights

When work-people have recourse to a strike, it is frequently because the hours of labor are too long, or the work too hard, or because they consider their wages insufficient. The grave inconvenience of this not uncommon occurrence should be obviated by public remedial measures; for such paralysis of labor not only affects the masters and their work-people, but is extremely injurious to trade, and to the general interests of the public; moreover, on such occasions, violence and disorder are generally not far off, and thus it frequently happens that the public peace is threatened. The laws should be beforehand, and prevent these troubles from arising; they should lend their influence and authority to the removal in good time of the causes which lead to conflicts between masters and those whom they employ.

But if the owners of property must be made secure, the workman, too, has property and possessions in which he must be protected; and, first of all, there are his spiritual and mental interests. Life on earth, however good and desirable in itself, is not the final purpose for which man is created; it is only the way and the means to that attainment of truth, and that practice of goodness in which the full life of the soul consists. It is the soul which is made after the image and likeness of God; it is in the soul that sovereignty resides, in virtue of which man is commanded to rule the creatures below him, and to use all the earth and ocean for his profit and advantage. *Fill the earth and subdue it; and rule over the fishes of the sea and the fowls of the air, and all living creatures which move upon the earth.* In this respect all men are equal; there is no difference between rich and poor, master

Reflecting cynicism regarding the Pope's friendliness toward labor, these caricatures by Joseph Keppler are moderate by comparison with cartoons published by blatantly anti-Catholic publications. "A Business Alliance," the drawing at the top, quotes Pope Leo XIII: "Bless you my children! I think we can work together nobly in America." The document lying at the Pope's feet cites the the pro-labor views of Cardinal Gibbons. Underneath is a caricature captioned "The New Ally of the Knights of Labor."

REVOLT AGAINST CONVICT LABOR

A long drawn out campaign against the competition of convict labor and the use of prisoners as scabs reached a dramatic climax in an uprising of Tennessee miners during a strike in 1891.

A storm broke in Briceville when forty prisoners who were employed as scabs built a stockade around struck coal property and proceeded to tear down the shacks that had previously served as living quarters for the miners. Angry armed workers stormed the stockade, rounded up the convicts and their guards, and placed them aboard a train to Knoxville.

Subsequently the Governor sent 163 convicts to Briceville under the protection of fourteen companies of troops. For a few months it looked like peace had been restored. On Halloween night, however, several hundred miners, faces covered by bandanas, silently closed in on the stockade, overpowered its guards, and set the prisoners free. A fuming, flabbergasted Governor had had enough. The mine owners capitulated to the strikers' demands and discontinued using convict labor.

(At the top is a scene in Knoxville during the miners' revolt against private use of convict labor. The cartoon below depicts trade union opposition to such labor as heartless hostility toward the rehabilitation of prisoners).

USE OF NEGROES
AS STRIKEBREAKERS

Antagonism toward Negroes as scabs, a persistent post-Civil War problem, exploded violently during a lockout of miners by Illinois coal operators in 1898.

Despite vigorous objections by Governor Tanner, the Chicago-Virden Coal Company and other mine operators lured Southern Negroes into the state by offering them free transportation and other inducements. (At the side is an advertisement posted in Birmingham, Alabama).

"If you bring in this imported labor," Governor Tanner warned the mine owners, "you do so . . . with the full knowledge that you will provoke riot and bloodshed." His words were disregarded. On October 12th a battle broke out when several hundred strikebreakers began to disembark at Virden. Seven miners and five company guards lost their lives; forty miners and four guards were wounded.

A large number of the miners were newly arrived immigrants who had found it difficult to get factory jobs because of discriminatory practices by unions and employers.

Imprisoned like circus animals, Southern convicts were privately guarded by their employers. Contract arrangements for such cheap labor, initiated by Southern states as a means of raising revenue after the Civil War, continued until the 1930's. (Some Northern states also engaged in similar exploitation of their prisoners.)

Under the Southern contract system convicts were farmed out in large numbers during harvest time. In the North prisoners were put to work manufacturing products in behalf of companies unwilling to pay regular wages to free workers. (The photo at the bottom was probably taken in the 1930's).

CARNEGIE'S "CALLOUS LOCKOUT"

Working in the Carnegie Steel Company mills near Pittsburgh was a brutalizing experience. Most of the men labored 12-hour days and sometimes longer than that. Their only holidays were at Christmas time and on July 4th.

The lack of safety equipment, along with fatigue and the speed-up, meant a regular death toll and a high rate of crushed limbs. The splashing of molten metal frequently left a trademark of burned flesh.

Recently arrived immigrants, paid less than $9 a week, were worse off than in Europe. A Hungarian clergyman who visited the Carnegie plants complained: "Wherever the heat is most insupportable, the flames most scorching, and smoke and soot most choking, there we are certain to find our compatriots bent and wasted with toil."

The skilled workers at Carnegie's Homestead plant belonged to the Amalgamated Association of Iron, Steel and Tin Workers, one of the strongest affiliates of the American Federation of Labor. The union's three-year contract, which provided a wage scale based on the price of steel billets, was expiring at mid-year.

Trouble loomed when the union resisted wage cuts on the ground that Andrew Carnege's ruthless practices, especially the strategy of flooding the market with cut-price billets to drive out competition, enriched the company while depressing wage rates.

Henry Clay Frick, the tough anti-labor general manager, responded by locking out the Homestead workers. Company guards were quickly sworn in as sheriff's deputies and a barbed wire fence three miles long and fifteen feet high was built around company property.

It was still dark early in the morning of July 6, 1892, as two barges were stealthily towed up the Monongahela River toward the Homestead works. On board were 300 Pinkerton agents, some of them ex-convicts, armed with Winchester rifles and other weapons. When the boats approached the mills, a volley of shots rang out from the shore. The locked out men were prepared for the enemy. There were casualties on both sides in the day long battle that ensued.

Unable to sink the barges with cannon fire, the workers poured oil on the water and set it ablaze. The Pinkertons, sensing they were trapped, ran up a white flag. They surrendered their arms and ammunition but once ashore they were stoned and clubbed by angry men and women as they were led away.

An ominous calm settled over the town while the victorious strikers awaited concessions from Frick.

Six days later 8,000 National Guardsmen marched into Homestead and placed the town under martial law. The mills were reopened with strikebreakers. In the months that followed the jobless men drifted away. Only a handful of the original workforce of 4,000 got their jobs back. Nothing of the union remained.

"Our victory is now complete and most gratifying," Frick jubilantly advised Carnegie. "Do not think we will ever have any serious labor trouble again. We had to teach our employees a lesson and we have taught them one that they will never forget." The great philanthropist and donator of public libraries replied: "Life worth living again . . . congratulate all round"

Forced to surrender, 300 Pinkerton agents hired to break the strike at Andrew Carnegie's Homestead plant are being led away by temporarily victorious workers. The strike was called because of wage cuts violating an existing agreement with the Amalgamated Association of Iron, Steel and Tin Workers.

Only a few years before Carnegie appeared to be one of the most enlightened of employers. "Peaceful settlement of differences," he declared in 1886, "should be reached through arbitration. I would lay it down as a maxim that there is no excuse for a strike or a lock-out until arbitration of differences has been offered by one party and refused by the other . . . To expect that one dependent upon his daily wages for the necessaries of life will stand by peacefully and see a new man employed in his stead is to expect too much."

WORKMEN CANNONADING THE BARGES.

SOLDIERS IN CAMP.

WORKMEN ATTACKING THE BARGES.

GREAT BATTLE OF HOMESTEAD.
Defeat and Capture of the
PINKERTON INVADERS
July 6th 1892.

Strikebreakers imported from Chicago and other cities are seen below as they milled about the shacks constructed for them on the grounds of the Homestead mills. Since they were shunned and despised by the locked out workers, they remained cooped up for weeks in their "Pottersville" shacks.

CARNEGIE'S GUARDIANS

Encamped at high points surrounding Homestead, National Guardsmen were kept "on the ready" for several months. At the side is a Carnegie plant photo taken after the strike was quelled.

THE PULLMAN STRIKE:
TEST OF INDUSTRIAL UNIONISM

The depression of the 1890's had a direct impact on the workers who lived in the model company town of Pullman outside Chicago.

On the surface, the town was run as smoothly as the luxurious Pullman railroad cars built here. In the words of George M. Pullman's press agent, the community was a place "where all that is ugly and discordant and demoralizing is eliminated and all that inspires self-respect is generously provided." In actuality paternalism cloaked not so subtle exploitation. All of Pullman's employees were required to live in the town and pay him a profit on just about everything—rents, gas and water, groceries, etc. Charges were even made for the use of church and library facilities.

With the onset of the depression, Pullman slashed wages and laid off 3,000 of his 5,800 employees. But rents and other charges were kept at the same high levels. The squeeze left most workers with less than $6 a week in take-home pay; one employee received a check for two cents after all deductions were made. A committee of workers who went to Pullman with a list of grievances was blandly told that there was no connection between wages and rent, between employer and landlord. Although the committee's members were assured there would be no retaliation, their leaders were summarily fired.

Incensed by Pullman's arbitrary actions, his workers had been flocking into the American Railway Union headed by Eugene V. Debs, a radically inclined idealist who had left a high post in the Brotherhood of Locomotive Firemen to promote industrial unionism among railroad men—i.e., unionism that encompassed all workers in the industry.

With the firing of their grievance spokesmen, the Pullman workers called a strike. This time Pullman retaliated by shutting down his plant. Arbitration was proposed by the union, but Pullman refused even to discuss the matter. "There is nothing to arbitrate," he said.

In the face of such treatment, the American Railway Union felt justified in waging a boycott to prevent hauling of Pullman cars rented to the railroads. Executives of 24 lines thereupon imported from Canada several hundred strikebreakers and secretly ordered them to hook up mail cars to Pullman cars, thereby laying the basis for a charge that the union was interfering with movement of the mails. The railroads also persuaded U. S. Attorney General Olney to swear in as special deputies about 3,500 men hired by the lines to keep the trains moving.

Violence ensued. Strikers clashed with the deputies, riots broke out, and property was destroyed. Although Illinois Governor John Altgeld insisted there was no

need to do so, President Cleveland sent federal troops into Chicago. "If it takes the entire Army and Navy . . . to deliver a postcard in Chicago, that card will be delivered," Cleveland warned. Still the strike remained solid, buttressed by sympathy walkouts by railroad workers throughout the nation.

195

After being sworn in and armed as deputies of the U. S. Department of Justice, strikebreakers were able to move engines despite obstruction by workers and sympathizers who even included a top-hatted gentleman. Below is a photograph of federal troops called out to protect the trains.

Use of the strikebreakers and troops was justified on the ground that they were needed to prevent violence and damage of railroad property. The strikers, however, contended that freight cars were burned and violence instigated by provocateurs hired by the railroads execu-

tives. This was suspected by Governor Altgeld and Mayor Hopkins of Chicago. In his notebook about the strike Henry Demarest Lloyd made the following entry:

"E. W. Bemis was told that Mayor Hopkins before leaving office procured affidavits showing that the burning of freight cars was done by railroad men; that the railroad men moved cars outside of fire limits, then burned them, inciting bystanders to participate. Hopkins, fearing these affidavits might be destroyed by some subsequent railroad mayor, took certified copies before leaving office." This evidence later disappeared.

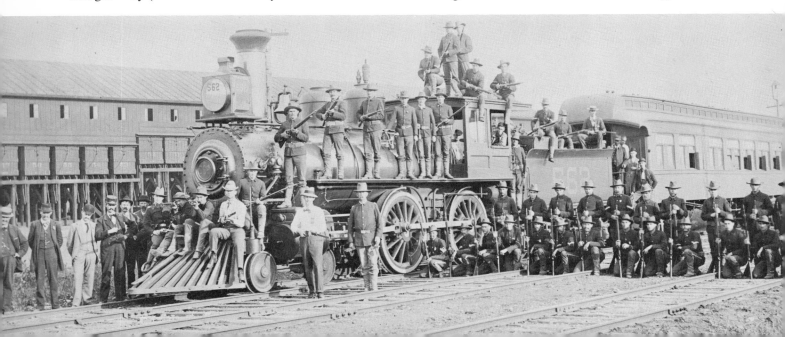

When angry strikers tried to stop troops from moving the trains, the White House decided this constituted insurrection against the government. At Cleveland's direction "law and order" was restored with the help of a blanket court injunction that tied the hands of the strikers in every conceivable way.

Debs and the American Railway Union were in a hopeless situation. They faced the full weight of the federal government and the courts. Public opinion was being poisoned by the press. The leaders of the rail brotherhoods and the American Federation of Labor turned a deaf ear to pleas for support. Gompers took the position that a proposal for a general strike was "inexpedient, unwise and contrary to the best interests of the working people." Convinced that defeat was unavoidable, Debs offered to end the strike in return for reinstatement of all workers, but this was rejected because there would be "no recognition of anarchism."

Debs was found guilty of violating the court injunction secured by the government and placed in prison for six months. Bereft of leadership, the strike collapsed.

Debs became a martyr. On returning to Chicago after serving out his prison term, he was met by a cheering crowd of more than 100,000. A contemporary writer said he was "the most popular man among the real people today . . . the victim of judicial lynch law."

The Pullman experience converted Debs to socialism. He was to run five times for the presidency on the Socialist ticket; in 1920 he received close to a million votes.

(Below Debs is being borne aloft by Governor Altgeld and other "anarchistic" union supporters.)

DEPRESSION VICTIMS

Sights such as these, photographed near the grounds of Chicago's glittering World Fair of 1893, cast a pall on the boast that "American civilization has truly reached a zenith of greatness."

HARD TIMES DURING
THE NOT SO GAY NINETIES

As the nation entered the last decade of the century, the outlook seemed relatively bright despite widespread discontent and unrest among farmers and workers. The Silver Purchase Act of 1890 offered hope of cheap money and the Sherman Anti-Trust Act appeared to place substantial restraints on big business. Moreover, the election of Grover Cleveland on a progressive Democratic ticket in 1892 augured better times for the masses. But the bright prospects of the decade were to quickly fade.

Hard times struck like an earthquake in 1893, signaling the start of the worst depression the country had known. Precipitated by a business panic due to over-speculation, it gripped the country for almost five years before it spent itself. Paralysis seized much of the business world; more than 8,000 commercial concerns with liabilities of $285 million failed between April and October of 1893. Many banks also toppled and some of the largest railroads went into receivership.

Almost overnight hundreds of thousands of workers found themselves jobless; their number rose steadily, reaching a peak close to four million. Ragged and hungry bands of jobless men began to haunt the city streets and swarm over the countryside.

The pay envelopes of those workers fortunate enough to remain employed became thinner and thinner. Resistance to wage cuts were futile—as Homestead and Pullman workers learned to their grief.

Despite the appalling amount of evidence of suffering during the depression, the nation was slow to recognize the need for providing relief.

"At Chicago last winter," a journalist reported in 1894, "the question of the relief of the unemployed was one which forced itself upon my attention by the barbarity of housing the casuals in the police stations and in the corridors of the City Hall. At first there was a disposition to . . . maintain that the American tramp deserved to be kicked by day and housed in the police-stations at night. But after various ministers, professors, and labor leaders had visited the police-cells and the City Hall, sufficient steam was generated to get the whole question of the relief of the distress taken in hand by a representative committee of citizens.

"For the first time in many winters the unemployed were furnished with work on the streets, by which they could earn their rations and pay for lodgings in a decent lodging-house . . . This year they were brigaded into street gangs three thousand strong, and set to work at the necessary work of cleaning the streets . . . It was found, contrary to general belief, that seventy-five per cent of the men out of work had resided in Chicago for more than five years. The unions did a great deal to support their own members, and the saloon-keepers, by their free lunches, fed a larger number of people than the public and private charities provided for; and so, by one way or another, the distress was tided over."

RELIEF LINES AND SOUP KITCHENS IN CHICAGO

The needy who swarmed to Chicago's relief centers and soup kitchens were barely able to subsist from day to day. During the evenings homeless men were permitted to sleep in city hall corridors.

For years it had been evident that the nation was headed for trouble, but there was scarcely any consciousness of this among men prominent in public life. One of the few to speak up with undisguised alarm was Senator John Ingalls. On the eve of the depression he warned Congress that trouble was brewing.

"We cannot disguise the truth that we are on the verge of a revolution . . . Labor, starving and sullen in the cities, aims to overthrow a system under which the rich are growing richer and the poor are growing poorer, a system which gives to a Vanderbilt and a Gould wealth beyond the dreams of avarice and condemns the poor to poverty from which there is no escape or refuge but the grave . . . The laborers of the country asking for employment are treated like impudent mendicants begging for bread."

INDICTMENT OF "RAPACIOUS CAPITALISM"

Published during the nadir of the depression, "Wealth Against Commonwealth," a scathing indictment of the methods used by large corporations to plunder the public, charged rapacious capitalism with blame for widespread human suffering. Author Henry Demarest Lloyd lashed out at the Rockefellers, the Carnegies, and the Morgans for thwarting the common good. For too long, he asserted, the nation had mistakenly assumed that unfettered pursuit of personal gain would inevitably benefit society as a whole. "In industry we have been substituting all the mean passions that can set man against man in place of the irresistible power of brotherhood . . . We have overworked the self-interest of the individual." Grasping businessmen who regarded themselves as responsible to no one but themselves operated on the arrogant principle of "the public be damned" and would go on doing so until "the vast multitudes who have been gathered together in modern production can . . . organize themselves" as a countervailing force in American society.

In return for cleaning the streets and performing other chores, Chicago's jobless were rewarded with free meals at kitchens run by charitable organizations. Married men were paid fifty cents a day for chopping wood.

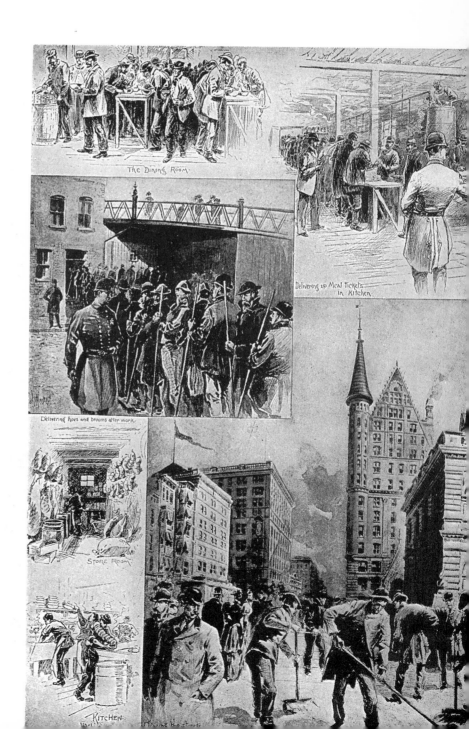

COXEY'S RAGTAIL ARMY MARCHES ON WASHINGTON

At the urging of "General" Jacob Coxey (seated in carriage at the left), a small army of depression victims began a march on Washington on Easter Sunday of 1894 to demand relief action by the federal government. As the march progressed, this motley collection of desperate down-at-the-heels men evoked more alarm than sympathy.

Coxey, a well-to-do businessman turned Populist, advocated the building of roads and other public works projects as means of providing jobs for the unemployed, but these ideas were ridiculed as crackpotism. When his army arrived in Washington it was subjected to derision and harassment.

Police prevented Coxey from delivering a speech in front of the Capitol. "Up these steps," he complained, "the lobbyists of trusts and corporations have passed unchallenged on their way to the committee rooms, access to which we, the representatives of the toiling wealth producers, have been denied. We stand here today in behalf of millions of toilers whose petitions have been buried in committee rooms, whose prayers have been unresponded to, and whose opportunities for honest, remunerative, productive labor have been taken away from them by unjust legislation which protects idlers, speculators, and gamblers."

Unable to march, "General" Coxey rode most of the way to Washington in a carriage that also provided temporary transportation for tired reporters who accompanied his "Army of the Commonweal of Christ". An intensely religious man, he frequently cited the Bible in his public pronouncements.

Arrested for "walking on the grass" surrounding the Capitol, Coxey, Christopher Jones, and Carl Browne peer from a police station cage. Browne, Coxey's principal aide, is seen below on horseback as the unemployed marchers converged on Washington; historians credit him with having proposed the march.

Most members of Congress were anxious to avoid a confrontation with the marchers, but Senator William Allen of Nebraska argued that their grievances should be heard by a Congressional committee.

These rare photographs are from the Ray Baker Collection at the Library of Congress.

Traveling by foot, by canal boat, and by rail, Coxey army units aroused fear of revolution in some quarters. No outbreaks of violence occurred during the march.

203

ADVERTISERS OF SOCIAL MISERY

"Coxey and his tatterdemalion followers," journalist W. T. Stead reported, "are laughable enough no doubt to those who from the stalls of full-fed comfort can only see the ludicrous side of weltering misery; but to the masses who suffer it is not surprising that they should appear in another and much more serious light. For they are sandwich-men of Poverty, the peripatetic Advertisers of Social Misery."

Trade unions as well as unorganized workers cheered the marchers onward. Speaking of Coxeyism, Edward Bellamy, author of the bestselling book "Looking Backward," wrote:

"The most significant feature of this industrial situation lies, not in the numbers of the marching bodies—which, of course, are trifling—but in the fact that it is evident that the laboring masses of people, the working classes, are deeply in sympathy with it. This has been shown, as of course every newspaper reader knows, by a series of demonstrations on the part of the workingmen—the poorer classes generally in the great cities, as well as the smaller districts along the line of march. It is also evidenced by the sympathetic attitude of the officials of the Knights of Labor, the Federation of Labor, and the Railway Union in the west, and especially in their attempt to assist the armies by threatening strikes if the latter's demands were refused. I have been much impressed by what the workingmen have said to me personally regarding their sympathy with the movement . . . while I was prepared for a surprise, it was even greater than I expected. They evidently think of their cause and believe that these armies are standing for their interests."

Discontent among Chicago's jobless fused outdoor demonstrations at which capitalism was excoriated.

THREADBARE RESPECTABILITY

Contrary to inaccurate news reports, relatively few of the men in Coxey's army were disreputable tramps. As these photos indicate, most were fairly typical American workers. Unlike some bands of unemployed that "bummed" around the country during the depression, they maintained discipline and kept up an air of threadbare respectability.

"You cannot find so much as a chicken feather among my men," Coxey boasted as he led the marchers past innumerable hen coops.

Writer Jack London can be seen peering toward the camera in the lower right hand corner of the photo at the top of the page.

These crude cartoons by Coxeyites express both their panaceas and prejudices.

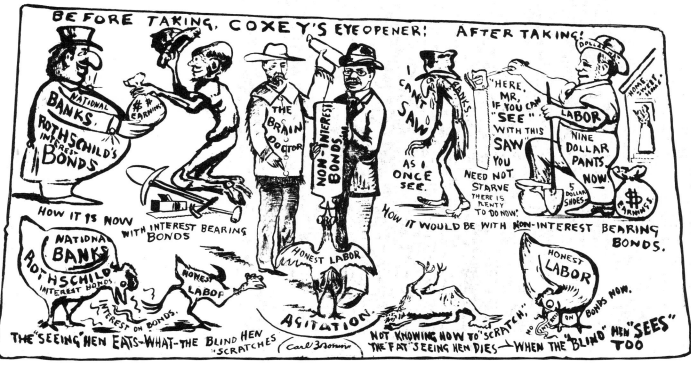

207

BRYAN'S PRESIDENTIAL BID

While William McKinley conducted his campaign for the presidency from the front porch of his Canton, Ohio, home in 1896, William Jennings Bryan went up and down the country exhorting farmers and workers to enlist in his battle against the evils of plutocracy.

In the famous "cross of gold" speech which won him the Democratic nomination, Bryan equated the basic interests of labor with his notions about bimetalism:

"Upon which side will the Democratic party fight; upon the side of the idle holders of idle capital or upon the side of the struggling masses? . . .

"The sympathies of the Democratic party . . . are on the side of the struggling masses . . . The Democratic idea has been that if you make the masses prosperous, their prosperity will find its way up through every class which rests upon them . . .

"Having behind us the producing masses of this nation and the world, supported by the commercial interests, the laboring interests, and the toilers everywhere, we will answer their [Republican] demand for a gold standard by saying to them: You shall not press down upon the brow of labor this crown of thorns, you shall not crucify mankind upon a cross of gold."

VOICE OF POPULISM

McKinley won with 7,000,000 votes as against 6,500,000 for Bryan. Tom Johnson, liberal Mayor of Cleveland, called the election "the first great protest of the American people against monopoly — the first great struggle of the masses in our country against the privileged classes. It was not free silver that frightened the plutocrat leaders. What they feared then, what they fear now, is free men."

Four years later Bryan again ran against McKinley unsuccessfully. This time he lost by about 850,000 votes and received 21 fewer electoral votes than during his first effort.

At the side is a photo of Bryan making a stump speech in Nebraska.

Skillful use of the full dinner pail stood the Republican party in good stead during the presidential campaigns of William McKinley and Theodore Roosevelt although Democrats felt that the big business pail overflowed with special privileges. Don Quixote Bryan was badly bruised in his tilts against the symbol.

UNDER THE LAST DEMOCRATIC ADMINISTRATION

HARD SELL POLITICS

"You Can't Fool the Workingman" (above) is a Republican reminder of the depression that afflicted the nation during Grover Cleveland's second term in the White House. The plea of Democratic boss David Hill ("Listen to me, my man. Return the Democratic party to power and let us again have those good times—the same as during the last Democratic administration") went unheeded.

In mobilizing sentiment against Bryan in 1896, the Republicans plucked at the strings of fear, warning the country of a dire future if William McKinley were not elected. Some firms placed orders for merchandise that was to be furnished only if Bryan was defeated and money lenders let it be known that mortgages on homes and farms would not be renewed if he became President. Shortly before votes were cast some manufacturers paid off their workers with the warning that production would shut down if he emerged as the victor. During the 1900 campaign such tactics weren't necessary; general prosperity took the wind out of Bryan's already sagging sails.

Despite the troubles ascribed to Republican policies, "Beneficent Bill McKinley" was twice elected President. Most of the strife depicted in this cartoon took place during the administration of fellow Republican Benjamin Harrison (1888-1892), when McKinley was a party leader.

Opposing concepts of the "free silver" issue kept cartoonists busy during presidential campaigns of the 1890's. Gold standard Republicans insisted that Bryan's silver coinage policy would sharply reduce purchasing power but his Populist supporters were convinced that bimetalism would solve the unemployment problem.

Brightening economic skies and mounting un-
easiness about Bryan's "soft money" policies combined to assure the election of Republican William
McKinley as "the advance agent of prosperity" who
could be relied upon to adhere to the gold standard
and promote American business interests.

HARUM-SCARUM BATTLE OVER MONEY

Free and unlimited coinage of silver, advocated by
Populists as a means of breaking the hold of monopoly
capitalism over the nation's economic life, had a fair
degree of labor support, particularly during William
Jennings Bryan's campaigns for the presidency, although Republicans warned workingmen that abandon-
ment of the gold standard would mean reduced wages
and lower living standards.

"In its essential reality," as W. E. Woodward pointed out retrospectively, "the McKinley-Bryan campaign
was a contest between men without money and men
with money. On one side were the dirt farmers, the
factory workers, the mechanics and laborers. On the
other side were the industrialists and stockholders, the
bankers and merchants . . . It was really a battle of
capital and labor, disguised as a fight over free silver.

"It is unfortunate that the Democratic-Populist party
should have risked its fate on an issue which was
obviously unsound. There were other questions of great
importance, such as the rise of trusts and monopolies,
the welfare of workers, the growth of towering fortunes,
the capture of coal, oil and timber lands by predatory
interests. But Bryan and his advisers decided unwisely
to concentrate on free silver, with the consequence
that a vast number of thoughtful men, who would have
been Democrats if the party had had a more comprehensive objective, cast their votes . . . for William
McKinley."

RIDICULE OF
BRYAN'S LABOR SUPPORT

Lampooning Bryan's presidential candidacy, the above cartoons envision what might happen if he were elected. Bryan is seen presiding over a cabinet composed of Secretary of War Jacob Coxey (leader of the 1894 march on Washington), Secretary of Interior Eugene Debs (president of the American Railway Union), Secretary of Navy John P. Altgeld (ex-governor of Illinois who remained a steadfast friend of labor), Secretary of State Mary Lease (feminine voice of the Populist movement), Secretary of the Treasury Benjamin Tillman (Southern spokesman of the Farmers' Alliance), and Secretary of Agriculture Dennis Kearney (California's firebrand labor leader).

Below is a cartoon ridiculing Samuel Gompers' support of Bryan.

214

CONTROVERSY OVER TARIFF PROTECTIONISM

Manufacturers and politicians alike appealed stridently to workingmen for support of high protective tariff walls. Although industry had out-stripped agriculture at home and was out-producing a great deal of competition abroad, the protectionist proponents justified their cause as beneficial to labor and the future economic progress of the nation.

Labor's attitude toward tariffs was usually determined by an industry's concern about foreign competition. Where imports threatened sales and employment, both employers and workers favored protection; where foreign trade did not directly affect an industry, unions tended to be indifferent toward import restrictions.

Republicans generally lined up on the side of high tariffs while Democrats preferred lower duties, but their differences were greatly exaggerated by partisan propaganda. Cartoons in Republican-biased newspapers went out of their way to create the impression that their party was on the side of the angels who shielded workers from the dumping of foreign goods made by European slaves while Democratic organs depicted Republicans as grasping, greedy ogres who profited outrageously from high tariffs.

Candidates for public office also engaged in exaggerations. "Our protective system," Benjamin Harrison assured the nation when he ran for President on the GOP ticket in 1888, "is a barrier against the flood of foreign importations and the competition of underpaid labor in Europe. Those who want to lower the dike owe it to those who live behind it to make a plainer statement of their purposes. Do they invite the flood or do they believe in the dike?"

Grover Cleveland, up for reelection, took a more cautious stand: "In a readjustment of our tariff, the interests of American labor engaged in manufacture should be carefully considered, as well as the preservation of our manufacturers . . . The question of free trade is absolutely irrelevant."

Harrison was elected, but four years later Cleveland had the misfortune of being returned to the White House on the eve of the worst depression of the century. The tariff issue arose again in 1896; this time arch-protectionist William McKinley was elected President.

Throughout this period the protectionists harped steadily on their altruistic concern for American labor, emphasizing that high tariff rates meant increased employment, "high" wages, and general prosperity. The factories of other industrial nations, it was contended, produced cheap goods because foreign wages were low; allowing such low-priced wares to enter the U. S. under free trade would force American wages down to foreign levels. At the same time advocates of lower duties on imports told the worker that high tariffs encouraged monopolies that kept prices up and wages down.

AUGURIES OF DOOM

Fearful of tariff reductions, protectionist Cassandras predicted "misery . . . for the American laborer" if "foreign wares are permitted to drown out our manufactures without restraint." Republican spokesman James G. Blaine put the matter this way:

"Were it possible for every voter of the Republic to see for himself the condition and recompense of labor in Europe, the party of free trade in the United States would not receive the support of one wageworker between the two oceans. It may not be directly in our power as philanthropists to elevate the European laborer, but it will be a lasting stigma upon our statesmanship if we permit the American laborer to be forced down to the European level."

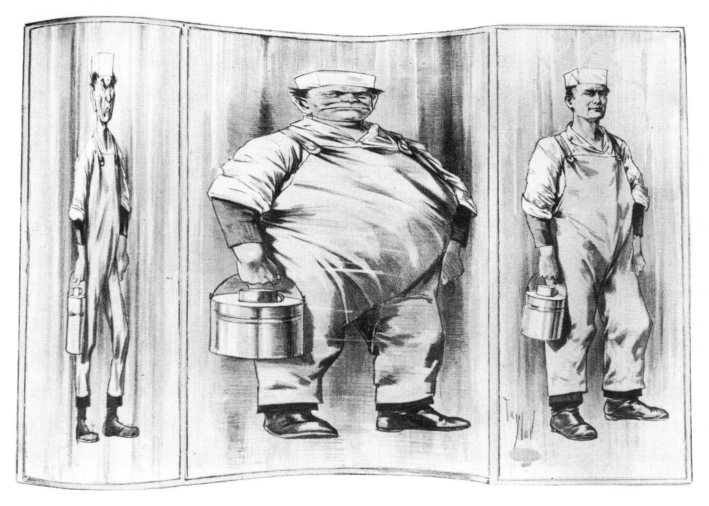

How labor stood to benefit by tariff policies depended on partisan mirrors and propaganda.

Democratic Free-Trade Means low wages, children in rags and ignorance.

Republican Protection Means good wages, happy homes and education for your children.

A GIANT IS BORN

More out of habit than necessity, manufacturers continued to beg for tariff protection although many of them could afford to sell their wares profitably at prices lower than those charged by their foreign competitors. As long as duties remained in effect, as ironmaster Abram Hewitt admitted, American rail makers went on piling up huge profits based largely on tariff subsidies. By the turn of the century he and Andrew Carnegie conceded that the time had come to abandon protection. Even President McKinley seemed to be of a like mind. "The period of exclusiveness is past," he told visitors at Buffalo's trade fair only a few hours before his assassination. "The expansion of our trade and commerce is the pressing problem. Commercial wars are unprofitable. . . . friendly trade relations will prevent reprisals."

As "Whittler For the World," the title Judge gave the cartoon below, Uncle Sam could not help but be pleased with the growth of overseas demand for American products. During the year in which this drawing appeared (1899) the U. S. produced eleven and a half billion dollars' worth of manufactured goods and more than five billion dollars' worth of agricultural products.

Most American industries were now strong enough to undersell foreign competition in European and Latin American markets.

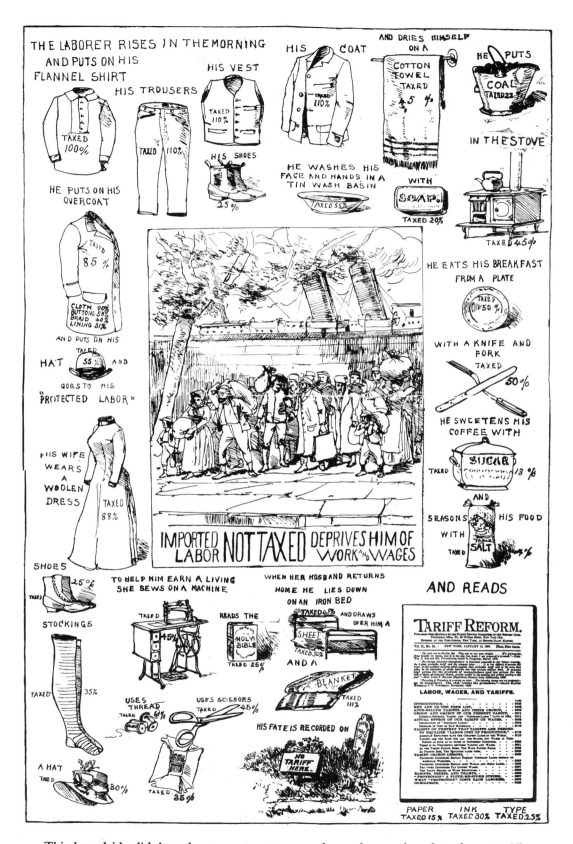

This broadside didn't make converts among workers who continued to favor tariffs.

BY H. C. DODGE.

YOU CAN'T
JOHN BULL-DOZE
ME—THIS TIME.

I am a little
workingman and what
I want to know is why the
big Republican is weeping for
me so? Why does he all at once
commence to shout in my behalf
and show a sympathy intense that
only makes me laugh? He never used
to think of me nor treat me with respect and now my wages suddenly he's
anxious to protect. Protect! Because
the Democrats, he says, will cut them
low. Excuse me if I mention,
"Rats!" and ask who told him so.
Four-fifths of all who labor
now are Democrats. Will
they destroy themselves to
please their foe by hurting
their own pay? Not much!
The little workingman
who learned a bit at school
laughs at the big Republican who takes him
for a fool Four y'rs
ago we he ard Free
Trade un to our
heart's content.
Now wh en the
same old game is
played we don't
scare for a
ce nt.

This
ballot is
for my
REAL
friends.

NO
WAR
TAX
ON
OUR
DINNER
PAIL.

THE REPUBLICAN PARTY
PROTECTING THE WORKINGMAN

Refuting tariff arguments was difficult because sentiments in behalf of protectionism were deeply rooted. Puck's editor commented:

"The fact is that this . . . whole high tariff business, honest enough in its inception, no doubt, has become an out-and-out swindle and humbug. It began in the 'protection' of certain industries . . . Now it goes wholly to the enriching of a few industries that are rich and strong, and daily growing richer and stronger. The capital invested needs no protection; but it is protected. Its employees are not protected; neither are the people who buy its products."

AMERICAN LABOR pays WAR TAXES on all these articles for the sole Benefit of TRUST, MONOPOLY & CO.

IMPORTED, DUTY FREE, by TRUST, MONOPOLY & CO. TO COMPETE WITH AMERICAN LABOR.

This cartoon points up the hypocrisy of monopolists who demanded tariff protection from low-priced foreign goods while advocating unlimited immigration of workers who were hired at wages lower than those customarily paid American laborers. "This situation is utterly unfair" charged a critic. "Our workingmen ought to have some protection from competition by immigrants who are willing to accept substandard wages... Our tariff and immigration policies penalize the humble American worker. He surely deserves equal participation in benefits conferred upon manufacturers."

Although alien labor contracts were no longer enforceable by the courts, it was still a common practice to hire workers abroad, transport them to the U.S., and pay them next to nothing until their passage fare and other expenses were completely repaid.

THE TRIUMPH
OF BIG BUSINESS

The growth of big business and big trusts placed labor at an enormous disadvantage. In earlier times it could bring effective pressure to bear on factory owners anxious to avoid strikes. But powerful corporations that dominated whole industries had little to fear from craft unions that could seldom do more than engage in poorly mounted skirmishes.

"As corporations grew and combined . . . business became more and more intricate and gigantic, more and more impersonal . . . [and] uncontrollable by society," according to Louis Adamic. "To be successful corporation managers had to become dehumanized . . . in their capacities as businessman. Indeed, it can scarcely be said that corporations were managed by men. They were operated almost purely by policy, which soon jelled into tradition, and which had little, if any, consideration for the human elements in business. The central aim of corporation policy was higher and higher profits. Such slogans as 'The public be damned' and 'Beat down the labor movement' were uttered by individuals prompted by the impelling impersonal, unsocial—in many cases distinctly anti-social—character of the corporations which they headed."

CORPORATE DOMINANCE

The enormous power of gigantic corporations became even greater after passage of the Sherman Anti-Trust Act in 1890 although the public was told that the law would hurt the economy and increase unemployment. Avowed purpose of the measure was to "protect trade and commerce against unlawful restraints and monopolies" but the trend toward trustification rolled onward inexorably into the twentieth century.

Ironically, judges who were disinclined to penalize big business under the terms of the Sherman Anti-Trust Act were quick to rule that union strikes and boycotts constituted violations of the law. A feeble instrument for maintenance of economic competition became a sharp-edged weapon against workers.

THE EXTRAVAGANT RICH LIVE IT UP

While a maelstrom of resentment was gathering momentum among workers and farmers, the extravagance of the idle rich seemed to have no limits, as Charles and Mary Beard have pointed out:

"At a dinner eaten on horseback, the favorite steed was fed flowers and champagne; to a small black-and-tan dog wearing a diamond collar worth $15,000 a lavish banquet was tendered; at one function, the cigarettes were wrapped in hundred dollar bills; at another, fine black pearls were given to the diners in their oysters; at a third, an elaborate feast was served to boon companions in a mine from which came the fortune of the host. Then weary of such limited diversions, the plutocracy contrived more freakish occasions—with monkeys seated between guests, human gold fish swimming about in pools, or chorus girls hopping out of pies.

"In lavish expenditures as well as in exotic performances, pleasures were hungrily sought by the fretful rich delivered from the bondage of labor and responsibility. Diamonds were set in teeth; a private carriage and personal valet were provided for a pet monkey . . . An entire theatrical company was taken from New York to Chicago to entertain the friends of a magnate and a complete orchestra engaged to serenade a child."

Revolt against such excesses is prophesied by artist William Ker in his painting "From the Depths."

John Barrymore drew this cartoon, "The Mill That Grinds Slowly," when he worked for Hearst's New York American in 1902. At the left side youthful workers are seen entering the machine of avaricious capitalism; at the right they emerge old and exhausted. Barrymore turned to acting after a brief stint as a cartoonist.

CHALLENGE OF VESTED INTERESTS

Seemingly the factory boss was hard put to cope with trade union pressure but the American Federation of Labor saw things differently. "On every hand," Sam Gompers pointed out in 1891, "we find organization and combination on the part of those who own or control wealth, and using their possessions to crush out the liberties, to stifle the voice, and pervert the rights of the toiling masses.... The combinations can only be successfully met and coped with by a compact and thorough organization of wage workers."

THE ENDURING IMPACT
OF SAMUEL GOMPERS

Thickset, sturdy-framed Samuel Gompers, president of the American Federation of Labor from its origin in 1886 until (except for one year) his death in 1924, was a labor leader in looks as well as in fact. Though short of stature, he was invariably the dominant figure at federation meetings. His voice had rich resonance as he boomed out his speeches. Dark eyes snapping behind rimless pince-nez glasses had a schoolmasterish quality that didn't quite harmonize with his unruly hair (black at first, but a mop of white in his later years). In his personal life he was unabashedly gregarious, drinking beer to excess, smoking odorous cigars, and visiting music halls whenever he had the chance.

As a boy Gompers knew poverty at first hand and he didn't much like it. He was born in London, the son of Jewish parents of Dutch origin. When his family settled on New York's East Side in 1863, he went straight to work, at 13, in a cigar factory. It didn't take him long to become a union member. As the youthful head of Cigarmakers Local 144, he demonstrated leadership qualities that resulted in his election as a national vice president.

First and foremost an advocate of craft unionism, Gompers played a major role in the establishment of the Federation of Organized Trades and Labor Unions in 1881, and its successor, the American Federation of Labor, five years later. Without his single-minded devotion to the federation for the rest of his life it is doubtful that the American labor movement would be the great force that it is today.

In his autobiography Gompers provides a vivid description of the men who joined with him in laying the basis for the American Federation of Labor in 1886:

"On May 18 there gathered in Philadelphia in the Donaldson Hall . . . the largest meeting of trade union executives I had attended up to that time. It was an impressive gathering of men of good presence and exceptional ability. Practically every man wore a silk hat and a Prince Albert coat. Each was a dignified and self-respecting journeyman who took pride in his trade and his workmanship. Yet we were all poor. Nobody had any money or any property.

"We shared with each other, traveled as cheaply as possible, and contented ourselves with very uncomfortable hotel accommodations. No labor man dreamed of Pullman conveniences in those days. The early labor leaders were tested by the ordeals of sacrifice and were tempered in spirit by an inextinguishable desire to help their fellows.

"Conspicuous among the group in Donaldson Hall were William Weihe, six feet six, the giant puddler; Joseph Wilkinson, the handsome tailor; P. J. McGuire, a lovable, genial companion . . . Henry Emrich, the eloquent leader of the Furniture Workers; and Adolph Strasser, the Bismarck of the Cigarmakers . . ."

(Gompers undoubtedly would have been somewhat less nonchalant had he realized that the photographer who took the above picture was a detective employed by a mining company.)

Gompers didn't mince words when he compared "the modest aspirations of workers with the greedy avarice of bloated trusts" but such bluntness opened him to vitriolic attacks. In the cartoon below he is depicted as "The Labor Pope." Whitelaw Reid, owner of the New York Tribune, is seen kissing Gompers' feet in the presence of surly union officers; comfortably seated at the extreme left is Terence Powderly, Knights of Labor Grand Master.

HUMBLE
BEGINNINGS

Looking back at his early experiences as the president and only full-time officer of the American Federation of Labor, Gompers wrote:

"The first little office, which was about ten by eight, had a door, a small window, and a brick floor. It was cold in winter and hot in summer. The furniture was make-shift, consisting of a kitchen table brought down from our scanty house furnishings and a box for my chair. My second boy, Henry, helped me when not in school . . .

"My daughter Rose had a child's writing desk that someone had given her. Henry took this down to the 'office,' put legs under it, and nailed it to the wall under the window. Thus equipped, with a box for a seat, Henry was busy during the summer all day long [preparing] wrappers for the paper and doing many errands . . . Just across the street was a grocery store, the friendly proprietor of which contributed empty tomato boxes which Henry transformed into files . . .

"However, as soon as we had a few pennies we tried to make improvements. We invested one dollar in pine wood and cuttings out of which to construct real files . . . It was some months later that I felt wealthy enough to buy a second-hand desk for $2.

"Money was scarce. There was not always enough for paper and ink. Henry remembers as one of his duties as office boy, going to the school around the corner to borrow a little ink until we could get money to buy a new bottle. Sometimes there was money to pay Henry his three dollars for his week's work, sometimes there was money to pay my week's salary. But whether there was money or not, in the morning we started to work with our lunch under our arms. If we had ten cents, we might ride back—if not, we walked. But we did the day's work, ate our sandwich apiece at noon, and got back home when we could. More often than not, it was midnight before I got home—there were meetings, speeches to make, conferences to attend, for the cause of labor is no easy mistress to serve . . ."

(Below is a 1915 photo of Gompers with his wife Sophia and daughter Sadie.)

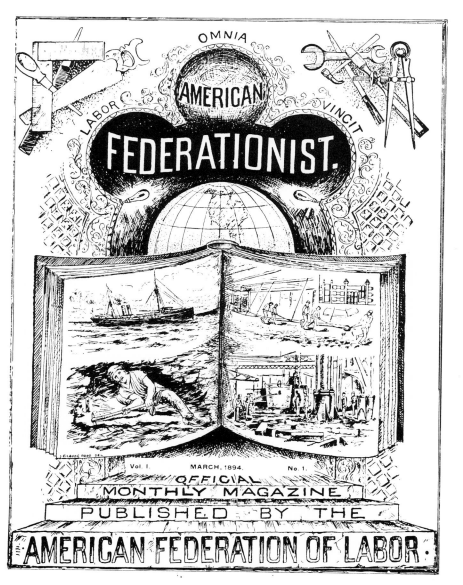

STEADY PROGRESS

Despite the depression of the 1890's, the AFL managed to keep growing fairly steadily. During previous depression periods unions barely managed to survive. Sensing that a national publication was urgently needed "in these difficult times," Sam Gompers launched the American Federationist on a shoestring budget; the first issue appeared in March, 1894. Some delegates to the convention of the following year insisted that the magazine be dropped but the executive council agreed to its continuation on a severely limited budget.

Like Gompers, the members of the executive council who shaped the early policies of the American Federation of Labor were representatives of the more powerful craft unions.

Seated in the photo at the top (probably taken in the late 1890's) are James Duncan (Granite Cutters), President Samuel Gompers, and John Mitchell (Mine Workers). Standing, left to right, are Secretary-Treasurer Frank Morrison (Typographers), Dennis Hayes (Bottle Blowers), James O'Connell (Machinists), Max Morris (Clerks), James Valentine (Molders), John Lennon, and Daniel Keefe.

In the front row of the 1909 picture at the bottom are Lennon, Duncan, Gompers, Mitchell, Morrison. In the rear row are Hayes, John Alpine (Plumbers), William Huber (Carpenters), O'Connell, Morris and Valentine.

HIERARCHY OF THE AMERICAN FEDERATION

BESET BY PANACEAS

Constantly plagued by nostrum peddlers and self-seeking politicians, the AFL kept finding itself hard put to concentrate on pure and simple trade unionism. In discussing this problem years later, Gompers wrote:

"In [all the] years of actively taking part in the making of the economic and political history of this nation, our federation has witnessed the birth, the struggle for life and the passing away of all sorts of political movements designed to save the republic from varying degrees of destruction; it has been coddled and mauled, petted and cajoled by the cohorts of particular brands of liberty; it has been assailed by isms and ologies without number; it has been baited with sugared doses for economic chills and political fevers; it has heard the dirge and attended the last sad rites over many a promising political corpse. It has been courted by all the allurements of the partisan politician; all the thralling visions of the emotional enthusiast have been pictured for its enticement; all the arts of the crafty self-seeker have been practiced to tempt it. But, despite all these, the American Federation of Labor has never been swerved from its non-partisan course."

In actuality the federation frequently flirted with politicians and reformers but it seldom lost sight of its primary aim—higher wages and better working conditions for its members.

THE SUNDAY TIMES-HERALD.

CHICAGO NOVEMBER 28, 1897.—FORTY-EIGHT PAGES.

AMERICAN FEDERATION OF LABOR.

History, Progress and Achievements of the Famous Organization of Workmen, Which Will Meet at Nashville in December.

Greatest Alliance of Bone, Sinew and Skill the World Has Ever Known—Has 600,000 Members and Is Gaining in Strength.

SAMUEL GOMPERS.
[President.]

P. J. M'GUIRE, PHILADELPHIA.
[First Vice President.]

JAMES DUNCAN, BALTIMORE.
[Second Vice President.]

JAMES O'CONNELL, CHICAGO.
[Third Vice President.]

M. M. GARLAND, PITTSBURG.
[Fourth Vice President.]

JOHN B. LENNON, BLOOMINGTON, ILL.
[Treasurer.]

FRANK MORRISON.
[Secretary American Federation of Labor, Washington, D. C.]

EDWARD HIRSH.
[President Baltimore Federation of Labor—International Typographical Union.]

THOMAS J. ELDERKIN, CHICAGO.
[Delegate Seamen's International Union.]

JOHN PHILLIPS.
[United Hatters of America, Boston.]

FRANK K. FOSTER.
[Tackmakers' Union, Boston.]

WHEN on Monday, Dec. 13, President Samuel Gompers calls the seventeenth annual convention of the American Federation of Labor to order in the hall of representatives in the state capitol at Nashville, Tenn., there will be gathered in that hall working men and women from every state and territory in the United States, several delegates representing the British trades union congress of Great Britain, and it is expected that Canada and Japan will also be represented. It will mark an epoch in the history of the American Federation of Labor, the greatest and strongest alliance of bone, sinew and skill the world has ever known.

The object of the American Federation of Labor is "to render employment and the means of subsistence less precarious by securing to the toilers an equitable share of the fruits of their toil." As a means to this end it proposes:

A free federation of all trade and labor unions in America; the establishment of self-governing unions of wage-workers in every trade and legitimate occupation; the formation of public opinion by the agencies of the platform, press and legislation, and the furtherance of civilization by securing to the toilers a reduction in the daily hours of labor; encourage the formation of local trade and labor unions, and the closer federation of such societies through the organization of central trade and labor unions in every city, and the further combination of such bodies into state, territorial and provincial organizations, to secure legislation in the interest of the working classes; the establishment of national and international trade unions, based upon a strict recognition of the autonomy of each trade, and the promotion and advancement of such bodies; to aid and encourage the labor press of America; and an American federation of all national and international trade unions to aid and assist each other, and furthermore, to secure national state and municipal legislation in the interest of the working people, and influence public opinion, by peaceful and legal methods, in favor of organized labor. The Federation of Labor endeavors to unite all classes of wage-workers under one head, through their several organizations, to the end that class, race, creed, political and trade prejudices may be abolished; that support, moral and financial, may be given to each other. It gives to any organization joining its ranks recognition in the field of labor in all its phases. It secures in cases of boycotts, strikes, lockouts, attentive hearing before all affiliated bodies and renders financial aid to the extent of its ability. It allows each organization to control its own funds, to establish and expend its own benefits without let or hindrance. It aims to allow—in the light of experience—the utmost liberty to each organization in the conduct of its own affairs consistent with the generally understood principles of labor. It has established intercommunication, created agitation, and is in direct correspondence with a corps of representative organizers throughout the country. It watches the interests of the workers in the national congress; it indorses and protests in the name of labor, and has secured vast relief from burdensome laws and government officials. It is in communication with reformers and sympathizers in almost all classes, giving information and enlisting their co-operation. It asks the co-operation of all wage-workers who believe in the principle of unity, and that there is something better in life than long hours, low wages, lack of employment, and all that these imply. Its existence is based upon economic law.

+ + +

Conservative and Influential.

THAT the American Federation of Labor is an organization of growing power and influence is due to the fact that its officers in the main have tried to be guided by reason and wise judgment in endeavoring to better the condition of the toilers whom they represent. This explains in good part why the federation has been steadily gaining in strength, stability and influence, while other organizations, that at times have held a more prominent place in the public eye, have either declined in numbers and power or gone to pieces altogether. To-day the American Federation of Labor is composed of sixty national and international trade unions, eleven state branches, eighty-one city central bodies, 458 local unions and has in round numbers a combined membership of 600,000 wage-earning men and women marching under its broad banner.

Fifteen years ago there were but fourteen national and international trades unions in the United States and Canada. Now there are seventy-eight, three having been formed in the past year. One of these, the Amalgamated Meat Cutters and Butchers' Workmen's National Union, which was formed of five locals at the Cincinnati convention, now has twenty-seven locals.

The stand taken by the federation in the recent agitation against "government by injunction" has attracted most attention. Because they believe in orderly and constitutional means of agitation, the officers of the federation have "appealed to all fair-minded molders of public thought, to our public men, to the clergy and to the press" to make a decided stand with them henceforth against the "novel and questionable" use of injunctions by the courts, which they hold to be subversive of popular liberty.

+ + +

A Great Federation.

THE American Federation of Labor does what all federations of labor unions do—attempts to give solidarity to the labor movement by getting the various sections of the labor army into touch with each other. It refuses to admit that occupation can be a barrier to the community of interest running through the wage-earning masses. From its inception it has taken the stand that, while unions of miners, sailors, shoemakers, cigar-makers and printers must each and all be left entirely free to govern themselves within their own borders, yet that between the members of all these unions there should be a bond as great as that between the members of the same union. The great aim and object of the federation is to strengthen that bond, and its method is by organization, education and inculcation, to place the labor movement upon a higher and more effective plane. The strength of a chain is in its weakest link, and the federation, therefore, endeavors to organize all labor, recognizing that while many nonunionists may be sympathetic with unionism, yet that the unorganized are far more exposed to the pressure of unjust conditions than are the organized, and being thus necessarily weaker in maintaining wages, keeping down hours and resisting other encroachments, are the source of constant danger to the organized as well as to themselves. And there is this that the American Federation of Labor has already done. It has largely swept away the old and foolish jealousy that existed between the skilled and the unskilled workmen; it has taught the great lesson that a man is a man, no matter whether he sets type or scales a ladder, whether he sews the garment together or sells it behind the counter, whether he makes the machine that spins the cotton or gathers the cotton in the fields. Whatever a man may be, so long as he works honestly and seeks to wrong no other man or to advantage himself at the cost of another, he is a man. The federation maintains this and seeks to swing them all into line regardless of how they may happen to be employed.

+ + +

Antecedents.

WHEN President Lincoln called for volunteers during the civil war none responded more patriotically than did the workingman. He laid down his tools of industry and took up the implements of war. After the close of the war the toiler realized that the political rights of a people are not more sacred than their economic rights and looked about for some means of relief. Organizations of workingmen had, in one way or another, been in existence in this country for years, for with the Mayflower came the founders of the American labor movement. The change of conditions now gave new strength to the many associations and unions which had weakened during the war, and they soon felt the necessity of amalgamation. In 1865 twelve men met in Louisville, Ky., took the first step beyond trade lines in the organization of labor in America by issuing a call to all organized bodies of workingmen to meet the following year in Baltimore, Md., where on Aug. 20, 1866, representatives from sixty labor organizations met and founded the National Labor Union.

The old National Labor Union issued but few charters, and the only one now in existence, signed by William H. Sylvis, for a local union in the town of Black River Falls, Wis., has since been presented to President Gompers of the Federation of Labor as a souvenir.

The next convention of this body was held in Chicago in 1867, where Z. C. Whaley, the president, advanced the ideas of a central head, all subordinate unions to be auxiliary to it, and to pay quarterly dues for its maintenance. Subsequent conventions were held in Pittsburg, 1868; New York City, 1868; Chicago, 1869; Boston, 1870; Philadelphia, 1871; and Columbus, Ohio, 1872. This last convention put a presidential ticket in the field, and rapid disintegration at once ensued. The great financial crisis of 1873 following, the resources of the unions were drained and the suspension of work decreased their numbers. No further steps were taken to form a national body until Aug. 2 and 3, 1881, when there assembled at Terre Haute, Ind., a number of gentlemen representing several national and international trades unions and the central labor bodies in the larger cities of the United States, and a call for a mass meeting was ordered printed and scattered broadcast. The gentlemen named in the circular as speakers were Senator Voorhees of Indiana, P. J. McGuire of St. Louis, Richard Powers of Chicago, L. A. Brant of Detroit, Mark L. Crawford of Chicago and Sam Leffingwell of Indianapolis, Ind. A call was here issued for a meeting of representatives of all trade and labor unions to meet in Pittsburg Nov. 15, 1881. One hundred and seven delegates, representing a quarter of a million wageworkers, responded to this call, and did not separate until they had established the "Federation of Organized Trades and Labor Unions of the United States and Canada." The meeting was called to order by L. A. Brant of Detroit, representing the International Typographical Union, and John Jarrett, president of the Amalgamated Association of Iron and Steel Workers of the United States and Canada, was elected chairman. The first legislative committe appointed was composed of Samuel Gompers, Cigarmakers' International Union, New York; William H. Foster, International Typographical Union, Cincinnati; Alexander Rankin, Iron Molders' Union, Pittsburg; Richard Powers, Lake Seamen's Union, Chicago, and Charles Burgman, Tailors' Union, San Francisco. This committee presented several measures to congress. One of importance creating a national bureau of labor statistics was passed in 1883. The secretaries were Mark L. Crawford, representing the Chicago Trade and Labor Assembly; H. H. Bengough, Pittsburg, Printers' Assembly, No. 1,636, K. of L., and W. C. Pollner, Cleveland, Ohio, Trade and Labor Assembly, who was also secretary of the Terre Haute meeting.

The second convention of the federation was held in Clev[illegible]d, Ohio, Nov. 21, 1882. At this meeting [illegible] manifesto was issued guaranteeing the [illegible] trial autonomy of each union, and, [illegible] deprecating antagonism to other labor [illegible] tions, made the qualities of a man [illegible] worker the only test of fitness and set u[illegible] no political or religious test of membersh[illegible].

The most notable [illegible]ature of the third convention, held in [illegible] York City on Aug. 21, 1883, was a decl[illegible]tion favoring arbitration as preferable [illegible] strikes, and the legislative committee [illegible] instructed to present a bill to congress [illegible] a national department of labor. S[illegible] were also taken to confer with the [illegible]ghts of Labor that thorough unifica[illegible] and consolidation might be had. [illegible] proposition was rejected by the Kn[illegible]s.

At the fourth [illegible]ention, held in Chi[illegible] propaganda [illegible] day and May 1, [illegible], fixed [illegible] a general [illegible] tion. The turbule[illegible] of the first [illegible] of that month in [illegible]cago, and the terrible consequences of t[illegible] memorable and fatal meeting on the Haymarket, where a bomb was thrown from behind the red flag of anarchy, created a violent reaction in the public mind. However, a number of unions were successful in securing the eight-hour system.

Washington was the scene of the fifth convention, held Dec. 8, 1885. Besides preparing for the eight-hour struggle important measures were taken to check the abuses of the boycott, so often levied upon trivial pretexts.

+ + +

Under the New Name.

AT THE sixth convention, held in Columbus, Ohio, Dec. 8, 1886, the old federation was dissolved, a more perfect plan of organization was adopted, and the name—American Federation of Labor—was chosen. A constitution was adopted stating the main objects of the organization to be:

The encouragement and formation of local unions, and the closer federation of such societies, through central trade and labor unions in every city, with the further combination of these bodies into state, territorial and provincial organizations; to secure legislation in the interests of the working masses; the establishment of national and international trades unions, based upon a strict recognition of the autonomy of each trade, and the promotion and advancement of such bodies; and the aiding and encouragement of the labor press of America.

The next convention of the American Federation of Labor, but the seventh consecutive annual gathering of delegates from trade and labor unions, was held in Baltimore, Md., Dec. 13, 1887. This convention represented 2,421 unions or branches, and a total membership of 600,340 members in good standing, as against 316,469 of the year previous, thus vindicating the wisdom of the change adopted at Columbus.

The eighth convention, held in St. Louis, Dec. 11, 1888, is memorable for the unanimity and enthusiasm with which the delegates fixed the date for the general inauguration of the eight-hour workday for May 1, 1890. To secure more efficient agitation it was resolved to call simultaneous mass meetings all over the country on four great national holidays, viz.; Washington's birthday, Feb. 22, 1889; July 4, 1889; Labor day, 1889; Washington's birthday, 1890. As illustrative of the interest taken in this action by the toilers it is a noticeable fact that the first series of these meetings embraced 240 cities and towns, the second 3[illegible], the third 420, and the fourth 526. The Labor day of the European workingmen was adopted at the suggestion of this convention of the American Federation of Labor.

Steps for an international congress were taken at the ninth convention, held in Boston, Dec. 10, 1889. An invitation was extended to the labor organizations of the world to attend an international labor congress in Chicago during the world's fair. A resolution of thanks to European workingmen for cordial indorsement of the proposed inauguration of the eight-hour workday was adopted and steps were taken to further such co-operation. Other resolutions indorsed the Australian ballot system and favoring an employers' liability law. A resolution looking to "the formation of a political labor party" was defeated. At this convention the executive council was empowered and selected the United Brotherhood of Carpenters and Joiners on which to concentrate all efforts to secure the adoption of the eight-hour day on May 1, 1890. The movement was successful in 137 cities, and benefited 46,197 workmen of that trade; in many others also the impetus thus given secured like benefit.

The tenth convention was held in Detroit, Dec. 8, 1890. There were present 103 delegates, representing eighty-three organizations. The national and international trade unions reported having established 913 locals during the year; also reported having had 1,163 strikes, of which 989 were succesful, 76 lost, and 98 compromised. All but one reported increase of wages from 7 to 25 per cent. The miners were selected as the next trade to move toward securing the eight-hour day. Most interest, for the time being, was provoked by action defining the attitude of the American Federation of Labor toward political parties seeking affiliation. This was the cause of the refusal of a charter of affiliation to the Central Labor Federation of New York City, because to that body the American section of the socialist labor party was attached. After protracted debate the action of the officers in refusing the charter of affiliation was indorsed by a large majority.

For the first time in the history of the general labor movement one of its conventions was held in the south, the scene being Birmingham, Ala. Its influence was of vast benefit to the organization in that section of the country. At this convention it was resolved to test the constitutionality of [illegible] ers charged with no offense against the law, but engaged in a contest with employers. An investigation of the sweating system was asked at the hands of congress; a protest against all convict labor that competed with free labor was entered, and the abolition of child labor demanded, as well as other legislation in the interest of the toiler.

+ + +

Recent History.

AN UNUSUAL interest is attached to the twelfth convention by reason of the fact that it met at Philadelphia in Independence Hall. It was the first time any labor organization had been permitted to hold its convention in that historic building. The convention took strong grounds against the use by national and state authorities of the military in labor disputes, as demonstrated in Homestead, Buffalo and Coeur D'Alene. It declared that "the powers, designed to rest with the people as expressed in the United States constitution, for the protection of life and property and guaranteeing the rights and liberties of the people have been diverted from the purposes of their authors and that the powers have been usurped by corporations." The convention demanded the creation of a board of commissioners to be elected by the people, the commissioners, in conjunction with the governors, to have sole power to call out the militia; declared against the Pinkertons, and for the enactment of laws prohibiting nonresidents from serving as peace officers in any community; advised, until these measures should be enacted into laws, unionists should not enter the militia or national guard.

The thirteenth convention was held in the council chamber, Chicago, Dec. 11, 1893, in the midst of the industrial depression. Notwithstanding this fact, there were ninety-five delegates present, representing as large a membership as at any time in the history of the federation. Among the resolutions approved were those favoring government ownership of telegraphs and telephones, institution of postal savings banks, better food and quarters for seamen, abolition of the "sweating" system and subcellars for bakers; judicial decisions inimical to labor were denounced, and a congressional investigation demanded; a "political programme" was referred to affiliated organizations; large sums of money previously loaned to organizations engaged in disputes were donated. This convention also authorized the publication of a magazine to defend the interests of labor. Its name is the American Federationist.

The great railroad strike was the chief topic of discussion at the fourteenth convention, held in Denver, Dec. 10, 1894, and resolutions of sympathy for the imprisoned leaders, denouncing the manner of their imprisonment without a jury trial, were adopted, and interference by congress demanded. A bill then before congress, to appoint a national commission of industrial inquiry, was approved; free coinage at a ratio of 16 to 1 indorsed, while a declaration in favor of free land, on an occupancy and use title, as well as against the patent monopoly, were adopted; bills to secure relief for seamen against unjust laws were approved and a committee sent to Washington to urge their adoption; legal attempts at compulsory arbitration were denounced and protests made against blacklisting by railways and the issuance of bonds without the consent of the house of representatives. Two fraternal delegates from the British Trades Union Congress of England were present. The most important question considered was that of political action and platform, in which it was proposed to commit the federation to state socialism; this movement was defeated. The headquarters of the federation were ordered removed from New York City to Indianapolis, Ind.

The fifteenth convention met in Madison Square Garden, New York City, Dec. 9, 1895. As general trade was just recovering from the long-continued industrial depression, no general movement looking to renewed efforts on behalf of the eight-hour day was inaugurated. Compulsory arbitration was again denounced and political party action was again discussed, and a constitutional law was adopted against it by an overwhelming vote. The demand for the initiative and referendum in the political field was reaffirmed. The executive council reported many disagreements between employer and empoye settled and victories achieved during the year.

The sixteenth convention met in Cincinnati, Dec. 14, 1896; 117 delegates were present. The officers' reports showed that affiliated unions had 100,000 more members than the previous year and 267 charters had been issued by the federation during 1896, against 141 the previous year. A referendum vote of affiliated unions ordered on "indiscriminate immigration. Sympathy for the Cuban insurgents was expressed; charges of [illegible] against President [illegible] confidence unanimously tendered him. Among other matters approved were the inauguration of an eight-hour day, which was set for May 1, 1898, and a levy of 1 cent per member of affiliated unions was ordered for the purpose of agitating the short-hour day. It was recommended that affiliated unions make their dues 50 cents per month as a minimum. The delegates presented the British delegate, Samuel Woods, with a diamond-set charm, and John Mallinson with a gold watch, as tokens of good fellowship and brotherly love existing between the two great federations of labor. The Erdman arbitration bill before congress was disapproved. The headquarters of the federation were changed from Indianapolis, Ind., to Washington, D. C. Resolutions were passed recognizing the union label as the mainstay of trades unions and the most far-reaching and earnest way of educating the people to mutual benefits, and forming a national label league, approving the suggestion that the head of the government labor department be made a cabinet officer; forbidding officers of the federation to use their official positions for political purposes; indorsing the stand of the Christian Endeavorers against Sunday work. A new rule declared that any union refusing to comply with orders of the federation within sixty days should be suspended.

+ + +

Its Business Methods.

THE annual conventions of the American Federation of Labor convenes at 10 o'clock a. m. on the second Monday in December at such place as the delegates may have selected at the preceding convention. The city central labor body in which the conventions are held usually makes arrangements for a meeting hall, hotel accommodations and a programme of entertainment for the delegates while attending the convention.

The reasons why the federation holds its conventions the second Monday in December, so near the holidays, may be summed up as follows:

1. December was chosen so that it shall be after the elections—national, state and municipal—which occur annually, and men are freed to a larger extent from political partisan prejudices and surroundings. The conventions formerly were held early in the year, but experience has demonstrated the wisdom of the change.

2. The second Monday in December was chosen because the United States congress meets on the first Monday in December of each year. Upon that day the President of the United States sends his message to congress, and it is published in full in all the papers of the country. If the American Federation of Labor conventions were held during that week reports to and the proceedings of the convention would either be unnoticed or so condensed as to practically amount to suppression.

About ten days before the annual conven-

WILLIAM B. PRESCOTT, INDIANAPOLIS.
[President International Typographical Union.]

JOHN M'BRIDE, COLUMBUS, OHIO.
[United Mine Workers.]

M. D. RATCHFORD, COLUMBUS, OHIO.
[United Mine Workers.]

GEORGE E. M'NEILL, BOSTON.
[Fraternal Delegate to the British Trades Union Congress, Birmingham, England.]

WILLIAM J. GILTHORPE, KANSAS CITY, KAN.
[Iron Ship Builders and Boiler-makers.]

HARRY WHITE.
[United Garment Workers of America, Boston.]

FUSATARO TAKANO.
[Delegate from Hougo-Tokyo, Japan.]

CHARLES L. [illegible] CITY, KAN.
[Brotherhood [illegible] Workers.]

JESSE JOHNSON.
[International Printing Pressmen's Union, Nashville, Tenn.]

MARTIN FOX, CINCINNATI.
[National President Iron Molders' Union of North America—Fraternal Delegate to British Trades Union Congress.]

HORACE M. EATON.
[Boot and Shoe Workers' National Union.]

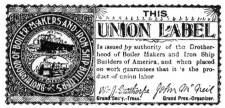

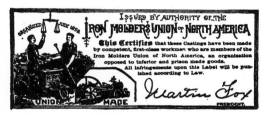

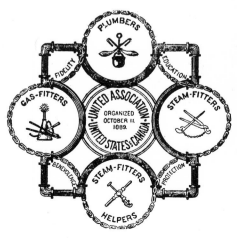

Labels of unions affiliated with the American Federation in 1903.

Above are officers of the Carpenters Union who attended a meeting in Detroit in 1904. On the facing page are delegates to a convention held in 1898.

Above are founders of the Brotherhood of Electrical Workers; at the side are Chicago officers of the union. The eight men in the photo at the bottom of the page established the Brewery Workers Union in 1886.

THE NEWSBOYS JOIN UP

Even newsboys were organized into unions. Above is a picture of Seattle youngsters all dressed up in their best clothes; typical "newsies" looked more like the boys in the photo directly underneath.

The New York messenger boys in the bottom thought it was a lark to go on strike for higher pay, but they regretted it when other teenagers got their jobs.

Hard knocks were good for youngsters in the opinion of Andrew Carnegie. "The millionaires who are in active control," he boasted, "started as poor boys and were trained in the sternest but most efficient of all schools—poverty." He held up as examples, besides himself, such men as John D. Rockefeller, George Pullman, Marshall Field, and George Westinghouse.

"Boys in the cities," an historian of the period tells us, "saw the stately mansions of these great men, saw their princely carriages, their gigantic offices. They read how these leaders of business . . . had acquired their rewards, and the ambitious set out to emulate them. Thus the ideals of our business leaders became the ideals of the great majority of the people, though only a few were themselves endowed with talent for leadership."

Celebrating Labor Day was a high-spirited experience.

Above are retail clerks at a convention held in 1892.

JOB PASSPORTS

Only a fully paid up member could obtain a travelling card entitling him to "fellowship" when he moved to another city. The card was especially valued because it assured continuity of union benefits.

Eligibility standards for "working cards" varied somewhat but most unions restricted membership to proficient craftsmen. In building construction and other highly organized trades there were tight union controls over who was qualified for employment, when, and under what conditions. Note the following rules in the working card at the side:

"Eight hours shall be a day's work, between 8 a.m. and 5 p.m. All work done after 5 p.m. shall be classed as overtime and must be paid for at double time; Sundays and legal holidays included.

"No member shall do piece work or sub-contract."

Such rules were considered necessary in order to maintain union standards but employers felt their rights were being usurped.

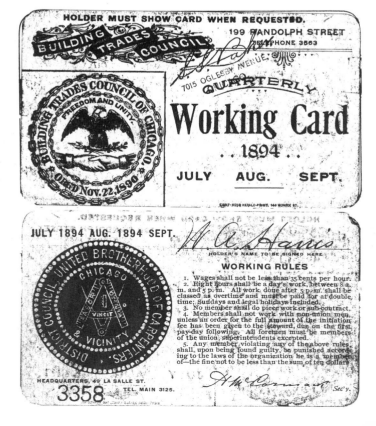

THE SOCIAL SIDE
OF UNION LIFE

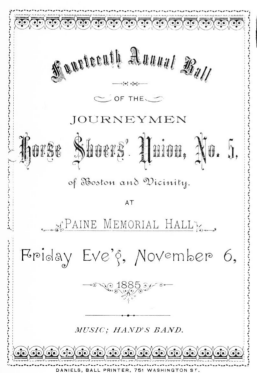

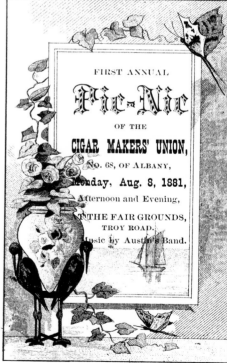

Social affairs were a convivial phase of union activity. They came as a welcome relief from the monotony of work. Balls, picnics, and excursions served not only to cement bonds of fraternalism but also to increase membership among workers not already in the fold.

Gregarious Samuel Gompers encouraged such festivities, but Knights of Labor leader Terence Powderly complained: "I will talk at no more picnics. When I speak on the labor question I want the individual attention of my hearers and I want that attention for at least two hours and in that two hours I can only epitomize. At a picnic where . . . the girls as well as the boys swill beer I cannot talk at all . . . If it comes to my ears that I am advertised to speak at picnics . . . I will prefer charges against the offenders for holding the executive head of the Order up to ridicule. . ."

TEAMWORK ON THE PLAYFIELD

Above is a 1905 photo of a soccer team composed of United Mine Workers who lived in the vicinity of Curry, Pennsylvania. The tieless youngster standing at the left is Philip Murray, future president of the Congress of Industrial Organizations. Below is a picture of Pressman Union members who participated in a Portland, Oregon, Labor Day picnic.

One of the most colorful figures in American labor history, fastidiously dressed "Mother Jones" (few knew her by her formal name, Mrs. Mary Harris Jones) frequently came to the help of strikers as a "hell raiser." In these photos she is seen with John Lawson, an organizer of the United Mine Workers (left at the top), and mustachioed Terence Powderly, long-time leader of the Knights of Labor. The adjoining article appeared in the Washington Star in 1930.

BATTLE FOR RIGHT.

Not "Humanitarian," She Once Said, but "Hell Raiser."

BY LEMUEL F. PARTON.

Once at a public meeting, a college professor referred to Mother Jones as a "great humanitarian." She interrupted him. "Get it right," she said. "I'm not a humanitarian, I'm a hell-raiser."

Dead in Silver Spring, Md., today, at the age of 100, Mother Jones probably would not wish to change this self-characterization. This writer had the privilege of knowing Mother Jones for many years and of frequently seeing her in action. The art of hell-raising as she practiced and expounded it was a dauntless and deathless battle for right as she saw it, and to her it provided an adequate philosophy of action. Anything other than action didn't interest her. "You don't need votes to raise hell," she told a gathering of women, seeking her views on suffrage.

Blended Sentiment and Fire.

Mother Jones was no shrieking virago. She was, instead, a soft-spoken, fastidiously dressed little old lady, with a white fichu and silver white hair, such as Cecil De Mille might have picked for "Way Down East." Born Mary Harris, in Cork, Ireland, she was the typical Celtic blend of sentiment and fire. She would croon old Irish songs to a miner's sick baby and then tie on her tidy little Victorian bonnet, with pansies on it, and lead a charge up a bleak hillside against guns, bludgeons or anything else that might lie ahead.

She loved to sit by the fireside with a cup of tea or perhaps making a bonnet for a miner's wife. She had been a dressmaker in Chicago and was skilled in needlework. She insisted that fighting miners' wives should wear bonnets, as shawls were to her the symbol of inferiority. Mother Jones must have outfitted whole legions of bonneted Amazons in the West Virginia and Pennsylvania coal fields. But, at that, there was little time for tea drinking and bonnet making. Mother Jones' life was spent mostly around blasted, slag-strewn mining dumps, in moldy jails, on scarred and desolate hillsides, with an occasional bullet whizzing through the scrub timber; down in the dark pits of coal mines, in forlorn miners' huts, in the textile mills and villages of the South, in dirty railway stations and on jerkwater trains—Mother Jones, with her neat little bonnet and a handkerchief always edged with lace.

Terror to Non-Union Men.

On the battle line she often wore two or three petticoats "to tie up the boys' heads with if they got hurt." And more than once she did rip off her undershirt to stanch the flow of blood for some fallen miner. The scourge of Attila was like nothing compared to Mother Jones leading an army of enraged women. Her method was to get them out with mops and brooms, with a large delegation making a frightful clatter pounding on tin wash tubs. This visitation, suddenly descending on a mine from the surrounding hillsides, was terrifying both to the mules and the non-union workers, usually stampeding both, with the women in pursuit.

THE LADIES HELP OUT

Even though it was considered "unbecoming for women to participate in public displays," the wives and sweethearts of workers joined in demonstrations, strikes, and Labor Day parades. Women who worked were especially active in the suffragette movement.

I drink only Union Beer.   **I drank Scab Beer.**

BRANDISHING THE BOYCOTT

Hard put to cope with powerful opposition from employers unwilling to raise wages or improve working conditions, both the Knights of Labor and the American Federation of Labor resorted to boycott campaigns that evoked alarm in contemporary cartoons.

Of all the activities of the Knights, none was more successful than their conduct of boycotts that curtailed workers' purchases of products manufactured by "unfair" employers. It remained, however, for the Federation to develop the technique of persuading the public at large to discontinue buying the goods of such employers.

In discussing labor's rationale for the boycott and resentment of restraining court injunctions, Samuel Gompers told a Congressional committee:

"The boycott is nothing more or less than the effort upon the part of labor to defend their friends and to withhold their friendship from those who are their enemies, who manifest particular enmity toward the effort of labor to secure improved conditions. 'Boycott' is a new term, but it is an old method. It is a method that has been employed from time immemorial. It is a perfect, legal, natural right for a man to prefer his friends to his enemies, and to act upon that, and have his actions conform to that sentiment; and we regard it as a perfectly lawful right, an inherent lawful right, of the workers to employ the boycott."

These views did not sit well with some members of the committee before which Gompers testified.

Union leaders usually threatened boycotts in fairly blunt language. But sometimes they resorted to intimidation in the following manner: "Of course if we cannot have other than ill will from your company we will have to be persistent and energetic in our efforts to acquaint our fellow workers and sympathizers with the matter in dispute between yourself and the union, and to urge the cooperation of all with greater alacrity and energy than ever before to bring you to realization that our fellow workers have rights which all are bound to respect."

Only an obtuse employer could fail to understand what these words meant.

How effectively boycotts were waged and possibly abused is suggested in a less than unbiased manifesto on the subject disseminated by the Manufacturers' and Employers' Association of San Francisco in the 1890's:

"The boycott is a crying evil of our times. Walking delegates have been bribed to boycott competitors, and walking delegates have exacted bribes for immunity from boycotts . . . When Cahn, Nickelsburg & Company introduced new machinery in their factory, a committee of expert manufacturers reported that the new rate on the new machines actually increased the wages of the operator, yet a boycott was levied. The 'Abend Post' is boycotted . . . Wellington coal is boycotted . . . Breweries are boycotted notwithstanding that the beer drivers in a body protested against the wrong and declared that they would no longer permit the Federated Trades to dictate what they should eat, drink, and wear, or read.

"This condition of things should no longer be tolerated. The boycott should be stopped . . . Watch your employees, and discharge boycotters. Patronize boycotted firms."

Boycotting of non-union goods engendered such intense feelings that cartoonists had conniptions similar to those of employers.

"The Big Boycott Windbag" (right) is an attack on "fools, fanatics, and unprincipled adventurers [who are] tempting honest laboring men into all manner of lawlessness and improper use of physical force . . . The boycott business is an extravagant, monstrous thing that the laws of a free country must crush out."

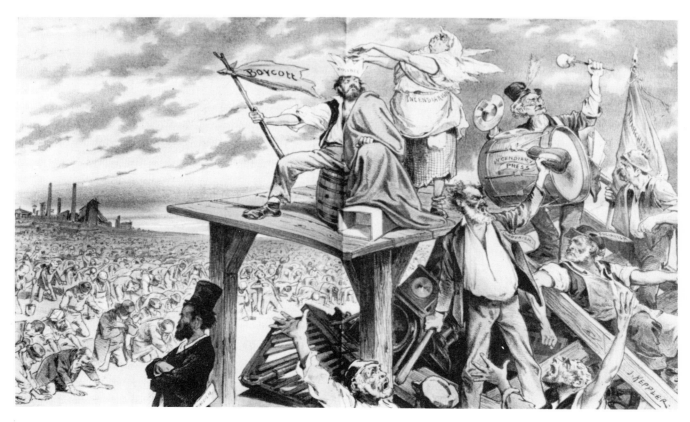

GOMPERS' ADVICE.

Tells Workmen Not to Buy Three-cent Bread.

HIS TALK ON BAKERS.

Denounces the Dealers Who Reduced the Price—Says There Was a Purpose.

Samuel P. Gompers, president of the American Federation of Labor, was greeted by an enthusiastic audience in Turn Hall last night, where he delivered an address on "The Struggles and Aims of the Labor Movement."

The audience was a large one for such an inclement night, and there were numerous women present. The latter occupied front seats, and they applauded the noted agitator's eloquent utterances as enthusiastically as did the men.

Mr. Gompers spoke at length on the labor question, taking occasion during the course of his remarks to deal with the local bakers' controversy. He scored the big bakers severely.

They Toil Like Slaves.

"The bakers work as no other workmen do," said he. "They work early and late, toiling like slaves. Some of them are compelled to board and live in the shops of the boss bakers, so that they can be always on hand, close to their work. Just think of it! These unfair master bakers, by putting cruel obligations on these poor men deprive them of the rights which we all hold dear—the rights of American citizenship. They are denied the privilege of marrying, denied the comforts of a happy home, not permitted to take a wife and be to her a good husband or make of her a good and helpful life partner.

"My friends, I have studied this baker question for years, and I am familiar with the history of the abuses heaped upon some of those poor workingmen.. I have seen a number of bakers attend meetings for the purpose of listening to addresses that might be of benefit to them, and I have noticed that before they had listened fifteen minutes to a speech their heads would fall forward on their breasts and the poor fellows would be fast asleep. This was the result of the long hours that they were compelled to work."

Referring to the local trouble, Mr. Gompers said: "I say to you, my friends, that the fight that is now being carried on by this trust, this biscuit factory, this Smith-Collins concern, against the international union, is an unmerciful one.

"Do you really believe that these fellows are giving you 3-cent bread just through being philanthropic? Nonsense! They remind me of a man going fishing. They bait their hooks with 3-cent bread and the working people who buy it bite like suckers."

Persuading the public to stop buying products sold at sharply reduced prices was more difficult than counteracting the argument that boycotts caused unemployment. The adjoining article is reprinted from a Buffalo newspaper of 1898.

Supplementing the boycott, the union label helped alert the public to the evils of unsanitary sweatshop conditions and bolstered the contention that union standards were a safeguard of consumer interests.

Pioneer standards were set in 1910 by labor and management members of the Joint Board of Sanitary Control charged with "improvement of shop sanitation, accident prevention and care for safety of workers and fire protection in buildings and shops."

The scope of sanitary control encompassed all needle trade shops organized by the Amalgamated Clothing Workers and the International Ladies Garment Workers Union.

TAYLOR'S SPEED-UP EFFICIENCY SYSTEM

Despite strenuous objections by trade unions, the scientific management techniques formulated by Frederick W. Taylor were adopted to achieve "maximum productivity." Based on the principle that more efficient use of labor and machinery could substantially increase profits, Taylorism incurred antipathy among workers who felt they were being treated impersonally as units of production.

Introduction of Taylor's rationalization techniques at the War Department's Watertown, New York, arsenal resulted in a strike by machinists and a Congressional investigation that produced a mass of conflicting testimony. In testifying on behalf of the railroad lines attorney Louis Brandeis claimed they could save a million dollars a day through Taylor's system but other witnesses contended that workers subject to his procedures were treated like machines and did not share in the gains that were made possible by increased efficiency.

For a while trade union opposition slowed up adoption of scientific management techniques, but manpower shortages during World War I led to the adoption of efficiency methods proposed by Taylor.

"Organized labor," as Philip Taft observed, "was fearful that [Taylor's] system would destroy its influence and undermine its position by eliminating standard earnings, valued craft skills, and joint [union-management] determination of tasks and wages. Especially threatening did it appear to the skilled trades which saw in Taylorism a means of eliminating the skilled worker . . ."

Taylor's system of "scientific management," a disciple explained, "is a direct outcome of his purpose to find a remedy for the labor problem that grew up coincidentally with and in consequence of the development of large-scale production."

An argument without words

TAYLORISMS

"My system is simply an honest, intelligent effort to arrive at absolute control in every department, to let tabulated . . . fact take the place of individual opinion; to develop team play to its highest possibility."

"One of the very first requirements for a man who is fit to handle pig iron as a regular occupation is that he shall be so stupid and phlegmatic that he more nearly resembles an ox than any other type of animal."

An Industry Epoch
CHANGING THE WORKS IN FORD EMPLOYEES
TO FIVE-DAY MOVEMENTS.

...HERE THEY ARE...

Lansing, Mich., August 1, 1900.

The following persons are now (or have been at some time during the past 23 months) employed by the Robert Smith Printing Co., State Printers of Michigan, and in such capacity have aided in the attempt to destroy Lansing Typographical Union No. 72. The persons whose names are printed in bold face type have been members of 72, and not only violated their solemn obligation, but rendered themselves particularly obnoxious to the Union men who have fought this battle to a finish. All Unions are warned not to admit to membership any person whose name appears below without notifying Lansing Union. Any person knowing of one of these applying for or holding a card, will confer a favor upon Lansing Union No. 72 by notifying them of the fact.

C. G. Abrahamson	Charles W. Kelly
Steve Allen	Eva Kenyon
Earl Ames	Samuel Klippert
Geo. Bayley	W. Lawrence
J. W. Beaty	Loyd Lockwood
Arthur Boles (machineist)	S. J. MacDonald
A. E. Brand	Robert Manwaring
John Brooks	J. W. Mason
James A. (Plug Hat) Brown	George Merritt
Charles W. Chandler	William Merritt
Miss Emma Cockburn	Charles Miller
Geo. Cornwell	J. W. Miller
Joe Davidson	Bert Moran
Charles Davis	B. F. Morrison
Oliver Diegel	Arthur G. Mortimer
Oscar (Kid) Diegle	James Ogden
Frank H. Doolittle	Charles F. Perkins
O. A. Douglas	Miss Maie Pike
T. B. Dowden	**H. D. Reprogle**
J. B. Duggan	R. J. A. Reynolds
A. E. Eldredge	C. M. Robbins

The Republican Candidate for Vice-President has a lively RAT-ification meeting in his own printing office.

"RATS" AND "SCABS"

Generally no fine distinctions were drawn, but strictly speaking a "rat" was an ex-union member who stayed on the job during strikes. A "scab," on the other hand, was—and, of course, still is—any worker who accepts employment in a struck plant.

Scabs, of course, were much more of a problem to the labor movement. They have been called many unprintable things, but Jack London's description, "written with barbed wire on sandpaper," has never been surpassed:

"After God had finished the rattlesnake, the toad, the vampire, He had some awful substance left with which He made a scab.

"A scab is a two-legged animal with a cork-screw soul, a water-logged brain, a combination backbone of jelly and glue. Where others have hearts, he carries a tumor of rotten principles.

"When a scab comes down the street, men turn their backs and angels weep in heaven, and the Devil shuts the gates of Hell to keep him out.

"No man has a right to scab so long as there is a pool of water to drown his carcass in, or a rope long enough to hang his body with. Judas Iscariot was a gentleman compared with a scab. For betraying his master, he had character enough to hang himself. A scab has not.

"Esau sold his birthright for a mess of pottage. Judas Iscariot sold his Savior for thirty pieces of silver. Benedict Arnold sold his country for a promise of a commission in the British Army. The modern strikebreaker sells his birthright, his country, his wife, his children and his fellow men for an unfulfilled promise from his employer, trust or corporation.

"Esau was a traitor to himself: Judas Iscariot was a traitor to his God; Benedict Arnold was a traitor to his country; a strikebreaker is a traitor to his God, his country, his wife, his family and his class."

Harvard president Charles W. Eliot had different notions. He once described the scab as "the hero of American industry."

One reason why Benjamin Harrison wasn't reelected President in 1892 was that Whitelaw Reid, his Vice Presidential running mate, incurred labor's wrath because his paper, the New York Tribune, "employed a large number of rats."

DON'T
WAIT FOR
EVOLUTION
DO
IT
NOW

Monkeys work Eight Hours in Nebraska
(See Session Laws 1905)

FIGHTING FOR THE
SHORTER WORK DAY

Agitation for reduction of the hours of work took on some of the characteristics of a holy crusade under the leadership of the American Federation of Labor. Its campaign for an eight hour day was both a popular rallying cry as well as an effective organizing technique.

"The answer to all opponents of shorter hours," declared Samuel Gompers in his favorite argument, "could well be given in these words: so long as there is one man who seeks employment and cannot obtain it, the hours of labor are too long. Hundreds of thousands of our fellows, through ever-increasing inventions and improvements in the modern methods of production, are rendered 'superfluous' and we must find employment for our wretched Brothers and Sisters by reducing the hours of labor or . . . [the trade union movement] shall be overwhelmed and destroyed."

But there were other reasons—the desire for greater leisure, for self-improvement, for conservation of health, for time to do as one chooses. In a nutshell, reduction in the hours of labor meant higher standards of living.

More implicit than explicit was the expectation that wages be kept at their existing level, but most employers objected on the ground that paying a worker as much for eight hours of labor as for ten (or more, for that matter) was equivalent to raising wages.

Mindful of earlier difficulties in achieving a general reduction of working hours, the AFL initially threw massive support behind a drive by organized carpenters for an eight hour day. Back-stopped by a large strike fund, the carpenters' campaign, begun in May, 1890, was largely successful. Within a year they could boast that their trade enjoyed an eight hour day in 137 cities. Other workers in the building trades followed suit. By the early 1890's many skilled workers were toiling less and earning more.

The movement for an eight hour day was bolstered in 1902 by a report of the U. S. Industrial Commission showing that excessive hours of labor resulted in diminished production, inferior quality of work, greater cost of operation, and unfavorable effects on the health of employees. The Commission recommended a shorter work day on the ground that it was desirable from the viewpoint of both labor and management.

The main argument against reducing the hours of work was that it would slow down output while increasing costs. In actuality this did not occur.

Regarding a study of 94 companies that instituted the five-day week during the 1920's, the National Industrial Conference Board stated: "It appears that nearly 70 per cent of these companies have suffered no loss in total output per week and are . . . obtaining greater production per hour than under the longer working schedule . . . This seems to indicate that management has not lost through the change and is actually operating with a lower unit cost of output."

In an article entitled "Why I Favor Five Days' Work With Six Days' Pay," auto manufacturer Henry Ford admitted in 1926: "Now we know from our experience in changing from six to five days and back again that we get at least as great production in five days as we can in six, and we shall probably get a greater, for the pressure will bring better methods. A full week's wage for a short week's work will pay."

A production expert reported: "Numerous investigations have shown that labor's efficiency has risen in specific cases when hours were decreased, so that as much or more was turned out per week under shorter hours as under longer. It is now a generally accepted principle that too long hours injure efficiency because of the evil effects of fatigue on the worker. This is especially true where the speed and quality of production depend on the skill of the individual. Even where the pace is set by automatic machinery . . . it is frequently found that spoilage, accidents, absenteeism, labor turnover and other factors are sufficiently reduced by shorter hours to make them worthwhile from the point of view of production."

Contrary to the impression encouraged by this Puck cartoon, entitled "In the Interest of Labor and Morality," workers favored enforcement of Blue Laws on the Sabbath. But the threat of unemployment left them no choice about Sunday work requirements. As for the five day movement that started after World War I, nothing seemed more absurd to the National Association of Manufacturers as recently as 1926.

IF YOU DON'T COME IN SUNDAY DON'T COME IN MONDAY.

THE MANAGEMENT

WILL THE

FIVE-DAY-WEEK

Become Universal?

IT WILL NOT!

For Numerous Specific and Fundamental Reasons Presented Herein

EXCELLENT BUSINESS TO CONTINUE INTO THE TURN OF THE YEAR, MANUFACTURERS REPORT IN NATION-WIDE TRADE SURVEY

A Summary of the Thirty-first Annual Convention of the National Association of Manufacturers Held in New York the first of this month

251

A FEW THOUGHTS FOR

A FEW THINKERS

'WE MEAN TO HAVE 8 HOURS'

The New York Times called the eight hour movement "un-American" and another paper warned that it would bring about "lower wages, poverty, and social degradation." But workers didn't think so. At union meetings they sang out lustily:

We mean to make things over
We're tired of toil for nought
But bare enough to live on; never
An hour for thought.
We want to feel the sunshine: we
Want to smell the flowers
We're sure that God has willed it
And we mean to have eight hours.
We're summoning our forces from
Shipyard, shop and mill
Eight hours for work;
Eight hours for rest.
Eight hours for what we will!

In the coalfields of Pennsylvania this was a favorite ditty:

We're brave and gallant miner boys who
work down underground
For courage and good nature no finer can
be found
We work both late and early, and get but
little pay
To support our wives and children in free
Amerikay.
If satan took the blacklegs, I'm sure 'twould
be no sin;
What peace and happiness 'twould be for
us poor working men.
Eight hours we'd have for working, eight
hours we'd have for play;
Eight hours we'd have for sleeping in free
Amerikay.

When employers weren't arguing that reducing the hours of work would encourage laziness, they heaped ridicule on the notion that ill-bred toilers would make constructive use of their leisure.

These satirical conceptions of shorter work day consequences amused readers of Puck.

THE AMERICAN WORKINGMAN OF THE FUTURE.

Rallying to a battle cry from artist Charles Dana Gibson, workers were demanding that museums remain open on Sundays, their only day of leisure. Ironically, trustees who saw no reason to object to Sabbath employment in factories felt it was blasphemous to encourage distraction from "proper observance of the Lord's Day." The popular creator of the "Gibson Girl," normally no firebrand on social issues, kept on harassing the Metropolitan Museum of Art until it finally opened its doors for a few hours on Sundays.

PERIL ON THE JOB

As mechanization of industry leaped forward, as machinery became more and more complicated, accidents increased to a marked degree. More than twice as many workers were being killed or injured than in Britain.

"The very nature of modern production," as Edison Bowers pointed out in an early study of industrial safety, "seemed to demand the hands and legs, arms and eyes and even lives of men and women. There are punch presses which smash fingers; metal shears which cut off hands; calendaring machines which tear off arms; giant rolls which smash bodies; falls which break legs; cave-ins which wrench backs; flying dust which blinds eyes. These are the concomitants of machine production."

For the workingman and his family such accidents had catastrophic consequences since the liabilities of employers were negligible. In the case of death the bereaved were sometimes offered, by way of consolation, a voluntary contribution toward funeral expenses. And in the case of incapacitation because of industrial injury a worker was occasionally given some extra pay for a short period.

In effect, the worker and his family were paying the price for industrial progress. An employer could, of course, be sued for negligence, but litigation was a slow, costly, and almost futile process. At least several years —often as many as five or six—elapsed between the time an accident occurred and judicial judgment was rendered. Besides the courts seldom ruled that an employer was accountable for damages unless it could be irrefutably demonstrated that he was to blame—usually a very difficult thing to prove. Moreover, employers were generally considered free from responsibility for accidents on the ground that hazards were normal risks of employment. Accepting the principle of laissez faire and complete freedom of action for both employer and employee, the courts generally took the position that a worker was free to leave a dangerous job or to demand higher wages because of the hazards of his employment.

President Theodore Roosevelt, on the other hand, contended (as did trade unionists) that accidents were part of the cost of production—like the cost of repairs or replacements of machinery. "It is neither just, expedient nor humane," TR declared in a denunciation of employer opposition to workmen's compensation legislation, "it is revolting to judgment and sentiment alike that the financial burden of accidents occuring because of the necessary exigencies of their daily occupation should be thrust upon those sufferers who are least able to bear it. When the employer starts in motion agencies which create risks for others, he should take all the ordinary and extraordinary risks involved."

The responsibility of industry was not definitely established until 1902 (long after precedents had been set by European nations) when Maryland passed a compensation law covering the injury of workers in mining, quarrying, and railroad transportation. Six years later Congress enacted, at the urging of President Roosevelt, the Employees Liability Act providing compensation for government workers.

Hardly more than a start in the right direction, these measures gave impetus to state-wide legislation. In 1909 Montana passed an accident compensation law applicable to various types of workers and other states began to follow suit. By 1922 Arkansas, Florida, North Carolina, and South Carolina were the only states without similar legislation.

"No monetary consideration," G. F. Michelbacher observed in arguing for adequate workmen's compensation laws, "can fully pay a worker for the loss of his eyes, his legs or his hands; it cannot compensate him for his mental suffering as he contemplates a life handicapped by the results of injuries or separated from the work which has been an important part of his daily existence. Nor can it modify the grief occasioned by the premature death or serious disablement of any member of a family."

The accident hazard was particularly acute for children working in industrial plants. "In the large stamping works and canning factories in a city like Chicago," Professor William Krohn told the National Conference of Charities and Correction in 1897, "not a day passes but some child is made a helpless cripple. These accidents occur after three o'clock in the afternoon. The child that has begun his work in the morning with a reasonable degree of vigor, after working under constant pressure for several hours, at about three o'clock becomes so wearied, beyond the point of recovery, that he can no longer direct the tired fingers and aching arms with a degree of accuracy. He thus becomes the prey of the great cutting knives, or of the jaws of the tin-stamping machine."

HUMAN CASUALTIES
OF INDUSTRIAL PROGRESS

"This man," said the Pennsylvania Labor Department in a 1903 description of the adjoining photograph at the top, "was injured in a railroad accident. He presents an excellent example of a man who maintains he is not in any respect physically handicapped."

The obviously retouched picture at the bottom right shows a legless miner.

On the left below is a Lewis Hine photo of a disabled factory worker; two of his four children are seen in the background.

TRAGIC VIGIL

For the families of miners each disaster was a harrowing experience. Wives and children gathered in silent groups waiting for news of loved ones who seldom escaped death. At the top is a scene outside the Mononagh Mine in West Virginia after an explosion in 1907.

Each new disaster had its common elements—the ominous mine whistle, the baleful church bells, and an eternity of waiting for news about survivors.

Victims of the Mononagh explosion could barely be identified.

Being buried alive was dreaded most of all. All too often attempts to rescue trapped men were futile because debris-choked tunnels were difficult to penetrate.

The risk of death—from sudden fall of rock, from gas, from explosions—was (and still is) a constant hazard. Especially dreaded was emission of deadly methane gas—"fire damp," the miners called it—so sensitive that a single spark from a shovel caused an explosion that incinerated anyone standing within fifty feet and set in motion secondary waves that compressed into a spear of flame traveling at 1,000 feet a second. Odorless monoxide gas was also dreaded; miners who breathed it fell asleep and died.

Only the lucky few were able to escape sudden death in mineshaft fires.

PENNSYLVANIA'S HUNGRY SLAVES OF THE MINE.

Tens of Thousands of Wretched Men and Their Families Starving, Hopeless and Facing a Black Future.

Miserable Wages and Only a Few Months' Work Each Year. Cheap Foreign Labor Making the Americans Desperate.

By Alfred Henry Lewis.

PITTSBURG, Pa., June 8.—What I saw would have dissolved an angel or made a fiend to weep. Being neither the supernatural one nor the other, I fear I sought the profane relief of oaths, as men do who find themselves in sight of outrage and cruel wrong they are helpless to redress. It was all, all horrible. Nor would I have believed that such things were in this country of America if I had not seen them. The memory, even, is like a tale told by a devil.

Yes, I will give you the story. But what then? You will only read what I write; you will not see what I saw. And therein lies the weakness of mere relation. The eye is the only avenue to sensibility, the only door to feeling. I might with ripest phrase recite the details of some accident by rail; how some overtaken wretch was caught and ground to death beneath the train. You would accept it with that thrill of mild, conventional horror proper to such crisis. But were you to see the wheels crush and mangle and tear some poor, helpless human bit to bloody rags and tatters, the very nightmare of it would steal your sleep for a month. But I will go on. And I will tell you my tale as coldly as I may. You shall then judge of what is wrong, and what the remedy.

There are two sorts of mines, "rail" mines and "river" mines. One feeds its product to the cars to be hauled away; the other to barges which float off down the Ohio, down the Mississippi. For these reasons the markets of the "rail" mine are different from the markets of the "river" mine. And also the activities of these two sort of mines differ, as do also their months of idleness and rest. Which all finally comes to have effect on the miners in their blasting and picking and coal digging; and, therefore, the distinction between "rail" mines and "river" mines is worth wearing in one's mind.

Tens of Thousands Slaves of the Lamp.

There are, speaking roundly, 35,000 coal miners in Western Pennsylvania, and 20,000 in neighboring Ohio. As many as 20,000 are also in West Virginia and hard by the same number in Illinois. These 95,000 slaves of the lamp are to represent as the bread winners for full 300,000 of our people. And what I set down as of hardship and starvation and overriding wrong in the grimy cases I have visited, exists also in devil's duplicate throughout all coal mine regions. What is bad in the "Pittsburg district", where 18,000 of the 35,000 miners of Western Pennsylvania dig and sweat out their dim lives, is equally extant as an evil wherever by drift or shaft the hunt for coal is made.

Fourteen miles from Pittsburg I travelled, seeking among the lamp-lit mines for that "prosperity" of McKinley's that certainly one found no trace of on the earth's surface hereabout, whereof manufactory and furnace one-half are sick and one-half dead, and none of them healthy at all. Yes, I sought "prosperity" in the bowels of the earth; it might make its lair among the mines. I went to Moon's Run, and Tom's Run, and Painters' Run. On Moon's Run, with 1,200 miners and three times as many folk, little and old, living by the mines, I found men and women and children, not in want, exactly—that would not be the story—I found them starving.

These people were thin and pinched and eaten by need of food. One might tell it in their drawn faces, with skins like parchment. One might see it in their eyes, large and wild and wolfishly bright. There were families of these mine folk. There had been no work for months and months. and months. There were households of five and six and eight, the aggregate earnings or gettings of any one of which had not reached $100 during the twelvemonth last past. And in many an instance not a splinter, not a penny of this had these mine people seen and handled. "The company" had sopped it up for what they "owed at the store" or for "rent" of a company house (hovel) before even it was earned. How these folk had lived I know not. They knew not themselves.

Sunk Into the Direst Poverty.

There they were, hopelessly ragged, and a prey to dirt, and, beyond all, hungry, thin, wan, grimy. Six and eight, and as high as ten, together in hovels unfit for swine, they presented a condition of life compared to which the lot of the peon of Mexico is the sublimation of worldly success. One would go to the mines of Siberia before one could find a fellow in misfortune to the miner of Moon's Run, as he

Extracts from Hearst's N.Y. Journal in 1897.

263

lies starving in his rags while this is written. This will be hard to believe, I know. The local papers say little or naught about it, for reasons I will leave you to guess. But my story is true. Come, oh, philanthropists! with your benevolent boats to India and your aid to Armenia, come to Moon's Run and put me to proof.

"How do you live?" I asked one of these gaunt wretches of Moon's Run.

There was a gulping agitation in his lean throat as if he swallowed something; a sob perhaps. Then he said:

"We don't live; we don't even exist. It has been terrible; it is terrible. Perhaps"—here a little flame of hope burned in his eye like a taper—"perhaps if they get that tariff bill passed times may be better."

There was a craving for some answer of encouragement in this last sentence. This man had voted for McKinley. He still thought that somehow, some time, "prosperity" might come. After "tariff" mayhap it would put in its belated appearance.

I had no heart to tell him what I thought—poor Hanna-buncoed creature. He will be starved to death long before any backwater of "prosperity" to rise from any high tide of "protection" comes flowing up his glen, but I could not tell him so.

Let me take you to Tom's Run, being specifically the town of Federal. Of all places there was the least suffering there. It will be more pleasant to show you Tom's Run than the other; it is less like a leper colony than Moon's Run. But, recurring to what I've said to starvation, and lest you deem the term one of exaggeration, let me first quote from a report made the other day by a State legislative committee on mine investigation. They speak of starvation, and while they speak but little they must have witnessed a deal of hunger to make them do so much. Your politician is ever and always alike, and in this "investigating" instance he will say as little as he may to offend the millionaire mine operators, for whom these poor mine people starve.

Report of a Legislative Committee.

Here is a line from the report. It excuses the "operator" while furnishing the fact of the starvation:

As to the condition of the mining business, it is unremunerative to both operators and employes alike, and is gradually becoming more so, resulting in the bankruptcy of the operators, and the poverty, destitution and distress, and, in many cases, the actual starvation of the miner.

There you have it, this starvation, from the timid lip of a legislative committee and quivering to please capital. It is the last thing the committee would admit if it could help it, but the hollow-eyed truth, foodless, helpless, hung on the members and haunted them to it.

But come away to Tom's Run, where the horrors are not so acute. As I said, Tom's Run, the town of Federal, presented the miner more prosperously than any region I invaded. Let me tell you of the coal miners at Tom's Run. There are 1,700 of them, and when they work they dig coal in eight mines. These are "rail" mines. And that means that from the 1st of November to the beginning of June work in these coal pits is suspended.

Mining here waits on lake navigation. It thus befalls that for the last eight years the mines of Tom's Run—and it is equally true of all "rail" mines—have been practically dead seven months in the year. The miners have had work for five months each year since '89; no more. This, mind you, is under the best of conditions, with no strike, no labor war, no fainting of trade to interfere.

Even when McKinley's prosperity gets here the mines of Tom's Run and all others of the great family of "rail" mines will work little, if any, over five months in twelve. Bear this in mind; it will aid in teaching somewhat the hard destiny of your coal miner.

Earnings of Tom's Run Miners.

"What is the price paid per ton to miners?"

This question I put to Captain Charles McDonald. Captain McDonald is a shrewd, deep Scotchman. He is sixty-one years old; hale, however, and wise. He is a leader among miners; this for his honesty, his wit and mental worth. Captain McDonald has dug coal, been pit boss, been mine superintendent and owned mines. He has also conducted a "company store." Since 1859, save for the five years he fought as an artilleryman for Uncle Sam in the civil war, Captain McDonald has lived and worked among the miners and the mines. No one could more worthily take the witness stand. "What do the miners get a ton for mining?" I asked.

"Fifty-four cents a ton," replied the Captain. "A few years ago they got as high as 71 cents; then it fell to 60 cents; now they get but 54 cents."

"Can a miner live and support his family on that?" "No," returned the Captain; "he cannot. Out of the 54 cents the miner is charged for oil and fuse, and squibs and powder, and blacksmithing and pick handles. This will amount at least to $1.50 a week, or about 8 to 10 cents for every ton he mines. He really gets but 44 cents or 46 cents a ton."

"How much can a man mine in a day?"

"A young man," responded the Captain, "while at his best, from the time he's twenty to forty-five years old, can, and do his swiftest, mine three tons a day. That would make $1.62 a day he would get at 54 cents a ton, or $9.72 a week. His deductions for oil, fuse, etc., might leave that $8.25 a week. This, of course, means steady work under the best of conditions."

"Taking work as it runs, how much the year round can a coal miner earn?"

"Why, as to the year round," replied the Captain, "you must know that mines do not run the twelve months. Now, some of our Federal mines opened to-day. Some will not open at all this season. None of them until to-day has been operated since last November. Thus, you see, a miner only works June, July, August, September and October—five months; say twenty-two weeks. At $8.25 per week, which would mean steady work and steady luck, the best coal miner makes $181.50 for the year's season. In the off seven months he may make $1.50 a week, as there's a little digging for the local markets. But this you can set down as fact: No miner can make more than $250 a year at 54 cents a ton. On that he must live and support his family. I don't go into the pit any more; I'm too old. But I know about it just as well as if I did."

The work was back-breaking, monotonous, and often exceedingly dangerous.

264

The faces of the men who mined for a living reflect the gloom of the shafts and tunnels in which they worked as long as twelve hours a day. Sometimes in ankle-deep water, sometimes lying on their backs, they hacked away at the coal deep in the bowels of the earth while rats scurried about seeking grain spilled from feed bags of the horses and mules that accompanied the men.

When top-hatted mine owners came avisiting, children swarmed to greet them, eager to be rewarded with shiney copper pennies. These photos were taken at about the turn of the century.

SHENANDOAH'S "STREET OF THE ROCKS"

Although scarcely an inviting community, Shenandoah, Pennsylvania, had housing standards somewhat higher than those of most coal towns. Besides it didn't have the suffocating constraints of a company town in which workers were paid off in tokens and scrip such as those seen below. Real money was rare in coal-company towns until unionization forced the discontinuation of private coinage.

GOOD FOR
FIVE CENTS.
IN MERCHANDISE AT
STORE 20.
———
GOOD ONLY TO AN EMPLOYE ON ACCOUNT OF LABOR PERFORMED.
———
THE COLUMBUS & HOCKING COAL & IRON CO.

Per

Probably only dimly aware of the squalor that hung like a pall over company towns, the children of coal miners enjoyed few of the pleasures of country life and none of the advantages of the city. "These villages," wrote James Albright in 1903, "lack the most elementary conveniences . . . The shacks in which the people live are unfit for human habitation . . . The miners are treated callously . . . They are forever in debt to company stores upon which they are utterly dependent for overpriced food, clothes, and supplies . . . The owners of the mines seem to control their very lives in every essential respect."

STRIKING WITH DIGNITY

All dressed up in their Sunday best, miners paraded silently during the 1902 coal strike. Their acceptance of President Roosevelt's arbitration proposal was treated disdainfully by operators who insisted that the government had no right to interfere. "The rights and interests of the laboring man," explained George Baer as spokesman for the owners, "will be protected and cared for, not by the labor agitators, but by the Christian men to whom God in His infinite wisdom has given the control of the property interests of this country." But Roosevelt's subsequent "big stick" threat to run the mines in the public interest forced the operators to accept arbitration.

In the opinion of Selig Perlman the strike was the "most important single event in the history of American trade unionism" because "for the first time a labor organization [had] tied up for months a strategic industry and caused . . . discomfort to the public without being condemned as a revolutionary menace to the existing social order calling for suppression by the government."

269

PRESIDENTIAL INTERVENTION IN BEHALF OF MINERS

Determined to end the great coal strike of 1902, ailing President Theodore Roosevelt took unprecedented action in summoning mine operators and union representatives to Washington. Leaning toward him in the above drawing is white-collared John Mitchell, leader of the United Mine Workers; truculent George Baer, spokesman of the coal industry is seen remonstrating with T.R. Among those seated nearby are U. S. Commissioner of Labor Carroll Wright and Attorney General Philander Knox.

In the absence of statutory power to settle labor disputes, Roosevelt had refused to intervene in the strike until acute suffering in the mine towns and mounting scarcity of coal convinced him that governmental action was unavoidable. Representatives of the operators and unions were called to the White House with the explanation that "the urgency and terrible nature of the catastrophe impending over a large portion of our people in the shape of a winter fuel famine impel me . . . to believe that my duty requires me to use whatever in-

fluence I personally can to bring to an end a situation which has become literally intolerable."

Mitchell agreed to arbitration by a Presidential commission, but Baer took an intransigent stand that infuriated Roosevelt. When Baer went so far as to rebuke the President for urging negotiation "with the fomentors of . . . anarchy and insolent defiance of the law," T.R. held his tongue with difficulty. "If it wasn't for the high office I hold," he said of Baer later, "I would have taken him by the seat and the breeches and the nape of the neck and chucked him out of the window."

At an early stage of the strike, Mitchell appealed to the National Civic Federation to facilitate a settlement, but tough-minded operators insisted they would deal with their workers only as individuals, not as a union. In rejecting a proposal by Mitchell to submit the issues in dispute to a group of prominent clergymen, Baer haughtily declared: "Anthracite mining is a business and not a religious, sentimental . . . or academic proposition."

JOHN MITCHELL, MINER'S HERO

Almost a folk hero to the men who dug coal, John Mitchell, leader of the victorious 1902 strike for an eight hour day, brought to the labor movement qualities of devotion and restraint that didn't quite jibe with the journalistic image of union leaders as demagogic, self-seeking men.

He began working in the mines when he was 12, joined the United Mine Workers when it was formed, rose through the union's ranks and became its president in 1898. Growth of the union under his leadership was spectacular; by 1908 it had 300,000 members.

His popularity was plainly evident when the workers of Shenandoah, Pennsylvania, greeted him with flags and banners during a visit he made to that town in 1902. In the photo at the side he is seen flanked by other union executives in a picture taken in New York late in 1906.

Generally regarded as Gompers' "crown prince," Mitchell seemed destined to become the head of the American Federation of Labor, but he quit the mine workers union in 1919 because of disagreement with other officers.

Membership eligibility didn't hinge on craft discrimination or other distinctions.

Proud to work alongside full fledged miners, youngsters gladly posed for photos such as those appearing in these pages. A few of the boys, apparently fearful that school authorities were after them, ducked out of the camera's range. These pictures were taken by Lewis Hine in Grafton, West Virginia, and South Pittston, Pennsylvania in 1908.

Although a notoriously dangerous occupation, coal mining employed more than 15,000 boys under sixteen years of age in 1910. They worked from 7 a.m. to 5:30 p.m. in the coal mines of western Pennsylvania.

"SHUT OUT FROM EVERYTHING THAT IS PLEASANT"

Somewhat typical of conditions under which youngsters worked in coal mines were those in the breaker room of the Hickory Colliery near St. Clair, Pennsylvania, described in the Labor Standard:

"In a little room in this big, black shed—a room not twenty feet square—forty boys are picking their lives away. The floor of the room is an inclined plane, and a stream of coal pours constantly in. They work here, in this little black hole, all day and every day, trying to keep cool in summer, trying to keep warm in winter, picking away among the black coals, bending over till their little spines are curved, never saying a word all the livelong day.

"These little fellows go to work in this cold dreary room at seven o'clock in the morning and work till it is too dark to see any longer. For this they get $1 to $3 a week. Not three boys in this roomful could read or write. Shut out from everything that's pleasant, with no chance to learn, with no knowledge of what is going on about them, with nothing to do but work, grinding their little lives away in this dusty room, they are no more than the wire screens that separate the great lumps of coal from the small.

"They play no games; when their day's work is done they are too tired for that. They know nothing but the difference between slate and coal."

In 1906, John Spargo described what he saw when he visited coal mines in Ohio:

"Work in the coal breakers is exceedingly hard and dangerous . . . From the cramped position [the boys] have to assume, most of them become more or less deformed and bent-backed like old men. When a boy has been working for some time and begins to get round-shouldered, his fellows say that 'He's got his boy to carry round wherever he goes.'

"The coal is hard, and accidents to the hands, such as cut, broken, or crushed fingers, are common among the boys. Sometimes there is a worse accident: a terrified shriek is heard, and a boy is mangled and torn in the machinery, or disappears in the chute to be picked out later smothered and dead. Clouds of dust inhaled by the boys lay the foundations for asthma."

Prodded by vigilant supervisors, "breaker boys" sat in the same position all day long as they removed slag and sorted coal by sizes. "The coal dust in the breaker sections is so thick," reported an investigator, "that it penetrates every portion of their lungs."

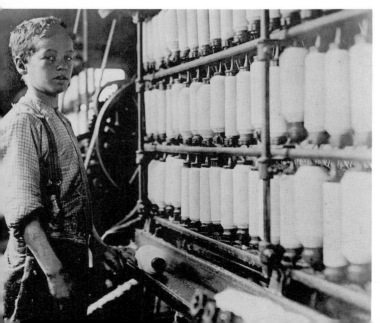

THE DISGRACE OF CHILD LABOR

Exploited without regard to their tender years, countless youngsters were working under conditions constantly fraught with danger to life and limb. Accidents occurred among them about three times as often as among adult workers. Many of those lucky enough to escape mortal injury sustained crippling disabilities and telltale scars for the rest of their lives.

The blight of child labor was widely prevalent—in dust-laden textile mills and pitch-black coal mines, in sweltering glass factories and fetid sweat-shop lofts, in filthy canneries and blazing hot tobacco fields. No industry, no region was without its "tiny hostages to rapacious capitalism."

Child labor had persisted throughout the nation's industrial growth but the public at large remained only dimly aware of its extent and its cruelties until the National Child Labor Committee began to publicize the unsavory facts that awakened the conscience of the country. The accompanying photographs by Lewis Hine, an ex-teacher, were taken for the committee between 1904 and 1910.

"The worst conditions," according to Harold Faulkner, "prevailed in manufacturing in which about 16% of the child workers were engaged. The picture of children kept awake during the long night in a Southern mill by having cold water dashed on their faces, of little girls in canning factories 'snipping' sixteen or more hours a day or capping forty cans a minute in an effort to keep pace with a never exhausted machine, of little ten-year-old breaker boys crouched for ten hours a day over a dusty coal chute to pick sharp slate out of the fast-moving coal, of boys imported from orphan asylums and reformatories to wreck their bodies in the slavery of a glass factory, or of a four-year-old baby toiling until midnight over artificial flowers in a New York tenement —these were conditions which might well shame a civilized people into action."

For years labor leaders had inveighed against the use of child workers, emphasizing that such exploitation was largely due to the unwillingness of employers to pay adults adequate wages. Humanitarian arguments were stressed, but trade unionists could not help but be alarmed by the growing displacement of adults by youngsters and the lowering of wage scales in the industries employing them.

So far as employers were concerned, child labor was a blessing in disguise. Instilling the work ethic in youngsters was good for their character and kept them out of mischief. Besides, as Charles Harding, president of the Merchants Woolen Company, told a Congressional committee: "There is a certain class of labor in the mills where there is not as much muscular exercise required as a child would put forth in play, and a child can do it about as well as a grown person . . . There is such a thing as too much education for working people sometimes. I have seen cases where young people are spoiled for labor by . . . too much refinement."

One textile employer wrote lyrically about the pleasures of child labor: "They seem to be always cheerful and alert, taking pleasure in the light play of their muscles; enjoying the mobility natural to their age. It was delightful to observe the nimbleness with which they pieced the broken ends as the mule-carriage began to recede from the fixed roller beam, and to see them at leisure after a few seconds' exercise of their tiny fingers, to amuse themselves in any attitude they chose till the stretching and winding-on were once more completed. The work of these lively elves seemed to resemble a sport in which habit gave them a pleasing dexterity."

As a direct result of the crusade launched by the National Child Labor Committee with the help of social welfare agencies and trade unions some states enacted restrictive legislation but the 1910 census showed that nearly two million children between the ages of 10 and 15 were employed on farms, in mines, and in factories. In principle the state laws sought to protect children from exploitation; in actual practice they did little to translate rights into realities. Few included effective enforcement provisions. Generally their wording was so ambiguous that employers could easily avoid compliance. Typical were laws stating that no child could be required to work more than ten hours a day—but which allowed employers to claim that extra work was voluntary.

In some states the only punishable abuses were those committed "knowingly." And in most states children could legally work at a younger age or for longer hours than provided by statute if they had their parent's consent, if they were orphans, or if they were supporting parents unable to work. Thus the laws failed to protect those youngsters most in need of protection.

In 1916 Congress passed a law prohibiting the shipment in interstate commerce of goods produced in factories employing children under 14, but this measure was declared unconstitutional by the Supreme Court two years later. In an effort to get around the court's ruling, Congress in 1919 attempted to use its taxing power to ban child labor by placing a 10% tax on the net profits of factories employing children under 14, but this action was also held unconstitutional.

Finally, in 1924, Congress approved and submitted to the states a proposed amendment to the Constitution prohibiting child labor. Although the amendment failed to secure ratification, its purposes were largely accomplished by New Deal measures enacted during the 1930's — notably by the Walsh-Healey Public Contract Act of 1936 prohibiting employment of boys under 16 and girls under 18 on practically all work connected with federal government contracts. Two years later the Fair Labor Standards Act of 1938 placed restrictions on employment of children in interstate commerce generally.

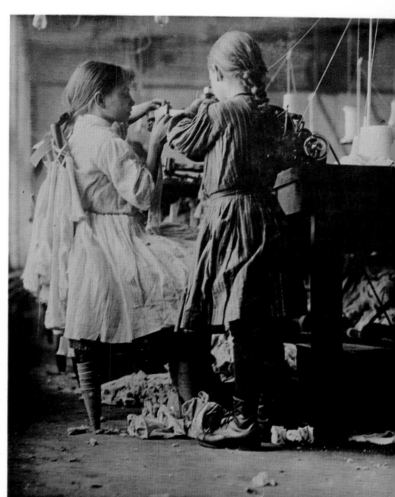

277

DRUDGERY THEIR LOT

Their normal development stunted, youngsters who worked in the textile mills grew up under conditions social reformers considered "debasing and shameful to society."

Aside from the fact that children were paid paltry wages at best, mill owners preferred them to adults not only because their speed and agility were greater but also because they adjusted to drudgery and discipline with little resentment. Some actually considered it a privilege to work alongside adults.

CHILD LABOR EXPLOITER

RICHARDS IN PHILADELPHIA NORTH AMERICAN

SWEAT SHOP

MAY IN DETROIT TIMES

Cheated of childhood, youngsters who worked in "infernally hot glass factories became physical wrecks within a few years." Since most were personally employed by blowers, an arrangement required by employers under union contracts, they were in effect "victims alike of the manufacturers and the skilled workers."

The "mold boys" either had to squat in a cramped position for hours at a time or, if they stood, had to stoop in their work in order to get close to the molds kept near the furnace. The "carrying-in boys" had to remain on their feet most of the time while "snapping-up boys" had to perform their chores near the fires which kept the glass molten.

YOUNGSTERS WHO TOILED IN THE GLASS FACTORIES

Sarcastically nicknamed "glory holes" because of their intense heat, glass factories observed few safety precautions. Many youngsters sustained injuries attributed to "personal carelessness" and "inattentiveness." Some night-shift operations were carried out merely by the light shed by open hearth furnaces.

Of one youngster a foreman said: "He's a good boy. Works all day and never complains."

These photos were taken by Lewis Hine in Grafton, West Virginia, in October, 1908.

SCENES IN CANNERIES

Reminiscent of cruel exploitation of children in England described by Charles Dickens in the 1840's, these haunting photographs by Lewis Hine show the realities of life in American canneries during the early 1900's.

An educator by profession, Hine had used his camera as an aid to teaching but he abandoned his occupation when he became convinced that pictures were more powerful than words and went to work as a photographer for the National Child Labor Committee.

While a foreman checks up on backsliders, women and children toil away busily at a Delaware food processing plant. Below is a photograph taken outside the factory at the end of the day; note that the boys at the left are displaying the knives they used in their work.

CHILDREN OF THE SOIL

Commercial farmers preferred to hire children because, as an Agriculture Department report explained, they "are short of stature and can pick tobacco leaves, cotton and cranberries without being fatigued . . . They're indefatigable."

Children under ten provided much of the manpower in Southern tobacco and cotton fields. Hours were long and the work tedious, but their employers saw to it that they wore hats as protection from the sun and were generously provided with cool drinking water.

More children were employed in agriculture than in all other occupations.

Hard put to sustain themselves on crops with poor yields, many Southern rural families turned to "back yard work" for supplementary income. Even children barely out of infancy were given chores. Below is a photograph of workers at a Massachusetts textile mill; note that children outnumber the adults. In later years textile unions insisted that employment of minors be limited to a greater degree than state laws stipulated.

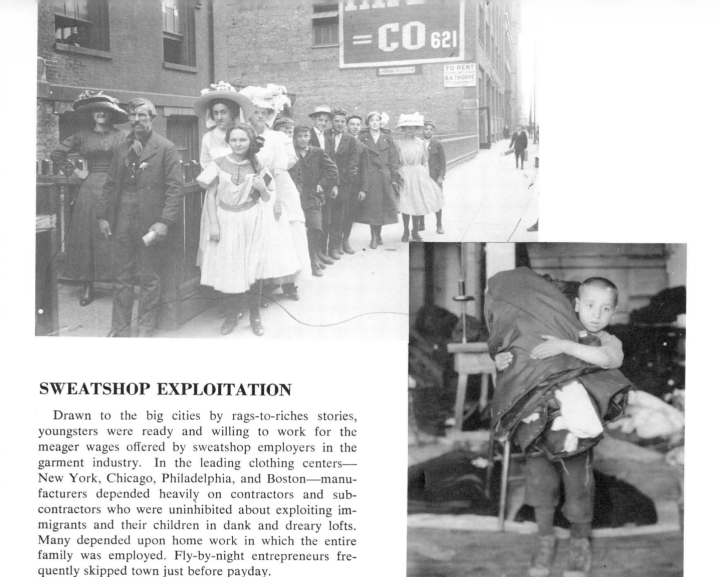

SWEATSHOP EXPLOITATION

Drawn to the big cities by rags-to-riches stories, youngsters were ready and willing to work for the meager wages offered by sweatshop employers in the garment industry. In the leading clothing centers—New York, Chicago, Philadelphia, and Boston—manufacturers depended heavily on contractors and subcontractors who were uninhibited about exploiting immigrants and their children in dank and dreary lofts. Many depended upon home work in which the entire family was employed. Fly-by-night entrepreneurs frequently skipped town just before payday.

"Capital has neither morals nor ideals," cried a critic of child labor slavery. The same, he added, could be said of the judicial system which continued to hold that federal restrictions in this area were unconstitutional restraints of states' rights and personal freedom. Despite vigorous opposition from employers, President Wilson in 1916 signed the first federal law placing controls over child labor but the Supreme Court killed the measure before it became generally effective.

THE ROAD TO DIVIDENDS

Expansion of vocational instruction in public schools accompanied gradual diminution of child labor in factories and growing controversy over union restrictions on apprentices. Employers complained they were handicapped by the reluctance of unions to cooperate in the training of young workers but labor leaders insisted that arrangements they proposed were disregarded or sabotaged by foremen. Below is a nineteenth century cartoon suggesting that shiftlessness was due to union indifference toward youngsters eager to learn useful trades.

Youngsters attending night schools could hardly bring to their classes the attentiveness their studies required.

Theoretically children were free to work only after school or during vacations but enforcement of compulsory education was exceedingly lax, especially in rural areas. In states like New York and Massachusetts night schools afforded opportunities for continuing the education of youngsters who legally entered the labor market when they were twelve years old, but a report about such schools charged that "their usefulness was minimal because children who have worked all day are too weary to benefit by instruction."

**UPWARD BOUND
AGAINST ODDS**

School facilities in many working class communities were "crude, depressing, and totally inadequate" in the opinion of a writer on the subject. Like other phases of American civilization, the educational system had not kept pace with the challenges posed by the industrialization and urbanization of the nation. Belatedly it was being recognized that the living conditions of the crowded slums made it imperative to institute curricula innovations capable of coping with such problems as health, hygiene, and recreation.

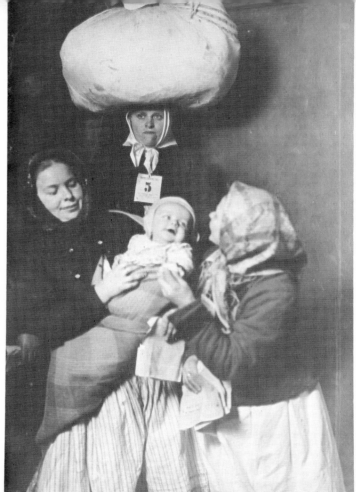

HOPEFUL NEWCOMERS

They came with babes in their arms, their worldly possessions on their backs, and hope in their hearts.

The torch held aloft by the Statue of Liberty glowed so brightly with its promise of hope to the dispossessed of many lands that Ellis Island's reception facilities were overtaxed.

During 1900 the number of immigrants who arrived was 448,572; in 1901 it was 487,918. The figure kept rising until it peaked at 1,285,349 in 1907.

ENDLESS STREAM

The inconveniences and hardships endured on the vessels that brought them to America hardly seemed to matter to the hundreds of thousands of immigrants who kept coming in an endless stream. Unlike previous newcomers, most were natives of eastern and southern Europe who made up in energy what they lacked in skill.

At the top is a photograph taken by Alfred Stieglitz in 1907. Beneath is a picture made about five years earlier.

STEERAGE CONDITIONS

Steerage passage was cheap, but conditions were deplorable. Men, women, and children were jammed together by the hundreds in compartments with the barest minimum of light, ventilation, and sanitary facilities. There, sometimes for several weeks or more, they ate, drank, cooked their food, answered calls of nature, and slept. Many who were healthy at the beginning of their voyage arrived so ill they were turned back by immigration officers.

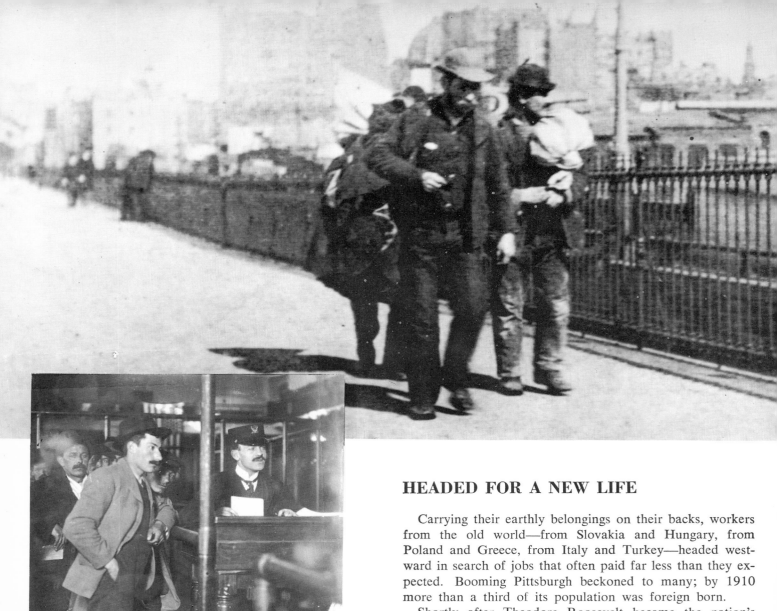

HEADED FOR A NEW LIFE

Carrying their earthly belongings on their backs, workers from the old world—from Slovakia and Hungary, from Poland and Greece, from Italy and Turkey—headed westward in search of jobs that often paid far less than they expected. Booming Pittsburgh beckoned to many; by 1910 more than a third of its population was foreign born.

Shortly after Theodore Roosevelt became the nation's President he appointed Terence Powderly, former leader of the Knights of Labor, the head of the government's greatly expanded immigration service.

Below are immigration workers and officials of the 1890's.

Eager to learn the language of their adopted homeland, immigrants attended after-work classes in great numbers. In many cities their enrollment exceeded the facilities of night schools. Special courses were given under the auspices of the Young Men's Christian Association and other social service groups. Some of the larger factories provided instructional courses within their plants. Below is a photograph taken at an English class for immigrant employees of the United States Steel Corporation plant in Pittsburgh, Pennsylvania.

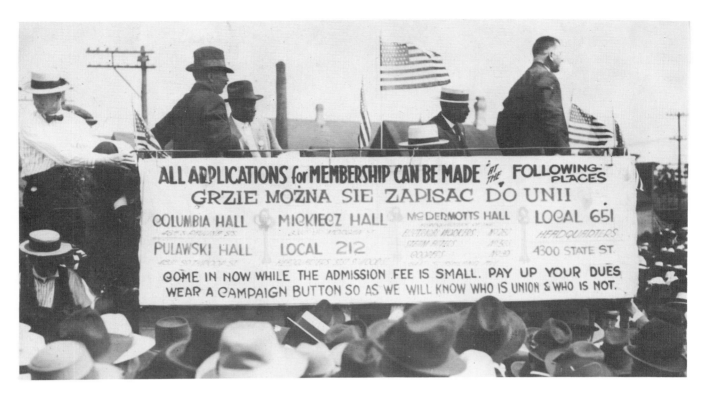

Unionization of immigrant workers unable to understand the English language or American ways required special recruitment techniques. In industries employing a large number of immigrants, unions organized foreign-language locals and these locals in turn sometimes banded together into groups such as the German Trades Circle, the United Hebrew Trades, and the Italian Chamber of Labor. Above is a photo taken during a membership drive of meat packers among Polish workers in Chicago. Below are participants in a 1909 parade.

Despite difficulties in organizing workers from different lands, unionization of the needle trades was pioneered by the men and women who laid the groundwork for the Amalgamated Clothing Workers and the International Ladies Garment Workers Union.

Placards expressing grievances in four languages are held aloft by Chicago clothing workers seen at the side. Below is a contingent of a May Day parade sponsored by Socialists in 1903.

Many unions were reluctant to open their doors to immigrants. They were effectively barred from skilled craft unions which stipulated that applicants for membership had to be full-fledged citizens; some unions required foreigners to pay excessively high initiation fees.

Union publications printed in various languages acquainted immigrants with their new environment and the ways by which their standard of living could be improved. "Advance," the organ of the Amalgamated Clothing Workers, was published in as many as six different languages. Some pamphlets of the United Mine Workers were printed in German, Italian, Polish, Greek, and French.

(When organization drives were stepped up among Mexican-Americans and Puerto Ricans during the late 1960's leaflets were printed in Spanish to bridge the language barrier.)

HOME, SWEET HOME

Many a tenement living room served as a family workshop in New York's East Side sweatshop district.

For clothing manufacturers intent upon cutting costs to the bone, the sweatshop system was ideal. They farmed out pre-cut garments to labor contractors who in turn arranged for sewing to be done on a piece-work basis by immigrants hard put to find regular employment. Since the income of a contractor was completely dependent on the margin between what he received for his services and what he paid his "sweaters," the latter had to toil night and day for paltry wages.

Sweatshop homework was also employed by cigar makers and producers of goods requiring unskilled drudgery (artificial flowers, beads, metal ornaments, etc.) Practical as well as humanitarian considerations motivated union opposition to such exploitation.

DRUDGERY FOR THE WHOLE FAMILY

In his autobiography, Samuel Gompers provides this vivid account of sweatshop exploitation during the late 1890's:

"Many of the Bohemians [who] moved into downtown New York . . . did not find it easy to learn English or to adjust themselves . . . As many manufacturers thought they had an advantage in the mold and filler system under which practically unskilled workers could produce cigars, soon they added the tenement feature which was an entirely different method from the old home work or factory work.

"The manufacturers bought or rented a block of tenements and subrented the apartments to cigar makers who with their families lived and worked in three or four rooms. The cigar makers paid rent to their employer for the living room which was their work space, bought from him their supplies, furnished their own tools, received in return a small wage for completed work sometimes in scrip or in supplies from the company store on the ground floor. The whole family—old and young had to work in order to earn a livelihood—work early and late, Sunday as well as Monday. The system was degrading to employer and workmen. It killed craft skill and demoralized the industry."

Regarding conditions a decade later, Gompers added: "I saw scenes that sickened me. I saw little children, six and seven and eight years of age, seated in the middle of a room on the floor, in all the dirt and dust, stripping tobacco. Little pale-faced children with a look of care upon their faces, toiling with their tiny hands from dawn till dark and even late into the night to keep the wolf from the door . . . Often they would be overcome with weariness and want of sleep, and fall over upon the tobacco heap. Shame upon such crimes; shame upon us if we do not raise our voices against them."

A Philadelphia sweatshop visited by the Reverend F. M. Goodchild in 1895 was barely 10 by 12 feet in size yet he found 8 men working in it. "The walls," he wrote, "are as grimy as though they had never known the use of a brush. The whole place wallows with putrefaction. It would seem that there had not been a breath of fresh air for five years. One whiff of the foulness is enough to give you the typhoid fever; yet what you cannot endure for minutes, these people live in from year to year."

Children helped their mothers pull basting
threads, string beads, and make artificial flowers.

Life in the slums was a bitter disappointment for those who had fled hardships in Europe only to find themselves imprisoned by grim realities in America. Wages for unskilled labor were so low and rents so high that many families had to crowd into squalid, ill-ventilated living quarters like those seen below.

GHETTO POVERTY

The flags came out on national holidays but the tenement poor hardly basked in the blessings enjoyed by more fortunate Americans. It was generally felt that slum dwellers had no one to blame but themselves for their plight; seemingly they were innately shiftless and lacked the will to improve their lot through industry and frugality.

The tenement courtyard was a haven for both mothers and children.

Even as the nation grew richer the lines of poor people grew steadily longer.

For youngsters scavenging made more sense than waiting for allotments.

Public bathing facilities were quite a novelty for workers who lacked running water in their tenement flats. Some employers who sensed the relationship between sanitation and manpower efficiency installed showerbaths in their factories. "We like to see our men freshen up at the end of the day," a foreman explained. "It's good for them and it's good for us." Some cities established public baths in slum neighborhoods.

Entrepreneurs of the streets.

MANPOWER IN TRANSITION

Men like these built great ships, constructed whole cities, levelled forests, laid railroads, burrowed through mountains, and even changed the course of rivers. Within the lifetime of most of these men the nation underwent extraordinary economic and industrial transformation.

In 1865 the U.S. was predominantly an agricultural country; by 1900 it had become the world's greatest industrial power. "Before 1865," according to Leo Huberman, "production was largely carried on by hand in homes or small shops; by 1900, production was largely carried on by machine in large factories. Before 1865, only one out of every six people lived in a city of over 8,000 inhabitants, and there were only 141 such cities; by 1900, one out of every three people lived in a city of over 8,000, and there were 547 such cities. Before 1865, the number of millionaires could be counted on the fingers of one hand; by 1900, it would have taken many hands to count them. Before 1865, business was smallscale, competitive, owned by individuals or partners; by 1900, business was large-scale, monopolistic, owned by corporations."

In 1902 the U.S. Industrial Commission boasted that "the changes and the progress since 1865 have been greater in many directions than during the whole history of the world before."

Oblivious to the hazards of their trade, construction men worked at dizzying heights. In his book "Skyscrapers and the Men Who Build Them," W. A. Starrett provides this comment:

"One passing a large metropolitan building under construction is apt to notice the young, virile men, with nonchalant manner, who so confidently go about their tasks. Few people stop to consider these same men after twenty-five or thirty years of this rigorous life. . They are hearty eaters and gulp their food, frequently carried to the job cold; or, if bought at the ubiquitous hot-dog stand, it is generally of the fried variety with little thought of the science of dietetics. Their inordinate use of tobacco and small attention to dental hygiene . . . leave them susceptible to the occupational ailments which their work sometimes engenders . . . The admiring spectator sees young men, but little realizes the shadow that an uncertain future is casting. He does not see the prematurely aged building mechanic, sometimes a pathetic figure, standing on the sidewalk week after week, in the furtive hope that a job commensurate with his now narrowed abilities is available for him."

BUILDING AMERICA'S GREAT SKYSCRAPERS

THE CARPENTER'S TRADE

Carpenters found their employment steadily curtailed by the use of ready-made parts put together at woodworking mills and by replacement of wood by steel and other material. To maximize opportunities for employment the Brotherhood of Carpenters and Joiners adopted the following credo: "Once wood, it is always the right of the carpenter to install it no matter what the material now used may happen to be."

"Year after year," complained Peter J. McGuire, a founder of the Brotherhood, "carpenter work is becoming less and less plentiful owing to recent innovations in architectural construction. With the introduction of iron and steel frames in the larger buildings, with iron and stone stair cases, tile floors and tile or metal wainscoting, with cornices and bay windows in many cases of other material than wood, and with numerous other changes going on . . . the increase and perfection of wood working machinery . . . the chances for the steady employment of carpenters are extremely uncertain."

As in earlier times, carpenters who helped build farmhouses and barns continued to hire out their services as self-employed artisans. In effect they were free-wheeling entrepreneurs who felt they had little in common with their counterparts in the urban building trades but their interests became intertwined when they went looking for work in the towns and cities and found they stood to benefit by union wage scales. (The above photograph was taken at an Ohio barn raising during the late 1880's.)

INDUSTRIAL EXPANSION

Electrical technology opened interesting new jobs in General Electric's Fort Wayne plant (above), but toilsome labor remained characteristic of employment in most factories. Work loads were constantly getting heavier and heavier. "The bosses drive the men to an extent that [British] employers would never dream of attempting," reported an English traveler. "The measure of a man's usefulness is his ability to perform more work in less time, regardless of monotony fatigue or occupational hazards." (Below is a photo of an early auto plant.)

The faces of these Pittsburgh steel workers bear witness to their toughness of body and spirit. Most were newly arrived immigrants from Slavic countries. "These hunkies are all right," a foreman told a visitor to a Homestead plant, "They work hard and you can trust them."

MAKING WAY FOR TROLLEY CARS AND SUBWAYS

Cities bursting at the seams could hardly keep pace with their transportation problems. In Manhattan trolley car tracks were being laid almost simultaneously with subway excavation work. The tumult and noise was so great that a New York Sun editorial bemoaned the fact that "city life has become . . . well nigh unbearable for anyone who does not stuff his ears with plenty of cotton padding."

Horse drawn street cars were rapidly giving way to electrically powered trolleys that required skillful repairmen. And telephone linemen who clambered up and down forty foot poles were familiar sights.

Except for skilled machinists, most railroad shopmen (and boys) worked long and hard for low wages. Average daily earnings were approximately $1.50 for a work-day that ranged between ten and twelve hours. Youngsters were lucky if their weekly pay envelope contained as much as $3.50.

RAILROAD "GANDY-DANCERS"

Unlike conductors and other railway "aristocrats of labor," the men who maintained the tracks were casual laborers hired on a daily basis at rock-bottom wage rates. These "gandy-dancers" were so far down in the pecking order that they were treated as though they were "expendable no-accounts." The train operating unions virtually ignored their existence until they final-ly set up their own union—the Brotherhood of Mainte-nance of Way Employees. For years the railroad owners took the position that their unskilled workers (many were Negroes) were not entitled to recognition as regular employees. (Above is a photo of a Pennsyl-vania Railroad track gang clustered around a shift-engine outside Pottsville, Pa.)

As electricity entered into the everyday life of the nation, linemen were kept exceptionally busy installing endless miles of power wires that transmitted current into homes, streets, and factories. One of the most dangerous of occupations, line work was considered so hazardous that insurance companies refused to provide coverage for this occupation. It was not uncommon for a lineman to risk his life stringing wires from fifty-foot poles for twelve hours a day, seven days a week for the munificent sum of 25c an hour—a wage rate somewhat higher than that paid most workers. Adjoining photos show a Philadelphia crew, linemen in Wyoming, and a Labor Day float.

MASS PRODUCTION OF HORSELESS CARRIAGES

A great deal of hand labor went into the manufacture of gasoline-powered Duryea automobiles (top photo) during the late 1890's. It remained for Henry Ford to greatly speed up production by using conveyor belts to carry parts on moving assembly lines. Below are pictures showing various phases of manufacture at Ford's earliest plants. At the bottom left is a 1913 photo of Model T cars being completed.

Detroit, a carriage-making center for many years because hardwood was plentiful in Michigan, was ideally situated for the new industry. It had ample labor and easy access to lumber, iron, and coal.

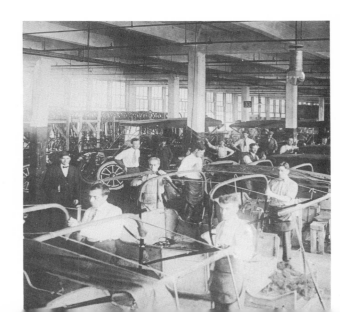

Construction of gauzy winged airplanes drew on the skills of machinists as well as jacks-of-all-trades. Fred Hewitt, who helped build Samuel Langley's plane in 1903 (above), later became the editor of the Machinists Journal. Below is an 1898 photo of Chicago's Haymarket Square; the statue standing in the center is a reminder of the tragedy that rocked the city during the previous decade.

LUMBERJACKS

Life was rough and adventurous for lumberjacks who hacked their way through the nation's great forests. The photo at the right shows several men pausing during their task of undercutting a 16-foot thick Douglas fir in Oregon. Standing on springboards inserted into the trunk, they used double-bitted axes and two-man saws. The picture at the bottom was evidently taken in 1883.

"The isolation of logging camps," according to Stewart Holbrook, "combined with an occupation so dangerous to life as to remove all but the toughest and most alert, conspired to produce a unique race of men whose dedicated goal was to let daylight into the swamp and thus, as they saw it, permit the advance of civilization."

Nomadic harvesters of the West led an uncertain existence. To meet the demand for seasonal labor, migratory harvesting crews moved northward across the plains during the summertime—working the wheat fields from Texas to the Canadian border. Below is a photograph showing seasonal workers loading grapes at the Buena Vista Vineyard in California. This picture was taken by Eadweard Muybridge in 1874.

Like migratory workers and lumberjacks, cowboys found life humdrum and dreary. Hardships, solitude, low pay, and long drives were central facts of their existence. They were up at 4 in the morning and usually worked till dusk. Their diet was principally beans, grease, and tough meat.

The cowboy's broadbrimmed hat served as shelter from rain, wind, and sun. His bandanna was his dust filter, towel, and napkin. Many an easterner who went west to plow and plant turned into a ranch-hand because he had no other choice when crop failures left him unable to meet his obligations.

Like these apple pickers and wheat harvesters, the great bulk of the people still lived close to the soil, but fewer and fewer of them farmed for themselves. Crop failures, high rates charged by the railroads, inability to keep up mortgage payments, and hard times forced many small holders of land to become hired hands.

PRODUCING
57 VARIETIES

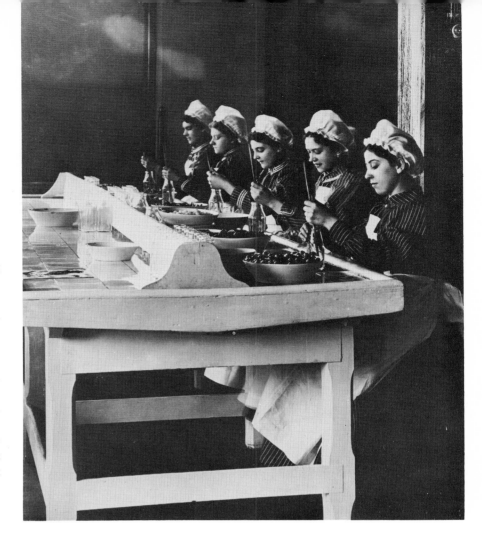

Preparing foods for processing under sanitary conditions was a fetish in the factories of Henry J. Heinz (seen standing on wagon in the photo below). His relations with employees also had a distinctly sanitized quality.

In his speeches, paternalistic H. J. preached mightily about the virtues of thrift and self-discipline. A master salesman of both his "57 Varieties" and his ideas of production efficiency, he stressed that "it is neither capital nor labor that brings success, but management, because management can attract capital and capital can employ labor."

Negroes constituted most of the tobacco industry's labor force. In 1903 many of them were working thirteen hours a day and earning only six to nine cents an hour.

Lowest paid of all were women and children who stripped stems from tobacco leaves, as seen above. Below are workers in a Richmond, Virginia, drying shop.

Black women employed by the tobacco industry were paid far less than other factory workers. Below are sorters at a Virginia warehouse. "As in the past," wrote Stephen Marcham in 1901, "Southern Negroes are exploited more than any other element in society. They may well have been better off under slavery. . . . now they must fend for themselves. Generally they are barred from all but menial jobs. . . . Most live in poverty."

THE REALITIES
OF MEAT PROCESSING

Meat processing scenes such as these are idyllic by comparison with those described by Upton Sinclair in "The Jungle," a muckraking novel about conditions in Chicago stockyards and packing plants published in 1906.

Along with millions of Americans, President Theodore Roosevelt was appalled by Sinclair's revelations. Congress quickly reacted to popular indignation by passing a stricter meat inspection law and a new Pure Food Act. Based on Sinclair's first hand observations of gruesome occupational diseases and hazards, "The Jungle" related how poisoned rats were shoveled into meat-grinding machines, how filth scraped from the floor was turned into "potted ham," and how government inspectors were bribed to pass tubercular cattle.

The most successful of contemporary muckraking books, "The Jungle" was highly praised both in the U.S. and overseas. Commented England's future Prime Minister, Winston Churchill: "This terrible book . . . pierces the thickest skull and the most leathery heart. . . . The issue between capital and labor is far more clear cut in [the United States] than in other communities or in any other age."

QUICK JURGIS WE MUST RECOVER THE BODY FROM THE LARD VAT

ALL STAR FEATURE CORP PRESENTS IN MOTION PICTURES
—UPTON SINCLAIR'S—
WONDERFUL STORY OF THE BEEF PACKING INDUSTRY
THE JUNGLE
FEATURING
GEORGE NASH - GAIL KANE
AND THE AUTHOR
5 DARING ACTS — 210 ASTOUNDING SCENES

"A Fertile Field For The Muck-Rake" is the caption Collier's gave the above picture of the sausage department of a Chicago packinghouse. At the side is a poster about a movie based upon Upton Sinclair's book. Meat packers insisted that their sanitary methods were similar to those seen in the photo below.

NIGHT AND DAY
WORK IN THE BREWERIES

Since beer consumption kept mounting steadily, there was seldom a shortage of work at the breweries but many of them required their men to live on the premises to assure the availability of manpower for both night and day chores.

Like the United Mine Workers, the Brewery Workers Union was organized along industrial rather than craft lines. Its membership included all types of workers employed in processing and distribution.

Mindful that most of their customers were workers, few breweries could afford to oppose unionization or overlook the advantage of placing the union label on their products.

Saloons often served as informal union meeting halls. In his autobiography Samuel Gompers relates that the AFL was "almost a peripatetic organization" during the 1890's because "we sometimes didn't drink enough beer to satisfy the saloon keepers."

LADIES OF THE SHOE FACTORIES

In New England shoe factories the majority of workers were women. "These operatives," reported an investigator of the Massachusetts Department of Labor in 1906, "are very conscientious. . . and considered more reliable than men. They perform their tasks quietly and rarely give their employers any trouble. Men who are paid more for the same work are often less productive."

As far back as the Civil War years, women became the mainstay of shoe factories. Above are delegates to the 1904 convention of the Boot and Shoe Workers Union. At the side and below are operatives in Lynn, Massachusetts, factories.

Resentful that women were being paid about one-third as much as men for similar work, members of the Women's Trade Union League (above) exasperated employers by insisting on equality of wages. But there was little discontent among typists and secretaries who felt satisfied with the new job opportunities open to them. Below are employees of the Metropolitan Life Insurance Company.

THE MINK BRIGADE
LENDS A HAND

Shocked by the exploitation of less fortunate members of their sex, a small but dedicated group of middle-class and well-to-do women organized the Women's Trade Union League for the purpose of "helping secure better working conditions . . . and higher wages for those women who are not being treated fairly."

Active participants in the League's campaigns included socially prominent women like Mrs. O. H. P. Belmont, Mrs. Willard Straight, Mrs. J. B. Harriman, Mrs. Eleanor Roosevelt; social workers Jane Addams (famed head of Hull House) and Mary McDowell ("Angel of Chicago's Stockyards"); and Wellesley College educators Vida Scudder and Ellen Hayes.

(The three stylishly dressed matrons in the photo at the bottom of this page were supporters of the League's Chicago branch. Left to right are Mrs. Isabelle Blaney, Mrs. Mary Willmarth, and Jane Addams.)

Spearheading the League's efforts was a handful of experienced labor leaders: Mary O'Sullivan of the Bookbinders Union; Mary Anderson, a clothing worker who later became director of the Women's Bureau of the Labor Department; and Rose Schneiderman, a seamstress who helped create the International Ladies Garment Workers.

When the League came into existence in 1905 most women workers were unorganized although in some trades—millinery, caps, ladies garments—they composed 75 to 90 percent of all employees. The conditions under which the majority of women toiled in the early 1900's were among the worst in the country— wages as low as $2 and $3 a week, a workweek ranging between 60 and 70 hours, lofts that were fire-traps. Some employers even required seamstresses to furnish their own needles and made deductions for damaged materials.

Although Samuel Gompers and other labor leaders gave the League their blessing, they provided relatively little practical support. Even Rose Schneiderman, a union activist, was skeptical about what could be accomplished. "I could understand why working girls joined the League," she said, "but I did not believe that women who were not wage-earners themselves understood the problems of workers."

Miss Schneiderman's attitude, as well as that of other trade unionists, changed when it became evident that many League members were not only sincerely imbued with the desire to aid those less fortunate than themselves, but also willing to join in the hurly-burly of strikes. To the bafflement of employers, fashionably dressed women turned up on picket lines. Moreover, they helped feed and clothe strikers, distributed leaflets, spoke at public meetings, posted bail for arrested workers, and engaged lawyers for their defense.

Above: Stylishly dressed Mrs. O.H.P. Belmont, wife of one of the nation's richest men, addressing an outdoor meeting of the Women's Trade Union League. Police were assigned to protect her "in case there is any trouble" but she insisted their presence was unnecessary since she knew "perfectly well how to deal with ruffians." Below: Members of the League are seen demonstrating in the Murray Hill section of Manhattan.

GOVERNMENT BY INJUNCTION

Almost blatantly biased in favor of employers, the courts placed formidable roadblocks in labor's path by handing down innumerable decisions restraining unions from striking, boycotting, or engaging in other activities considered illegal means of interfering with freedom of enterprise.

Ironically, the Sherman Anti-Trust Act, passed in 1890 to curb business monopolies, became the basis for some of the most serious onslaughts against labor. The strike of the American Railway Union against the Pullman Company in 1894, for example, was enjoined on the ground that it constituted a conspiracy in restraint of trade within the meaning of the Sherman Law. Injunctions granted by the courts led to the arrest of several hundred strikers and imprisonment of their leaders.

Even more alarming from the viewpoint of labor's longtime interests was the decision of the Supreme Court in the anti-boycott suit brought against the United Hatters Union by the Loewe Company, a Danbury, Connecticut, hat manufacturing firm. The court held that the union's boycott of Loewe's products constituted a restraint of trade conspiracy under the Sherman law and awarded triple damages totaling $252,000 to the Loewe firm. (A facsimile of a check for $175,000 paid to Walter Gordon Merritt, Loewe's lawyer, appears above.)

And a few years later another Supreme Court decision, handed down in the suit of the Buck Stove & Range Company against the AFL, held that inclusion of the firm's name in a "We Don't Patronize" list was a violation of the Sherman Law. Officers of the Federation were forbidden even to speak or write anything critical of the Buck Company or the court's decision.

Injunctions of the type sanctioned by the Danbury and Buck Stove decisions, Gompers contended, made it possible for the government to dissolve any labor organization under the Sherman Act. "Injunctions as issued against workmen," he complained, "are never applied to, or issued against, any other citizens of our country . . . These injunctions in labor disputes are an indirect assertion of a property right in workmen engaged in a legitimate effort to protect or to advance their natural rights and interests."

Subsequently the American Federation of Labor pressured Congress into passing the Clayton Anti-Trust Act which ostensibly removed labor from the scope of the Sherman Act and limited the right of the courts to issue injunctions. Gompers jubilantly—but prematurely—hailed the Clayton law as a "Magna Charta" for labor because it established the legal principle that "the work of a human being is not a commodity or article of commerce." Subsequent judicial decisions, however, completely nullified the gains unions had anticipated.

For all the fine words in the Clayton Act, it did not provide specific safeguards to assure protection of labor. As the U. S. Supreme Court later pointed out, the law did not contain any provision exempting a trade union or its members "from accountability where it or they depart from . . . legitimate objects and engage in an actual combination or conspiracy in restraint of trade."

As late as 1928 Professor Thomas Reed Powell caustically commented: "Congress has thus far acquiesced in the decision that the Clayton Act . . . restrained the federal courts from nothing that was previously proper. A statute full of words that seemed a balm to labor turned out upon interpretation to be chiefly a bane . . ." Not until the National Labor Relations Act became the law of the land in the 1930's did wage earners get a genuine "Magna Charta."

THE "YELLOW DOG" CURSE

Manacling workers to "yellow dog" contracts sanctioned by the courts continued to frustrate the growth of the trade union movement.

In essence these contracts required workers to agree not to join a union or otherwise participate in any concerted action considered objectionable by management. Usually the stipulation applied to the duration of employment, but in a surprising number of cases a longer period was specified. "In case my service is terminated," many workers were required to pledge, "I will for one year thereafter in no way annoy, molest or interfere, directly or indirectly, with your customers, property, business or employees."

Below is a proclamation authorizing the wholesale blacklisting of workers who refused to deny or renounce membership in an Idaho miners union charged with being "criminal in purpose." Although state authorities could not substantiate their charges against the union, 400 miners were held prisoners in a stockade maintained by the Standard Oil Company under the muzzles of federal rifles. Conditions comparable with those of Civil War days in the Andersonville concentration camp resulted in the death of four men.

At the side is a yellow dog notice posted by a Massachusetts employer in 1912.

NOTICE

TO ALL WHOM IT MAY CONCERN:

THE G. EDWIN SMITH SHOE COMPANY, an Ohio corporation, having its works, its principal office and doing business at Columbus, Ohio, contracts with its employes with the express understanding that each person employed by it is not a member of the Boot and Shoe Workers' Union nor a member of the United Shoe Workers of America; that such person will not become a member of the Boot and Shoe Workers' Union nor become a member of the United Shoe Workers of America while an employe of THE G. EDWIN SMITH SHOE COMPANY; that THE G. EDWIN SMITH SHOE COMPANY is run non-union and agrees with such person that it will run non-union while such person is in its employ; that if at any time while employed by THE G. EDWIN SMITH SHOE COMPANY such person wants to become connected with the Boot and Shoe Workers' Union or any affiliated organization, or wants to become connected with the United Shoe Workers of America or any affiliated organization, such person agrees to withdraw from the employment of THE G. EDWIN SMITH SHOE COMPANY; and that while an employe of THE G. EDWIN SMITH SHOE COMPANY such person will not make any effort amongst its employes to bring about the unionizing of that Company's shoe manufacturing plant against that Company's wish.

THE G. EDWIN SMITH SHOE COMPANY.

PROCLAMATION.

WHEREAS, The following notice has been served upon the mine-owners of Shoshone County by the duly constituted State authorities, by whom martial law has been declared, to wit:

"TO THE MINE-OWNERS OF SHOSHONE COUNTY:

"Certain Organizations or Combinations existing in Shoshone County have shown themselves to be criminal in purpose inciting and, as organizations, procuring property to be destroyed, and murders to be committed, by reason whereof it has been twice necessary to declare martial law in Shoshone County:

"You are therefore notified that the employment of men belonging to said or other criminal organizations during the continuance of martial law must cease. In case this direction is not observed, your mines will be closed."

Therefore, in order to carry into effect the spirit of the foregoing notice and restore the industries of the district as far as possible, it becomes necessary to establish a system by which miners who have not participated in the recent acts of violence and who are law-abiding people, may obtain work, and, that order and peace may be established, the following is promulgated for the guidance of all mine-owners and employes in the affected district:

All parties applying for underground work in any of the following mines will be required to obtain from Dr. Hugh France, the duly appointed and authorized agent for the State of Idaho for this purpose, or his deputy, at Wardner or at Wallace, a permit authorizing said person to seek employment in any of the following mines: Bunker Hill & Sullivan, Last Chance, Empire State-Idaho, Consolidated Tiger and Poorman, Hecla, Mammoth, Standard, Helena-Frisco, Gem, Morning, Hunter and such others as may be hereafter included in the above list. Parties applying for such permits must be prepared: First, to deny all participation in the riots of April 29, 1899, in Shoshone County and, Second, to deny or renounce membership in any society which has incited, encouraged or approved of said riots or other violation of public law.

Mine-owners must refuse employment to all applicants for underground work who do not present a duly signed permit authorizing the same. Such permits will be deposited in Mine-owners' office subject to periodical inspection.

All parties now under employment by any of the mines above named will be required to procure within ten days from this date the permits above referred to as a condition to their remaining in the service of their respective companies.

BY ORDER OF THE GOVERNOR AND COMMANDER IN CHIEF, BARTLETT SINCLAIR,

Examined and approved: H. C. MERRIAM, Brig. Gen. U. S. Army.

State Auditor.

Dated May 8th, 1899.

BLATANT LABOR-BAITING

Animosity toward unions was generated by cartoons like these. Labor was, of course, vulnerable to criticism but some attacks went far beyond the bounds of even minimal fairness. Contrary to the message conveyed by Leslie's skull of death, for example, nothing remotely sinister was the occasion for this cartoon. Underneath "It Means Death" is this explanation: "While walking delegates are holding up plans for public and private improvements, labor and capital are both facing ruin."

The drawing at the upper right, sardonically captioned "A Triumph of Civilization," appeared in Harper's Weekly during a St. Louis streetcar strike in the summer of 1900. The disagreeable fellow on the left turned up after the 1877 railroad strikes.

To Strike   Struck   Stricken

CLOSED

H. Mayer.

W. A. Rogers.

RATIONALE FOR STRIKES

Employers considered strikes reprehensible means of attaining improper ends, but from labor's viewpoint they were inalienable expressions of lawful protest.

"While some may assert that the strike is a relic of barbarism," declared Samuel Gompers in an outburst of excessive zeal, "I answer that the strike is the most highly civilized method which the workers, the wealth producers, have yet devised to protest against the wrong and injustice, and to demand the enforcement of the right.

"The strike compels more attention and study into economic and social wrongs than all the essays that have been written . . . It establishes better relations between the contending parties than have heretofore existed; reconciles laborers and capitalists more effectually, and speeds the machinery for production to a greater extent; gives impetus to meaningful progress . . .

"I trust that the day will never come when the workers, the wealth producers of our country and our time will surrender their right to strike . . ."

336

So far as employers were concerned strikes were motivated more by capriciousness than by genuine interest in the workingman's welfare. In a scathing criticism of labor unions a trade association charged:

"It is contrary to the most cherished American ideals to require workingmen to forfeit their right to be free citizens.... When they are forced to become union members they are unable to do as they choose; they must do the bidding of men who are solely interested in feathering their own nests...by collecting dues which they personally pocket.

"Besides union membership has a repressive effect on individual initiative and equality of opportunity."

Strikebreaking was "a precarious but distinctly profitable occupation."

Private guards (below) were legally authorized to maintain law and order.

ANGUISHED OUTCRY
AGAINST "UNION AUTOCRATS"

So far as Harper's Weekly was concerned "the liberty, safety and the very life of the private citizen" was being strangled by the labor trust.

"The general public is between the upper and the nether millstones. Between extortion at the hands of Beef Trust and starvation at the hands of the beef labor trust, there is small choice and great distress. The very candy we eat is under the eye of the unions . . .

"As a result of this warfare, the work of the world is no longer done by slaves or serfs, or by the poor; it is done by autocrats who are not content with a normal and profitable scale of wages, but have forced prices to the breaking-point and employers to the point of bankruptcy . . .

"The laboring man having conquered equality has not been satisfied with his just desserts, but has forced his way on to despotism. Not only the commerce and the manufacturers and the general business prosperity of the country are at his mercy, but the liberty, safety, and the very life of the private citizen are in his clutch. How long will the public endure this strangle-hold?"

THE LABOR DESPOT.

THE supreme tyrant of the labor organizations is the walking delegate, the well-fed, well-paid official who performs the functions of a general overseer, and whose fiat is expected to be obeyed without protest or murmur. Not a few of the disastrous strikes of recent years were prolonged, if they were not instigated, by these representatives of the worst elements of discontent. Happily American workingmen seem now to be losing their respect for this class of petty despots, and it is hardly probable that they will be able in future to exercise any such autocratic power as they have so injuriously employed in the past.

It was the peculiarity of the recent great strike in London that it was spontaneous, that it was based upon a real grievance, was entirely free from coercive excesses on the part of would-be bosses, and that it had, from first to last, the genuine sympathy of the great body of the people. The sole obstacle to a settlement was the obstinacy of the dock companies, upon whom the demand for slightly increased compensation was made by the striking laborers. Against these stubborn dock directors were arrayed the merchants, the ship-owners, and all the high officials in church and state, such men as Cardinal Manning, the Lord Mayor, the Bishop of London, and Sir John Lubbock interfering actively in behalf of the strikers, while Lord Randolph Churchill and other men in official life ably championed their cause in public addresses. It was inevitable that, thus sustained, the men on strike should ultimately gain a substantial victory. It will be well if American workingmen shall learn the lesson that, with a just cause, and abstaining from all disorderly and offensive methods, they, too, can depend upon public sympathy, and will be much more likely to win their way than when pursuing an opposite course.

Seemingly trade union officers were bloated plutocrats who imposed their will on workers with even greater callousness than employers. Some "walking delegates" were, of course, susceptible to pay-offs for closing their eyes to violations of union rules but those who did so possibly were sensible enough not to go swaggering about looking like Diamond Jim Brady. The above cartoon appeared in the pages of Leslie's Illustrated Weekly.

THE LABOR TRUST BUGABOO

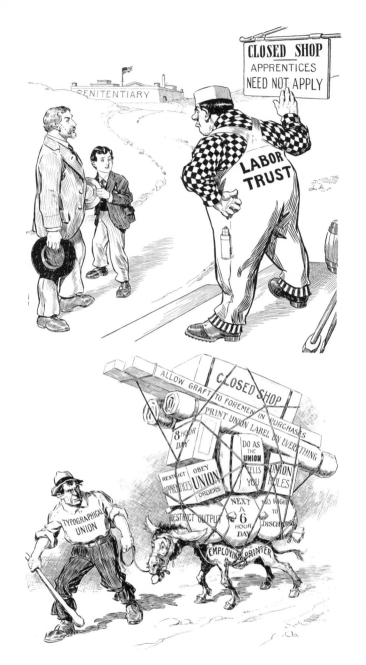

Berating of unions as "trusts," a spin-off of anti-labor court decisions based on the Sherman Anti-Trust Act, was becoming a ritualistic editorial exercise in leading newspapers and magazines.

Irresponsible labor leaders who abused their power were at least partially to blame. Samuel Parks, boss of New York building workers at the turn of the century, attracted notoriety because of his strong-man tactics. "Some [employers]," he once boasted, "did not believe unions would be good for them, and I gave them a belt on the jaw. That changed their minds." When he was arrested for extortion, he was bailed out by a former chief of police to the accompaniment of cheers from union members.

The constructive purposes of trade unionism—improvement of working conditions, reduction of the hours of monotonous toil, attainment of a higher standard of living—were generally disregarded by the press. If they were mentioned, it was usually as the object of attack rather than sympathy. In varying degrees, now in outright abuse and again in ridicule, workers were held up as ignorant malcontents led by autocratic union officers arrogantly seeking to dictate to employers. Complained Harper's Weekly in 1903:

"It has come to this—that even when we eat, it is by the grace of the walking delegate. The milk that comes to us in the morning is brought by a union milk-wagon driver, who took it from a union trainman, who brought it from the country in a union-made can and a union-made car. In most cases, the bread we eat in the morning is delivered by a union man, who had it from a union shop, where a union baker made it from union-made flour. The meat we order comes by the same channel; and that channel may be stopped at any moment, on any pretext, by almost any union, through a direct or a sympathetic strike . . ."

Even musicians were subject to "arbitrary union bosses . . . insensitive to the finer things of life."

THE DUBIOUS ROLE OF THE CIVIC FEDERATION

Organized for the purpose of "establishing right relations between employers and workers," the National Civic Federation enjoyed the cooperation of the American Federation of Labor but aroused hostility from some unions.

Industrialist-politician Mark Hanna and Samuel Gompers were the leading figures of the movement. Prominent participants included Grover Cleveland and Harvard's Charles Eliot (representatives of the public), Charles Schwab and John D. Rockefeller, Jr. (representatives of employers), and John Mitchell of the United Mine Workers, James O'Connell of the Machinists Union, and James Duncan of the Granite Cutters (representatives of labor).

In justifying the AFL's cooperation, Gompers pointed out that the civic group provided labor with a forum through which employers and the public could be convinced that unions were a constructive force.

But critics skeptical of the Civic Federation's sincerity regarded it as an agency which blunted union militancy and transformed labor leaders into appeasers of big business. Morris Hillquit, a Socialist active in the trade union movement, considered the organization a "subtle and insidious poison . . . [which] robs . . . [the AFL] of its independence, virility, and militant enthusiasm; it hypnotizes or corrupts its leaders, weakens its ranks, and demoralizes its fights."

The National Civic Federation is the direct outgrowth of the Chicago Civic Federation, organized in November, 1893, and having for its object the concentration of all forces then laboring to advance the municipal, philanthropic, industrial and moral interests of Chicago, the significant title, "Clearing House of Reforms," being frequently applied to the organization in its infancy. This movement was inaugurated immediately after the World's Fair, when lax municipal gov-[...] federation, held in Chicago, 1900. Compulsory arbitration had a prominent place on the program but the confer-[...] the employers' class. His first experience in railroad service was that of shoveling gravel on a construction [...] The committee also provided for the organization of permanent boards of conciliation to use their good offices wherever possible before strikes should be declared and to endeavor to settle strikes under way. Local branches have been organized in New York, Chicago, St. Louis and Cleveland. The establishment of local organizations in every industrial center during the coming year is contemplated.

When John Mitchell stepped down as president of the United Mine Workers to become an executive of the civic group, officers of his union voiced objections to such "collaboration."

As unions grew more powerful, employers previously committed to the National Civic Federation's policies turned hostile toward labor and the group devoted its attention more and more to the menace of radicalism. AFL officers gradually withdrew from active association with the organization, but it was not until 1935 that formal ties were cut.

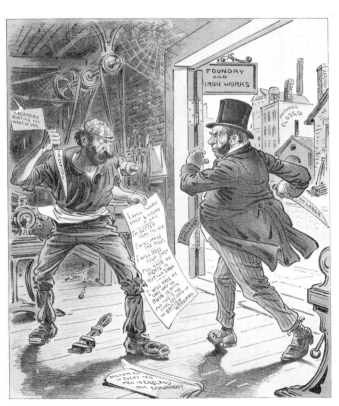

HANNA AS A POLITICAL INVENTOR.

His Machine for Manufacturing Public Sentiment.

"HANNA THE HARD-HEARTED"

Mark Hanna didn't fare at all well at the hands of cartoonists who considered him labor's enemy despite his conciliatory efforts through the National Civic Federation. His Democratic opponents seldom missed an opportunity to remind workers that he showed no high regard for their interests while he amassed his huge fortune as owner of coal and iron mines, steel mills, lake and streetcar companies, and a shipyard.

Primarily responsible for the selection of William McKinley as the Republican party's presidential favorite, Hanna bluntly demanded big business backing for McKinley as the protector of property rights against radical doctrines.

Rising discontent encouraged candidates for public office to identify themselves with working class sentiments. The above picture was probably taken in Salida. Colorado, during local elections in the early 1900's. Below are New York demonstrators with placards making distinctly unorthodox demands.

ROOSEVELT'S "SQUARE DEAL"

Essentially middle-class oriented, Theodore Roosevelt's Square Deal offered workers more of a fair shake than the policies of previous Republican Presidents. While he was scornful of labor radicalism, he spoke up in behalf of trade unionism. "I believe," he said, "that all men who are benefited by the union are morally bound to help to the extent of their power in the common interests advanced by the union."

Regarding court decisions that were hamstringing labor, he took a bold stand: "It is all wrong to use the injunction to prevent the entirely proper and legitimate actions of labor organizations in their struggle for industrial betterment, or under the guise of protecting property rights unwarrantably to invade the fundamental rights of the individual. It is futile to concede, as we all do, the right and necessity of organized effort on the part of wage-earners and yet by injunctive process to forbid peaceable action to accomplish the lawful objects for which they are organized and upon which their success depends."

Roosevelt was on friendly personal terms with Samuel Gompers although they differed markedly on some issues. Once during an argument, TR exploded: "But I am the President of the United States!" Gompers, unawed, shot back: "And I, sir, am President of the American Federation of Labor." Their relations cooled later when Roosevelt pointedly ignored a detailed "Bill of Grievances" drafted by the American Federation of Labor.

Labor support of Roosevelt during the 1904 campaign, when the above poster was circulated, contributed to the defeat of lackluster Judge Alton B. Parker, the Democratic candidate. When TR ran for President on the Progressive ticket in 1912 he had substantial labor support but Woodrow Wilson, who endorsed the 8-hour day, was elected.

QUEST FOR POLITICAL POWER

At both national and local levels politically ambitious men were courting the labor vote with unusual vigor. While workers tended to vote Democratic, they did not constitute a solid block that could be taken for granted or, for that matter, delivered.

In his unsuccessful efforts to secure the Democratic Presidential nomination in 1904 and attain the governorship of New York two years later, publisher William Randolph Hearst assiduously solicited support from workers who were repeatedly reminded that his newspapers championed their cause.

Hearst's San Francisco Examiner shouted foul when Abe Ruef, boss of that city's powerful Union Labor Party (the first labor party to gain control of an American city) was indicted for bribery. He is seen below listening to advice from his attorney.

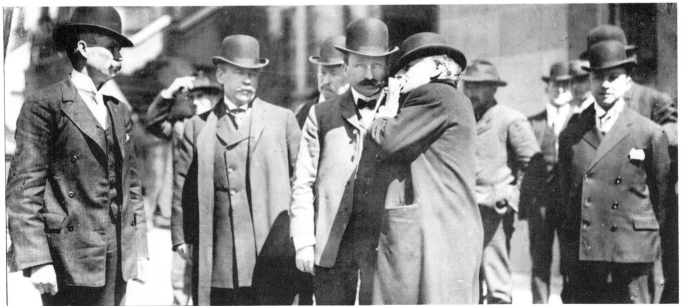

FOOD AND RELAXATION

The prices charged by "Bob's Quick Lunch" seem ridiculously low by 1972 standards, but in actuality they were high for workers who rarely earned more than $1 a day. Beer was selling at a penny a glass in saloons like the one seen below. In more genteel establishments a higher price included the equivalent of a free lunch. For workingmen saloons provided more than beer; here they relaxed and swapped stories. Here, too, gripes about low wages often led to union action. Saloons run by ward heelers were also the focal point for political activities.

DEBS' CAMPAIGN FOR THE PRESIDENCY

Baldheaded Eugene Debs, founder of the American Railway Union who led the abortive Pullman strike in 1894, is seen peering out of the Socialist "Red Special" he rode during one of his campaigns for the presidency. Standing near him (fourth and fifth from the left) are John and Tom Mooney. Below is a picture of Debs with railroad workers and a photo of admirers who visited the "Red Special" when it stopped at Danville, Illinois. Debs polled only 96,000 votes during his campaign in 1900 but subsequent support, especially among workers, increased; he won 402,000 votes in 1904, 421,000 in 1908, and 901,000 in 1912.

Their faith in Debs united Socialists behind him. These sketches of delegates to the party's 1912 convention include IWW leader Bill Haywood, labor lawyers Morris Hillquit and Meyer London, Victor Berger (a Socialist member of Congress), J. Stitt Wilson (Socialist mayor of Berkeley, California), James Maurer (president of the Pennsylvania Federation of Labor).

DISRUPTIVE ELEMENTS

Further left than the Socialist Party, the Socialist Trade and Labor Alliance, founded by Daniel DeLeon in 1895, sought to band together "those masses who cannot directly be reached by . . . [political] activities." Labor leaders scoffed at the Alliance, but they couldn't ignore its disruptive infiltration of some unions. Dogmatic DeLeon, a master of vituperation, considered the American Federation of Labor "nothing but a masked battery behind which the capitalist class can encompass . . . the work of enslaving and slowly degrading the working class."

Though the Alliance exercised some influence among radically inclined labor groups in Chicago and New York, its threat to the AFL didn't materialize. It did, however, succeed in exacerbating relations between trade unions and the Socialist movement in general. After its demise, DeLeon kept on berating "labor fakirs" through the Socialist Labor Party, an organization that remains active to this day.

A doctrinaire forerunner of Lenin and a sworn enemy of the wage system, DeLeon regarded trade unions as the nuclei of revolutionary Socialism. Anyone who disagreed with this concept or expressed doubts about the desirability of "proletarian rule" was subjected to a torrent of abuse. Moderate Socialists who favored cooperation with AFL unions were treated with no more tolerance than "bosses who oppress the masses."

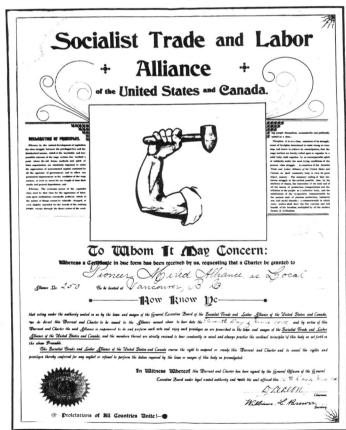

UNION LABOR IN LABOR POLITICS

TO THE DELEGATES OF THE CENTRAL TRADES AND LABOR UNION AND THE BUILDING TRADES COUNCIL, AND TO EVERY MEMBER OF ORGANIZED LABOR IN ST. LOUIS AND ELSEWHERE:

ours. A "financial flurry" they called it. All would soon be over! said the newspapers. Don't lose confidence! said the bankers! Prosperity will soon return! prophesied the politicians and statesmen.

The Result of Frenzied Business Speculation.

It was not a "flurry." It is one of those genuine crises which strike the capitalist business world after every period of frenzied financiering and wild business speculation. Today the factories and workshops are closed, or operate with reduced labor forces. It is estimated that nearly two million men and women are at present out of work. Men—citizens of a free country—are compelled to beg, to eat at charity soup-houses, and to sleep on the cement floors of our police stations. Others lose all hope, and in their despair give up their life in self-destruction. Only a week ago five young workingmen committed suicide in one day in our great city of St. Louis, because they could not find employment.

Millions in Misery Under Stars and Stripes.

These are terrible conditions. At least ten million men, women and children in our great Republic of the Stars and Stripes are living in misery and want. Mothers' hearts are bleeding when looking at their suffering little ones. Starvation in the wealthiest country on earth has become chronic with many thousands of honest, industrious working people.

The full-dinner pail has become a phantom, a myth. The voice of prosperity has been silenced. Like a tornado the financial panic swept over this great and wealthy country of

GROWING SOCIALIST STRENGTH

Above is an extract from a leaflet urging trade unionists to back the Socialist Party line espoused by Eugene Debs.

Workers who admired Debs and felt victimized by the inequities of life were susceptible to Socialist arguments although the American Federation of Labor scoffed at "the impractical idealism of unattainable utopian aims."

During the 1870's the Socialist movement provided a training ground for Samuel Gompers, Adolph Strasser, Peter J. C. McGuire, and other labor leaders, but when the AFL was founded they turned their energies to attainment of its "here and now" goals.

Do It Now!

TIE UP THE TOWN!

Let that be your answer to Farley, Phelan and the Furies

TIE UP THE TOWN

Don't Feed Scabs.   Don't Have Scab Protectors.   Don't Serve the Scab-Hearted Herd of Cowards.

Guns May Bristle.   Guns are for Scabs.   Scabby Gunners.

TIE UP THE TOWN

Janitors, Cooks, Teamsters, Printers, Carpenters, Servants, Clerks,—Don't Serve the Scabs. Don't Serve the Cowards Who Serve Scabs.

TIE UP THE TOWN

Misery is Misery. This is the old fight between the rich and the poor. Where do you stand!   With the rich, if you serve the Scabs. You serve the Scabs, if you work at all.

Tie Up the Town.   Not bad to do that.   Not hard to do that.

EASY TO TIE UP THE TOWN

You are miserable when any are miserable, so DON'T RIDE. DON'T WORK. Don't do a thing but TIE UP THE TOWN.

JUST DON'T! THAT'S THE GAG—DON'T!

Soldiers, Police, Judges, have to be miserable with you in misery if you

TIE UP THE TOWN   TIE UP THE TOWN

TIE IT UP!   TIE IT UP NOW!   TIE IT UP!

Of course you could have voted the Socialist Ticket last time and you would not have to tie it up now, but

TIE IT UP.   TIE IT UP NOW.   DO IT NOW.

Hear

WALTER MacARTHUR

at EQUALITY HALL, 139 Albion Ave.

Bet. 16th and 17th, Valencia and Guerrero Sts.

Under the Auspices of the 'Socialist Party

SUNDAY, MAY 12th, 1907, 8 p. m.

SUBJECT: "TRADES UNIONISM; ITS ESSENCE; ITS EFFICIENCY."

Never mind about your boiled shirt!   Don't phone that you can't come!
Don't ride a car, but come. Admission Free

DO IT NOW!

For six months in 1907 trolley car service in San Francisco was disrupted by a Socialist-sponsored strike for higher wages and an eight hour day. Violent clashes with imported strikebreakers ended in thirty-nine deaths and more than five hundred injuries.

352

UPRISING OF THE GARMENT WORKERS

New Yorkers were treated to some unexpected sights and sounds during the 1909 uprising of 20,000 unorganized shirtwaist and other garment makers who went on strike for higher wages and better conditions. Sparked by a spontaneous rebellion in a few shops, the strike spread to 500 within 24 hours, much to the bewilderment of employers who had for years been indifferent to persistent grumbling about low pay and sweated toil.

Newspaper reports of deplorable working conditions, militant picketing by attractively garbed women, and strong-arm tactics by the police readily convinced the public that the dressmakers were unfairly treated. Reluctantly most of the employers gave in, granting the strikers virtually all the demands made in their behalf by the International Ladies Garment Workers Union.

The 1909 uprising was but a preliminary to a greater struggle a year later when an even larger number of apparel workers left their jobs. This time the union succeeded in winning higher wages, improved conditions, and about 50,000 more members.

The two short strikes changed New York's clothing industry from a chaotic and oppressively sweated trade to one strongly organized and subject to discipline under the terms of a joint union-management "protocol." (A prime promoter of the "protocol" was arbitration mediator Louis Brandeis, whose later appointment to the Supreme Court was bitterly opposed by business.)

Almost simultaneously cloak and suit workers in Chicago were striking under the leadership of men and women who laid the basis for the Amalgamated Clothing Workers.

"You ladies must remain steadfast," skull-capped Samuel Gompers told the striking shirt-waist workers at a Cooper Union meeting that triggered the "Uprising of the Twenty Thousand." Enthusiastic participation in the strike, amply evident in the photo below, kept up morale until substantial concessions were made by employers. A labor leader previously indifferent about the unionization of women conceded admiration for their "capacity to do and dare for their rights."

The protests of striking garment workers became bolder as they marched during winter months.

Despite police efforts to break up their demonstrations, public support of the rebellion escalated.

FERMENT IN CHICAGO

Ignoring freezing weather, more than ten thousand Chicago clothing strikers marched through the main streets of Chicago in December 1909 in protest against low wages and "harsh exploitation" by garment manufacturers.

At the side is a scene at the graveside ceremony for Charles Lazinskas, a striker who died of wounds inflicted by police. A huge funeral parade preceding the burial "preserved a strange and frightening silence . . . no dirge sounded and not an outcry was heard."

Leaders of the strike became founders of the Amalgamated Clothing Workers union.

A typical sweatshop operator, Harper's Weekly told its readers, "is not a toiler, not a merchant, not a producer, not even a dealer in anything but human endurance. He is a contractor, and the name 'sweater' by which he is commonly called is indicative of the character of his employment . . . To him it matters little how small the price of the work is if he can secure enough of it, for he looks out for his own pay first, and pays the workmen whom he employs whatever is left. He serves no purpose whatever in the economy of civilization beyond the mere convenience . . . of the manufacturer."

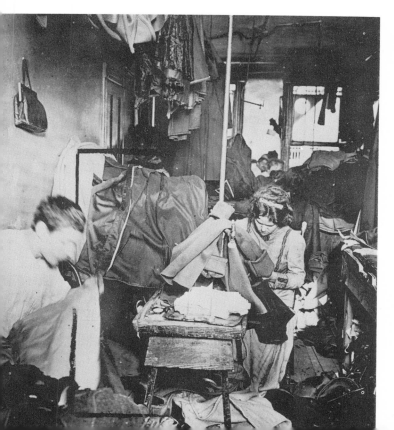

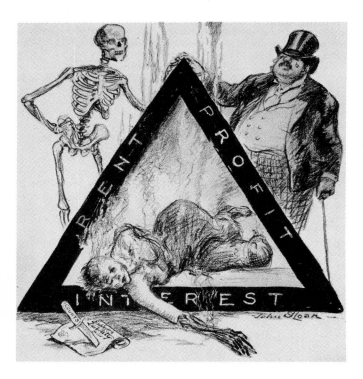

THE TRIANGLE FIRE TRAGEDY

It was Saturday afternoon, March 25, 1911. In New York City the first touch of spring warmed the air. Children were playing hide-and-seek among the old trees in Washington Square Park.

Suddenly there was the muffled sound of an explosion and passersby saw dark smoke oozing from the Asch Building on Greene Street. A few hours later the charred bodies of 154 employees of the Triangle Shirtwaist Company, mostly young women, covered the sidewalk.

As fire raged through the top three floors of the building, about fifty girls frantically hurled themselves out of the windows. The remainder were burned to death. Heaps of bodies were found piled against emergency doors that were kept bolted, as one newspaper explained, "to safeguard employers from the loss of goods by the departure of workers through fire exits instead of elevators."

By existing standards the owners of the Triangle Company weren't accountable for the tragedy despite evidence that they had skimped on safety precautions and had placed their equipment in a manner that blocked access to fire hose and a flimsy fire escape. Ironically, only nine days before the holocaust the dangers that lurked in the city's cloak and suit shops were discussed in a New York Call article based on a report prepared for the Joint Board of Sanitary Control, a labor-management group created after a strike by the International Ladies Garment Workers Union in 1910.

The Triangle tragedy alerted a previously indifferent public to shocking factory conditions that had been ignored or condoned and a clamor went up for remedial action. At the insistence of trade unions, business groups, and prominent citizens such as Henry L. Stimson, Henry Morgenthau, Sr., and the Reverend John Haynes Holmes, the New York State legislature authorized a Factory Investigating Commission to make an intensive study of hazardous working conditions. The chairman and vice chairman of the commission were two young members of the legislature who were beginning auspicious careers in American political life: Robert F. Wagner, Sr., and Alfred E. Smith. Among the inspectors they hired were Frances Perkins and Rose Schneiderman, women destined to play an important role in the history of American labor. The findings of the commission became the basis of far-reaching safety laws enacted by New York and other states.

Present day regulations regarding factory inspection, fireproofing, and sprinkler systems are largely traceable to the martyrdom of the 154 workers who perished on March 25, 1911.

Rosie Safran, one of the survivors of the Triangle tragedy, provided a graphic account of her experiences:

"I heard somebody cry 'Fire!' I left everything and ran for the door on the Washington Place side. The door was locked and immediately there was a great jam of girls before it. The fire was on the other side, driving us away from the only door that the bosses had left open for us to use in going in or out. They had the doors locked all the time.

"The fire had started on our floor, and quick as I had been in getting to the Washington Place door, the flames were already blazing fiercely and spreading fast. If we couldn't get out we would all be roasted alive. The locked door that blocked us was half of wood; the upper half was thick glass. Some girls were screaming, some were beating the door with their fists, some were trying to tear it open. Someone broke out the glass part of the door with something hard and heavy, I suppose the head of a machine. I climbed or was pulled through the broken glass and ran downstairs to the sixth floor, where someone took me down to the street.

"I got out to the street and watched the upper floors burning, and the girls hanging by their hands and then dropping as the fire reached up to them. There they were dead on the sidewalk. It was an awful, awful sight, especially to me who had so many friends among the girls and young men who were being roasted alive or dashed to death.

"One girl jumped from the ninth floor and her clothing caught on a hook that stuck out from the wall on the eighth. The fire burned through her clothing and she fell to the sidewalk and was killed. Another girl fell from the eighth to the sixth floor when a hook supporting a sign caught her clothes and held her."

Charred bodies of victims of the Triangle Shirtwaist fire alerted the nation to factory fire hazards due to blatant disregard for human safety. The tragedy set off a chain reaction that led to stringent industrial codes with severe penalties for violations.

BREAK WITH THE PAST

No longer passively willing to accept paltry wages and degrading working conditions, women were throwing off nineteenth century shackles with a vivacity that animated other unorganized workers.

Below is Philip Reisman's painting of the shirtwaist makers strike in 1909. Clara Lemlich, one of the leaders, is seen in the center; standing at her left is Samuel Gompers.

Confident that their strength lay in sustained collective action, clothing workers made extraordinary headway despite temporary setbacks, court injunctions, and police harassment. A strike victory by Chicago tailors in 1915 (above) was clear evidence of increasing power. The photos below were taken during strikes of the period.

LEADERS OF THE NEEDLE TRADES

Like most members of their unions, the majority of the officers were men and women who had escaped from persecution or economic hardship in foreign lands. At the top are members of the first executive board of the Amalgamated Clothing Workers. Seated at the extreme left is Fiorello La Guardia, who later blossomed as the "Little Flower" Mayor of New York. To his right are Bessie Abramowitz, Sidney Hillman and Joseph Schlossberg. (Hillman, who married Miss Abramowitz shortly after this photo was taken, became the union's president; Schlossberg served as secretary-treasurer for many years.)

At the side, with hands in pockets, is Meyer London, ILGWU attorney who was elected to the U.S. House of Representatives during World War I. Below are early officers of the union.

Morale of garment workers was sustained at picnics which offered social recreation as well as opportunities for speeches and discussions about the benefits to be derived from trade union cohesiveness. "Our social functions have worked wonders in breaking down national and religious differences," a union organizer boasted. Above is a photograph of youthful David Dubinsky (reclining on a tree limb), future leader of the International Ladies Garment Workers Union, with fellow workers who joined with him in a successful revolt against sweatshop conditions in their industry.

HIGH NOON AT CRIPPLE CREEK

Mobbed by vigilantes, striking Colorado miners were rounded up and herded into bull pens during open warfare between the Western Federation of Miners and the Mine Owners Association.

Low wages, intolerable conditions, and disregard of a constitutional amendment requiring the legislature to enact an 8-hour-day law angered the workers into calling a massive strike at the mines adjoining Cripple Creek.

At the insistence of the mine owners, Colorado's governor sent into the area a thousand troops under the command of General Sherman Bell, a former Roosevelt Rough Rider who ordered arrests of union officers and invasion of their headquarters. Predictably, the Western Federation of Miners retaliated. In the violence that followed 33 persons were killed and scores injured, but the mine owners held the upper hand decisively.

Abetted by vigilantes and deputized mine guards, General Bell's troops forced most of the strikers out of the state. Some were deported on trains, others were marched out of the area and warned not to come back.

To make sure that there wouldn't be any more trouble, the editor of the Victor Record, a newspaper friendly to the strikers, was arrested after his offices were wrecked. Jacketless editor George Kyner is seen with his arms upraised in the photo at the side.

364

THE SHAMEFUL LUDLOW MASSACRE

The brutal massacre that took place at Ludlow, Colorado, on April 20, 1914, had its origins much earlier.

For years the coal miners of the state had lived and worked under appalling conditions. Their wages were barely sufficient to keep them from starving in their wretched shacks on the twisted, gnarled canyons near the mines. How they lived, what they ate, even what they did was subject to company rules, company stores, and company guards. For all practical purposes they were serfs of the mine owners who ran Huerfano and Las Animas counties as though they were private fiefdoms dominated by the Colorado Fuel and Iron Company, a property of John D. Rockefeller.

Most of the miners were immigrants from eastern and southern Europe. Some were Mexicans brought in as strikebreakers ten years earlier. But the weight of common misery pushed aside old antagonisms, ethnic differences, and language barriers. Although fearful of reprisals, they joined the United Mine Workers in large numbers.

The union's leaders didn't want a strike. What they wanted, they told the mine operators, were the rights to which the men were entitled under Colorado statutes limiting the length of the work day, requiring adequate safety precautions, payment of wages in cash instead of scrip, and freedom to organize without being blacklisted. The operators were in no mood for such nonsense; they refused to deal with the union in any way. Acting in concert, they began laying in arms and hiring additional guards late in the summer of 1913.

On September 22nd twelve thousand miners struck. Within a few hours armed patrols proceeded to evict them from the company owned hovels in which their families lived. Those who did not move fast enough found their scant possessions thrown into the mud. The day was rainy and a slashing north wind blew gusts of damp snow against makeshift caravans that headed for tented camps the union had set up at Ludlow and other nearby points. It was, a reporter wrote, "an exodus of woe, of a people leaving known fears for new terrors, a hopeless people seeking new hope, a people born to suffering going forth to new suffering."

Heavily armed guards and poorly equipped workers clashed frequently as the strike dragged on. After a 12-hour battle on October 26th between 700 strikers and a detachment of private guards and deputy sheriffs, Colorado's governor sent National Guard troops into the Ludlow area "to preserve the peace." The militia's role, the governor explained, was to protect miners who wanted to work and "prevent any attacks" by one side against the other.

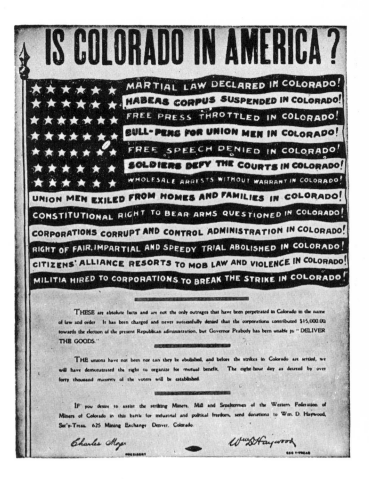

Reporters who interviewed the strikers in the bleak Colorado coal fields heard "heart-breaking tales about cold-blooded cruelty by ruthless mine owners . . . who seemed to lack any sense of humanity."

Hearses were in such short supply that coal wagons had to be used for funeral services of massacre victims.

COLD-BLOODED MURDER

An uneasy peace ensued, exacerbated by the unconcealed pro-coal operator bias of a National Guard commander who continued to make life uncomfortable for the strikers. Against the governor's orders, the ranks of the Guardsmen were filled out with company hirelings and the militia resumed the harrassing tactics of the old company patrols under the direction of Lieut. Karl Linderfelt, previously a deputized sheriff on intimate terms with the mine operators. A machine gun mounted on a car served as a primitive tank; nicknamed the "Death Special," it sprayed bullets at random when it was driven past the tent colonies.

As tension mounted, some miners dug out pits to provide their families with shelter against gunfire, and the leader of the Ludlow strike camp, Louis Tikas, tried to dampen down the passions of his men. There was no trouble the day before the massacre in April, 1914. It was Greek Easter Sunday; gibes rather than shots were exchanged with the troops.

But the next morning the Ludlow area was swarming with Linderfelt's militia. The strikers quickly prepared to meet an attack by taking positions that would draw fire away from the colony. At about 10 a.m. there were several explosions; moments later shots rang out on all sides. The Battle of Ludlow had begun.

During a lull in the fighting in the evening, while some families slept, the militia suddenly turned to the tent colony, setting fires and spraying the area with bullets. As flames swept through the canvas, panic spread; women with skirts afire ran in search of safety, many clutching infants. In the morning the charred bodies of eleven children and two mothers were found near one tent.

The death toll included, in addition, miners who were shot during the assault on the camp. Tikas was killed while being held by the militia; when he was brought before Lieut. Linderfelt he was smashed down with a blow from the officer's rifle.

Vengeful reaction came swiftly. Infuriated strikers, reinforced by fellow workers from nearby New Mexico, attacked mines throughout the area. In the ten days following the Ludlow massacre 46 men were killed, the great majority of them company guards. On appeal from the governor, President Wilson sent in U. S. Army units and an uneasy peace was established.

But the strike went on. The President offered to mediate—the mine operators refused. The President proposed a specific formula for settlement—the operators spurned it. Instead they recruited a large number of scabs and took other measures to starve out the strikers.

A year later a Presidential Commission on Industrial Relations confirmed almost every union charge against the mine operators, their private guards, and the state militia, but the strike was long lost by then.

Most of the miners were immigrants from eastern and southern Europe; some had been brought in as strikebreakers a decade before. The tents were provided by the United Mine Workers when the striking miners were summarily evicted from company-owned houses during a driving rain.

Survivors of the massacre turned out en masse for the funeral of Louis Tikas, a leader of the miners beaten to death while a prisoner of the militia. A burial service in his honor wasn't held until federal troops restored order.

Grim remnants of the massacre. Charred household furnishings were all that remained of the strikers' tent colony after it was attacked and set ablaze by militiamen without justification in the opinion of a Presi-dential commission that later investigated the Ludlow tragedy. The soldier in the foreground is standing a few feet away from an underground shelter that became a deathtrap for eleven children and two women.

TROOPS AT LUDLOW

Training their guns directly at the tent colony, state militiamen abetted by coal company guards took up firing positions under the command of Lieut. Karl Linderfelt, previously a deputized sheriff on unusually friendly terms with the mine operators.

National Guardsmen were sent into the Ludlow area to "preserve the peace," Colorado's governor explained, but they proceeded to perform functions quite similar to those of the coal company guards.

Coal company guards were permitted to serve alongside militiamen who were supposed to maintain order "solely in the public interest." Below is a picture of workers who sought revenge after the Ludlow massacre; some were fellow miners from nearby states.

Fearless Wobbly leaders were determined to overthrow capitalism through "one big industrial union" despite their vulnerability to persecution. Above, left to right, are Adolph Lessig, William Haywood, and Carlo Tresca. The aims, structure, and methods of their organization were completely at odds with those of the American Federation of Labor.

THE WOBBLIES RAISE THE
BANNER OF INDUSTRIAL UNIONISM

More violent in their slogans than in their actions, the Wobblies—the Industrial Workers of the World—were waging a lost battle as European war clouds edged ever closer to American shores. The country was in no mood to tolerate troublemakers of any type, let alone men who openly espoused radical notions at a time when the nation felt threatened by barbaric forces.

Organized on the initiative of the rambunctious Western Federation of Labor, the IWW grew out of a Chicago meeting in 1905 that brought together leaders of left wing labor and political groups such as Daniel DeLeon, sharp-tongued theoretician of the Socialist Labor Party; Eugene Debs, frustrated founder of the American Railway Union who had become the Socialist Party candidate for President; and Charles Sherman, general secretary of the United Metal Workers.

Dominant figure of the Chicago meeting was massive, stoop-shouldered, one-eyed "Big Bill" Haywood, head of the delegation from the Western Federation of Miners. When he called the meeting to order he came straight to the point. "Fellow workers," he shouted, "this is the continental congress of the working class. We are here to confederate the workers of this country into a working class movement that shall have for its purpose the emancipation of the working class from the slave bondage of capitalism." He meant it and so did the men who cheered his words. They were out to overthrow capitalism and replace it with their curious mixture of communism and syndicalism. The uncompromising preamble to the constitution they adopted could not have been more blunt:

"The working class and the employing class have nothing in common. There can be no peace so long as hunger and want are found among millions of working people and the few, who make up the employing class, have all the good things of life. . .

"It is the historic mission of the working class to do away with capitalism. The army of production must be organized, not only for the everyday struggle with capitalists, but also to carry on production when capitalism shall have been overthrown. By organizing industrially we are forming the structure of the new society within the shell of the old."

Diverse and disparate elements in the IWW couldn't agree on how "the new society" should be achieved but they were essentially united in their scorn of AFL craft unionism as a bulwark of the status quo that blocked the path to industrial justice. "The rapid gathering of wealth and the centering of the management of industries into fewer and fewer hands," the IWW contended, "make the trade unions unable to cope with the ever-growing power of the employing class, because the trade unions foster a state of things which allows one set of workers to be pitted against another set of workers into the belief that the working class has interests in common with their employers. . ."

Accordingly, the IWW sought the creation of "One Big Union" encompassing both skilled and unskilled workers organized along broad industrial lines—manufacturing, mining, transportation, building, etc.—so powerful that a grievance of workers in a single shop could bring on a strike that would paralyze a whole industry. And some day all workers in all industries would be able to throw off the yoke of capitalism.

Instead of the AFL's slogan "A fair day's wage for a fair day's work," the Wobblies inscribed on their banner the motto "Abolition of the wage system."

For a while the IWW had limited success. Its greatest strength was among laborers so poorly and so badly treated that they were ready for desperate tactics — miners, lumberjacks, migratory harvest hands, and textile mill workers.

The shrillness of the Wobblies in their demonstrations was muted at bucolic Sunday outings conducted with Edwardian propriety.

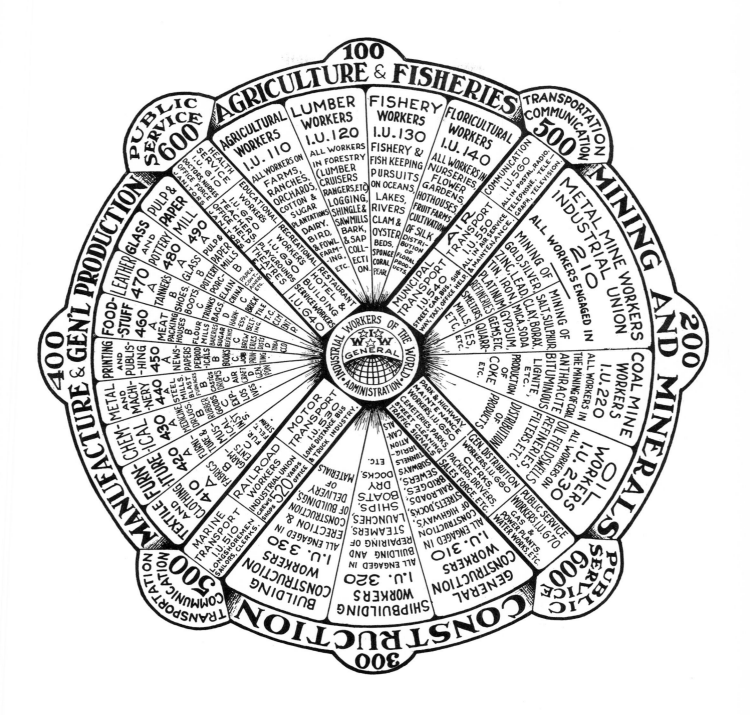

FATHER HAGERTY'S "WHEEL OF FORTUNE"

This classification of workers by industries was basis for the IWW's "One Big Union" plan. It was drafted by Father Thomas Hagerty, a nonconformist mine parish priest who helped draw up the organization's constitution. Suspended from his religious duties because he insisted that Marxian tenets were compatible with Catholicism, he became the editor of "Voice of Labor," organ of the short-lived, socialistic American Labor Union sired by the Western Federation of Miners. "Tall, massive, erect," Eugene Debs said of him, "he could command attention anywhere . . . He has ready language, logic, wit, sarcasm, and at times they roll like a torrent and thrill the multitude."

373

"We Have Fed You all A Thousand Years."

BREAD LINES OR PICKET LINES?
TO DESPAIR — TO PROSPERITY

THE WORLD FOR THE WORKERS
ONE BIG UNION OF ALL THE WORKERS
I.W.W.
LOW WAGES
LONG HOURS
MILITARISM
ROTTEN CONDITIONS
SPEED-UP SYSTEM

DONT BUY JOBS • READ THE INDUSTRIAL WORKER
EMPLOYMENT OFFICE

WHAT TIME IS IT?
ORGANIZATION
ORGANIZE NOW
ORGANIZE RIGHT
TIME TO ORGANIZE
JOIN THE I.W.W.

I.W.W. INDUSTRIAL CODE
4 hr. Day (Jobs for Everyone)
Security of Income
Abolition of the Wage System
Production for USE and not FOR PROFIT
A New Social Order Based on the Scientific Administration of Industry
ABUNDANCE for Workers
NOTHING for Parasites

I.W.W. WHAT WE STAND FOR
MORE WAGES
BETTER WORKING CONDITIONS
SHORTER HOURS
EMANCIPATION
SOLIDARITY
ABOLITION OF THE WAGE SYSTEM
ABOLITION OF UNEMPLOYMENT
SHOP DEMOCRACY
GOOD PAY OR BUM WORK
THINK IT OVER
JOIN THE ONE BIG UNION
FIGHT FOR THE FULL PRODUCT OF YOUR LABOR

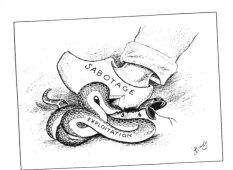

SABOTAGE
EXPLOITATION

WAKE UP!
LONG HOURS
POVERTY
WAGE SLAVERY
JOIN the I.W.W.

INDUSTRIAL UNIONISM
ABOLITION OF THE WAGE SYSTEM
JOIN THE I.W.W.
FREEDOM from WAGE-SLAVERY
FOR INFORMATION ADDRESS I W W 1001 W MADISON ST CHICAGO ILL U S A

IWW
ONE BIG UNION OF ALL THE WORKERS
THE GREATEST THING ON EARTH
FOR INFORMATION ADDRESS I W W 1001 W MADISON ST CHICAGO ILL U S A

374

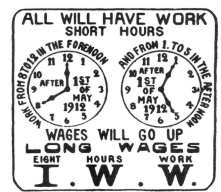

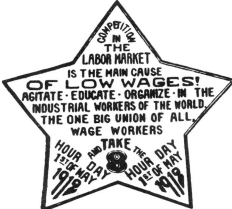

Flamboyant "stickerettes" such as these — pasted conspicuously on fences, telephone poles, store windows — left the public uneasy about the subversive nature of the IWW.

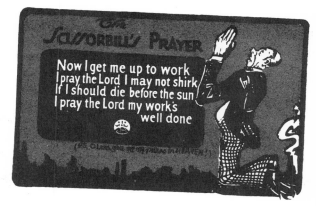

FRAMEUP OR REVENGE?

The IWW was barely under way when it had to suspend virtually all of its organizing activities because of the imprisonment of Haywood, Charles Moyer, president of the Western Federation of Miners, and George Pettibone, an ex-miner (seen left to right in the photograph at the top) on the charge that they had murdered former Idaho Governor Frank Steunenberg. Convinced that Haywood and Moyer were being railroaded to the gallows because they were radical labor leaders, the IWW devoted most of its energies to raising legal defense funds in their behalf.

National interest in the case was heightened by the roles played by Senator William Borah as the prosecuting attorney and Clarence Darrow as the defense counsel. In trying to prove that Haywood, Moyer, and Pettibone had conspired to kill Steunenberg out of revenge for his repression of Idaho miners, Borah relied chiefly on patently suspect testimony by Pinkerton detective James McParlan, key witness in the Molly Maguires trial back in 1875, and Harry Orchard, a miner with a shady background.

Haywood, Moyer, and Pettibone were acquitted, but they parted company with bitterness toward each other because of differences that surfaced during their trial. Soon thereafter the Western Federation of Miners broke away from the IWW and the Socialists followed suit. From here on out anarchistic direct-action elements led by Haywood came to dominate the organization.

McParlan's boast that the accused men "will never leave Idaho alive" infuriated Eugene Debs.

"Well, by the gods, if they do not," he wrote, "the governors of Idaho and Colorado and the masters from Wall Street, New York, to the Rocky Mountains had better prepare to follow them.

"Nearly twenty years ago the capitalist tyrants put some innocent men to death for standing up for labor. They are now going to try it again. Let them dare! There have been twenty years of revolutionary education, agitation, and organization since the Haymarket tragedy, and if an attempt is made to repeat it, there will be a revolution and I will do all in my power to precipitate it. The crisis has come and we have to meet it . . .

"If they attempt to murder Moyer, Haywood and their brothers, a million revolutionists at least will meet them with guns."

(Seated in the center of the courtroom picture below are Darrow, Haywood, and Pettibone.)

JOE HILL'S MARTYRDOM

A legend was born when the body of Joe Hill, poet laureate of the Wobbly movement, was carried through the streets of Chicago on Thanksgiving Day of 1915. At Graceland Cemetery, 30,000 mourners heard eulogies spoken in nine European tongues.

In a very real sense Joe Hill had made the IWW a singing movement. He was the author of dozens of Wobbly songs that became extraordinarily popular. These songs were written in "tough, humorous, skeptical words [that] raked American morality over the coals"; they were sung lustily at innumerable strikes and demonstrations long after his death.

Joe Hill died a martyr. He was executed by a five-man firing squad in the yard of the Utah State Penitenitary. That was the penalty he paid for allegedly killing a Salt Lake City grocer.

"The main thing the state has against Hill," his lawyer claimed, "is that he is an IWW and therefore sure to be guilty." Many who were convinced he had been framed packed protest meetings throughout the world. Among those who sought to prevent or delay his execution were President Wilson, the Secretary of State, the Swedish Ambassador to the U. S., Samuel Gompers, and the daughter of the president of the Mormon Church.

For reasons that remain obscure, Hill was reticent about the facts of his life. When he was asked for some biographical data, he scoffingly replied that he was a "citizen of the world" who had lived on "the planet Earth." Prior to his arrest for murder he had evidently organized a successful strike against a Utah construction company but the facts as to this matter are somewhat unclear.

A day before he was executed, he sent to Bill Haywood in Chicago a terse telegram: "Goodbye Bill. I die like a true blue rebel. Don't waste any time mourning. Organize!"

Few of the thousands who mourned Joe Hill's death knew him personally. But those who sang his verses and kept his name alive were legion; for them he was a folk hero—"a man who never died" because what he wrote was "full of lilting laughter and keen-edged satire, full of fine rage and finer tenderness; simple, forceful and sublime songs; songs of and for the worker, written in the only language he can understand ..."

CASEY JONES—THE UNION SCAB
By Joe Hill

The Workers on the S. P. line to strike sent out a call;
But Casey Jones, the engineer, he wouldn't strike at all;
His boiler it was leaking, and its drivers on the bum,
And his enigne and its bearings, they were all out of plumb.

CHORUS

Casey Jones kept his junk pile running;
Casey Jones was working double time;
Casey Jones got a wooden medal,
For being good and faithful on the S. P. line.

The Workers said to Casey: "Won't you help us win this strike?"
But Casey said: "Let me alone, you'd better take a hike."
Then some one put a bunch of railroad ties across the track,
And Casey hit the river with an awful crack.

Casey Jones hit the river bottom;
Casey Jones broke his blooming spine,
Casey Jones was an Angeleno,
He took a trip to heaven on the S. P. line.

When Casey Jones got up to heaven to the Pearly Gate
He said: "I'm Casey Jones, the guy that pulled the S. P freight."
"You're just the man," said Peter; "our musicians went on strike;
You can get a job a-scabbing any time you like."

Casey Jones got a job in heaven;
Casey Jones was doing mighty fine;
Casey Jones went scabbing on the angels,
Just like he did to workers on the S. P. line.

The angels got together, and they said it wasn't fair,
For Casey Jones to go around a-scabbing everywhere.
The Angels' Union No. 23, they sure were there,
And they promptly fired Casey down the Golden Stair.

Casey Jones went to Hell a-flying.
"Casey Jones," the Devil said, "Oh fine;
Casey Jones, get busy shoveling sulphur;
That's what you get for scabbing on the S.P. line."

SCISSOR BILL
By Joe Hill
(Tune: "Steamboat Bill")

You may ramble 'round the country anywhere you will,
You'll always run across the same old Scissor Bill.
He's found upon the desert, he is on the hill,
He's found in every mining camp and lumber mill.
He looks just like a human, he can eat and walk,
But you will find he isn't, when he starts to talk.
He'll say, "This is my country," with an honest face,
While all the cops they chase him out of every place.

CHORUS

Scissor Bill, he is a little dippy,
Scissor Bill, he has a funny face.
Scissor Bill should drown in Mississippi,
He is the missing link that Darwin tried to trace.

And Scissor Bill, he couldn't live without the booze,
He sits around all day and spits tobacco juice.
He takes a deck of cards and tries to beat the Chink!
Yes, Bill would be a smart guy if he only could think.
And Scissor Bill, he says: "This country must be freed
From Niggers, Japs and Dutchmen and the gol durn Swede."
He says that every cop would be a native son,
If it wasn't for the Irishman, the sonna fur gun.

Scissor Bill, the "foreigners" is cussin';
Scissor Bill, he says: "I hate a Coon";
Scissor Bill is down on everybody
The Hottentots, the bushmen and the man in the moon.

Don't try to talk your union dope to Scissor Bill,
He says he never organized and never will.
He always will be satisfied until he's dead,
With coffe and a doughnut and a lousy old bed.
And Bill, he says he gets rewarded thousand fold,
When he gets up to Heaven on the streets of gold.
But I don't care who knows it, and right here I'll tell,
If Scissor Bill is goin' to Heaven, I'll go to Hell.

THE INTERNATIONALE
By Eugene Pottier
(Translated by Charles H. Kerr.)

Arise, ye prisoners of starvation!
Arise, ye wretched of the earth,
For justice thunders condemnation,
A better world's in birth.
No more tradition's chains shall bind us,
Arise, ye slaves; no more in thrall!
The earth shall rise on new foundations,
We have been naught, we shall be all.

REFRAIN

'Tis the final conflict,
Let each stand in his place,
The Industrial Union
Shall be the human race.

We want no condescending saviors,
To rule us from a judgment hall;
We workers ask not for their favors;
Let us consult for all.
To make the thief disgorge his booty
To free the spirit from its cell,
We must ourselves decide our duty,
We must decide and do it well.

The law oppresses us and tricks us,
Wage systems drain our blood;
The rich are free from obligations,
The laws the poor delude.
Too long we've languished in subjection,
Equality has other laws;
"No rights," says she, "without their duties,
No claims on equals without cause."

Behold them seated in their glory,
The kings of mine and rail and soil!
What have you read in all their story,
But how they plundered toil?

Fruits of the workers' toil are buried
In the strong coffers of a few;
In working for their restitution
The men will only ask their due.

Toilers from shops and fields united,
The union we of all who work;
The earth belongs to us, the workers,
No room here for the shirk.
How many on our flesh have fattened!
But if the noisome birds of prey
Shall vanish from the sky some morning,
The blessed sunlight still will stay.

Sung lustily, such "hymns of hope and hate" were popularized in the IWW's "Little Red Songbook," a scarlet-covered pamphlet fitted to the size of an overall pocket.

WORKERS OF THE WORLD, AWAKEN!
By Joe Hill

Workers of the world, awaken!
Break your chains, demand your rights.
All the wealth you make is taken
By exploiting parasites.
Shall you kneel in deep submission
From your cradles to your graves?
Is the height of your ambition
To be good and willing slaves?

CHORUS:

Arise, ye prisoners of starvation!
Fight for your own emancipation;
Arise, ye slaves of every nation,
In One Union grand.
Our little ones for bread are crying,
And millions are from hunger dying;
The end the means is justifying,
'Tis the final stand.

If the workers take a notion,
They can stop all speeding trains;
Every ship upon the ocean
They can tie with mighty chains.
Every wheel in the creation,
Every mine and every mill,
Fleets and armies of the nation,
Will at their command stand still.

Join the union, fellow workers,
Men and women, side by side;
We will crush the greedy shirkers
Like a sweeping, surging tide;
For united we are standing,
But divided we will fall;
Let this be our understanding—
"All for one and one for all."

Workers of the world, awaken!
Rise in all your splendid might;
Take the wealth that you are making,
It belongs to you by right.

WORKERS OF THE WORLD
(Air: "Lillibulero")
By Connell

Stand up, ye toilers, why crouch ye like cravens?
Why clutch an existence of insult and want?
Why stand to be plucked by an army of ravens,
Or hoodwink'd forever by twaddle and cant?
Think of the wrongs ye bear,
Think on the rags ye wear,
Think on the insults endur'd from your birth;
Toiling in snow and rain,
Rearing up heaps of grain,
All for the tyrants who grind you to earth.

Your brains are as keen as the brains of your masters,
In swiftness and strength ye surpass them by far;
Ye've brave hearts to teach you to laugh at disasters,
Ye vastly outnumber your tyrants in war.
Why, then, like cowards stand,
Using not brain or hand,
Thankful like dogs when they throw you a bone?
What right have they to take
Things that ye toil to make?
Know ye not, workers, that all is your own?

Rise in your might, brothers, bear it no longer;
Assemble in masses throughout the whole land;
Show these incapables who are the stronger
When workers and idlers confronted shall stand.
Thro' Castle, Court and Hall,
Over their acres all,
Onwards we'll press like waves of the sea,
Claiming the wealth we've made,
Ending the spoiler's trade;
Labor shall triumph and mankind be free.

WAGE WORKERS, COME JOIN THE UNION
(Tune: "Battle Hymn of the Republic")

We have seen the reaper toiling in the heat of summer sun,
We have seen his children needy when the harvesting was done,
We have seen a mighty army dying, helpless, one by one,
While their flag went marching on.

CHORUS

Wage workers, come join the union!
Wage workers, come join the union!
Wage workers, come join the union!
Industrial Workers of the World.

O, the army of the wretched, how they swarm the city street—
We have seen them in the midnight, where the Goths and Vandals meet;
We have shuddered in the darkness at the noises of their feet,
But their cause went marching on.

Our slavers' marts are empty, human flesh no more is sold,
Where the dealer's fatal hammer makes the clink of leaping gold,
But the slavers of the present more relentless powers hold,
Though the world goes marching on.

But no longer shall the children bend above the whizzing wheel,
We will free the weary women from their bondage under steel;
In the mines and in the forest worn and helpless man shall feel
That his cause is marching on.

Then lift your eyes, ye toilers, in the desert hot and dear,
Catch the cool winds from the mountains. Hark! the river's voice is near;
Soon we'll rest beside the fountain and the dreamland will be here
As we go marching on.

WE WILL SING ONE SONG
By Joe Hill
(Air: "My Old Kentucky Home")

We will sing one song of the meek and humble slave,
The horn-handed son of the toil,
He's toiling hard from the cradle to the grave,
But his master reaps the profits from his toil.
Then we'll sing one song of the greedy master class,
They're vagrants in broadcloth, indeed,
They live by robbing the ever-toiling mass,
Human blood they spill to satisfy their greed.

CHORUS

Organize! Oh, toilers, come organize your might;
Then we'll sing one song of the workers' commonwealth,
Full of beauty, full of love and health.

We will sing one song of the politician sly,
He's talking of changing the laws;
Election day all the drinks and smokes he'll buy,
While he's living from the sweat of your brow.
Then we'll sing one song of the girl below the line,
She's scorned and despised everywhere,
While in their mansions the "keepers" wine and dine
From the profits that immoral traffic bear.

We will sing one song of the preacher, fat and sleek,
He tells you of homes in the sky.
He says, "Be generous, be lowly, and be meek,
If you don't you'll sure get roasted when you die."
Then we'll sing one song of the poor and ragged tramp,
He carries his home on his back;
Too old to work, he's not wanted 'round the camp,
So he wanders without aim along the track.

We will sing one song of the children in the mills,
They're taken from playgrounds and schools,
In tender years made to go the pace that kills,
In the sweatshops, 'mong the looms and the spools.
Then we'll sing one song of the One Big Union Grand,
The hope of the toiler and slave,
It's coming fast; it is sweeping sea and land,
To the terror of the grafter and the knave.

62D CONGRESS }
2d Session } HOUSE OF REPRESENTATIVES { DOCUMENT No. 671

THE STRIKE AT LAWRENCE, MASS.

HEARINGS

BEFORE

THE COMMITTEE ON RULES

OF THE

HOUSE OF REPRESENTATIVES

ON

HOUSE RESOLUTIONS 409 AND 433

MARCH 2-7, 1912

VICTORY AT LAWRENCE

The IWW reached the crest of its power in the textile workers' strike that enveloped Lawrence, Massachusetts, in 1912.

Although the industry's profits were greater than ever, the owners of Massachusetts' textile mills decided to reduce wages when the state legislature enacted a law limiting the work week of women and minors to 54 hours. The average earnings of most mill hands—largely foreign-born—was less than $9 a week at the time. To make matters worse, newly established speed-up systems had greatly increased production pressures.

On January 12th thousands of angry, unorganized men, women, and children spontaneously began pouring out of the Lawrence factories.

The factory owners refused even to consider the worker's grievances. "There is no strike in Lawrence, just mob rule," declared William W. Wood, president of the American Woolen Company. "To pay for 54 hours' work the wages of 56," he added, "would be equivalent to increasing wages and that the mills cannot afford."

Since the strikers could barely manage to live on their already meager wages, they closed ranks behind the leadership of Joseph Ettor and Arturo Giovannitti, experienced organizers of the Industrial Workers of the World, in protests that won public sympathy and ultimately forced the employers to offer settlement terms which virtually met all the workers' demands.

An exodus of the strikers' children attracted so much adverse publicity for Lawrence that the mayor ordered the police to prevent any more youngsters from leaving the city. Margaret Sanger, one of the backers of the exodus, told a Congressional committee: "Out of 119 children [sent to New York] only four had underwear on . . . their outerwear was almost in rags." Upon their arrival in New York the youngsters were given clothes contributed by supporters of the strike. Below is a photo of an arrested Lawrence worker.

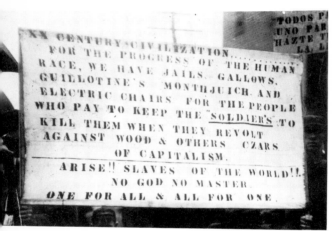

MILITARY INTERVENTION

"They cannot weave cloth with bayonets," Ettor reminded the workers. "By all means make this strike as peaceful as possible. In the last analysis, all the blood spilled will be your blood . . . You can hope for no success on any policy of violence . . . Violence necessarily means the loss of the strike."

As pickets approached the gates of the Atlantic mills in below-freezing weather, streams of ice cold water were trained on them from fire hose on adjoining roofs. When the strikers retaliated by hurling back pieces of ice, 36 of them were arrested and summarily sentenced to a year in prison.

SCORNFUL SMUGNESS

Considering their long hours and meager wages, the Lawrence workers had ample reason to be dissatisfied with their lot, but Judge W. E. Rowell, before whose court many of the Lawrence strikers were summoned, thought otherwise.

"I shall," Judge Rowell loftily declared, "make an assertion that I realize will meet with the scorn of all the gentlemen and ladies from abroad who have so kindly interested themselves in our affairs of late — namely, that the foreign working people in Lawrence have been before this strike, and will be after it is over, decidedly prosperous, happy, though perhaps not quite contented . . ."

These words didn't jibe with an official state report showing that malnutrition and premature death were common among the textile workers.

Following discovery of dynamite caches at three different points in Lawrence—a cemetery lot, a tailor shop and a shoe store—the strikers were promptly (too promptly as it later turned out) denounced for resort-

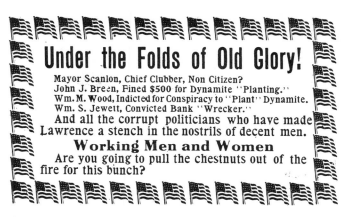

ing to terroristic tactics. "When the strikers use or prepare to use dynamite," declared the New York Times, "they display a fiendish lack of humanity which ought to place them beyond the comfort of religion until they have repented."

But the Times and other papers backtracked when evidence proved that the head of the American Woolen Company was one of the persons who had tried to involve the strikers in bombing plots.

TRUMPED UP CHARGES

The strikers suffered a heavy blow when leaders Joseph Ettor and Arturo Giovannitti were clapped in jail on the trumped up charge of "accessories" to the murder of Anna LaPizzo, a picket shot during a clash between workers and the police.

Publicized as martyr-like victims of a crude frameup, Ettor and Giovannitti perhaps did more good for the strike inside of jail than they could have done on the outside. Their arrest not only served to make the workers more determined to persevere but also attracted greater sympathy for the strike. Moreover, as these broadsides suggest, the IWW was now in a better position to step up agitation among textile workers.

STRIKE
Quash The Indictment
Against Ettor & Giovannitti

The Spirit of Lincoln

FELLOW WORKERS—CITIZENS—COMRADES:

Do not let the Capitalist Editors befog the present situation for you. In the present disclosures revealing the Dynamite Planting by the Contemptible WOOD and his Gang of Hirelings, do not forget the real motive of the PLANT. Capitalist Editors say it was to discredit the strikers—that was only part of it—the bigger motive was TO GET EXCUSE to ARREST ETTOR AND GIOVANNITTI. The Dynamite Planter was sent to plant the dynamite in Ettor's headquarters—only his unfamiliarity with the building caused it to be left on the other side of the partition in the cobbler's shop.

This was a week before Ettor and Giovannitti were arrested for murder. When one PLANT failed the dastardly crew put up another. They started the disturbances that led to the killing of Anna LaPizzo. The whole thing is now exposed.

Innocent men have spent eight months in jail. Demand an IMMEDIATE special session of the court and the quashing of the indictment against Ettor and Giovannitti.

And furthermore demand of Governor Foss and your state government a thorough investigation of the conduct of Judge Mahoney, Judge Brown and District Attorney Atwill, who are accused of "white-washing" and shielding these criminals of wealth. Demand these things—and DEMAND THEM NOW.

If Ettor and Giovannitti are not released from jail by September 30, all the workers, whether organized or unorganized, ARE URGED TO STRIKE until these innocent union men are released.

ETTOR-GIOVANNITTI DEFENSE COMMITTEE.
Central Bldg., Lawrence, Mass.

LABOR IS WATCHING

GET READY FOR THE GENERAL STRIKE
THE TRIAL IS ON!

ETTOR, GIOVANNITTI AND CARUSO

Occupy a **Steel Cage** in the center of the Salem Court Room. The presumption of **innocence** is entirely **destroyed**. The men are dragged into Court **Shackled together.** Humiliation and insult is thus added to the many wrongs these men have suffered. Not one of the 30,000 mill workers of Lawrence have been called upon to testify against them. Not a decent citizen of Lawrence has the prosecution called. **Policemen, Militiamen, Thugs, Detectives, Dynamiters, and Spies** are the star witnesses of the State.

Honest men's **lives must not, will not, be jeopardized on such evidence.**

We have the **power** to wrench the bloody hands of Capitalism from the throats of innocent men. The Woolen and Cotton trust shall not judicially commit murder.

There is nothing the Ruling Class fear as much as a **strike,** A **GENERAL STRIKE.**

Workers of France saved Durand. We'll save Ettor, Giovannitti and Caruso.

GET READY!

ETTOR-GIOVANNITTI DEFENSE COMMITTEE.

ORDEAL OF JUSTICE

Court proceedings against Ettor and Giovannitti were held in Salem, Massachusetts, scene of the witchcraft trials in the 1690's. A reporter covering the case wrote: "It would be impossible to find a more suitable locale. The Massachusetts authorities are repeating the witchcraft trials. The three defendants are brought into court daily locked in portable cages . . . a stunt that is supposed to convince the jurors that these men are desperate characters . . . Today's unfortunate witches do not ride brooms; they are disguised as Wobblies and locked up like wild animals."

Long after the strike was won the jury brought in a verdict of "Not guilty."

DEFEAT
AT PATERSON

Marching with high spirits encouraged by the Lawrence victory, the striking silk workers of Paterson, New Jersey, responded to IWW agitation with rash confidence of success.

The strike began early in 1913 when several hundred workers walked out of the Doherty mills in protest against the introduction of four-loom speedup machinery that reduced both wages and employment. As the strike widened, it gradually embraced all of Paterson's silk mills and dye works.

The city's mill owners draped the streets with American flags attached to posters that boasted "We live under this flag; we fight for this flag, and we will work under this flag." The striking workers replied with shouts: "We wove this flag; we dyed this flag; we won't scab under this flag."

At the bottom is a photo of Elizabeth Gurley Flynn,

Joan of Arc of the Industrial Workers of the World, speaking at a demonstration held in nearby Haledon because Paterson's authorities refused to permit labor meetings in their city.

Suppression of civil rights was a major factor in the strike's defeat. Forbidden by local authorities to meet, march or picket, most workers were forced to remain in their homes. Those who ventured out risked arrest. In all, 2,238 workers were charged with unlawful assembly or disorderly conduct. Merely for permitting friends to sit on a bench in front of his house, one striker was fined more than he earned in a week. For standing on the opposite side of the street while beckoning to men in the mills to come out, several workers were arrested on the ground of unlawful assembly and jailed in default of $500 bail. In some cases bail ran as high as $5,000. "The brutality of the police in arresting strikers

at any pretense, clubbing them into insensibility when they resisted, and breaking up their picket lines was notorious," according to historian Foster Dulles.

The apogee of the strike was its dramatization by a thousand Paterson workers who participated in a gigantic pageant staged in New York's Madison Square Garden. Conceived by a youthful journalist named John Reed, the pageant drew upon the talents of distinguished writers, artists, and actors. John Sloan painted the scenery and Robert Edmond Jones designed the setting; others who helped out were Walter Lippmann and Mabel Dodge.

Fifteen thousand spectators sat enthralled as the pageant depicted the strike with dramatic realism. A reporter described the spectacle this way:

"The big mill aglow with light in the dark hours of early winter morning, the shrieking whistles, the din of machinery dying away to give place to the 'Marseillaise' sung by a surging crowd of 1,200 operatives, the fierce impassioned speech of an agitator, the sending away of the children, the great meeting of desperate, hollow-eyed strikers—these scenes unrolled with a poignancy that no man who saw them will ever forget."

Above is a photograph of key figures of the Paterson strike. Left to right are IWW leaders Pat Quinlan, Carlo Tresca, Elizabeth Gurley Flynn, and Adolph Lessig. Below is a picture of a protest demonstration in New York.

FIGHTING FOR FREE SPEECH

"For Wobblies," as Melvyn Dubofsky observes in his history of their movement, "free speech fights involved nothing so abstract as defending the Constitution, preserving the Bill of Rights, or protecting the civil liberties of American citizens. They were instigated primarily to overcome resistance to IWW organizing tactics and also to demonstrate that America's dispossessed could, through direct action, challenge established authority. To workers dubious about the results achieved by legal action and the reforms won through political action, the IWW taught the effectiveness of victories gained through a strategy of open, yet nonviolent confrontations with public officials."

The Wobblies paid dearly for their participation in such confrontations but in the opinion of Roger Baldwin, founding father of the American Civil Liberties Union, the IWW fights for free speech constituted "a chapter in the history of American liberties like that of the struggle of the Quakers for freedom to meet and worship, of the militant suffragists to carry their propaganda to the seats of government, and of the Abolitionists to be heard . . . The little minority of the working class represented in the IWW blazed the trail in those ten years of fighting for free speech [1908-1918] which the entire American working class must in some fashion follow."

Great splotches of blood covered the trail in Everett, Washington, in the winter of 1916.

Trouble began when about forty Wobblies, mostly lumberjacks, were rounded up by vigilantes, taken to the edge of town, stripped of their clothes, and forced to run the gauntlet between rows of men armed with spiked bats and pick handles. Sheriff Donald McRae wielded one of the thicker clubs.

On the following Sunday a towboat arrived at Everett's docks with 150 high spirited Wobblies. As they tried to land, they were met by a fusillade of shots from vigilantes. In the ensuing fray, five workers were killed and thirty-one wounded. The toll for the vigilantes—two dead and nineteen wounded.

"Who fired the first shot is really unimportant," as Dubofsky points out, "What is significant is that public authorities and private citizens had attempted to deny Wobblies their constitutional rights . . . even at the cost of violence, bloodshed, and death."

(At the top is a photograph taken at memorial services for the five Wobblies who lost their lives during Everett's "Bloody Sunday.")

BITTER HARVEST
FOR MIGRATORY WORKERS

The debasing living and working conditions of migratory farm hands were readily susceptible to IWW agitation among hop pickers of Wheatland, California, in the summer of 1913. A revolt against meager wages, lack of sanitary facilities, and inhuman overcrowding at the huge E. B. Durst Ranch resulted in a strike of several thousand angry workers led by a small group of Wobblies.

During a heated argument with a delegation that demanded improvement of conditions, Durst summarily fired all of its members. Later a peaceful meeting of the pickers was disrupted by a sheriff, several deputies, and the county's district attorney. When the workers refused to comply with the sheriff's order to disperse, a deputy fired a shot that precipitated a riot in which two pickers, a deputy, and the district attorney lost their lives. Upon encountering workers fleeing from the scene, novelist Jack London was reminded "of nothing so much as the refugees after the [San Francisco] earthquake. When I did get one of them to tell about the affair [he] spoke of it as . . . a spontaneous, unpremeditated explosion."

For a week terror reigned in Yuba County. Scores of the strikers were rounded up, beaten, and imprisoned. Two leaders were convicted of murder on the ground that their agitation had created "a climate conducive to violence" but no serious effort was made to bring to justice the killers of the workers.

Beneath the picture of Wheatland pickers at the top is a Sacramento Bee cartoon entitled "A Plague O' Both Your Houses." Editorially the paper commented: "California has had enough of [both] the IWW . . . and the shameful conditions at the Durst hop yards." An official commission headed by Senator Frank P. Walsh placed chief blame on exploitation and cruel treatment of the migratory workers.

(The photo at the bottom of the page shows strawberry pickers in Virginia, circa 1910.)

VIGILANTE PATRIOTISM IN ARIZONA

By the simple process of equating strikes with treason, vigilantes egged on by employers often took the law in their own hands. In some instances such action was considered justified because of IWW agitation; it made little difference that AFL unions committed to support of the war were involved; of even less consequence, seemingly, were legitimate labor grievances.

The situation in Arizona had a variety of disturbing elements in 1917. Stubborn unwillingness of copper mine operators to improve employment conditions, shorten hours or raise wages played into the hands of IWW organizers who sought to displace the Mine, Mill and Smelters Union, an AFL affiliate to which many of the miners belonged.

When a strike by most of the state's 30,000 miners became inevitable, their employers went to considerable pains to create the impression that it was fomented by IWW agents of Kaiser Wilhelm. This was uppermost in the minds of two thousand vigilantes who rounded up 1,200 strikers, forced them aboard cattle cars, took them across the state line, and abandoned them in a New Mexico desert where they remained without food, water or shelter for several days before they were rescued.

Despite indignation over the illegal mass deportation action he had encouraged, Sheriff Harry Wheeler wasn't the least penitent. "If we are guilty of taking the law into our hands," he advised Arizona's attorney general, "I can only cite to you the Universal Law that necessity makes . . . I would repeat the operation any time I find my own people endangered by a mob composed of 80% aliens and enemies of my Government." Almost half the deportees were American citizens; only a handful were technically enemy aliens.

At gun point, the miners were deported by Bisbee's self-appointed "protectors" to the "complete satisfaction of the town's leading citizens."

FANNING THE FLAMES OF DISCONTENT

At outdoor meetings Wobbly leaders delivered fiery speeches that drew large crowds as well as undercover police agents who were often mystified by exhortations in foreign languages. The accompanying pictures, discovered in Justice Department files at the National Archives, were taken during meetings held in New York's Union Square shortly before World War I. "Bread or Revolution," says the card sticking out of the hat worn by the man at the side. In the picture at the bottom youthful Joseph Ettor, organizer of the Lawrence strike, is seen addressing a noontime gathering.

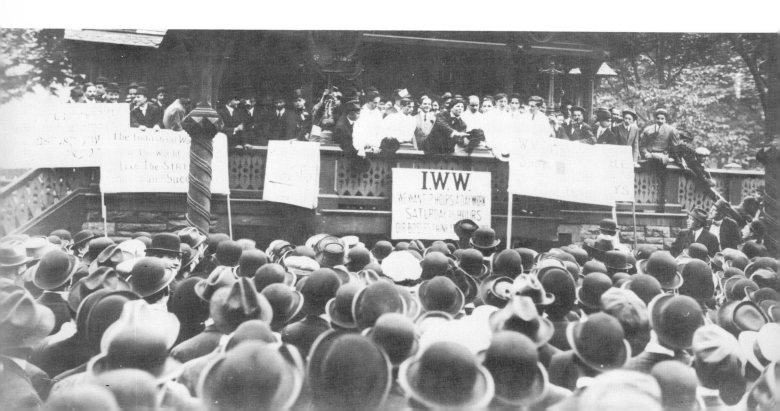

Hostility toward the Wobblies reached a fever pitch when the U. S. declared war on Germany in April, 1917.

Their threats to shut down factories and sabotage crops sent tremors down patriotic spines throughout the country. It didn't matter that there was little evidence that they actually disrupted wartime production; it was enough that they were avowed troublemakers. In any case their efforts to organize unions among foreign born workers could hardly be tolerated in an atmosphere inflamed by xenophobia. Hundreds were rounded up and jailed merely on the grounds of suspicion—along with scores of conscientious objectors.

Below is an IWW broadside depicting Haywood languishing in jail while Samuel Gompers dined with Italy's King during a good will mission in Europe.

Confident that the McNamara brothers were not responsible for the Los Angeles Times explosion, Samuel Gompers posed with them for the above photograph.

Almost completely wrecked by the explosion, the newspaper's building was a hollow shell. Below is a courtroom scene during the trial of the McNamara brothers.

DYNAMITE VENGEANCE BY THE McNAMARA BROTHERS

A stunning blow was dealt the IWW and the labor movement in general when John J. McNamara, secretary of the International Association of Bridge and Structural Iron Workers, and his brother James admitted dynamiting the Los Angeles Times building in 1910.

Although the McNamaras weren't Wobblies, their crime was linked to the IWW because it had rallied boisterously to their defense and even threatened a general strike in protest against their prosecution. Moreover, newspaper accounts of the bombing played up IWW advocacy of "direct action" as sanction of the explosion in which twenty persons lost their lives.

Prior to their confession the McNamaras had so righteously claimed complete innocence of the crime that both the IWW and the AFL were certain that the brothers were being framed. The AFL, to which the Bridge and Structural Workers were affiliated, took especially vigorous steps for the McNamaras' defense, raising several hundred thousand dollars for legal expenses. Simultaneously, to the embarassment of the AFL, Wobblies set up a hue and cry in behalf of the brothers.

Convinced that the McNamara case "demonstrated beyond doubt that no legal safeguard can be invoked to protect any member of the working class who incurs the enmity of the employers by standing between them and the unlimited exploitation of the workers," the IWW took the position that the AFL "did not come to the assistance [of the brothers] as it should have done."

Extra-legal means used in the proceedings against the McNamaras aroused apprehension. "Sound the alarm . . . to the working class!" Eugene Debs exclaimed. "There is to be a repetition of the Moyer-Haywood-Pettibone outrage upon the labor movement. The secret arrest of John McNamara by a corporation detective agency has all the earmarks of another conspiracy to . . . discredit and destroy organized labor."

Defense lawyer Clarence Darrow contended that a gas leak was responsible for the explosion of the Los Angeles Times building, but prosecuting attorneys amassed a great deal of evidence showing that the McNamaras were motivated by hatred of publisher Harrison Otis because he was responsible for keeping Los Angeles an open shop town, having been denounced by the AFL as "the most unfair, unscrupulous and malignant enemy of organized labor in America."

The McNamaras' sudden admission of guilt came as a shock to all who felt they had been unfairly persecuted. Samuel Gompers, who had steadfastly stood by the brothers, was a shaken man when he heard the news. "It won't do the labor movement any good," he muttered as he held back tears. In the opinion of historian Patrick Renshaw, "the IWW suffered most in the aftermath of the McNamara case . . . [because] it was the most militant labor movement."

CONFLICT IN MICHIGAN

The presence of American flags in strikes by workers affiliated with the American Federation of Labor didn't make any difference to employers intent upon smashing unionization efforts as the handiwork of radicals.

These pictures were taken in Calumet, Michigan, at the start of a peaceful strike by copper miners in 1913. A week later the city was invaded by several hundred armed guards hired by the mine operators. In clashes between guards and workers two of the latter were killed and a score of others were beaten up. Subsequently several thousand state militiamen were called in and Calumet became an armed camp.

Adamant in their unwillingness to deal with unions of any type, the mine operators refused to mediate demands of the workers for wage increases and the eight hour day. After several months of hardship, the workers gave in and went back to their jobs.

The presence of Mother Jones and other sympathizers lifted the spirits of the Calumet strikers even though the town was ringed by troops.

The strike was broken by the tragic death of seventy men, women, and children during a panic caused by a false fire alarm at a Christmas party.

BRUTALITY IN NEW JERSEY

Another grisly example of strikebreaking violence took place during a 1915 strike by workers of the Middlesex, New Jersey, plant of the American Agricultural Chemical Company.

"According to the stories of all the witnesses except the deputies," the New York Times reported, "the train halted, the strikers were permitted to inspect it, and they were leaving it cheering because they had found no one arriving to take their places, when forty deputies . . . rushed from the fertilizer plant out on to the railroad property, firing revolvers, rifles and shotguns as they ran.

"The strikers stood aghast for a moment. As many among them screamed and fell wounded, the others fled into the marsh which surrounds the plant, and the deputies, according to witnesses, pursued, firing again and again . . .

"Between the groups lay wounded men, some of whom tried to creep toward the strikers, while cries and groans arose from the marsh."

Two strikers were killed; 16 others were shot in the back. Most of the deputies were strikebreakers hired from a New York detective agency. Their claim that the first shots were fired by the workers was refuted by a local police officer:

"These deputies lie if they say the strikers fired at them. How could the strikers shoot when they had no weapons? They were thrown into a panic by the attack of the deputies, some taking to the highlands and others to the marshy lands. It was those who ran through the marsh that suffered. The deputies butchered them. It is impossible to describe how they slaughter-

ed those unarmed, defenseless men. The strikers were shot and beaten and then shot again. The deputies kept firing until their leader signalled them to stop and then they returned to the Williams & Clark property without attempting to aid the injured men groaning all over the marsh."

THE BLOODY BATTLE OF BAYONNE

Intent on revenge for the killing of several strikers, workers at Standard Oil's refinery in Bayonne, New Jersey, hurled rocks at Bergoff strikebreakers "who were so vicious and unreliable" according to the U. S. Commission on Industrial Relations, "that the officials of the company themselves say that their presence was sufficient to incite a riot . . .[they] shot without provocation at anyone or everyone who came within sight . . . the killing of at least three strikers and the wounding of many more [during the 1915 strike] is directly chargeable to these privately employed guards."

The Rockefellers washed their hands of any responsibility with the explanation that they were merely owners of Standard Oil stock and had not engaged in the formulation of labor policies. Subsequently, however, they followed the advice of Mackenzie King, Canada's former Minister of Labor, by establishing "far-sighted company union programs."

Below is a photo of Bergoff strikebreakers who participated in the Bayonne conflict.

A Bayonne worker fires a revolver at strikebreakers armed with Winchester rifles.

THE FRAME-UP OF
MOONEY AND BILLINGS

Five minutes after the above photograph was taken atop San Francisco's Ferry Building on July 17, 1916, a bomb exploded among bystanders watching a Preparedness Day parade about a mile away, killing ten persons and wounding forty others.

Among those gazing down from the roof were Tom Mooney and his wife Rena. On the following day they and three others—Warren Billings, Edward Nolan, and Israel Weinberg — were charged with the bombing. To all indications they were arrested because they had figured conspicuously in both labor unrest and radical activities.

For years Mooney had been a thorn in the side of the powerful United Railroad Corporation because of his efforts to organize San Francisco's streetcar workers. Only a few days before the Preparedness parade he and his wife led an unsuccessful walkout of conductors that disrupted transportation in the heart of the city. His prosecutor, District Attorney Charles Fickert, had been elected to office with the backing of employers who pressed him to adopt a "get tough" policy toward trade unions.

Mrs. Mooney, Nolan, and Weinberg were acquitted but Mooney and Billings were convicted on flimsy evidence provided by witnesses described as a prostitute, a drug addict, a psychopathic liar, and a woman suffering from spiritualistic hallucinations. Mooney was sentenced to the gallows; Billings was given a life sentence.

Convinced that a miscarriage of justice had taken place, labor groups throughout the country organized a massive campaign in behalf of Mooney and Billings. Although the AFL had some reservations about their radicalism, it demanded that "they be given a new and fair trial in order that a jury, the composition of which [should be] . . . above suspicion, may pass upon evidence by witnesses whose character warrants credence in their testimony and around whom there hangs no cloud of past viciousness, depravity and attempted subornation of perjury."

Such pressure resulted in a special investigation by a commission appointed by President Wilson. Its report concluded that "the atmosphere surrounding the prosecution and trial of the [Mooney] case is ground for disquietude . . . There can be no doubt that Mooney was regarded as a labor agitator of malevolence by the utilities of San Francisco and he was the special object of their opposition . . . The utilities against which Mooney directed his agitation, or who suspected him of mischievous activity, undoubtedly sought 'to get' Mooney." Subsequently Mooney's death sentence was commuted to life imprisonment.

As the years dragged on much of the courtroom testimony was recanted by one witness after another; several admitted they had been "coached" by the police. The most important recantation was that of an itinerant acrobat-waiter who had sworn he had seen Mooney and Billings at the place of the bombing.

Even the trial judge came to admit he had misgivings. In a belated statement he acknowledged: "We must have been slightly crazed by the hysteria of the time to have accepted for a moment the preposterous contention . . . that the alleged dynamiters . . . fully aware that they were being shadowed by private detectives, rode straight down a cleared street in the face of an upcoming parade."

In 1939 California Governor Culbert Olson gave Mooney a full pardon and released Billings by commuting his sentence to the twenty-three years he had already served in prison.

Above are photographs taken during the abortive street car strike in which Mooney and his wife participated a week before the parade bombing. The inset shows them facing each other near a motorman who stalled his car in the middle of traffic. A group of strike agitators, including Billings and Mrs. Mooney, managed to disconnect trolleys while urging indifferent conductors and motormen to quit work. The incident soured Mooney's relations with local labor leaders who felt he had acted prematurely. Below is a courtroom scene. Left to right are Mrs. Mooney, Mrs. Israel Weinberg, attorney Maxwell McNutt, Mooney, and attorney Bourke Cockran.

Right to left, top to bottom: New York Mayor James J. Walker during a visit he paid Mooney at San Quentin prison; Israel Weinberg being grilled about his role in the bombing "conspiracy"; Mooney and Billings after their release in 1939; Mooney leading a San Francisco celebration parade a day after he was pardoned by Governor Olson. Among those in the front line behind Mooney are his wife and Harry Bridges.

BIRTH OF THE
LABOR DEPARTMENT

Only hours before he was succeeded by Woodrow Wilson on March 4, 1913, President William Howard Taft signed the bill creating the U. S. Department of Labor but Democrats could claim chief credit for Congressional passage of the measure.

It remained for President Wilson to appoint the nation's first Secretary of Labor, an ex-miner named William B. Wilson, and to lay a firm foundation for the new agency. "The great guiding purpose of the Department of Labor," Secretary Wilson announced when he took office, "is the promotion of the welfare of the wage earners of the United States . . . by improving their working conditions and advancing their opportunities for profitable employment . . . in harmony . . . through realization of the highest ideals of industrial justice."

Initially the department's offices were in the building seen at the top. The adjoining photo shows Secretary Wilson flanked by Immigration Commissioner Anthony Caminetti and Terence Powderly, former Knights of Labor leader who served as an aide to Wilson.

TAFT SIGNS BILL FOR DEPARTMENT OF LABOR

Not in Hearty Accord With the Measure, But Wishes to Aid Wilson.

President Taft early this morning signed the bill creating a new Department of Labor. He took this step in opposition to Charles Nagel, his secretary of Commerce and Labor. Mr. Nagel opposed the bill largely because he thought that some of its provisions are unconstitutional, that the new department will have little or no authority not now given to the bureau of labor, and that many of the bureaus transferred to the new department do not belong there.

President Taft was inclined to sympathize with many of the contentions of Mr. Nagel. In addition, he said that he thought Congress was making a big mistake in not rearranging the bureaus of the different departments so as to bring those of proper relation into the departments to which they naturally belong.

Done in Wilson's Interests.

At the last minute, however, the retiring President concluded that he would not interfere with President Wilson adding another member to his cabinet, and signed the bill. Mr. Wilson has stated that he is prepared to name the new cabinet officer along with the other nine, which is taken to mean that he has selected William B. Wilson of Pennsylvania for Secretary of Labor.

HARVEST YEARS DURING THE WILSON ADMINISTRATION

Flanked by President Woodrow Wilson and Secretary of Labor William B. Wilson, Samuel Gompers couldn't help but beam with pride as a parade of workers marched past them. There was much to celebrate during President Wilson's administration:

• Establishment of the Labor Department "to foster, promote, and develop the welfare of the wage earners of the United States, to improve their working conditions, and to advance their opportunities for profitable employment."

• Creation of the Children's Bureau, the U. S. Employment Service, and the Conciliation Service within the Labor Department.

• Creation of the U. S. Industrial Commission to investigate the causes of strikes.

• Establishment of the 8-hour day by the Adamson Act. Although the law applied only to railroad workers, it helped pave the way to a shorter day for workers in other industries.

• Passage of the LaFollette Seamen's Act improving working conditions on American merchant vessels.

• Passage of the Clayton Act expressly designed to exempt unions from antitrust suits and judicial injunctions. The law was hailed as "Labor's Magna Charta" but subsequent Supreme Court decisions construed it so narrowly that its aims were nullified.

• Creation of the War Labor Board to settle disputes by mediation and conciliation.

• Participation of labor leaders in the formulation of government policies.

Greatly encouraged by the favorable climate provided by government support, especially in the World War I years, membership in unions doubled between 1912 and 1919, rising from 2,500,000 to 5,047,000. During this period the railway clerks bounded from 5,000 to 71,000; membership in the electrical workers union leaped from 32,000 to 131,000; meat cutters and butchers rose from 7,000 to 85,000.

Simultaneously substantial economic gains were made. Average hourly earnings in manufacturing increased from 22 cents in 1915 to 48 cents in 1919. However, a steady rise in living costs cut into the gains. Between 1914 and 1918, for example, food prices rose 64%.

HISTORIC OCCASION

Trade union leaders as well as high government officials were on hand when Samuel Gompers, trowel in hand, laid the cornerstone for the new headquarters of the American Federation of Labor in Washington, D. C.

Dedication ceremonies on July 4, 1916 were highlighted by an address by President Wilson and a parade led by officers of the thirty-five unions. Gomper's son Henry, who had been the Federation's first office boy, carved the lettering of the cornerstone.

The shovel wielder in the photo at the side is Frank Morrison, longtime secretary of the AFL. Looking on are bare-headed Secretary of Labor William B. Wilson and Gompers.

Furiously busy during the wartime years, Sam Gompers seemed "downright indefatigable."

EMANCIPATION OF
MARITIME WORKERS
FROM BONDAGE

Amid outcries of anguish from shipping interests that had long profited from conditions somewhat similar to indenture, President Wilson signed into law the Seaman's Act of 1915 sponsored by Senator Robert M. LaFollette, Wisconsin Republican.

Applicable to all American vessels and foreign ships in U. S. ports, the new law abrogated imprisonment as a penalty for desertion, made owners liable for infliction of corporal punishment, required more adequate safety regulations, and forbade the allotment of wages to creditors.

Passage of the law instituting these reforms culminated a tenacious campaign Andrew Furuseth launched back in 1894. "At the time," as Joseph Rayback has pointed out, "the American sailor's condition was at its worst. He lived under the full control of the captain at sea; he was unable to quit his job at will for fear of being punished as a deserter; and he was unable to join in concert to improve his condition on pain of being punished as a mutineer. In addition, he had become the prey of the 'crimp,' a combination shipping master and boardinghouse keeper. The crimp had obtained control of the sailor's employment by taking the sailor into his boardinghouse between jobs and keeping him there until he ran up a huge board bill. When the bill was large enough, the crimp provided the sailor with a voyage, making him sign over several months' pay, which the shipping company paid as soon as the ship cleared, keeping the sailor in a perpetual state of peonage."

A tall, gaunt Norseman who served as president of the Seamen's Union from 1908 to 1937, Furuseth was idolized as an unselfish labor leader, but shipowners considered him a "foreign-born agitator who created dissension and dissatisfaction among a class of men [who were] content, properous and happy." Once, when he was threatened with imprisonment because of his militancy, he remained unruffled: "They cannot put me in a smaller room than I have always lived in. They cannot give me plainer food than I have always eaten. They cannot make me lonelier than I have always been."

Energized by the friendly climate of Wilsonian policies, labor could now flex its muscles more openly than in previous years. A new wave of organizational activity followed passage of the Clayton Act of 1914 which exempted unions from prosecution as conspiracies in restraint of trade and limited the use of injunctions by federal courts but it later turned out the law was at best a "mere statement of fine principles."

(Above are field offices of the United Textile Workers on the outskirts of Atlanta, Georgia, in 1915. Below are New York trolley car workers "passing the hat" during a strike in 1913.)

HELPING MAKE THE WORLD SAFE FOR DEMOCRACY

Representatives of Allied nations who attended the AFL's 1917 convention heard President Woodrow Wilson speak out boldly in behalf of labor's hard-won rights. "While we are fighting for freedom," he declared, "we must see [to it] . . . that labor is free, that the conditions of labor are not rendered more onerous by the war, and . . . that the instrumentalities by which the conditions of labor are improved are not checked."

Earlier in the year, shortly before the United States declared war on Germany, organized labor placed itself squarely behind Wilson's crusade to make the world safe for democracy. The AFL executive council, representatives of 79 affiliated unions, and the rail brotherhoods closed ranks behind a ringing manifesto:

"We the officers of the national and international trade unions of America . . . hereby pledge ourselves in peace and in war, in stress or in storm, to stand unreservedly by the standards of liberty and the safety and preservation of the institutions and ideals of our Republic. In this solemn hour of our nation's life, it is our earnest hope that our Republic may be safe-guarded in its unswerving desire for peace; that our people may be spared the horrors and the burdens of war; that they may have the opportunity to cultivate and develop the arts of peace, human brotherhood, and a higher civilization. But despite all our endeavors and hopes, should our country be drawn into the maelstrom of the European conflict, we . . . offer our services to our country in every field of activity to defend, safeguard, and preserve the Republic of the United States of America against its enemies whomsoever they may be, and we call upon our fellow workers and fellow citizens in the holy name of Labor, Justice, Freedom and Humanity, to devotedly and patriotically give like service."

In return for labor's cooperation during the war, the Wilson administration adopted a policy distinctly favorable to the trade union movement. Moreover, union leaders were accorded a voice in the determination of broad national issues as well as representation in government agencies dealing with military production. Union officers served prominently in the formulation of the policies of the Council on National Defense, the War Labor Board, and other official bodies.

The War Labor Board — a body composed of representatives of unions, employers, and the public—encouraged collective bargaining, backed the right of workers to organize in trade unions, and helped settle disputes. Never before had the government actively promoted the interests of workers.

The war years saw a rapid expansion of organized labor. Spectacular gains were made by unions in industries affected by the needs of the armed forces—shipbuilding, munitions, railroads, mining, and clothing. Substantial advances were also made by electrical workers, carpenters, longshoremen, teamsters, and merchant seamen. Simultaneously large groups of semi-skilled workers were for the first time brought within the trade union movement.

Critics of Wilson's friendliness toward labor in general and the "Big Four" (the railroad brotherhoods) in particular considered his policies a recipe for "trouble-making," but cartoonist Maurice Becker hailed enactment of the Adamson eight-hour day law as a boon for the nation's railroad workers.

SCORN OF
RADICALISM

Despite obstruction by the Industrial Workers of the World, the labor movement remained steadfast in its patriotism. IWW halls were shut down and their publications were suppressed. In June 1917 the federal government indicted the whole top leadership of the organization under wartime espionage laws; 150 were jailed. Were it not for such harassment, the IWW might well have become a powerful force in the opinion of labor historian Philip Taft.

Labor wasn't conscripted but in some communities workers considered "slackers" were subjected to disagreeable coercion. In shipbuilding yards construction was geared to a feverish pace. Below are steelworkers who participated in a Pittsburgh Liberty Bond parade.

20 AT HOME TO 1 IN THE TRENCHES

It takes the best co-operative efforts of from six to twenty workers at home to properly equip and maintain one American soldier at the front.

For each soldier boy, weighing on an average, 150 pounds, our factories, mills, mines, farms, etc., must furnish four tons of supplies per annum; including clothing, food, arms, ammunition, transportation, airplanes, etc., etc.

The manufacturers of this community are doing their bit. With consistent help and encouragement for their wage-earning partners and themselves, from all classes of the people,

AMERICAN INDUSTRY CAN AND WILL WIN THIS WAR FOR HUMAN LIBERTY

Breeders of industrial war at home must be eliminated. National co-operation is the slogan to insure victory for Democracy over Autocracy.

AGITATION WHICH DELAYS OUR WAR INDUSTRIES IS 'MADE IN GERMANY'

In the first seven months after America's entrance into this war for human freedom, enemy agitators in our midst caused 283,402 workers to lose 6,285,519 days of production. Our war industries were heavily handicapped by this unpatriotic strife.

LET US ALL PULL TOGETHER TO WIN THE WAR QUICKLY

These wartime propaganda posters were prominently displayed in factories.

THE HAND THAT THREATENS OUR INDUSTRIAL LIFE

More than 32,000 American industrial plants have been placed at the disposal of the government to win this war. Their effectiveness must not be hampered by enemy agitators who cause bad feeling between wage-earners and wage payers. Every community is interested in promoting industrial prosperity.

THE SHOT THAT WILL WIN THE WAR

United action by America's industrial partners will shorten and win this struggle for human freedom. It is the heaviest shot our Democracy can fire at wage-earners' and wage-payers' common foe — Autocracy.

EVERY LOYAL WORKER AND EMPLOYER CAN RIDE TO VICTORY UNDER THE EAGLE'S WINGS WITH UNCLE SAM

Despite skepticism about their suitability for mechanical occupations, women took the place of their husbands and brothers in large numbers. Organized labor had mixed feelings about the great influx of women into industry. While it was recognized that their employment was necessary, it was feared they would undermine working standards. Most unions continued to bar women from their ranks.

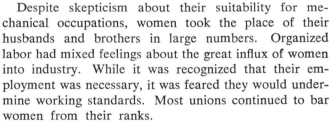

When the war ended, Congress authorized establishment of the Women's Bureau "to formulate standards and policies which shall promote the welfare of wage-earning women, improve their working conditions, increase their efficiency, and advance their opportunities for profitable employment."

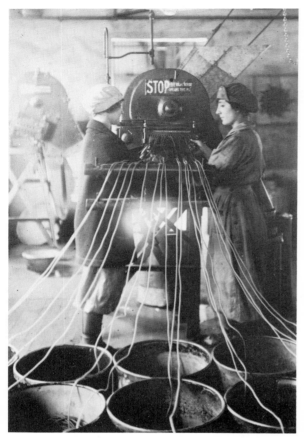

The nimble fingers of women at the Dupont explosives plants increased production manifold, keeping the Allied troops amply supplied. Although total employment at these plants rose from 5,500 to 55,000 in 1918, the accident rates declined steadily because of safety precautions.

FREE EMPLOYMENT BUREAU A BLESSING FOR UNEMPLOYED

Thousands of Positions for Workers Without Any Fee Being Charged for Job.

DEPARTMENT DOING SATISFACTORY WORK

Plan to Cover Whole State Advocated by Well Known Writer "Progress."

A most important department of the State at the present time is that of the free employment bureaus, maintained in three of our leading centres of population. This department is doing a most effective but a quiet work, one in which there is very little noise.

There are some people who believe that it is the province of the State to provide work for all its citizens, but only a few really hold to this doctrine at the present time. The general idea is that the State should keep its hands off and let the people settle their industrial affairs for themselves. The latter idea has always been the prevailing one and that alone accounts for its strength and popularity. Where a custom or institution has long held its position it becomes embedded, so to speak, in the minds of the people and finally it becomes so firmly established as to be considered permanent.

But progress must be made just the same and if the State has not as yet taken up the question of furnishing employment it has at least attempted to find employment, and the reports for the past four years, or since the free bureau has been established, show that there has been a pretty good success made along that line. The three bureaus are located at Boston, Springfield and Fall River, and have found positions for some 43,000 people since starting. They actually filled 68,780 positions, but in many cases individuals were helped to position more than once, and this accounts for the fact that it only took 43,000 applicants to fill the 68,780 jobs.

Taken as a general proposition it can be stated that supply and demand do not run even, so far as labor is concerned, in our present system of society. Still it is not as bad as it might be, as the jobs offered foot up a respectable total when compared to applications for work. In four years there were more than 195,000 applications for work, while during the same time the three bureaus were able to offer over 172,000 positions. That only some 68,780 of these were filled only proves that, in many cases, the people looking for employment were unable to fill the qualifications. This happens often and is bound to happen as long as industry is conducted as it is

Monthly Market Letter.

They issue a monthly market letter at Boston, giving the people who are interested an idea of the situation in the so-called labor market every 30 days. This letter, for the month of April last, shows that the conditions during that month were rather below normal compared to other years. The average number seeking employment during April this year was 131 as compared with 112 last year, while the demand was only 74 compared to 81 last year. This means the daily figures for every day that the office was open during April. The daily average number of positions reported filled were 48 this year as compared to 56 last year. There was a good demand during the past April for industrial help in some few trades, but in the building trades it was not as good as last year. There was a good demand for farming help, but there was only a limited supply at the rate of wages offered. It is said, too, that the number of unskilled people out of work seems to be increasing, rather than diminishing, and that many of these refuse to accept what is offered in the shape of work. As for female help there is a big demand, especially from factories, but not many women are willing to take such work, probably due to some extent to the conditions attached to much of this work.

This monthly report for April does not give much encouragement to those who have nothing to sell but their labor and, of itself, it shows that the state of business in the country in general is not as bright as it might be. This free employment bureau is in a position to tell to a nicety just what is doing in nearly all fields of labor, as it has patrons in some 20 or more States who send to Boston, off and on, for all classes of help. It is a first class barometer and is the first to feel the ups and downs of business. When times are good there is a big demand for help and when times are other than good there is a small demand. April should be one of the best of all months, as it is then that all new enterprises are well under way, and especially is this true of all out door life.

This monthly letter is a good thing in its way, as it keeps the public informed on the main question, but a feature of all such letters that ought to arouse thought on the part of the more intelligent among the workers is that much used phrase "labor market." It is true that there is a labor market and the term has to be used in the State employment service as much as elsewhere, but when the working-man comes to rightly understand it he will have a much better idea of his true status in society than ne has at present. The term labor market means that labor is a commodity bought and sold in the market the same as cattle in the cattle market, or cabbages in the cabbage market, or potatoes in the potato market, and as no commodity can put a price on itself it follows that the price of labor will be fixed by supply and demand, the same as all commodities. To the man able to think this is a statement of fundamental import.

Applicants Stand in Line.

Naturally it is the unskilled who look to the employment bureau to find them jobs in the largest number and that there are plenty of these looking for work every day and all day is evident by the great number who stand in front of the officer much of the

(This article appeared in a Lynn, Mass., newspaper in May, 1911.)

HUMAN RESOURCES

Enlisting the nation's man and woman power was greatly facilitated by the U. S. Employment Service established in 1918. Almost overnight it opened 800 field offices but most of them were shut down when the Armistice took effect.

Assisting workers obtain private employment through public agencies made slow headway after the war except in states like Wisconsin (where these photos were taken) and Massachusetts.

Despite questionable practices and the high fees they charged, private employment agencies were permitted to flourish without being subject to regulation. Not until the passage of the Wagner-Peyser Act in 1933 was the federal government authorized to help the states set up free employment services.

Skilled wartime workers were earning so much that the Los Angeles Times and other papers made them the butt of cartoons such as these. Some unions were setting up their headquarters in buildings that seemed to ape the architecture and decor of fashionable clubs.

HELMSMEN OF THE LABOR DEPARTMENT

Surrounded by his top aides, Secretary of Labor William B. Wilson could lay claim to solid achievements by the Labor Department during the hectic war years.

By the time "Puddler Jim" Davis (seen at the side with Secretary of Commerce Herbert Hoover) succeeded Secretary Wilson in 1921, the department was credited with advancing the basic interests of the nation's wage earners to a substantial degree.

An ex-iron worker, Secretary Davis (seen below with John L. Lewis), guided the department through its postwar adjustments and into the period of uncertain prosperity during three Republican administrations (Harding, Coolidge, and Hoover).

Davis' successor, William Doak, former president of the Brotherhood of Railroad Trainmen, took over the task of running the Labor Department during the first two years of the depression Thirties.

(Among the Wilson aides in the photo at the top are Roger Babson, Felix Frankfurter, Mary Van Kleeck, Louis Post, Mary Anderson, Ethelbert Stewart, Hugh Kerwin and Samuel J. Gompers).

AN INTERNATIONAL BILL OF RIGHTS

Keenly appreciative of the wartime role of trade unions, President Wilson prevailed upon the Paris Peace Conference to accord labor a substantial voice in the formulation of post-war policies.

An International Commission on Labor Legislation —a body composed of Allied union leaders headed by Samuel Gompers—laid the basis for the International Labor Organization in a notable Bill of Labor Rights approved by the signers of the Versailles Peace Treaty. The document endorsed the right of association by workers, equal pay for equal work, unrestricted mi-

gration, inspection of factories, and similar principles.

The International Labor Organization, a League of Nations affiliate, was empowered to promote the improvement of working conditions throughout the world. Although Gompers had long been distrustful of governmental intervention in labor affairs, he threw his support behind the Organization, but it was not until 1934 that the U. S. became a member of the ILO.

Secretary of Labor William B. Wilson (above) presided at the first ILO meeting, held in Washington, D. C., in October, 1919.

"WET" OR "DRY"

"VOTE WET FOR MY SAKE!"

"VOTE DRY FOR MINE!"

Shall the Mothers and Children be Sacrificed to the Financial Greed of the Liquor Traffic?

IT IS UP TO YOU, VOTER, TO DECIDE

VOTE DRY

Labor and Beer.

When You Invade a Man's Habits, What Happens?

By Samuel Gompers,
PRESIDENT AMERICAN FEDERATION OF LABOR.

I AM not an advocate of drinking. I am not an advocate of wine drinking, or even of beer drinking.

Yet I am an anti-prohibitionist. Not an anti-prohibitionist of mere mushroom growth, but one opposed to prohibition, steadfastly and in principle, for more than forty years. And still I think I may honestly say that I have done as much as most men, and much more than many men, in the furtherance of the cause of temperance.

And it is as a worker for temperance—for the right and true temperance—that I wish to say that I consider the foisting of prohibition upon this country against the palpable wish of the large mass of the people, to be, in times like these, worse than a crime; it is a blunder. And moreover, a blunder charged with danger and loaded with disastrous probabilities.

The world today lies torn and tortured and tempest-tossed. All peoples of the earth have been upset and unsettled. The minds of men are excited and unstrung. Subtle, or open, discontent exists throughout the earth. From the bloody Bolshevism of Russia to the economic unrest of the still stable countries, it is there for the least observing to see and the most unthinking to recognize.

It is a singularly unfortunate moment to upset further a country by an invasion of personal liberty and a fatuous attempt to reorganize, by force, the daily habits of its citizens. The very fact that in some cases these habits are harmful is, of course, not sufficient excuse for the autocratic rule that attempts to control the daily lives of those in whom such habits are without harm.

This is no attempt, as it is no time, to deal radically with the evils of drink. They exist, and they should be corrected. But to rescue the few and bring disaster to the many is a policy too fatuous to admit of discussion. A general on the battlefield does not turn all his soldiers into stretcher-bearers. He wins the battle first and aids the wounded afterward.

That is precisely the condition that confronts us in this country today.

POSTWAR PROHIBITION

Despite opposition by organized labor, ratification of the Eighteenth Amendment, and subsequent enactment of the Volstead Law marked the culmination of a temperance campaign backed by employers who blamed absenteeism and reduced efficiency on excessive drinking.

A hastily mobilized "No beer, no work" movement was all but ignored by Congress. In testimony before the Senate Judiciary Committee, Samuel Gompers spoke out in behalf of the right of workers to continue "the habit, the necessity" of drinking beer with their dried-out lunches. Referring to the days when he was a cigar worker, he testified: "I know what a glass of beer meant to me in the midday, in the factory full of dust, full of foul air . . . Take the man who works in any industrial establishment for eight or nine hours or more a day; how welcome beer is to him cannot be known except to those who have had industrial experience of the type I have described."

Prohibition, Gompers argued, was discriminatory class legislation because workers were deprived of beer while rich men could continue to draw upon their well stocked cellars of wines and whiskeys for many years to come.

419

Welcome Them Back to Their Jobs

"--on the dying echo of your resounding cheers"

WHEN the fanfare of trumpets and the drummer's steady tattoo to the regular step, step of our victorious returning crusaders dies down,

When the admiring, enthusiastic observers have cheered themselves hoarse, and dispersed after the last ranks have passed in file,

When the boys, flushed with victory, return to their homes and reappear in civilian dress,

What will you offer them? What remains of the dying echo of your resounding cheers?

The least you can do is to let them have their old jobs, or better jobs if possible. They left your store, your office, your factory, to fight your battles, to preserve your safety, to protect you, your family and your property.

They return with the pride of accomplishment, with the sense of a duty well done.

Welcome Them Back to Their Jobs

The Boot and Shoe Workers' Union stands for an American welcome to all who have fought and sacrificed that American ideals may prevail in the world.

The Boot and Shoe Workers' Union in industry stands for those principles for which the world is praying and hoping— the banishment of warfare and the peaceful adjustment of disputes.

The Boot and Shoe Workers' Union stands for the upbuilding of the community, civic and industrial peace, progress to the manufacturer, uninterrupted earnings and prosperity to the workers.

The Boot and Shoe Workers' Union stands for the intelligent exercise of the power of reason in industrial relationship. Our boys have fought that reason and not might shall prevail in the world.

The Boot and Shoe Workers' Union
256 Summer Street, Boston.

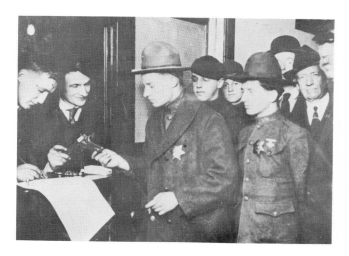

SEATTLE'S GENERAL STRIKE

National Guardsmen were on the ready when the nation's first citywide general strike erupted in Seattle early in 1919. Responding to a call from Seattle's Central Labor Committee, 60,000 workers left their jobs. For five hectic days local industry was almost completely paralyzed. The strike arose out of a demand by shipyard machinists for an increase in their wages, but Mayor Ole Hanson blamed it on a Bolshevik plot.

A strong wave of hostile public opinion convinced Seattle labor leaders to withdraw support of the strike.

The photo at the right shows an ex-doughboy who went to work as a department store clerk.

BOSTON'S UNPRECEDENTED POLICE STRIKE

Still jittery because of Seattle's general strike earlier in the year, Bostonians were distinctly nervous when their policemen went on strike in September, 1919.

Although policemen in Los Angeles, St. Louis, Jersey City, and a score of other cities had organized into unions without encountering serious objections, Boston Police Commissioner Edwin Curtis was angered by efforts of members of his force to affiliate their social club with the American Federation of Labor. Regarding this as a breach of discipline, he suspended 19 leaders despite the club's assurance that its members would continue to "do their duty as police officers in the future as in the past."

Outrage at Curtis' arbitrary action precipitated a strike by 1,500 policemen (about 85% of the force) on September 9th. The first day passed with relatively minor acts of vandalism, but serious trouble erupted when units of the state guard began patrolling the city on the following day. In clashes between the soldiers and "rioters," eight persons were killed and a score wounded. On the third day Governor Calvin Coolidge sent several thousand additional militiamen into the city and asked Secretary of War Newton D. Baker for the help of federal troops.

Coolidge turned a deaf ear to appeals for peaceful settlement of the strike. "There is no right to strike against the public safety by anybody, anywhere, any time" he told Samuel Gompers in a terse telegram that brought him into national prominence and placed him on the road to the White House.

Some newspapers were convinced that Communism had taken root in Boston. "Bolshevism in the United States is no longer a specter," said the Philadelphia Evening Public Ledger. "Boston in its chaos revealed its sinister substance. In their reckless defiance of the fundamentals of morality, in their bullying affront to the structure of civilization, wherein do the police of New England metropolis differ from the mad minority which overthrew Kerensky and ruined Russia. Only an arrant casuist, a fatuous hair-splitter, can proclaim a shade of contrast. The nation has chosen. If ever it was vague in its conception of the Bolshevist horror, its vision is clear-cut now. So is the issue. Defiled Boston has seen to that."

Thanks to Coolidge and Curtis, Boston was snatched from the "clutches of Communism." The striking policemen decided it was their patriotic duty to go back to work. (Below are leaders of the strike.)

REVOLT OF THE ACTORS

New Yorkers didn't have to buy tickets to see Ethel Barrymore, Eddie Cantor, Marie Dressler, Ed Wynn or other stage stars in the summer of 1919. They could be seen on the picket line of the newly organized Actors Equity Association.

For years actors had been subject to crass exploitation. Although they had to participate in rehearsals that sometimes lasted as long as six weeks, they weren't paid for such work. To make matters worse, some rehearsals didn't culminate in paid employment; it was not unusual for producers to abandon a play while it was being readied for performance. Morever, actors

were even required to furnish their own costumes.

Prior to the strike the Actors Equity Association, formed to put an end to such exploitation, persuaded theatrical procedures to sign an agreement assuring a minimum of two weeks of employment, but the producers subsequently reneged on their promise and refused to negotiate with Actors Equity on the ground that it "threatens the profession with a closed shop."

A strike that started in New York in August, 1919, and spread to other cities was so effective and evoked so much unfavorable publicity for the producers that they signed a contract within a few weeks.

Actresses and chorus girls who took to the sidewalks of New York's Times Square attracted a great deal of attention. Some marched to City Hall, where Ethel Sadler delivered a speech from the pedestal of Nathan Hale's statue.

At the right is Ethel Barrymore, one of the strike's leading figures.

The Actors Equity Association became affiliated with the American Federation of Labor after the charter of the White Rats Actors Association, a vaudeville group, was withdrawn in 1919.

George M. Cohan was one of the few popular entertainers who regarded unionization as a personal affront.

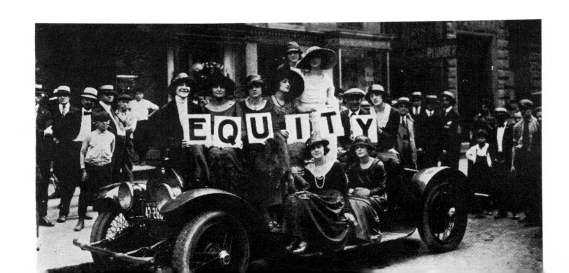

FRICTION AMONG THE ARTISTES

Most members of the White Rats Actors Union, predecessor of Actors Equity Association, were vaudeville entertainers but under the terms of the union's charter, ratified by the AFL in 1911, it had exclusive jurisdiction over "all parts of theatrical production occurring behind the footlights and in front of the scenery after the same has been placed in position by the stage mechanics . . . and any forms of entertainment known as either legitimate, variety or vaudeville." By the time Actors Equity was formed the White Rats were past their heyday but they were unwilling to be superseded; Gompers, ordinarily a stickler for strict observance of jurisdictional authority, compelled the Rats to give up their charter.

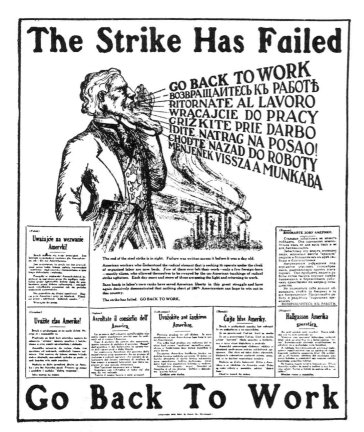

The strike had barely begun when its "failure" was proclaimed by the U. S. Steel Corporation in posters printed in eight different languages.

THE GREAT STEEL STRIKE

Unlike Seattle's general strike and Boston's police strike, the steel strike of 1919 was no local affair. It involved a battle between the nation's most powerful industrial aggregation and more than 300,000 workers in eight states.

"Conditions in the steel mills at the time," according to Foster Dulles, "fostered universal discontent and underscored what labor leaders declared was an imperative need for unionization if the workers expected any consideration of their grievances. Wages remained low in spite of wartime advances and were steadily falling further behind the continued rise in living costs. A twelve-hour day, six days a week, was still in effect for something over half the labor force, and the average working week was just under sixty-nine hours. Among the highly diversified immigrant groups that made up the majority of employees, living conditions were a bitter travesty upon the promise of a more abundant life which had drawn them to the Land of Opportunity."

The first step leading to the strike was the formation of an organizing committee composed of representatives of twenty-four AFL unions whose crafts had elements of jurisdiction in the steel industry. By the fall of 1919 more than 100,000 workers had joined the Amalgamated Association of Iron, Steel and Tin Workers (almost defunct since the Homestead strike was smashed in 1892) and the time seemed ripe for action.

Demands made upon the steel companies called for union recognition, abolition of the twelve hour day, wage increases sufficient to guarantee "an American standard of living", and the right of collective bargaining. But attempts to open negotiations with Elbert Gary, chairman of the U. S. Steel Corporation, were futile. He took an inflexible position: "Our corporation and subsidiaries, although they do not combat labor unions as such, decline to discuss business with them." Other steel firms took the same stand.

The strike started on September 22nd. Within a week about 300,000 men had stopped working.

The steel industry wasn't caught by surprise. On the day the strike began the New York World reported: "In the Pittsburgh region thousands of deputy sheriffs have been recruited at several of the larger plants. The Pennsylvania State Constabulary has been concentrated at commanding points. At other places the authorities have organized bodies of war veterans as special officers. At McKeesport alone 3,000 citizens have been sworn in as special police deputies subject to instant call. It is as though preparations were made for war."

War was indeed waged by the hated Pennsylvania police—"The Cossacks"—in the Pittsburgh area. They rode their horses straight into groups of strikers, clubbed anyone within reach, invaded homes of "agitators", and broke up meetings at the slightest excuse. Scores of workers were arrested without warrants and imprisoned summarily.

HARASSMENT

Mounted police were uninhibited about harassing steel workers and sympathizers. Rudolph Dressel was standing in front of a Homestead barbershop when "the state constabulary on duty . . . stopped directly in front of me and demanded that I move on . . . Before I had time to comply I was struck on the head."

SOLIDARITY

Strike pickets included sympathetic war veterans and union leaders. Seen at the side are Philip Murray, future head of the CIO; James Maurer, president of the Pennsylvania Federation of Labor; peering from behind Mother Jones is bare-headed William Z. Foster, secretary of the committee that organized the strike.

ARRESTS

Many strikers were rounded up and jailed on trumped-up charges. Even reporters were arrested as "suspicious persons found trespassing on privately owned property."

427

THE "COSSACKS" RIDE AGAIN

Despite martial law repression by mounted "Cossacks," the morale of the steel workers remained high until the tables were turned by large-scale use of strike-breakers, many of them Negroes who had come north during the war.

RELUCTANT BELLES TAKE A WALK

Above are some of the eight thousand New England telephone operators who also went on strike in 1919. Unwillingness of plant men to cross the ladies' picket lines "showed convincingly what can be done when workers stand together in solidarity". After a six-day tie-up the operators won higher wages. In the same year 35,000 New York garment workers (30,000 were women) left their jobs when their employers turned down demands for a shorter work week; below are strikers who went back to work after concessions were won.

VICTIMS OF HYSTERIA

The Industrial Workers of the World found themselves hounded down by Justice Department agents as well as vigilante groups.

A raid on an IWW hall in Centralia, Washington, ended in the death of several persons, the lynching of Wesley Everest and imprisonment of seven Wobblies (upper left) for 25 years. Hysteria ran rampant in Centralia for a week; more than 1,000 persons suspected of being Wobblies were arrested.

All the furniture of the IWW headquarters in New York (lower left) was smashed during a raid by police seeking evidence of "dangerous . . . seditious activities."

THE I. W. W. OF SPECIAL PRIVILEGE---THE REPUBLIC'S MOST SERIOUS MENACE

Drawn for LABOR by Former Congressman JOHN M. BAER

OUTBREAK OF THE RED SCARE

Skillfully exploited, the postwar Red Scare ushered in an era in which there was far less concern with making the world safe for democracy than with making America safe from Bolshevism.

To be sure, there were disturbing manifestations of radicalism here and there but they hardly were such a clear and present danger to the republic as to warrant the hysteria whipped up by the raids conducted by Justice Department agents, the arrest of thousands of aliens, the enactment of "criminal syndicalism" and "anti-sedition" laws, and wild accusations that emanated from investigations by the Overman Committee of the U. S. Senate and the New York legislature.

Attorney General A. Mitchell Palmer was practically certain that the country was at the brink of disaster. "Like a prairie fire," he asserted, "the blaze of revolution was sweeping over every institution of law and order . . . It was eating its way into the homes of the American workman, its sharp tongues of revolutionary heat were licking the altars of the churches, leaping into the belfry of the school bell, crawling into the sacred corners of American homes, seeking to replace marriage vows with libertine law, burning up the foundations of society."

Communism, judging by disquieting press reports, was just around the corner. "Outside of Russia," warned the Literary Digest, "the storm center of Bolshevism is in the United States".

Labor unrest largely unrelated to radicalism was given a sinister cast that employers did not neglect to embellish. "The American businessman," as Frederick Lewis Allen points out in his informal history of the 1920's, "had come out of the war with his fighting blood up, ready to lick the next thing that stood in his way. He wanted to get back to business and enjoy his profits. Labor stood in his way and threatened his profits. He had come out of the war with a militant patriotism; and mingling his idealistic with his selfish motives, after the manner of all men at all times, he developed a fervent belief that 100-per-cent Americanism and the Welfare of God's Own Country and Loyalty to the Teachings of the Founding Fathers implied the right of the business man to kick the union organizer out of his workshop. He had come to distrust anything and everything that was foreign, and this radicalism he saw as the spawn of long-haired Slavs and unwashed East Side Jews. And, finally, he had been nourished during the war years upon stories of spies and plotters and international intrigue . . . His credulity had thus been stretched until he was quite ready to believe that a struggle of American laboring men for better wages was the beginning of an armed rebellion directed by Lenin and Trotsky . . ."

HOLY CRUSADE OF COMPANY UNIONISM

The post-war Red Scare fitted in perfectly with the massive campaign against trade unionism that employers launched under the flamboyantly patriotic banner of "The American Plan."

On its face the plan was motivated by a patriotic desire to protect the American way of life but in actuality it was designed to stamp out unionism—and it almost succeeded. Organized labor lost ground steadily throughout the 1920's; by the end of the decade practically all the gains won during the war years were gone.

"The American Plan" had its roots in an intensive drive in behalf of "open shops"—i.e., non-union shops. As early as 1919, William Barr, president of the National Founder's Association, could boast: "A partial but careful survey of irresistible activities in behalf of the open shop shows that 540 organizations in 247 cities of 44 states are engaged in promoting this American principle in employment relations. A total of 23 national industrial associations are included in these agencies. In addition, 1,665 local chambers of commerce are also pledged to the principle of the open shop."

By 1921 "The American Plan" had all the trappings and driving force of a great national movement. "Never before," reported Savel Zimand, "has America seen an open shop drive on a scale so vast as that which characterizes the drive now sweeping the country. Never before has an open-shop drive been so heavily financed, so efficiently organized, so skillfully generalized. The . . . drive flies all the flags of patriotic wartime propaganda. It advances in the name of democracy, freedom, human rights, Americanism."

Unions, employers contended, were obsolete. "They may have been justified in the long past," declared Elbert Gary, chairman of the U. S. Steel Corporation. ". . . I think the workmen were not always treated justly." But now there was "no necessity for labor unions"; "no benefit or advantage through them will accrue to anyone except the union labor leaders . . . The existence and conduct of labor unions, in this country at least, are inimical to the best interests of the employees, the employers, and the general public." Another captain of industry was no less blunt about the matter: "Unionism is opposed to efficiency. It destroys the esprit de corps . . . In its very essence it is antagonistic to the employer, it sets labor and capital into two distinct and inimical camps."

Sponsors of "The American Plan" spoke loftily of its purposes. The nation's employers were called upon to "break the shackles that have been forged upon the wrists of those who labor" and free their employees from "the false leadership of designing pirates who

parade in the guise of the workingman's friend." Rugged individualism was stressed: "Every man [ought] to work out his own salvation and not be bound by the shackles of organization to his own detriment."

The "yellow dog" contract became, ostensibly, a ticket to salvation. "We will not," declared A. M. Glossbrenner of the Indiana Manufacturers Association, "employ any individual in any part of the plant that does not sign an individual contract in which it is expressed that he is not and will not become a member of a labor organization while in our employ."

432

STICK TO YOUR JOB

The man who jumps from one job to another never learns enough about any particular class of work to become valuable in it.

EVERY BUSINESS HAS THREE PARTNERS

Capital—The Employer
Labor—The Employe
The Public—The Consumer

No industry can thrive if <u>Co-operation</u> among the <u>three</u> is lacking.

No business can succeed that has a dishonest or indifferent partner.

Each partner owes a duty to the others.

YOU ARE ONE OF THE PARTNERS

The open shop movement thrived on such posters.

WE ARE HUMAN 'ROUND HERE

OUR employes ARE NOT looked upon as mere cogs in the machines. They are the human masters of our machines.

They are looked upon as human beings with brains, hearts, hands and ambitions to do things. They are our WORKSHOP PARTNERS.

At the same time as employers, we are SOMETHING MORE THAN A MEAL TICKET. DON'T TRY TO PUNCH US FULL OF HOLES.

LET US HELP EACH OTHER

THE 4-LEAF CLOVER OF INDUSTRY

The business men and all good citizens in this community are in favor of industrial co-operation. We believe that co-operation is the life-giving stem of prosperity for those who pay wages, those who receive wages and those who spend the wages paid by our American factories, mines, mills, shops, etc.

Industrial peace is needed to win this war for democracy. Agitators are breeders of treason and this community has no room for them.

433

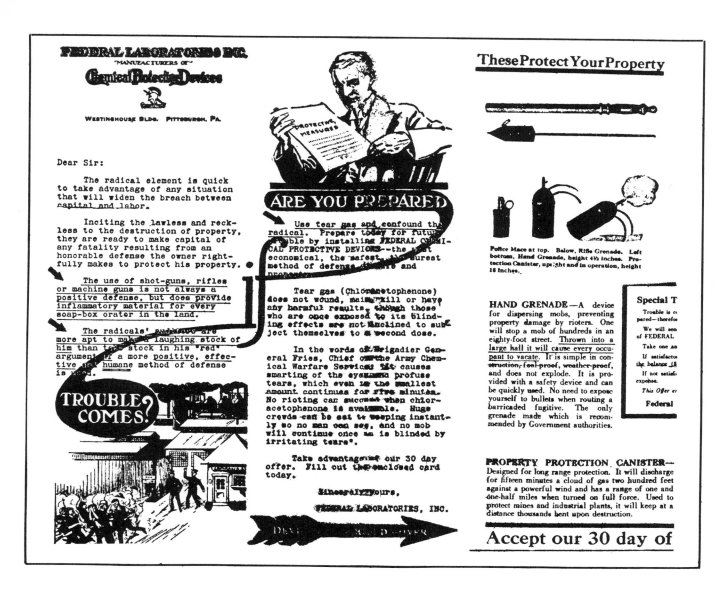

MERCHANDISING STRIKEBREAKING EQUIPMENT

A principal supplier of munitions for industrial use, Federal Laboratories Incorporated had close ties with strikebreaking entrepreneurs.

Eugene Ivey, a Southern manager for Federal, also ran the Atlanta office of the Railway Audit and Inspection Company. Harry Reston, vice president of Railway Audit, boasted in a letter to a prospective spy:

"Our organization is a very large one, covering the whole of the United States. We are engaged in what we call 'human engineering and work of general efficiency.' All large corporations such as mills and manufacturing plants desire to know what their employees are doing, what they are thinking about, and how they are conducting themselves both at work as well as outside of the plant after working hours.

"It is very difficult for the head of a plant to know conditions in his plant. If he could go and work among his employees without being known to them he could get very valuable information which would assist him in correcting some condition which might be bad. He cannot do this but he can do the next best thing— that is to call on such a concern as we are and have us send him a man who can become the eyes and ears of the head of the plant. In this way he can in almost every case, correct trouble before it breaks and causes either a strike or a very much dissatisfied condition amongst his employees . . . The manufacturer wants to know who his loyal employees are . . . On the other hand, he likes to find out who is disloyal in order that he may eliminate the ones who are undesirable."

During a street car strike in 1920 Railway Audit furnished men whose duties were "to obtain information as to the sentiment of the men toward the strike and furnish data which would be of value to the officers of the company in conducting the breaking of the strike."

UNDERCOVER SERVICES

The "Industrial Co-ordination" and "Production Engineering" services performed by the Sherman firm included espionage and strikebreaking for U. S. Steel, the American Woolen Company, and other employers.

In an indiscreet book entitled "Harmony in Industry," John F. Sherman told of spies who filed daily reports on union members, spread dissension among workers after winning their confidence, and caused the firing of "trouble-makers."

At the side are extracts from reports compiled for the Oliver Mining Company, a U. S. Steel subsidiary. They were brought to light by Frank Palmer, a resourceful labor journalist of the Federated Press.

Such undercover operations paid off quite handsomely during the 1920's.

2/2/22

One William Keenan came to Hibbing early in 1921 as Secretary of the Hibbing Central Labor Union (same as trades assembly) and also acted as delegate of the Hibbing Building Trades Council. He has been very active indeed in organization matters and is regarded as quite radical. His paid position was recently abolished, but he continues his activities. He has been quite busy of late organizing the building laborers and hod carriers.

When he came to Hibbing he was regarded as quite a competent man in the agitation line and has lived up to that reputation entirely. He came the e from St. Paul where he was reputed to be active in the same line. Our record shows him to have been the delegate of Local 132, Building Laborers and Hod Carriers of St. Paul, to the St. Paul trades assembly in 1920, and in that same year represented the same local as delegate to the Rochester Convention of the Minnesota State Federation of Labor.

Will you make careful inquiries as to his past? Has he a police record? Has he ever been indicted in the state court? Has any action ever been brought against him there for non-support or for divorce? Has he ever figured in any of the late radical activities there or in any of the labor troubles such as the street car strike? Any information you can get concerning him will be much appreciated.

CPP

RUPARCHICH (Ruparcich), FRANK S.,
118 East Hemlock.
Miner at Shenango Mine. Joined the American Federation of Labor. 12/19/18.
Member of Chisholm I. U. M. M. S. W. 2/28/19.
In good standing in union. 3/8/20.
Left service of Oliver Iron Mining Company in March 1919.
Joined I. U. M. M. S. W. 1/5/19; paid last dues May 1920-dropped. 1/13/21.
Donated 25¢ in support of Proletarec. 2/17/21.
Is satisfied with last election that two of their (laboring men) candidates were elected over steel trust nominees. 7/28/22.
Writes in Prosveta paper dated 8/7/22 advising the laboring men to stick together.
Writes in Prosveta that Oliver Iron Mining Company dismisses men without cause and if men are not for company's interests, also if over 45 years of age and worn out they are not kept either. 9/7/22.
Writes in Prosveta re-labor conditions, wages, etc., regarding employers towards laboring men. 12/9/22.
Writes in Prosveta in 11/3/23 issue.

WEEKLY SUMMARY OF LABOR ACTIVITIES IN DULUTH AND VICINITY

AND ON THE IRON RANGES FOR WEEK ENDING SATURDAY SEPTEMBER 20th, 1924.

BESSEMER, MICHIGAN.

September 14th. At a meeting of Bessemer Branch of Metal Mine Workers' Industrial Union, No. 210, of the I. W. W., today, it was decided to approve the action of Iron River, Michigan, branch in discontinuing the Upper Michigan District Committee of the I. W. W. and transferring the balance of the treasury of that organization to the recently organized Minnesota, Wisconsin and Upper Michigan District Committee with Headquarters in Duluth, because it was considered that the Duluth office could handle the business of the organization more efficiently, especially among the miners in the iron mining districts of the said states. The recommendation of the board of directors of orkers' Socialist Publishing Company for the employment of Lauri Masmi as field representative of the I. W. W. in the above mentioned district was also approved.

DULUTH, MINNESOTA.

September 14th. A. J. Heal, of Crookston, deputy president of the Order of Railway Conductors, and L. D. Kiser, of St Paul, of the Brotherhood of Railroad Trainmen legislative committee, conducted a meeting today for the purpose of organizing a LaFollette-Wheeler Club.

These cartoons about company unionism during the 1920's suggest why a contemporary critic charged that "The American Plan is a facade for repressing the labor movement. The gains made during the Wilson administration are being wiped out." Above is "The Company Union Holds A Meeting," a cartoon by Fred Ellis.

REPRESSION BY THE COURTS

Labor suffered increasingly at the hands of a hostile judiciary. Many of the gains it won during Wilson's administration were vitiated by a whole series of post-war court decisions.

In the case of Duplex Printing Press Company vs. Deering (1921) the Supreme Court upheld an injunction preventing members of a national union from boycotting an employer. The Justices ruled that the exemptions of the Clayton Anti-Trust Act applied only to workers directly involved in a controversy, not to members of affiliated unions engaged in boycotting. Again, in the case of United Mine Workers vs. Coronado Coal Company (1922), the court held that unions were in every respect like corporations and hence subject to the Sherman Anti-Trust Act.

Generally the decisions of the Supreme Court reflected the philosophy of William Howard Taft, its Chief Justice from 1921 to 1930. He did not disguise his feelings about "the irresponsibilities of labor unions." As far back as 1909 he declared in his Presidential inaugural address:

"Another labor question has arisen . . . in respect to the power of the federal courts to issue injunctions in industrial disputes. As to that, my convictions are fixed. Take away from the courts, if it could be taken away, the power to issue injunctions in labor disputes, and it would create a privileged class among the laborers and save the lawless among their number from a most needful remedy available to all men for the protection of their business against lawless in-

vasion. The proposition that business is not a property or pecuniary right which can be protected by equitable injunction is utterly without foundation in precedent or reason. The proposition is usually linked with one to make the secondary boycott lawful. Such a proposition is at variance with the American instinct, and will find no support, in my judgment, when submitted to the American people."

One of the relatively few court decisions that came down on the side of labor was that of New York Supreme Court Justice Robert F. Wagner in the case of Schlesinger vs. Quinto. This case involved a complaint by the International Ladies Garment Workers Union that the Cloak and Suit Manufacturers Protective Association had breached a contract under which weekly wage rates were supposed to replace piecework compensation. Justice Wagner's opinion is especially interesting as a commentary on equality of bargaining power in an industrial society:

"While the application [of restraint on an employer] is novel, it is novel only in the respect that for the first time an employees' organization is seeking to restrain their employers' organization from violating a contractual obligation.

"It is elementary, and yet sometimes requires emphasis, that the door of a court of equity is open to employer and employee alike. It is no respecter of persons—it is keen to protect the legal rights of all. Heretofore the employer alone has prayed the protection of a court of equity against threatened irreparable illegal acts of the employee. But mutuality of obligation compels a mutuality of remedy. The fact that the employees have entered equity's threshold by a hitherto untravelled path does not lessen their right to the law's decree."

JUDICIAL MUZZLING

Taking their cue from Supreme Court decisions under Chief Justice William Howard Taft, judges handed down innumerable injunctions. Gompers inveighed against "judicial muzzling" at the National Industrial Conference but U.S. Steel chairman Elbert Gary grinned urbanely.

MILITANCY ON
THE RAILROADS

Railway labor also suffered a disastrous blow at judicial hands.

Following a Railway Labor Board decision authorizing wage cuts totaling $60 million, 400,000 shopmen—boilermakers, sheet metal workers, machinists, electricians, and carmen—went on strike early in July, 1922. Even before they put down their tools, Attorney General Harry Daugherty laid the groundwork for a court order against the strike "on the grounds [that] it is a conspiracy and an interference with interstate commerce" although he was officially advised that "a proceeding involving bitterly contested questions of employer and employees should not be begun unless clear warrant of law for it exists. It is not enough that some authority or plausible reason may be found for it . . . There can be no question that by common law as expounded by the courts a mere strike, leaving out all elements of force, intimidation, secondary boycott, etc., is not illegal . . . [Moreover] it is well known that the Congress definitely refused to set up compulsory arbitration under the terms of the [Railroad Transportation] Act of 1920."

President Harding denounced the strikers as violators of law and enjoined them from interfering with the operations of the railroad. Encouraged by this support, the railroads proceeded to hire thousands of strikebreakers. Many, according to the New York Times, were "thugs, gunmen, sharks, second-story men and ex-bootleggers . . . The bum who a year ago panhandled his way from park to park and into one jag after another has for the last several months been a personage. Sought after and welcomed by all the rival strikebreaking organizations, fly-by-night detective agencies, fake industrial bureaus and upstart employment headquarters, he has been depended upon to help break the strike and keep it broken."

Attorney General Daugherty was clearly determined to break the strike at any cost. "So long and to the extent that I can speak for the government of the United States," he declared, "I will use the power of the government within my control to prevent the labor unions of the country from destroying the open shop."

Just as the strike was about to collapse early in the fall it was delivered an extraordinary coup de grace. Acting at the request of Attorney General Daugherty, Federal Judge James Wilkerson (who owed his bench appointment to Daugherty) issued the most sweeping injunction ever laid down in a labor case. It not only enjoined strike activities of every sort but also prohibited any form of aid to the strikers "by letters, telegrams, telephones, word of mouth, oral persuasion, or suggestion, or through interviews to be published in newspapers or otherwise . . ."

The breadth of Judge Wilkerson's prohibitions, the scope of the actions restrained, and the conditions under which the injunction was obtained so angered the entire labor movement that an AFL call for a general strike was only narrowly averted.

DISCONTENT OVER RISING LIVING COSTS

While working class parents march in protests against increased living costs, New York youngsters raid a cinder pile near the East Side. Such scenes took place during hard times after World War I.

Ironically, the prosperity of the twenties was accompanied by heavy unemployment, particularly in industries in which technology outran consumer ability to purchase high priced goods.

Between 1920 and 1929 machines displaced 3,272,000 men in manufacturing, railways, and coal mining; while many were gradually reabsorbed by the economy, more than a million workers remained jobless.

In New York unemployed and low-paid workers hard put to make ends meet joined in protests against inflation, rising rents, and evictions. In the photo at the side an organizer of the Anti-Rent League is seen enrolling members.

Convinced that Sacco and Vanzetti were convicted chiefly because of their radical views, many persons in and out of the labor movement demanded that they be given a new trial. In 1927, after their case had dragged on interminably, they were sent to the electric chair.

"If it had not been for this thing," said Vanzetti in his last words, "I might have lived out my life, talking on street corners to scorning men. I might have died unmarked, unknown, a failure. Now we are not a failure. This is our . . . triumph. Never in our full life can we do such a work for tolerance, for justice, for man's understanding of man, as now we do by an accident. Our words—our lives—our pains—nothing! The taking of our lives—lives of a good shoemaker and a poor fish-peddler—all! The last moment belongs to us—that agony is our triumph!"

In New York City a crowd gathered in Union Square on the day Vanzetti and Sacco were to die. Someone hung out of an office window a sign reading, "Vanzetti Murdered!" At this awful moment, according to the New York World, "the crowd responded with a giant sob. Women fainted in fifteen or twenty places. Others, too, overcome, dropped to the curbs and buried their heads in their hands. Men leaned on one another's shoulders and wept. There was a sudden movement in the street to the east of Union Square. Men began to run around aimlessly, tearing at their clothes and ripping their straw hats, and women cried in anguish."

THE PASSION OF NICOLA SACCO AND BARTOLOMEO VANZETTI

Two obscure Italian workingmen—Nicola Sacco and Bartolomeo Vanzetti—became martyrs of the Red Scare under circumstances that appeared to be more closely related to their radicalism than to positive proof that they had killed a factory paymaster during a holdup in South Braintree, Mass., on April 15, 1920.

For years Sacco and Vanzetti had been agitators among immigrant workers. At the time of their arrest they were in the midst of stirring up protests over the death of an Italian printer who had been subjected to "strong-arm interrogation" by Justice Department agents.

During their trial Judge Webster Thayer frequently alluded to their radicalism. "This man," he said of Vanzetti in remarks to the jury, "although he may not actually have committed the crime attributed to him, is nevertheless morally culpable because he is the enemy of our existing institutions . . . [his] ideals are cognate with crime."

STRIKES IN THE SOUTH

Long smoldering flames of bitterness flared up among Southern textile workers in 1929.

Above is a photo of Gastonia, North Carolina, mill hands who went on a strike spawned by the National Textile Workers Union, a Communist group. Their grievances were low pay, long hours, "stretchout" production methods, and unsanitary toilets.

In nearby Marion later in the year deputized strikebreakers opened fire at pickets fleeing from tear gas fumes. Six workers were killed and 25 wounded. Below is a photograph of funeral services at which an old mountain preacher expressed the sentiments of the strikers. "I trust, O God," he prayed, "that those friends will go to a better place than this mill village . . . Dear God, what would Jesus do if He were to come to Carolina?"

It made no difference to the mill owners that the Marion strike was organized by the United Textile Workers, an AFL affiliate. Snarled a company president: "I cannot see that there is any difference between this so-called conservative union and the Communist union at Gastonia."

National Guardsmen called out by Governor Max Gardner weren't deterred by the invective hurled at them by Gastonia mill girls who "didn't act like ladies."

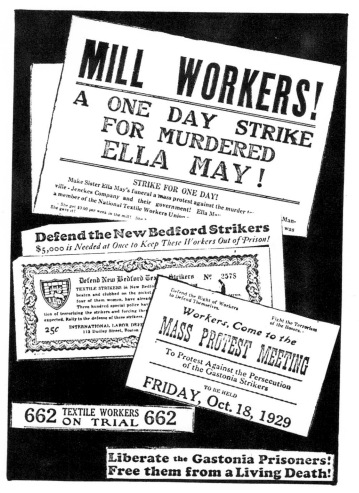

Conditions in Southern textile mills described by novelist Sinclair Lewis won sympathy for the strikers.

At the side are extracts from leaflets about the Gastonia strike. Ella May, a 29-year-old mother of five, was murdered while on her way to a union meeting. "Lord-a-mercy!," she cried out as vigilantes pumped shots toward her in broad daylight. One of the leaflets quoted a poignant ballad she had written:

> They locked up our leaders, they put them in jail,
> They shoved them in prison, refused to give them bail.
> The workers joined together, and this was their reply:
> We'll never, no, we'll never let our leaders die

These words became a rallying cry as the strike dragged on to its doomed end.

TEXTILE TROUBLES

Wielding both clubs and tear gas, Passaic police attacked both workers and sympathizers during New Jersey's eight-month long textile strike of 1926. The strike began with a walkout of workers employed at the Botany factory in Passaic but it soon spread to other textile mills in the area.

Albert Weisbord, left-wing leader of the strike, was a Harvard Law School graduate who had worked in a silk mill. Because of his devotion to their cause, Polish workers nicknamed him "Little Jesus."

COUNTERATTACK

While most unions lost ground to open shop employers, the Amalgamated Clothing Workers managed to make substantial gains. Composed largely of women who joined the labor force in large numbers during the late war, the union fought its way to supremacy in the men's clothing industry despite the anti-union climate of the 1920's.

President Sidney Hillman brought to collective bargaining ability as a negotiator who seldom demanded more than he knew an employer could afford to grant and firmly insisted that workers abide by their contractual agreements.

POLITICAL TRAIL BLAZING

Embittered by the setbacks of the post-war years—the witch hunts, the strike defeats, the depression of 1921-22, and the rise of company unionism—labor faced a bleak outlook as the elections of 1924 approached. Whatever influence it had in the Democratic Party was now at rock bottom; that was plainly evident in the party's nomination of John W. Davis, a Morgan partner, for the Presidency. As for Republican standard bearer Calvin Coolidge, no one had any illusions as to his conservatism on economic and social issues.

In short, labor had no place to go politically until it decided to take a fling at unabashedly partisan politics by endorsing Progressive Senator Robert M. LaFollette for the Presidency. For the AFL this meant a sharp break with its long standing aversion to engaging in independent political action; traditionally its officers had personally backed candidates of the major parties without making commitments for the federation as a whole.

Mainstay of LaFollette's support was the Conference For Progressive Political Action representing the International Association of Machinists, the railway brotherhoods, about two dozen national unions, eight state labor federations, the Farmer-Labor Party of Minnesota, the Socialist Party, the Farmers Union, the Non-Partisan League, and an assortment of liberal and reform groups.

The platform on which LaFollette ran was a mixture of farmer and labor demands directed at breaking the power of big business over the government, the courts, industry, and agriculture. It called for public ownership of the nation's water power, heavy inheritance taxes, reduction of taxes on individuals, lowering of tariffs, and farm relief. On behalf of labor, the platform demanded abolition of the injunction in industrial disputes, statutory recognition of the rights of unions, adoption of a child labor amendment, and repeal of the Esch-Cummins Railway Act.

Considering the handicaps of the Progressive Party, particularly its lack of funds and precinct machinery, the LaFollette ticket did surprisingly well. It ran up a vote of 4,822,000 (17% of the total)—the largest vote accorded a third party since the Republican Party made its debut back in 1856.

Coolidge got an easy popular majority but LaFollette received 59% as many votes as did Democrat Davis. Besides carrying Wisconsin, LaFollette ran second in California, Oregon, Minnesota, Iowa, North and South Dakota, Montana, Wyoming, Idaho, and Washington.

But a campaign that had opened in a mighty burst of enthusiasm and optimism ended in disillusion; the nation's labor vote clearly could not be delivered. Convinced of the futility of independent political action, the AFL returned to its cautious non-partisan policy.

In the picture at the top Samuel Gompers is shaking hands with "Fighting Bob" in the presence of the Senator's dapper eldest son. Below LaFollette is seen mapping campaign strategy with his running mate, Senator Burton Wheeler of Montana (seated in center), and David Niles. Looking on are Basil Manly and Robert LaFollette, Jr., who later succeeded his father in the U.S. Senate. During the New Deal days, Niles served as an aide to Roosevelt in relations with unions.

447

FEDERATION LEADERS

Seemingly unfazed by the difficulties they were encountering during the early 1920's, Gompers and other AFL leaders appeared to be in high spirits when the photo at top was taken. The woman beaming at the side in the front row is Florence Thorne, Gompers' devoted secretary for many years.

Below is a photo of the executive council's nucleus. In the front row, left to right, are Daniel Tobin (Teamsters), Gompers, Frank Morrison (AFL Secretary-Treasurer) and Matthew Woll (Photoengravers). Standing in the back are Thomas Rickert (Garment Workers), Frank Duffy (Carpenters), James Duncan (Granite Cutters), and Joseph Valentine (Moulders). Woll was generally regarded as Gompers' "crown prince," but succession was to go to William Green.

FAREWELL TO SAMUEL GOMPERS

The death of Samuel Gompers in 1924 was a great loss to the American Federation of Labor. Only a few months before he expressed his final wish. "I want to live for one thing alone—to leave a better labor movement in America and in the world than I found it in when I entered, as a boy, the field of industrial and humane struggle for the right." In accordance with his wishes, his casket was draped with the American flag he had taken to the annual conventions of the AFL.

WILLIAM GREEN TAKES OVER

Affable, apple-cheeked William Green, Gompers' successor as president of the American Federation of Labor, promised "to find a basis of accommodation, harmonize conflicting opinions, [and] settle differences which arise . . . among the family of organized labor." This was to prove somewhat more difficult than he realized at the time, but during the 28 years he reigned over the house of labor he remained steadfast in his adherence to the fundamental principles of trade unionism laid down by Gompers.

William Green was born into a mine family in Coshocton, Ohio, in 1873. His parents, Welsh immigrants, were as poor as their neighbors. At 16, lacking the money to follow his religious bent into the Baptist ministry, young William entered the mines beside his father. He had leadership qualities other miners quickly recognized and he gradually rose through the hierarchy of the United Mine Workers from local secretary to president of the Ohio district.

William Green was an all-around citizen, a joiner, a good fellow. He became an active member of the Elks, the Masons, and the Odd Fellows.

In 1913 he was elected secretary-treasurer of the United Mine Workers. That same year a vice presidency of the AFL became vacant; it was scorned by John Mitchell, then president of the UMW, who passed it on to Green. After Gompers' death in 1924, none of the powerful union heads who sat on the AFL executive council wanted any of the others to become the federation's president. Easygoing Bill Green turned out to be acceptable to all.

His accession was generally praised as evidence of the AFL's respectability and for a few years this seemed to be his principal concern. (Below he and other executive council members are seen during a West Point visit in 1926). But he gradually took a bolder stance as it became evident that the AFL was taking a beating at the hands of anti-union employers.

CLASHES WITH COMMUNISTS

Conflicts between unionists and Communists raised serious difficulties in some industries. The Communist-fostered Trade Union Educational League succeeded in capturing control over several New York needle trade locals. Racketeers who managed to infiltrate unions in the service trades also gave labor a black eye.

Participation in labor-oriented ballets and plays was part of the curriculum at the Bryn Mawr Summer School for Women Workers launched in 1921 with the help of trade unions and the National Women's Trade Union League. The object of the school was "to offer young women of character and ability a fuller opportunity to study liberal arts subjects in order that they may widen their influence in the industrial world . . . and increase the happiness and usefulness of their own personal lives."

Below is a photo taken during an evening session at the Rand School of Social Science in New York City. Leading sponsors of the school were the Amalgamated Clothing Workers and the International Ladies Garment Workers Union.

The Workers Education Bureau, a clearinghouse backed by the AFL, received help from historians Charles and Mary Beard and economist Stuart Chase. Brookwood College, wholly devoted to workers' education, was in operation at Katonah, New York.

CATASTROPHE IN THE COAL FIELDS

Appalling evidence of poverty in coal mine towns reflected the inevitable consequences of cut-throat competition, and rising consumption of oil, gas, and hydroelectricity. As markets dwindled, innumerable mine shafts were boarded up and hundreds- of thousands of miners faced unemployment or drastically reduced wages.

Coal operators broke their union contracts freely and the minefields became strike-torn battlegrounds. The United Mine Workers was confronted by the gravest crisis in its history; its membership plummeted from 500,000 in 1920 to 150,000 in 1929.

Conditions in the areas dominated by the Pittsburgh Coal Company, the nation's largest producer, deteriorated to an almost unbelievable degree. Upon returning from a visit to "Hell-in-Pennsylvania," a New York Daily News reporter wrote in 1925:

"I have . . . seen horrible things there; things which I almost hesitate to enumerate and describe. I can scarcely expect my story to be believed. I did not be-lieve it myself when the situation was first outlined to me. Then I went into the coal camps of western and central Pennsylvania and saw for myself . . .

"Many times it seemed impossible to think that we were in modern civilized America. We saw thousands of women and children, literally starving to death. We found hundreds of destitute families living in crudely constructed bareboard shacks. They had been evicted from their homes by the coal companies. We unearthed a system of despotic tyranny reminiscent of Czar-ridden Siberia at its worst. We found police brutality and industrial slavery. We discovered the weirdest flock of injunctions that ever emanated from American temples of justice.

"We unearthed evidence of terrorism and counter-terrorism; of mob beatings and near lynchings; of dishonesty, graft, and heartlessness . . .

"The mine fields are a bubbling cauldron of trouble. If it boils over—and it threatens to do so—blood must flow freely and many lives pay the forfeit."

"UNFIT FOR HUMAN HABITATION"

Like other workers who lived in squalid company towns, coal miners were subject to eviction if they participated in strikes or complained about housing conditions considered "unfit for human habitation."

"The position of the miners in company-owned houses is anomalous," the U. S. Coal Commission reported in 1922. "They are not tenants and have no more rights than a domestic servant who occupies a room in the household of the employer. The documents which pass for leases often give the company control over the social life of the families who live in the houses owned by the company . . ."

A typical lease required a Pennsylvania coal miner to agree "not to use, allow, suffer, or permit the use of said premises, or the private ways or roads . . . for any purpose other than going into [and out of] said premises from the public road . . . and, further, to do no act or thing whereby any person or persons whomsoever may be invited or allowed to go or trespass upon said premises, or upon said private ways or roads, or upon other grounds of the lessor, except physicians attending the lessee and his family; teamsters or draymen moving lessee and his family belongings into said premises or away from the same; and undertakers with hearse, carriages and drivers, and friends, in case of death of the lessee or any member of his family."

In short, occupants of company towns were virtually shut off from contact with the outside world—a point elaborated by attorney Winthrop Lane. In his book "The Denial of Civil Liberties in the Coal Fields" he wrote in 1924:

"These towns are not the independent, many-sided communities that most small towns are. They exist for the coal mines. They are the adjuncts and necessary accompaniments of an industry. In them everything is owned by the company that is extracting the coal. They stand on company land; they were built by the company; the store, the movie theater, the amusement hall, the little bank if there is one, the cafe, the ice cream parlor—all are run by the company. The school is often a company-built project, and so is the church; sometimes the company supplements the salary of the teacher and helps to maintain the minister. Roads leading through the town are private property. Not infrequently the post office is a corner of the company store and the man who sells crackers and meat is the postmaster. These towns are not incorporated. The company is responsible for whatever exists in the nature of a public utility—the supply of water, the lighting, the sanitation and so forth."

Fellow workers only marginally better off were good samaritans during strikes crushed by troops called out at the urging of coal operators.

On the eve of a massive strike in 1922, Secretary of Commerce Herbert Hoover saw no reason for federal mediation: "The government's position has long been known to be that sooner or later there would have to be a showdown in the mine fields. Its attitude is that if a strike must be, it must be, and the sooner the issue is disposed of the better."

DIFFICULT TIMES

These top officers of the United Mine Workers had much to be worried about when this photo was taken in 1922; the union was then experiencing a sharp decline in membership. Left to right are Thomas Kennedy (secretary-treasurer), P. T. Fagan (president of District 1), John L. Lewis (national president), Philip Murray (vice-president), and John Brophy, an organizer who later sought to wrest leadership of the UMW from Lewis. Both Murray and Brophy were to play leading roles in the CIO during the New Deal years.

"King Coal," a cartoon by Daniel R. Fitzpatrick, accompanied a St. Louis Post-Dispatch editorial denouncing mine operators who employed gunmen.

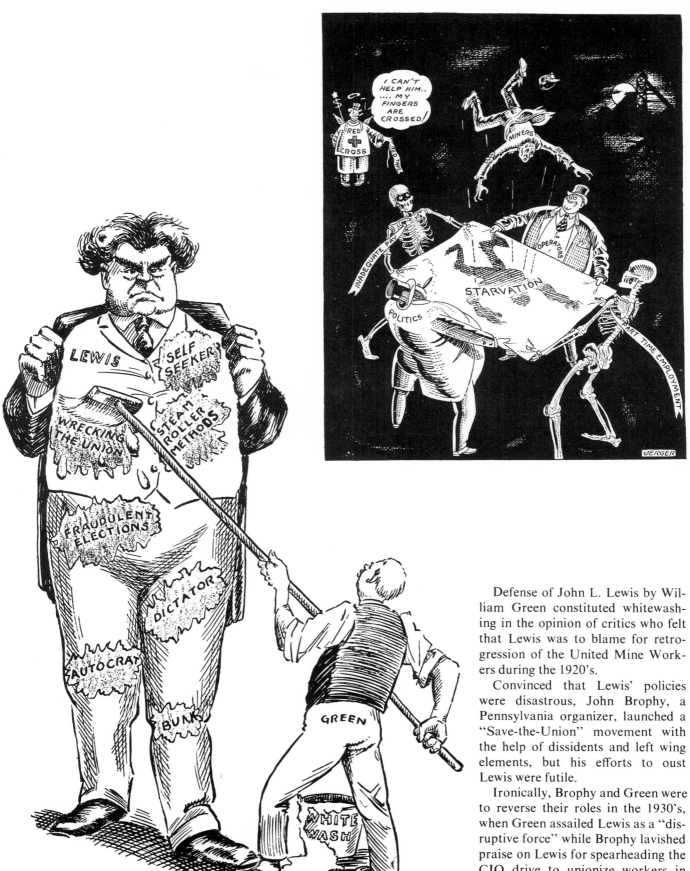

Defense of John L. Lewis by William Green constituted whitewashing in the opinion of critics who felt that Lewis was to blame for retrogression of the United Mine Workers during the 1920's.

Convinced that Lewis' policies were disastrous, John Brophy, a Pennsylvania organizer, launched a "Save-the-Union" movement with the help of dissidents and left wing elements, but his efforts to oust Lewis were futile.

Ironically, Brophy and Green were to reverse their roles in the 1930's, when Green assailed Lewis as a "disruptive force" while Brophy lavished praise on Lewis for spearheading the CIO drive to unionize workers in mass production industries.

ONSLAUGHT OF THE GREAT DEPRESSION

The plunge from "normalcy" to adversity that followed in the wake of the stock market collapse of October, 1929, did not shake President Hoover's optimism that all would soon be well. But as business failures increased, as factories drastically curtailed production, and as unemployment figures began to mount, it quickly became evident that the nation was entering a period of unparalleled depression.

While the economy careened downward, Hoover kept on escalating his rhetoric. "The fundamental business of the country," he declared in October, 1929, "is on a sound and prosperous basis." In January, 1930, he said there were "definite signs" that the nation had "turned the corner." On March 7th he was sure that "All evidences indicate that the worst effects of the crash upon unemployment will have been passed during the next sixty days." In May he announced "We have now passed the worst and with continued unity of effort we shall rapidly recover."

Even as Hoover said these things publicly he was privately conceding to Republican leaders that he anticipated a severe depression but all he was willing to do about it was go through almost meaningless motions. Shortly after the Wall Street crash, for example, he hurriedly called to the White House a brigade of prominent businessmen—including Henry Ford, Owen Young, Alfred Sloan, Pierre du Pont, and Myron Taylor—in whose behalf he blandly announced that they had agreed not to encourage any "movement for wage reduction." Hours later he met with top labor leaders—William Green, John L. Lewis, William Hutcheson, John Frey, Matthew Woll, and A. F. Whitney—and prevailed upon them to recommend that "no movement beyond those already in negotiation should be initiated for the increase of wages." Labor kept its promise but pay envelopes got thinner and thinner.

Meanwhile public incredulity was turning into panic. The American dream had become a nightmare. "We are not in a mere business recession," Senator Robert Wagner warned Congress. "We are in a life and death struggle with the forces of social and economic dissolution."

All over the country unemployment grew by leaps and bounds. By the spring of 1930—six months after the crash—over four million persons were out of work. The figure kept rising until it reached a peak of 15 million in 1935.

So devastating were the effects of the depression that even captains of industry spoke harsh words about the economic system that had previously served them so well. Owen D. Young, chairman of the General Electric Company, labeled unemployment "the greatest blot on our capitalistic system."

JULY, 1930: *Let's See . . . "*

DECEMBER, 1930: *" . . . a very serious problem . . . "*

JUNE, 1931: *"We have it . . . "*

DECEMBER, 1931: *"There Is No Work!"*

458

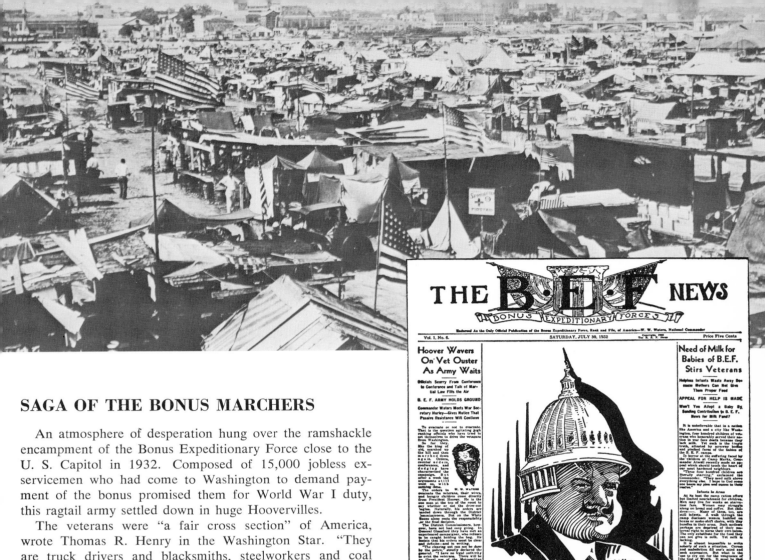

SAGA OF THE BONUS MARCHERS

An atmosphere of desperation hung over the ramshackle encampment of the Bonus Expeditionary Force close to the U. S. Capitol in 1932. Composed of 15,000 jobless ex-servicemen who had come to Washington to demand payment of the bonus promised them for World War I duty, this ragtail army settled down in huge Hoovervilles.

The veterans were "a fair cross section" of America, wrote Thomas R. Henry in the Washington Star. "They are truck drivers and blacksmiths, steelworkers and coal miners, stenographers and common laborers. They are black and white. Some talk fluently of their woes. Some can muster only enough English to tell where they came from and why. The Georgia drawl mingles with the characteristic patois of the New York sidewalks . . . But they nearly all have one thing in common—a curious melancholy, a sense of the futility of individual struggle, a consciousness of being in the grip of cruel, incomprehensible forces."

When Congress adjourned without conceding their demands many of the veterans gave up and went home. But several thousand stayed on because they had no place to go.

RESISTING EVICTION

The bonus marchers were peaceful enough until the capital's policemen sought to eject them from their tar-paper shanties. In the clashes that ensued two veterans were killed and eighteen were injured. But President Hoover felt relieved. "Thank God," he said "we still have a government that knows how to deal with a mob."

A LOST CAUSE

Acting under orders from President Hoover, troops led by General Douglas MacArthur succeeded in laying waste to the ex-servicemen's encampment. The Army accomplished its mission, but Hoover's reputation as a great humanitarian went up in the flames that set aglow the sky over Washington.

Long lines of hopeless, humiliated men were melancholy sights in most large cities. If you were hungry you didn't let pride stand in the way of a free meal—usually a bowl of soup and a crust of bread provided at charity kitchens sponsored by the Salvation Army and local relief agencies.

BREADLINES

EVERYWHERE

Some businessmen offered the government strange advice about how to feed the needy. John Nichols, president of the Oklahoma Gas Utilities Company, suggested to his friend Patrick Hurley, Hoover's Secretary of War, that restaurants be urged to dump left over food into five-gallon containers. The local unemployed could earn this food by chopping wood or performing other chores.

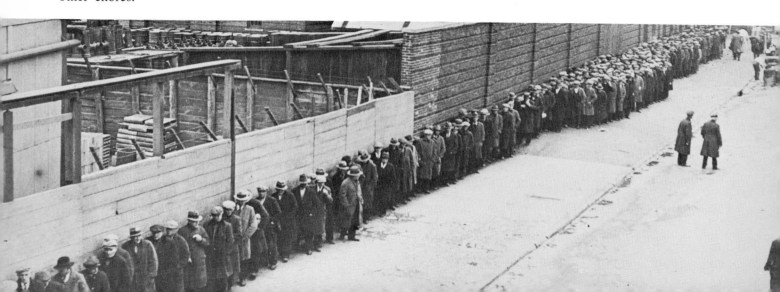

HOMES OF THE DESTITUTE

Hoovervilles sprang up in abandoned lots everywhere. Countless thousands of families lived like vagrants in shacks put together with packing case boards, rejected pieces of corrugated metal, strips of tar-paper and similar gleanings from city dumps. Seattle's makeshift colony (top photo) was neat by comparison with the huts erected in New York's tenement district as seen in the photo at the side.

In the South the dispossessed were permitted to live in tent communities on city outskirts.

HENRY FORD
ON UNEMPLOYMENT

I HAVE always had to work, whether any one hired me or not. For the first forty years of my life, I was an employe. When not employed by others, I employed myself. I found very early that being out of hire was not necessarily being out of work. The first means that your employer has not found something for you to do; the second means that you are waiting until he does.

We nowadays think of work as something that others find for us to do, call us to do, and pay us to do. No doubt our industrial growth is largely responsible for that. We have accustomed men to think of work that way.

In my own case, I was able to find work for others as well as myself. Outside my family life, nothing has given me more satisfaction than to see jobs increase in number and in profit to the men who handle them. And beyond question, the jobs of the world today are more numerous and profitable in wages than they were even eighteen years ago.

But something entirely outside the workshops of the nation has affected this hired employment very seriously. The word "unemployment" has become one of the most dreadful words in the language. The condition itself has become the concern of every person in the country.

When this condition arrived, there were just three things to be done. The first, of course, was to maintain employment at the maximum by every means known to management. Employment—hire—was what the people were accustomed to; they preferred it; it was the immediate solution of the difficulty. In our plants we used every expedient to spread as much employment over as many employes as was possible. I don't believe in "make work"—the public pays for all unnecessary work—but there are times when the plight of others compels us to do the human thing even though it be but a makeshift; and I am obliged to admit that, like most manufacturers, we avoided layoffs by continuing work that good business judgment would have halted. All of our non-profit work was continued in full force and much of the shop work. There were always tens of thousands employed—the lowest point at Dearborn was 40,000—but there were always thousands unemployed or so meagerly employed, that the situation was far from desirable.

When all possible devices for providing employment have been used and fall short, there remains no alternative but self-help or charity.

I do not believe in routine charity. I think it a shameful thing that any man should have to stoop to take it, or give it. I do not include human helpfulness under the name of charity. My quarrel with charity is that it is neither helpful nor human. The charity of our cities is the most barbarous thing in our system, with the possible exception of our prisons. What we call charity is a modern substitute for being personally kind, personally concerned and personally involved in the work of helping others in difficulty. True charity is a much more costly effort than money-giving. Our donations too often purchase exemption from giving the only form of help that will drive the need for charity out of the land.

*T*HE unemployed man is every one's concern, Henry Ford says — most of all the man's own concern. Being unemployed does not need to mean being out of work. There may be work even though one may not be hired to do it. Mr. Ford begins today a discussion of Employment, Charity and Self-Help as the three courses open to us in present conditions. He does not believe in routine charity because, he says, it is neither kind nor helpful. It does not get under the load or tackle the cause. He describes here a method he has followed. In the next issue of this publication he will discuss Self-Help.

Our own theory of helping people has been in operation for some years. We used to discuss it years ago—when no one could be persuaded to listen. Those who asked public attention to these matters were ridiculed by the very people who now call most loudly for some one to do something.

Our own work involves the usual emergency relief, hospitalization, adjustment of debt, with this addition—we help people to alter their affairs in common-sense accordance with changed conditions, and we have an understanding that all help received should be repaid in reasonable amounts in better times. Many families were not so badly off as they thought; they needed guidance in the management of their resources and opportunities. Human nature, of course, presented the usual problems. Relying on human sympathy many develop a spirit of professional indigence. But where co-operation is given, honest and self-respecting persons and families can usually be assisted to a condition which is much less distressing than they feared.

One of our responsibilities, voluntarily assumed—not because it was ours, but because there seemed to be no one else to assume it—was the care of a village of several hundred families whose condition was pretty low. Ordinarily a large welfare fund would have been needed to accomplish anything for these people. In this instance, we set the people at work cleaning up their homes and backyards, and then cleaning up the roads of their town, and then plowing up about 500 acres of vacant land around their houses. We abolished everything that savored of "handout" charity, opening instead a modern commissary where personal I O U's were accepted, and a garment-making school, and setting the cobblers and tailors of the community to work for their neighbors. We found the people heavily burdened with debt, and we acted informally as their agents in apportioning their income to straighten their affairs. Many families are now out of debt for the first time in years. There has appeared in this village not only a new spirit of confidence in life, but also a new sense of economic values, and an appreciation of economic independence which we feel will not soon be lost. None of these things could have been accomplished by paying out welfare funds after the orthodox manner. The only true charity for these people was somehow to get under their burdens with them and lend them the value of our experience to show them what can be done by people in their circumstances.

Our visiting staff in city work has personally handled thousands of cases in the manner above described. And while no one institution can shoulder all the burden, we feel that merely to mitigate present distress is not enough—we feel that thousands of families have been prepared for a better way of life when the wheels of activity begin turning again.

But there is still another way, a third way, so much better than the very best charitable endeavor that it simply forbids us to be satisfied with anything less. That is the way of Self-Help, which I shall discuss in the next issue of this publication.

Prepared and paid for by the Ford Motor Company as a contribution to public welfare.

Henry placed this advertisement in the Literary Digest of June 11, 1932.

EMPTY DAYS

For millions of Americans who were jobless, life was a dreary succession of listless days. William Green reported that in Detroit "men are sitting in the parks all day long and all night long . . . muttering to themselves." In New York City homeless men slept in the subways and hallways.

Are U. S. Business Leaders Morons?

ARE our business leaders morons?
Are they incapable of meeting evils begotten by their own activities?

Must they be regarded as irresponsible citizens, concerned only with money-making?

Are they willing to be accepted and adjudged as incapable of exercising business statesmanship?

Do our industrialists, financiers and other men of large affairs rate themselves as less competent than our politicians to grapple with social problems created by the economic revolution now under way?

Have those playing a foremost part in revolutionizing modern industry no qualms about making such a confession as this:

"Business is business. The objective of industry is to make money. We are determined to make money. We concentrate solely on that aim. If we are satisfied that a billion-dollar merger will mean greater profits, we go ahead and engineer it.

"One of the easiest ways to cut down expenses being to cut down salary and wage rolls, we of course lay men off right and left. If elderly workers have become less nimble because of their long years of service, they are the logical ones to be dropped first. Naturally, the greater resources at the command of the enlarged combinations are unstintedly used to acquire the very latest labor-saving machinery, enabling us to dismiss still more wage earners.

"In our eyes the most valuable executive is the one who can produce the most with the least amount of labor—the smallest number of workers and the smallest payroll. Our up-to-the-minute methods make it feasible for us to dispense with enormous numbers of workers—it is not uncommon for us to instal one machine which enables half-a-dozen men to do what formerly took half-a-hundred or even a hundred men.

"Yes, we know that through our creation of gigantic enterprises—manufacturing, distributing, retailing and every other kind—and through our vast expenditures on research, on invention, on machinery, we have caused grave dislocation of employment; but instead of being criticised for all this technological unemployment, we should be commended, since it is conclusive proof of our mastery of the science of management. What happens to all the hordes of workers we release is not our concern. Our responsibility begins and ends with running our business with surpassing efficiency, which means with a minimum of human labor.

"No, the unemployment thus created does not enter in any way into our calculations. Our bounden duty is to exercise every ounce of ingenuity we possess to do away with jobs, not to create them. Our objective is money, more and more money, not more and more men, but fewer and fewer men.

"We are much too engrossed in increasing profits to give a thought to what happens because of our reducing the number of workers. How to take care of unemployment is a problem for others to solve. Let George do that. Politicians talk as if they know how to solve the problem. Very well, let them go ahead and do it. Anyway, we haven't the time to bother with it. It isn't our worry."

American industry may disclaim that it *talks* that way, but it cannot disclaim that, collectively, it has *acted* that way.

Industry hasn't one organization, representing its best brains, devoting itself seriously, systematically, scientifically, to handling the whole subject of employment and unemployment.

There is no co-ordinated machinery for co-operating with the workless to find work. Industry feels perfectly free to dismiss breadwinners by the hundred and by the thousand without giving a thought as to how these breadwinners may succeed or fail in earning bread for themselves and their families.

This far-reaching evil cannot be airily dismissed with the superficial remark, "Panics always cause unemployment. There will soon be work for all."

The disturbing truth is that our economic revolution had released an abnormal number of workers even during our period of greatest prosperity. It is a commentary upon how this whole problem has been neglected that neither government nor industry has taken the pains even to keep track of the extent of unemployment from month to month, from season to season. It has been nobody's business to lie awake cogitating what happens to breadwinners denied opportunity to earn their bread.

Let industry take heed of this warning, written on the wall in starkly clear handwriting:

If industry itself confesses its indifference or its inability to wrestle with the problem of unemployment, including the older workers, depend upon it that the politicians will step in.

FORBES implores the best brains in industry and finance and business to get together before public opinion induces the politicians to institute drastic measures. We still have more faith in America's business statesmanship than in America's political statesmanship

This blunt editorial appeared in Forbes magazine in April, 1930.

BITTER FRUIT

You were lucky if you lived in a community that furnished needy families with free food. The choice was usually limited to fruits and vegetables close to decaying stage—but at least it wasn't necessary to sign a pauper's oath to qualify for such handouts. "I'd steal before I'd let my kids starve," a desperate laborer told a reporter.

Selling apples on street corners was thinly disguised begging. Buyers were expected to pay more than the price on the placard.

EROSION OF
THE HUMAN SPIRIT

Despair etched the faces of tens of thousands of up-rooted rural families forced off their farms by debt or drought. "The land of more than 500,000 of our farms is so poor," reported the Farm Security Administration, "that it means actual starvation for the families dwelling on them." Farm income dropped from $4.1 billion in 1930 to $1.5 billion in 1936. Tenants and sharecroppers were hit worst of all.

Their homes foreclosed, their savings gone, hundreds of thousands of destitute families loaded up their meager belongings and took to the open road in search of fruitful soil, of relief handouts, of jobs. Prosperity was supposed to be just around the corner but all they found were the seeds of despair and the grapes of wrath.

BEWILDERED NOMADS

Many families in acute distress took to living in tents. Some clustered together in camps lacking the most elementary conveniences. For food they were dependent on handouts, on what they could find in garbage dumps, and, in many instances, on what they could steal. Because they were transients, they were generally considered ineligible for public relief aid.

Foreclosures and bankruptcies multiplied at a dizzying pace as home owners fell hopelessly in debt.

VOICES OF REBELLION

The jobless and destitute who beseiged city halls and state capitols were turned away empty handed.

Hoover set a stubborn face against allocating federal funds for relief purposes. "I am opposed," he said, "to any direct or indirect government dole." Official subsidization of idleness was "an abhorrent notion" he could not in good conscience sanction. In his thinking the public interest was best served by reliance on private charity in times of social distress. Local relief, he suggested, should be kept as distasteful as possible to avoid encouraging shiftlessness and dependence on society.

(Jobless packinghouse workers are seen below as they marched through Chicago's stockyard district.)

"LAST HIRED, FIRST FIRED"

Unemployment among Negroes in the slum areas of New York, Chicago, Detroit, and other Northern cities was far greater than elsewhere. Many employers fired blacks to make room for whites who were willing to do menial work for low wages. Moreover, discrimination operated against Negroes in the distribution of relief, especially below the Mason-Dixon line.

Harlem and other Northern ghettoes were bursting at the seams because about 1,300,000 Negroes had migrated from the South since World War I only to find that de facto segregation was almost as bad as what they had previously experienced. Even when there were jobs during the 1920's they were usually the last to be hired; invariably they were given the least pleasant chores and few were allowed to do skilled work.

Victimized by the depression to a greater degree than whites, Negroes, were easily susceptible to the slogans of the International Labor Defense, a Communist front group that came to the aid of the Scottsboro boys and other blacks who didn't get a fair break at the hands of "lily-white justice."

A Negro song of protest went this way:

> Trouble, trouble, had it all mah day . . .
> Can't pawn no diamonds,
> Can't pawn no clo'
> An' boss told me,
> Can't use me no mo'.
> Rather get me a job, like white folks do.
> Trampin' 'round all day
> Say, 'Nigger, nothin' fo' you.'

For all practical purposes union doors remained closed to Negroes. Although the AFL opposed racial discrimination in principle, this policy had inconsequential effect on unions that kept tight control over whom they admitted into their ranks. An inevitable result was frustration and anger that played into the hands of Communist groups as well as anti-union employers who experienced little difficulty in drawing upon Negroes as a primary source of scab labor.

Winning the support of Negro workers in the unorganized mass production industries was to present a formidable challenge to the CIO. Simultaneously New Deal policies on civil rights were to play an important role in breaking down some of the formidable barriers to racial equality.

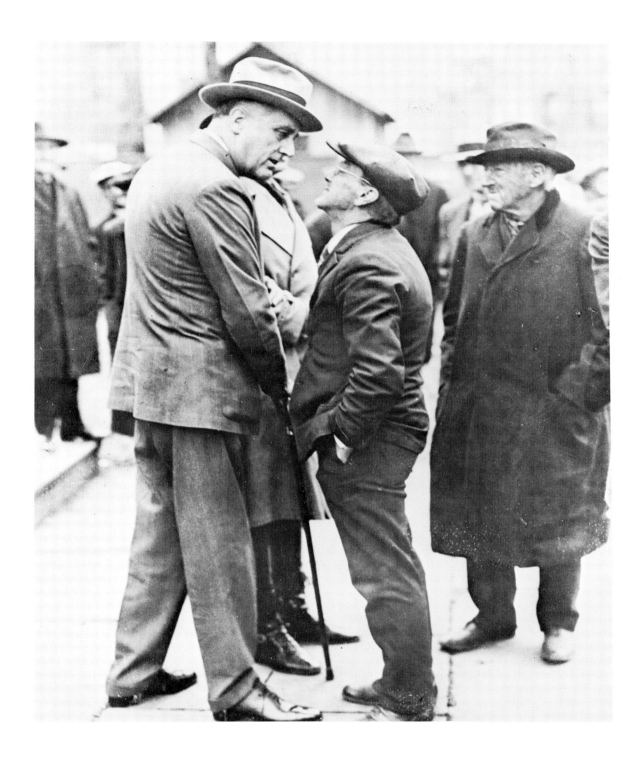

PRESIDENT ROOSEVELT LAUNCHES THE NEW DEAL

Seemingly a confidante of the man in the street, Franklin D. Roosevelt brought to the presidency a resolute determination to reverse the depression and establish long overdue economic and social reforms. "Our greatest primary task," he declared in his inaugural address on March 4, 1933, "is to put people to work. This is no insolvable problem if we face it wisely and courageously. It can be accomplished in part by direct recruiting by the government itself, treating the task as we would treat the emergency of a war."

MAN OF THE PEOPLE

From the moment Roosevelt became President he raised the spirits of the nation by giving top priority to the three R's of the New Deal—Relief, Recovery, and Reform. Breaking sharply with Republican policies, he turned the government around and attacked the depression with breath-taking boldness.

NEW CODES FOR OLD

A sharp break with laissez faire traditions, the multi-purposed National Industrial Recovery Act, boldest of New Deal measures, infused the nation with a hectic sense of excitement and hope.

"The law I have just signed," President Roosevelt explained "was passed to put people back to work—to let them buy more of the products of farms and factories and start our business going at a living rate again.

"In my inaugural I laid down the simple proposition that nobody is going to starve in this country. It seems to me to be equally plain that no business which depends for existence on paying less than a living wage to its workers has any right to continue in this country . . ."

General "Ironpants" Johnson, administrator of the NRA, is seen delivering a speech at a meeting of the American Newspaper Guild; he is flanked by Morris Ernst, the union's lawyer, and the Guild's founding president Heywood Broun.

477

RENEWAL OF CONFIDENCE

In exhorting the nation to support the NRA codes, President Roosevelt explained:

"Throughout industry, the change from starvation wages and starvation employment to living wages and sustained employment can, in large part, be made by an industrial covenant to which all employers shall subscribe. It is greatly to their interest to do this because decent living standards widely spread among our 125 million people eventually means the opening up to industry of the richest market the world has even seen. . .

"This is the principle that makes this one of the most important laws that has ever come from Congress because, before the passage of this law, no such industrial covenant was possible.

"I am fully aware . . . that wage increases will eventually raise costs. But I ask that management give first consideration to the improvement of operating figures and to the greatly increased sales to be expected from the rising purchasing power of the public. This is sound economics and good business. The aim of this whole effort is to restore our rich domestic market by raising its vast consuming capacity."

Of even greater importance from labor's viewpoint was an NIRA provision guaranteeing workers the right to organize or join unions of their own choosing. Section 7a stated:

"Employees shall have the right to bargain collectively through representatives of their own choosing, and shall be free from the interference, restraint, or coercion of employers of labor, or of their agents, in the designation of such representatives or in self or-

ganization or in other concerted activities for the purpose of collective bargaining or other mutual aid or protection."

This phrasing gave an almost debilitated labor movement a new and unexpected lease on life. Old unions began to flex their flabby muscles and new unions burst into action all over the country. The greatest gains took place among workers in coal mining, the garment trades, and the auto, rubber, steel, and textile industries.

But many employers made a farce out of Section 7a by organizing company unions they controlled lock, stock, and barrel.

"Although real gains were achieved by labor under the NIRA," according to Mark Starr, "the high hopes raised by the act were never realized. The immediate problem was enforcement of the labor provisions and of the codes, and this the federal government seemed unable to accomplish. National and local boards were set up to enforce the act, but they were soon swamped with complaints and proved inadequate. As the fact dawned upon labor that the NIRA was no short cut to a better day and that its enforcement was primarily their own responsibility, the number of strikes increased rapidly. The number of workers directly involved in strikes, which had sunk to 158,000 in 1930, increased to over a million in 1933 and considerably more in 1934. It was not only failure of government adequately to enforce the act, but also the refusal of business in many cases to obey the law that caused many of these strikes."

SETTLING LABOR-MANAGEMENT DISPUTES

Constantly beset by problems, NRA was hard put to satisfy the claims and counterclaims of both labor and management. Dishevelled Clarence Darrow (second from the left) is seen above as he presides at a hearing of the NRA Board of Review he headed; seated at his right is Charles E. Russell, a prominent Socialist. Below is an advertisement dealing with an NRA problem the National Labor Board was trying to settle.

FAREWELL TO ALMS

Employment provided by the Work Progress Administration gave millions of jobless men a sense of self-respect while they constructed innumerable public buildings, parks and playgrounds, hospitals, schools, and sewage systems. Jobless teachers, actors, artists and writers were also given WPA employment.

YOUTH GETS A HELPING HAND

An adjunct of the WPA nursed into existence by Mrs. Roosevelt, the National Youth Administration helped young people get "their chance in school, their turn as apprentices, and their chance for jobs."

Establishment of the agency arose out of anxiety about the acute problems youth suffered during the depression. "A needy youngster looking for work in the 1930's," according to Cabell Phillips, "was constantly confronted by this exasperating paradox: You can't get a job without experience and you can't get experience without a job. Young people were coming into the labor market at the rate of 1,750,000 a year. More than two-thirds of them went a year or more without finding a job. In 1935 those in the 16 to 24 age bracket (some three to four million) represented about a third of the total unemployed. Unable to continue their education, they haunted employment offices, loafed disconsolately or took to the road as migrants."

THE CIVILIAN
CONSERVATION CORPS

Enlistees in the Civilian Conservation Corps—mostly youngsters who had been roaming the streets in futile search for jobs—were put to work clearing forests, planting trees, draining marshlands, and preventing floods, They were paid a dollar a day, in addition to maintenance, but were required to allot $25 a month to dependents or needy relatives.

"No one," Roosevelt declared in a speech about the CCC, "will ever be able to estimate in dollars and cents the value to the men themselves, and to the nation in morale, in occupational training, in health, and in adaptability to later competitive life."

During a visit to a CCC camp, Roosevelt, was accompanied (top left) by Secretary of Interior Harold Ickes, Secretary of Agriculture Henry Wallace, brain truster Rexford Tugwell, and Robert Fechner, head of the CCC. Fechner, a former vice president of the Machinists Union, is seated to the right of FDR.

$522,000,000 Road Bill Signed

President Paves Way for Three-Year Plan
to Continue Recovery Steps.

WASHINGTON, June 18 (A. P.).—President Roosevelt
today signed the Hayden-Cartwright bill authorizing
22,000,000 for road cons...

15, 1934.

**OVER AND UNDER THE RIVERS:
TWO MIGHTY PROJECTS START**

Triborough Bridge and Midtown Hudson Tunnel Are Speeded
To Create Employment and to Ease Traffic Burden

HERALD TRIBU

**Moses Projects
Vast Play Area
In East River**

Municipal Recreation Spot
as Big as Central Park
Expected to Open in '36

0-Acre 'Fill' Proposed

VOL. LXXXIV....No. 2

**JONES PICTURES RFC
AS AID TO NATION
IN DEPRESSION WAR**

**U.S. To Mobilize 40,000
Jobless School Teacher**

Plans Illiteracy Campaign To Help Unemployed
2,000,000—Also To Help Unemployed
Fit Selves For Trades

NEW YORK SUN, MONDAY, JANUARY

RFC Gets $50 Million More

But Roosevelt Restricts Cash Withdrawals
to 500 Million Until Feb. 1, 1935.

WASHINGTON, Jan. 22 (C. P.).—Cash withdra...

THE WEATHER
Today: Rain
Tomorrow: Probably rain and
much colder

VOL. XCIII No. 31,829

**R.F.C.'s Spending
Spurt Starts Year
At 32 Million a Day**

Levine
As O'C
Shout

Tribune

EDITION

SUNDAY, AUGUST 19, 1934.

**Roosevelt Assures Loan
For a City Power Plant
That May Sell to Public**

BEYOND RELIEF: THE LARGER TASK

Hopkins Sees as the Three Ultimate Goals: A Maximum of Private Employment; a Permanent
Structure of Public Works to Take Up the Slack; and Unemployment and Health Insura...

Jobs were provided on a score of fronts through a bewildering maze of agencies.

SOCIAL SECURITY PROTECTION

A keystone measure of the New Deal, the Social Security Act of 1935 laid the foundations for unemployment insurance, old age pensions, aid to dependent children, rehabilitation of the physically handicapped, and improvement of public health. Funds for unemployment compensation were provided through a federal tax on payrolls.

Among those who surrounded President Roosevelt when he signed the act were Representative Robert Doughton, Senators Robert Wagner and Robert LaFollette, Jr., Secretary of Labor Frances Perkins, and Representative David J. Lewis.

In the picture below social security pioneers John R. Commons (right) and Edwin Witte are seen at a ceremony at which Voyta Wrabetz, chairman of the Wisconsin Industrial Commission, gave N. B. Ruud the state's first unemployment compensation check on August 17, 1936. Wisconsin was the first state to establish an unemployment insurance system.

Special to THE NEW YORK TIMES.

Social Security Bill Is Signed; Gives Pensions to Aged, Jobless

Roosevelt Approves Measure Intended to Benefit 30,000,000 Persons When States Adopt Cooperating Laws—He Calls the Measure 'Cornerstone' of His Economic Program.

WASHINGTON, Aug. 14.—The Social Security Bill, providing a broad program of unemployment insurance and old-age pensions, and counted upon to benefit some 30,000,000 persons, became law today when it was signed by President Roosevelt in the presence of those chiefly responsible for putting it through Congress.

Mr. Roosevelt called the measure "the cornerstone in a structure which is being built but is by no means complete." He was referring to his program for economic rehabilitation.

He added that the present session of Congress would have become historic had it done nothing beyond completion of this law. The text of the measure as originally introduced was published in THE NEW YORK TIMES Jan. 18.

The President said he hoped that three members of a board provided by the law to supervise the social projects could be named before the Congress session ended.

He gave no indication of the persons he had in mind for these posts, but it was reported that among possible appointees are Arthur J. Altmyer, Assistant Secretary of Labor, and Murray Latimer, chairman of the Railroad Pensions Board, an organization now in abeyance because the Supreme Court declared unconstitutional the law establishing the board. The third member will be a political appointee.

The signing took place in the Cabinet Room of the White House offices, where motion picture and still photographers had been invited to record the event as a result of the President's desire to obtain the widest possible publicity for the measure, which he said had not received due publicity because of the press of other news.

Among about thirty persons who stood grouped around the President as he read a statement and then signed the act were Secretary Perkins, Senator Wagner, who was one of the first advocates in Congress of legislation of this character; Representative Lewis of Maryland, co-author with Senator Wagner of the bill; members of the Senate Finance Committee, headed

Continued on Page Four.

UNEMPLOYMENT INSURANCE

484

Snooping—Tagging

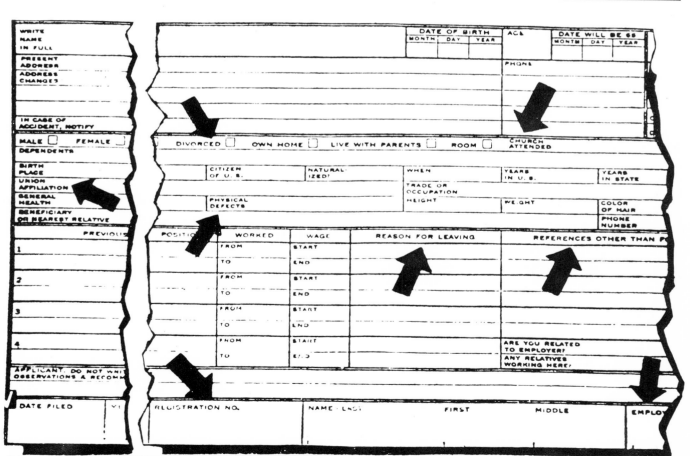

AROUND HIS NECK HE WORE A TAG

Each Worker Would Be Required to Have One for the Privilege of Suffering a Pay Cut Under the Social Security Act Which Is Branded as a 'Cruel Hoax'

FAKES

Items like these were used to discredit social security legislation. At the right is a leaflet employers placed in pay envelopes. Underneath is a privately contrived registration form publicized by the Hearst papers as though it was a government - issued document.

NOTICE

Deductions from Pay Start Jan. 1

Beginning January 1, 1937, your employer will be compelled by law to deduct a certain amount from your wages every payday. This is in compliance with the terms of the Social Security Act signed by President Franklin Delano Roosevelt, August 14, 1935.

The deduction begins with 1%, and increases until it reaches 3%.

To the amount taken from your wages, your employer is required to pay, in addition, either an equal or double amount. The combined taxes may total 9% of the whole payroll.

This is NOT a voluntary plan. Your employer MUST make this deduction. Regulations are published by

SOCIAL SECURITY BOARD

WASHINGTON, D. C.

FACSIMILE OF APPLICATION ON WHICH WORKERS WOULD BE FORCED TO REGISTER UNDER NEW DEAL'S SOCIAL SECURITY PROGRAM

The Arrows Indicate Some of the Information Sought, Prying Into Intimate Secrets of the Worker's Life

Both Frances Perkins and Eleanor Roosevelt were to exert enormous influence on New Deal social welfare and labor policies.

The first woman ever named to a Cabinet post and the first Secretary of Labor not to be drawn from the hierarchy of organized labor (which induced a furor in the AFL), Madam Perkins was a one-time social worker who had served as New York State's Industrial Commissioner. Because of her background she was inclined, in the opinion of Arthur Schlesinger, Jr., "to be more interested in doing things for labor than enabling labor to do things for itself; and her emphasis as Secretary was rather on the improvement of standards of work and welfare rather than on the development of labor self-organization. But this was in part a result . . . of the long indifference of the labor movement to improving its position through legislative action . . . For Madam Secretary the overriding objective, once emergency problems of hunger and want had been met, was to construct a permanent system of security through social insurance."

Not content with presiding over White House social functions, Mrs. Roosevelt shattered First Lady traditions by taking an activist role in implementing New Deal reforms.

Top: Sidney Hillman, leader of the Amalgamated Clothing Workers who became a trouble-shooter for President Roosevelt. Center: William Green and Matthew Woll conferring with FDR. Bottom: Green chatting with Senator Robert Wagner, author of the National Labor Relations Act.

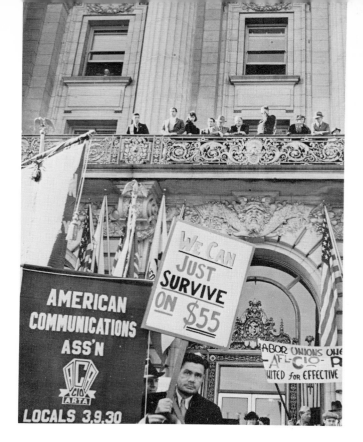

RUMBLINGS ON THE LEFT

Beset by critics on both the left and the right, the New Deal found itself simultaneously charged with doing too much and too little. Leftist elements fanned the flames of discontent among the unemployed in California (upper left) and Kansas (right). In New York, Socialist leader Norman Thomas (bottom) called for "more far-reaching economic reforms" while Communist marchers denounced "American imperialism" as a threat to the security of Soviet Russia. Unlike the Communists, Socialists considered the New Deal well-intentioned but short-sighted in its policies and programs.

Panaceas devised by Upton Sinclair (upper left) and Dr. Francis Townsend attracted enormous followings. Dr. Townsend's plan had the virtue of grade school simplicity: payment of $200-a-month pensions to all persons over sixty years of age would reinvigorate the economy and create jobs for the unemployed. In 1935 there were 10,000 Townsend Clubs with a reported membership of 5,000,000. Sinclair's Epic (End Poverty in California) formula called for employment of the jobless by self-supporting cooperatives run along Socialist lines.

Townsend Plan supporters John L. Lewis, president of the United Mine Workers, and Senator Burton K. Wheeler, the Progressive Party's candidate for the Vice-Presidency in 1924, are seen at the left with Dr. Townsend. Other allies of the movement were the Rev. Charles Coughlin, founder of the National Union for Social Justice, and Dr. Gerald L. K. Smith, a rabble-rousing clergyman.

FORMULA
FOR EDEN

Born in the depths of the depression, the Technocracy movement hatched by eccentric engineer Howard Scott stirred messianic excitement. If, Scott argued, politicians and businessmen would abdicate to high-minded technicians, the nation's economy could achieve full employment, full production, and abundance for all.

In a Technocratic society unencumbered by the profit system, consumption would be scientifically balanced with production in such a manner that every family would get the equivalent of $20,000 a year in return for a four-day, twenty-hour work week.

Scott proposed that work energy ("ergs") become the primary basis of both money and prices.

Stuart Chase saw in Technocracy "the most arresting challenge which the American industrial system has ever faced." But the movement dissolved when it became evident that Scott's statistics and charts lacked credibility.

PITCHED BATTLE IN MINNEAPOLIS

These pictures tell the story of the violence that occurred during the strike of Minneapolis truck drivers in May 1934. Adamant refusal by local employers to comply with Section 7a of the NRA Act frustrated settlement efforts by Farmer-Labor Governor Olson and the National Labor Board.

TROOPS FIRE ON FLEEING OHIO STRIKERS
213,000 ON STRIKE; VIOLENCE GROWS
STRIKE PERILS COAST, CITIZENS FLEE

Bitter struggles marked the rise of organized labor during the New Deal years.

While employers were generally not at all averse to reaping the benefits accorded them by National Recovery Administration codes forbidding price cutting and other "unfair" trade practices, most went out of their way to avoid compliance with NRA strictures regarding the treatment of labor. A few, like Henry Ford, flatly refused to adhere to Section 7a requirements, but many employers simply set about organizing company unions that could be counted upon to do their bidding. Predictably, organized labor's response was a wave of strikes, especially in mass production industries.

STRIFE INCREASES

"Today labor stands patient and hopeful," the Cleveland Plain Dealer told its readers in 1933. "Never has there been a period of depression so free from labor strife. Unemployment has harassed it. Closed factories have taken away its livelihood. But, in the face of enormous hardship, labor has showed its good citizenship and sturdy American stamina. Labor deserves a salute." Less than a year later, jobless men were rioting in the streets of Cleveland.

BLOODY THURSDAY
IN SAN FRANCISCO

On the sidewalk lay the dead bodies of a long-shoreman and a ship's cook. About a hundred other workers were injured during a brutal battle with San Francisco police on "Bloody Thursday"—July 5, 1934.

Trouble had been brewing up and down the west coast ever since longshoremen became aware of their rights under the National Industrial Recovery Act. They had lots of grievances, but most of all they were fed up with the "blue book" and hiring hall practices which perpetuated blacklisting and blatant favoritism. Antipathy toward the "shape-up system" was expressed this way by Harry Bridges, an ex-seaman who emerged as spokesman for the longshoremen:

"We have been hired off the streets like a bunch of sheep standing there from six o'clock in the morning, in all kinds of weather; at the moment of eight o'clock, herded along the streets by the police to allow the commuters to go across the street from the Ferry Building, more or less like a slave market in some of the Old World countries of Europe."

But San Francisco employers were in no mood to tolerate a massive strike that tied up the city's port. It was at their behest that Mayor Angelo Rossi called out the police on Bloody Thursday. In retaliation a general strike paralyzed San Francisco for four days until employers and longshore workers agreed to arbitration terms through which the men won most of their demands.

LEADERS OF MARITIME WORKERS

Formation of the National Maritime Union under the leadership of Joseph Curran (above) set in motion forces that were to make American seamen the highest paid of all who sail the seven seas.

Insurgent elements in the AFL-affiliated International Seamen's Union rallied behind Curran's rough-and-tumble militancy. By the time the NMU held its first convention in the midst of widespread strikes on east coast ships, its ranks included 30,000 seamen who had switched allegiance from the ISU. The goals of the new union included unification of all maritime workers "regardless of creed, color, nationality, or political affiliation."

During the first few years of its existence the NMU was beset by difficulties from within and without. To charges that it was Communist-inspired, Curran replied that "ours is not a political organization, it is not committed to the support of any political program . . . it is controlled by the rank and file." In time such charges diminished as leftwing elements in the union were purged.

At the top of the adjoining column are leaders of the AFL Seamen's Union who locked horns with Curran in jurisdictional battles; Harry Lundeberg, president of the union is the central figure.

Harry Bridges, president of the West Coast Longshoremen's Union, is seen at the bottom. He and his wife are in a discussion with the union's attorney. Bridges, an Australian-born longshoreman, rose from the ranks during the 1934 maritime strikes.

Even tear gas and police clubs couldn't stop picketing of Rochester, New York, factories by members of the Amalgamated Clothing Workers. Clashes finally ended when employers agreed to negotiate with the union and comply with labor relations requirements of the National Recovery Administration's newly formulated codes.

THEY KNEW WHAT THEY WANTED

Expressing their feelings in no uncertain terms, pickets outside a cotton mill in Greensboro, Georgia, jeered at company guards.

Encouraged by NRA codes establishing minimum wages and maximum hours, thousands of textile workers poured into union ranks in 1934, but many mill owners resisted collective bargaining. A general strike encompassing almost the entire textile industry broke out in September. Hours after it started troops with fixed bayonets began charging at pickets outside mills in North Carolina and Georgia. Scores of organizers were arrested and fourteen workers were killed. After three weeks of near-civil war, the strike was halted at the urging of President Roosevelt, but settlement proposals made by an investigating board he appointed were ignored by a majority of employers.

SIGNS OF THE TIMES

Outspoken placards like those seen at the side helped win an election at the Rutter-Rex factory in New Orleans. Below is a photo of Mrs. Gifford Pinchot, wife of Pennsylvania's newly-elected governor, in the vanguard of a demonstration in Allentown. Seated in the photo at the bottom are Jacob Potofsky and Joseph Schlossberg, leaders of the Amalgamated Clothing Workers union.

Prior to unionization by the Amalgamated Clothing Workers, sweatshop conditions prevailed in Allentown and Lancaster shirt factories. "In many instances," a state investigator reported, "the working hours are 60 to 72 a week. The Pennsylvania law limits the hours for women and children to 54. But it is being violated constantly . . . A number of cases have been reported where child workers were forbidden to stop work long enough to eat lunch. Boys and girls were fired for taking a bite out of a sandwich."

Some Allentown child workers were so young that their employers provided places for them to "hide out" when factory inspectors came around. One shop boarded up its windows so that passers-by could not see the children working on Sunday.

STARING DOWN THE SCABS

Hostility is barely concealed by these striking coal miners blocking access to a company store at Ducktown, Tennessee. Led by John L. Lewis, the revitalized United Miner Workers union was rapidly regaining much of the strength lost during difficult times in the 1920's.

HOLLYWOOD STARS GO UNION

Movie actors were also organizing along trade union lines. Above is a photo taken during an unpublicized meeting of founders of the Screen Actors Guild in 1933. Seated left to right are Alan Mowbray, Lucille Gleason, Boris Karloff, Ralph Morgan, and Noel Madison. Behind them are Kenneth Thomson, Jimmy Gleason, Ivan Simpson, Richard Tucker, Clay Clement, Claude King, Alden Thomson, Bradley Page, Morgan Wallace, and Arthur Vinton.

Below is a picture of members of the Guild's board of directors during the late 1940's: Edward Arnold, Walter Pidgeon, Jane Wyman, Dick Powell, Robert Montgomery, George Murphy, Ronald Reagan, Lucille Ball, Robert Taylor, and Gene Kelly.

The Guild's roster of presidents has included Ralph Morgan, Eddie Cantor, Robert Montgomery, Edward Arnold, James Cagney, George Murphy, Walter Pidgeon, and Charlton Heston.

CREATION OF THE
NEWSPAPER GUILD

Roly-poly Heywood Broun seemed to enjoy haranguing newspaper publishers.

"After years of holding down the easiest job in the world I hate to see other newspapermen working too hard," he told readers of his widely syndicated column in 1933. "It embarrasses me even more to think of newspapermen who are not working at all." Noting that printers and other craft-union members were better off than editorial workers, he became convinced that newsmen needed a union. "There should be one," he wrote. "Beginning at nine o'clock on October 1, I am going to do the best I can to help in getting one up."

But newsmen throughout the country who had been thinking along similar lines didn't let unionization wait that long. Locals began springing up in Cleveland, New York, and Chicago. A few months later Broun became the first president of the American Newspaper Guild. Subsequently he had little time for poker, horse races, and his other favorite pastimes.

Below is a photograph of Broun with members of the executive board of the American Newspaper Guild.

CHICAGO'S LABOR CHIEF Says...

"Excellent Union conditions prevail on the Herald and Examiner and the Evening American. These newspapers are deserving of the support of all American Federation of Labor men and women."

John Fitzpatrick

PRESIDENT, CHICAGO FEDERATION OF LABOR

CHICAGO HERALD AND EXAMINER
CHICAGO AMERICAN

GROWING PAINS

While a few of the early Newspaper Guild contracts were negotiated harmoniously, most were won through strike action.

The Hearst papers capitulated in Chicago and Milwaukee only after a protracted battle in which Guild members "demonstrated extraordinary tenacity" despite lack of support from entrenched craft unions.

At the side is a photo of Guildsmen who put out their own paper during a newspaper strike in Philadelphia.

SPIES INCORPORATED

Hearings of the Senate's Civil Liberties Committee headed by Senator Robert M. LaFollette, Jr., produced shocking revelations of ruthless efforts by employers to smash unions and intimidate workers through espionage and strong-arm tactics. A committee report covering the period 1933-1937 disclosed that 2,500 leading corporations relied on spies, stool pigeons, and agents to carry out anti-union activities.

Subpoenaed records of three detective agencies specializing in "industrial security" showed that they employed 3,871 operatives to report on union affairs, stir up trouble, and generally frustrate labor organization activities. Most of the operatives infiltrated unions and some even managed to become union officers. One group of companies spent more than $9,440,000 for spies, strikebreakers, and munitions.

Senator LaFollette displayed a photo of the Memorial Day massacre during hearings which convinced his committee that tragedy had not been provoked by demonstrators, that they could have been disbanded without loss of life, and that the subsequent investigations by Chicago authorities were prejudiced.

"The public cannot afford to let . . . industrial espionage go unnoticed," the committee declared. "Through it private corporations dominate their employees, deny them their constitutional rights, promote disorder and disharmony, and even set at naught the powers of government."

The record of the committee was studded with confessions by labor spies and strikebreakers, admissions by plant managers, and indiscreet letters showing that scores of corporations were grossly contemptous of collective bargaining.

2432 VIOLATIONS OF FREE SPEECH AND RIGHTS OF LABOR

Senator LA FOLLETTE. Mr. Young, have you found that industrial strife and strikes have been helpful in increasing your industrial business?

Mr. YOUNG. Yes, I would say; but the percentage would be relatively small, very small.

Senator LA FOLLETTE. Do you make any special effort to get business when strikes are threatened or under way?

Mr. YOUNG. Well, I think I would put it this way: if there is impending possibility of riot, we would make an effort to have the equipment available.

Senator LA FOLLETTE. I did not mention a riot; I mentioned strikes.

Mr. YOUNG. Well, strikes are only one cause of a riot. I wouldn't limit it to that, Senator; I would say to any cause of a riot.

Senator LA FOLLETTE. Do you make a special effort to get busine. in connection with strikes?

Mr. YOUNG. Not any more so than we would with bank hold-ups or——

Senator LA FOLLETTE (interposing). Do you make such an effort?

Mr. YOUNG. That is a part of our sales work, to get business where there is a demand for our product.

Senator LA FOLLETTE. Do you make a special effort to get it in view of strikes or contemplation of strikes?

Mr. YOUNG. I wouldn't say a special effort; I would say a normal effort.

S_____der

501

VIGILANTES ROAM THE STREETS

Weapons used by vigilantes during strikes were often obtained from arsenals stocked by anti-union employers, according to findings of the LaFollette Committee. Above is a photo of "citizen-police" roaming the streets of Ambridge, Pennsylvania, during the Spang-Chalfant strike in 1933. Below is a picture of "loyal workers" who blocked off access to a Monroe, Michigan, steel plant during a strike in June, 1936. It later turned out that many of these "loyal workers" were imported strikebreakers.

These photos, taken in October 1933, show deputized gunmen of steel companies attacking pickets outside the Spang-Chalfant Tube plant in Ambridge, Pennsylvania. Bullets felled fifteen of the fleeing strikers as tear gas billowed through the streets. One worker, shot in the back, died while being rushed to a hospital. Terror reigned in Ambridge for weeks.

BERGOFF'S STRIKEBREAKERS

·Strong-arm strikebreaking, an increasingly lucrative business, was also denounced by the LaFollette Committee. Its investigation disclosed that detective agencies and firms specializing in industrial security drew heavily on the services of gangsters whose chief source of income had dried up since the repeal of prohibition in 1933.

Unlike labor spies, strikebreakers operated out in the open, relatively speaking, although their association with employers remained clandestine. Their worth was measured by the number of strikers they were able to put out of commission with weapons such as brass knuckles and rubber truncheons.

The Bergoff Industrial Service, a major supplier of strikebreakers, boasted that it helped smash 300 strikes between 1905 and 1935. During the strikes against Goodyear, Firestone, and Goodrich in 1934 Bergoff developed the stratagem of creating back-to-work drives which appeared to be supported by "loyal" workers. In actuality these drives were organized and run by professional strikebreakers and spies furnished by Bergoff. Their effectiveness in the Remington-Rand strike of the following year wielded such satisfactory results that they became the principal component of the "Mohawk Valley Formula" endorsed by the National Association of Manufacturers.

A confidential prospectus of services offered by the Bergoff agency included these details:

STRIKE PREVENTION DEPARTMENT

"This department is composed of men possessing natural leadership qualifications. Men of intelligence, courage, and great persuasive powers to counteract the evil influence of strike agitators and the radical element.

UNDERCOVER DEPARTMENT

"Our undercover department is composed of carefully selected male and female mechanics and workpeople. They furnish accurate information of the movements and contemplated actions of their fellow employees.

OPENSHOP LABOR DEPARTMENT

"This department is composed of an organization equipped to supply all classes of competent mechanics and workpeople to keep the wheels of industry moving during a strike.

PROTECTION DEPARTMENT

"This department is composed of big, disciplined men with military or police experience, for the protection of life and property."

At the side are candid camera photos of some Bergoff operatives. Peering out of an auto is "Chowderhead" Cohen; his "266 pounds of stoolpigeon" earned him both derision and hatred.

BATTLE OF THE OVERPASS

Ford Company "service men" didn't pull their punches when they encountered Walter Reuther, Richard Frankensteen, and other union men on May 26, 1937.

Armed with a permit allowing them to distribute leaflets, Reuther and Frankensteen (third and second from the right in the above photo) were standing on an overpass near the Ford River Rouge plant when they were attacked, knocked to the ground, stomped on, and kicked in the groin.

In uncontroverted testimony about what happened, Reuther told of his experience: "I made an attempt to protect my face by shielding [it] with my crossed arms. In the meantime I was being pounded in all parts of the head and upper body. Then I was knocked to the ground, where I was kicked and also beaten on the head again . . . And at a signal from the leaders I was thrown on my back on the concrete . . . I was kicked again in the head, temples, all parts of the upper body, and an attempt was made to hold my legs apart to kick me between the legs, but I squirmed enough so that they were not able to do that very successfully . . . I finally found myself lying beside Richard Frankensteen, who at that time was lying face down with his coat up over his head . . . [later] I was thrown down the stairway."

A few hundred feet away, some UAW members who were distributing handbills were also attacked.

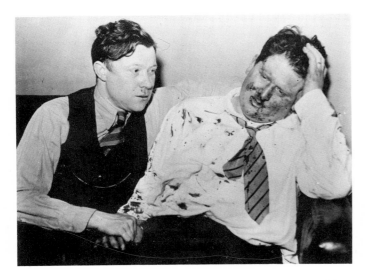

CHICAGO'S MEMORIAL DAY MASSACRE

Resistance to unionization by "Little Steel" companies came to a ghastly climax on Memorial Day, 1937, "the blackest day of modern labor history." Ten workers were slain and a hundred injured when 150 South Chicago police attacked an impromptu parade of Republic Steel strikers and their families.

The police "charged like a bunch of demons," Harry Harper testified. "No one had a chance in the world. I was knocked down by the impact of the officers surging forward. I received a blow that struck me in the face. I went down. I tried to get up and blood was streaming out of my left eye. It also affected the right eye partially but I still had a little vision. I managed to run a little, covering my face with one hand. With the right eye I could see officers charging in a circle, shooting with revolvers—not up but right into the crowd— I realized the danger I was in.

"I feared I was going to be shot so I fell into a hole. Before I fell into this hole I saw people being mowed down, like with a scythe . . . As I fell into this culvert there was a party lying there already. He said to me, 'Help me, buddy. I am shot.' And I said, 'I am helpless. I cannot help you.' I could not stay there much longer because just then a gas bomb fell into my face. It was choking me so I made one more attempt to go into the safety zone. But then I lost all sense of reasoning . . ."

Some of the strikers defended themselves by hurling stones at the police but most fled. Seven of the ten who lost their lives were felled by bullets that entered their bodies from the rear. Thirty of the marchers wounded by shots included a woman and three minors; 28 others were so badly beaten that they required hospitalization and 30 more sustained injuries requiring medical treatment. The police claimed that 35 of theirs were injured; three required hospitalization.

There is no evidence that Republic Steel had instigated the massacre but it had a close working relationship with South Chicago's police department. Republic president Tom Girdler had made extensive preparations for a violent conflict. Early in May he authorized the expenditure of $50,000 for munitions and by the end of the month Republic's private police force included 370 men backstopped by 552 pistols, 245 shotguns, 64 rifles, 143 gas guns, 2707 gas grenades, 178 billies, and 232 night sticks, and 58 gas billies.

Investigation by the Senate's Civil Liberties Committee, based in part on Paramount newsreel photos of the massacre, confirmed that the marchers had not provoked the attack. "The encounter of May 30th should never have occurred," the Committee concluded. "The loss of life cannot be defended as having been in defense of property . . . the very presence [of police] in unusual numbers invites disorderly incidents which in turn magnify themselves into clashes that produce death beatings."

The police charged at the Memorial Day marchers with riot sticks flying. Seemingly "crazed with passion," they showered blows indiscriminately, brutally attacking even the fallen. Some marchers found themselves the target of blows by several policemen. "One strikes him across the face, using his club as he would a baseball bat. Another crashing it down on top of his head and still another is whipping him across the back. Then one gives the fallen a final smash on the head before moving on to the next job."

PROTECTION OF COLLECTIVE BARGAINING UNDER THE NATIONAL LABOR RELATIONS ACT

Undeterred by Supreme Court nulification of NRA, the New Deal nudged labor ahead under the terms of the National Labor Relations Act authored by Senator Robert F. Wagner. Far and away the most significant American labor law ever enacted, the new measure guaranteed workers "the right to self-organization, to form, join, or assist labor organizations, to bargain collectively through representatives of their own choosing, and to engage in concerted activities for the purpose of collective bargaining or other mutual aid or protection."

Unlike Section 7a of the National Industrial Recovery Act, the Wagner law unequivocally encouraged the organization of bona fide trade unions and laid the basis for effective safeguards.

Employers were expressly forbidden to engage in unfair practices such as restraint of employees in their self-organization and collective bargaining activities, inter-ference with the operation of any union, discrimination against workers through employment conditions aimed at discouraging membership in a union, and refusal to bargain collectively with the duly elected representatives of employees.

Power to prevent such interference with the right of workers to bargain collectively was placed in the hands of the newly established National Labor Relations Board composed of labor and employer members. Although hamstrung by the refusal of many business firms to comply with the Wagner Act on the ground that it was unconstitutional, the board settled several thousand grievance cases during its first hectic year.

Finally, in April, 1937, the hand of the National Labor Relations Board was strengthened by a Supreme Court ruling that held workers were entitled to rights similar to those enjoyed by employers.

UNCLE SAM Protects You!

YOU CAN'T BE FIRED FOR JOINING THE UNION

THE WAGNER ACT (NATIONAL LABOR RELATIONS ACT) IS STILL LAW

- It Guarantees Your Right To Join a Union
- It Protects You Against Discharge or Discrimination

The Danville workers have united with Marshall Field and Erwin.
They are now negotiating for the benefits and protection of a union contract.

Cone Workers Join the Army of FREE LABOR
Enjoy Real Industrial Democracy

GET A SECRET, GOVERNMENT, LABOR BOARD ELECTION
SIGN A BLUE PLEDGE CARD TODAY

Tune In: Special Labor Day Broadcast, Governor Broughton, CIO & AF of L Leaders.
Monday — WBIG — 10:45 A. M.

TEXTILE WORKERS UNION OF AMERICA, CIO

National Labor Relations Board

OFFICIAL BALLOT

To determine the representatives for collective bargaining purposes for the employees of *NEW YORK BUTCHERS DRESSED MEAT COMPANY, Division of Armour & Company,* as described in Notice of Election, dated May 18, 1937.

1. This is a secret ballot.
2. Make your choice of organization to represent you by marking "X" in one square only.
3. Do not sign your name.
4. If you spoil your ballot, return it to the Board's agent and get a new one.
5. Fold your ballot to conceal the "X" you have made and deposit it personally in the ballot box in the presence of the Board's agent.

Do you Desire to be Represented for Purposes of Collective
Bargaining by the

Amalgamated Meat Cutters and Butcher Workmen
of North America, A. F. of L.?

YES	NO
☐	☐

This is a secret ballot and must not be signed

Workers Know Your Rights!

The President wants you to Join the Union.

The National Labor Relations Board, official U. S. Government agency created by the last session of Congress, has the legal power to hold an election in your plant, to let the workers decide for themselves which organization shall serve as their collective bargaining agency.

This is how the 11,000 General Electric workers in Schenectady, N. Y. defeated the fake company union and instead voted themselves into the United Electrical and Radio Workers and gained recognition from one of the most powerful employers in America. You, too, can do likewise.

The Steel Workers Organizing Committee just wrested the first 10 percent wage increase from the Steel Corporations in years, which started a train of wage rises throughout America. This is how you came to get yours.

But there is more where this came from. And you are entitled to more.

Your employer is compelled by Federal law to recognize your union as soon as a majority in your plant votes for it. Your employer is also forbidden by law to fire you for union activity. Even the most powerful U. S. Steel Corporation no longer dares fire workers for union activity. They have learned their lesson.

Backed by the most powerful unions in America, you elected a President of the United States. Now the Committee for Industrial Organization, of which John L. Lewis is Chairman, is helping you elect yourselves a Steel Workers Industrial Union.

How to get it:

1) Fill out the attached Application Blank. Seal in attached envelope. Drop in nearest mail box. No postage required.
2) As soon as a majority of you mail these in, the Union will demand that the National Labor Relations Board hold an election in your plant. Your employer will then be compelled to recognize your union.

One Big Industrial Union for All Workers in the Steel and Wire Industry

Sign this Application Now.
Tomorrow may be too late.

Don't wait for the other fellow.
Do it today. Hundreds have already done it.

NO INITIATION FEE

Here's How!

1. Fill out this Application.
2. Tear out carefully.
3. Seal and mail in attached envelope.

No postage required.
Only the Union has your vote.
The employer cannot reach you.
You have nothing to fear.
This is YOUR Declaration of Independence.

DO IT NOW!

AMALGAMATED ASSOCIATION OF IRON, STEEL
AND TIN WORKERS OF NORTH AMERICA
(Steel Workers Organizing Committee)
3600 GRANT BUILDING : PITTSBURGH, PA.

E. J. LEVER, Field Director
Philadelphia, Pa.

Date........................19.......

I hereby accept membership in the Amalgamated Association of Iron, Steel & Tin Workers of North America, through the Steel Workers Organizing Committee, and of my own free will hereby authorize the Steel Workers Organizing Committee, its agents or representatives to act for me as a collective bargaining agency in all matters pertaining to rates of pay, wages, hours of employment, or other conditions of employment.

Employed by ....
(Name of Company) .... (Department)

If not working check ☐

Name ....
Address ....
City ....

A Message to You
from the
PRESIDENT!
•
Use this Envelope for your reply.   No postage required.

Quick to take advantage of New Deal friendliness, both AFL and CIO unions launched intensive organization drives that seemed to have President Roosevelt's personal endorsement.

The favorable Supreme Court verdict on the constitutionality of the Wagner Labor Relations Act was a crushing blow to employers who had resisted compliance with the law. "Employees have as clear a right to organize and select their representatives for lawful purposes," the Court ruled, "as [a company] has to organize its business and select its own officers and agents. Discrimination and coercion to prevent the free exercise of the right of employees to self-organization and representation is a proper subject for condemnation by competent legislative authority. Long ago we stated the reason for labor organizations. We said that they were organized out of necessities of the situation, that a single employee was helpless in dealing with an employer...that union was essential [for workers] to deal on an equality with their employer..."

No tears were shed at funeral services for unfair labor practices. San Francisco maritime laborers burned hated "fink books" while steel workers sank an E.R.P. (Employee Representation Plan) casket in a river flowing past a Bethlehem Steel plant in Pennsylvania.

FINIS

INDUSTRIAL UNIONISM THE KEY

BIRTH OF THE COMMITTEE FOR INDUSTRIAL ORGANIZATION

Greatly invigorated by the New Deal, the trade union movement was "busting out all over," as one old timer put it. Workers were joining up by the tens of thousands, many of them entirely on their own initiative.

Some of the biggest gains were being made by unions that had suffered serious losses during the previous decade. Within the first few months of the NRA, the United Mine Workers added 300,000 new members and negotiated agreements in the formerly non-union coalfields of Kentucky and Alabama. By the middle of 1934 the membership of the International Ladies Garment Workers Union had trebled to 200,-000 and the Amalgamated Clothing Workers was larger by 50,000 members.

Simultaneously, the AFL sent scores of organizers into the automobile, rubber, steel and textile industries. Much progress was made through the establishment of temporary "federal" unions which were supposed to be split up between existing craft unions, but there was little inclination to heed the demand of United Mine Workers president John L. Lewis to mount an aggressive drive for organization of workers in mass production into industry-wide unions.

Lewis was not alone in his conviction that "the time has arrived when common sense demands that the . . . policies of the American Federation of Labor must be molded to meet present-days needs" by providing "for the organization of workers in mass-production and other industries upon industrial and plant lines, regardless of . . . claims based upon the question of jurisdiction."

On November 9, 1935, the leaders of seven other AFL-affiliated unions who agreed with Lewis joined hands in the establishment of the Committee for Industrial Organization "to foster recognition and acceptance of collective bargaining . . . in basic industries; to counsel and advise unorganized and newly organized groups of workers; [and] to bring them under the banner and in affiliation with the American Federation of Labor as industrial organizations."

But the Committee soon found itself in difficulties. AFL president William Green denounced it for fostering "dualism" and demanded that it discontinue its activities. In August 1936 the unions affiliated with the CIO were read out of the AFL; shortly thereafter the group changed its name to the Congress of Industrial Organizations.

"DUALISM AND DISUNITY"

The gulf between John L. Lewis and William Green was considerably wider than the aisle that separated them at a National Recovery Administration meeting in Washington. Ironically, Green endorsed industrial unionism long before Lewis had spoken out on the subject. "The organization of men by industry rather than by craft," Green declared in 1917, "brings about perfect organization . . . The causes of jurisdictional disputes are considerably decreased and in many industries can be eliminated altogether . . . When men are organized by industries they can concentrate their economic power more advantageously than when organized into craft unions."

Even after Green became the president of the AFL in 1924 he expressed similar thoughts but when Lewis launched the CIO Green felt that this constituted defiance of AFL policies and would foster "dualism and disunity."

Green was anxious to avoid an open break with Lewis forces. He took the position that the latter were dutybound to dissolve the CIO. "It is not," he asserted, "a question of the industrial union or craft union, and if I had the power of Providence himself I would place upon that statement all the emphasis I possess. That is not the issue . . The real issue, my friends, is this: Shall the American Federation of Labor, the organized labor movement of America, follow democratic procedure? Shall the movement be governed by majority rule? Shall the will of the majority of the membership of organized labor be the supreme law of the American Federation of Labor? That is the issue."

JOHN LLEWELLYN LEWIS

Nothing so became craggy-faced, bushy-browed John Llewellyn Lewis, president of the United Mine Workers and founder of the CIO, as his grimace during inspection of mine conditions.

"CAPTAIN OF A MIGHTY HOST"

Lewis never tired of identifying himself in terms that workers could easily understand:

"The thing that gives me strength is the fact that I am able correctly to interpret the aims of my people. I know the psychology of the coal miner. I know about his dreams and his ideals and trials and tribulations. I have lived with coal miners. I am one of them. My family has been associated with the mining industry for a century and a half and an understanding of the miners' problems is inbred in me . . .

"I have laid down in a mine tunnel with my face in a half inch of water, and pulled my shirt up over my head, expecting to die the next minute in an explosion I heard coming toward me. And when God performed a miracle and stopped that explosion before I died, I think it gave me some understanding of what men think about and how they suffer when they are waiting to die in a coal mine explosion. . .

"When I speak, I speak the thoughts of the membership of the United Mine Workers of America, because I understand them. I remain true to them and they remain true to me. . .

"As an individual, my opinions and my voice are of no more consequence in our world of affairs, or in the coal industry of the country, than the voice or the opinions of any passerby on the street. It is only when I am able to translate your dreams and aspirations into words that others may understand, that my tongue possesses any strength or my hand has any force.

"I have never faltered or failed to present the cause or plead the case of the mine workers of this country. I have pleaded your cause from the pulpit and the public platform; in joint conference with the operators of this country; before the bar of state legislatures; in the councils of the President's cabinet; and in the public press of this nation—not in the quavering tones of a feeble mendicant asking alms, but in the thundering voice of the captain of a mighty host, demanding the rights to which free men are entitled."

Key figures of the CIO: Sidney Hillman, Homer Martin, Lee Pressman, Lewis, and John Brophy.

In the adjoining pictures Lewis is seen with labor economist Leo Wolman and Pennsylvania Governor Gifford Pinchot (above) and New York Mayor Fiorello La Guardia (below).

LEADERS OF THE CIO'S INDUSTRIAL ASSAULT

As originally constituted, the CIO included, besides Lewis, seven union leaders who were convinced that the time was ripe for an intensive organization drive among workers in mass production industries:

Charles P. Howard, president of the International Typographical Union.

Sidney Hillman, president of the Amalgmated Clothing Workers of America.

David Dubinsky, president of the International Ladies Garment Workers Union.

Thomas F. McMahon, president of the United Textile Workers of America.

Harvey Fremming, president of the Oil Field, Gas Well, and Refinery Workers of America.

Thomas H. Brown, president of the International Union of Mine, Mill, and Smelter Workers.

Max Zaritsky, president of the Cap and Millinery Department of the United Hatters, Cap and Millinery Workers International Union.

Unlike other members of the committee, Howard, its secretary, and Zaritsky served as individuals without committing their organizations to CIO aims.

When the unions associated with the committee were expelled from the AFL in 1937, the top CIO leaders were the men seen in the above photo. Seated left to right are Sidney Hillman, James Carey (Radio Workers), John L. Lewis, and Philip Murray (Steel Workers). Standing in the rear are Emil Rieve (Textile Workers), R. J. Thomas (Auto Workers), Reid Robinson (Mine Mill and Smelter Workers), and Sherman Dalrymple (Rubber Workers). Murray and Hillman were vice-presidents and Carey secretary.

ORGANIZING IN THE OPEN FIELDS

Organization meetings frequently had to be held in the open fields because public halls could not be rented in towns dominated by anti-union employers. In one community the YMCA agreed to let a meeting be held in its gymnasium but at the last minute this was barred; the board of directors caved in to pressure from a company on which the YMCA was dependent.

Unwillingness of some local authorities to permit meetings was another problem, particularly during strikes, even though the Norris-LaGuardia Act protected the right of workers to publicize "the existence of, or the facts involved in, any labor dispute, whether by advertising, speaking, patrolling, or by another method not involving fraud or violence."

Inability to establish contact with workers and propaganda attacks on the CIO as a "Communistic organization" often resulted in election defeats for which the unions were taunted in newspaper ads.

This is how a textile mill owner publicized the fact that the majority of his workers decided they didn't want to join the CIO.

VICTORIOUS STEEL WORKERS

It was in the steel industry—the country's most basic industry—that the CIO concentrated its first organizing drive. Long a bastion of anti-unionism, steel had been festering with workers' grievances ever since the great Homestead strike was smashed in 1892.

In 1936 the average annual wage of a steel worker was $560, a third of the amount needed for a minimum standard of living. Working conditions were among the worst in the country. And living conditions were oppressively subject to the will of the steel companies. Many workers resided in company-owned homes, bought their food in company-owned stores, read company-owned newspapers, even worshipped in company-built churches.

Thus the steel industry was fertile ground for the CIO's Steel Workers Organizing Committee, headed by Philip Murray, a long-time vice president of the United Mine Workers.

The SWOC drive began in earnest in the mid-summer of 1936. Despite powerful employer opposition, or-

ganizers invaded the small shanty towns along the Monogahela River, flocked into Youngstown, Aliquippa, Gary, into the Middle West and South, wherever the furnaces of the great steel trust flamed and smoked into the sky.

"For the first time in the history of the United States," a financial weekly reported, "industrial management is faced with a labor movement which is smart and courageous, wealthy and successful—a movement, moreover, which is winning its [unionization] battle by applying a shrewd imitation of big business organization and technique."

Such thoroughness paid off. In March 1937 the U.S. Steel Corporation suddenly changed its life-long policy of opposition to organized labor and recognized the SWOC as bargaining agent, raised wages 10%, and established an eight-hour day. This success was followed by similar victories in other "Big Steel" plants. By July 75% of steel had been organized.

HIGH PRESSURE ORGANIZATION

As the SWOC intensified its organization drive, steel workers flocked to join up in plants with long standing anti-union policies. At the top on the right is a photo of Michael Musmanno addressing a 1936 meeting held at McKeesport, not far from Carnegie's Homestead mills, where unionism was stamped out in the great strike of 1892.

Jones-Laughlin workers are seen (photo on the right) voting for union recognition in an election supervised by the National Labor Relations Board in May, 1937. At the bottom, left, Benjamin Fairless, president of the Carnegie-Illinois Steel Corporation, is shaking hands with Philip Murray as they sealed an historic collective bargaining agreement in 1938. Standing directly behind Murray is Van A. Bittner, a field director of SWOC. The beaming gentleman in the center is David McDonald, who succeeded Murray as the president of the union.

ERUPTION OF SIT-DOWN STRIKES

Symbolic of the times, the massive sit-down strike of auto workers that broke out in December 1936 forced General Motors to come to terms with the CIO's fledgling United Auto Workers. The strike started at the Fisher plant in Flint, Michigan, but quickly spread to Detroit, Cleveland, and Toledo. Instead of walking out of the factories, the men sat down at their work benches and refused to leave until they had won union recognition and higher pay.

Throughout the 44-day strike, patrol, commissary, and sanitation committees maintained discipline. No smoking was allowed on production floors and liquor was prohibited. Supplies and food were provided by friends and relatives.

When guards tried to enter some plants, they encountered a hail of soda bottles, coffee mugs, and iron bolts. Police who returned with tear gas were driven back by streams of water from fire hoses. The "Battle of the Running Bulls" was won without any violence.

Hopelessly frustrated, General Motors obtained a Michigan court injunction for ejection of the strikers as trespassers on private property, but Governor Frank Murphy, sympathetic with the workers and fearful of bloodshed, was unwilling to order in the militia. Instead he called together officials of GM and the United Automobile Workers and persuaded them to negotiate. Not all of the strikers' demands were met but, as in the case of the "Big Steel" settlement, another anti-union bastion was captured. Chrysler and other auto companies capitulated several months later.

The success of the auto workers' sit-down techniques led to a wave of similar strikes in rubber factories, textile mills, and even department stores.

519

HOME WASN'T
LIKE THIS

Sit-downers in General Motor's factories made themselves at home despite the lack of normal conveniences. Car seats provided sleeping as well as lounge facilities. Although the strikers were deprived of heat during freezing weather, their morale remained high. "For seventy-five years," Upton Sinclair told a reporter, "big business has been sitting down on the American people...I am delighted to see the process finally being reversed." (Adjoining photos were taken at the Fisher plant in Flint, Michigan.)

GRIPES AND FRUSTRATIONS

Merchants who suffered losses during the auto strikes felt that the workers held out too long. Above is advice a Detroit restaurant offered its customers. Below are pickets displaying a sign offering "safe passage" to employees of the Kohler Company plant in Wisconsin. The company's aggressive anti-unionism frustrated the United Auto Workers for several decades.

THE LIE-DOWN VERSION
OF THE SIT-DOWN TACTIC

Woolworth sales girls who had no place to sit simply took to horizontal positions that attracted a great deal of publicity.

Charges that property rights were grossly violated didn't faze the strikers. "What more sacred right is there in the world today," demanded one labor leader, "than the right of a man to his job? This property right involves the right to support his family, feed his children and keep starvation away from the door. This is the very foundation stone of American homes . . . the most sacred, most fundamental property right in America."

The CIO didn't officially endorse sit-downs—or lie-downs—but it didn't go out of its way to discourage them until the need for such tactics ended when employers complied with the collective bargaining requirements of the National Labor Relations Act.

"Hello Momma. We're makin' history" is the caption Denys Wortman gave the adjoining cartoon.

522

FIGHTING FOR SURVIVAL

Determined to back up their husbands' demands for higher wages, wives were not at all lady-like when strike tensions mounted. These photos were taken during steel and auto conflicts in 1936-37.

"These Americans are afraid of Henry Ford," a New York newspaper asserted in its story about the above picture. "The man works for Ford. He has just joined the CIO . . . [We] wanted to photograph a Ford union man with his family. He said yes—this way. In the Ford empire few men feel free."

FEAR OF FORD WAS VERY REAL

Intimidated by Ford's efforts to prevent unionization, some employees took to wearing masks at public demonstrations and even in the privacy of their homes during visits by newspaper photographers.

"To keep the union out," the United Automobile Workers charged, "the Ford Service Department organized a system of surveillance that can only be compared to the Nazi Gestapo or the Russian Communist GPU . . . Ford agents took the license numbers of all the cars parked in the neighborhoods of Detroit union halls day or night.

"Harry Bennett, head of the Ford Service Department, boasted half his personal staff men were undercover spies in the union.

"Ford workers who were fired for joining the union were offered their jobs back if they would play along with the company.

"A priest, who was a Regional Director of the National Labor Relations Board, caught two Ford servicemen spying on a union meeting.

"Workers' overcoats were searched while they worked. Lunch buckets were ransacked. Ford spies stood around in bars, hotel lobbies, supermarkets, restaurants, listening for scraps of conversation which were turned in to the Service Department.

"Any worker suspected of belonging to the union was fired.

"When this became hazardous because of the operation of the law guaranteeing workers the right to belong to a union, a Ford service man testified before the NLRB, that 'if we could not get anything on a man—we'd frame him'."

Unlike employers who dodged compliance with the National Labor Relations Act, Henry Ford was bluntly hostile. "We shall never recognize the United Auto Workers or any other union," he declared. "Labor union organizations are the worst thing that ever struck the earth . . . they take away a man's independence . . . I have heard no complaints from our men. There is nothing a union can give them they haven't got. I haven't given the Wagner Act a thought. We've always had it in force."

Peaceful picketing during a Ford strike in April, 1941, erupted into violence when a worker tried to cross a picket line. Detroit News photographer Milton Brooks won a Pulitzer Prize for the picture below.

WORKING TO WIN THE WAR

The attack on Pearl Harbor brought government, labor, and management together in a common cause. Jointly they mounted a massive war production program that was to play a decisive role in defeating the Axis powers.

Immediately after the U. S. entered the war, the AFL, the CIO, and the railroad brotherhoods gave the nation a "no strike" promise which most workers faithfully lived up to. (Some strikes did, of course, occur but only 1/100 of 1% of all working hours between 1941 and 1944 were lost because of them).

Substantial contributions to winning the war were made as a result of labor's participation in and implementation of the programs carried out by the War Production Board, the National War Labor Board, and the War Manpower Commission. Recommendations by union leaders on the national level and by workmen on the local level (via thousands of labor-management factory committees) led to marked improvement in production efficiency although manpower shortages, absenteeism, and other problems created acute difficulties. An output rise of nearly 90% between 1941 and 1945 made possible such achievements as the

production of 300,000 airplanes, 71,000 naval vessels, 45,000,000 tons of merchant shipping, 2,700,000 machine guns, 86,000 tanks, and 2,500,000 trucks.

According to Secretary of Labor Frances Perkins, President Roosevelt was "enormously impressed" by what he saw during semi-secret wartime visits to factories and shipyards. "He was [especially] enthusiastic about the speed, skill and precision of the workers of America. He was delighted and heartened by the warmth and affection of their spontaneous welcome to him when, unannounced and unexpected, [he] turned up in the middle of a factory and said, 'Hello, what are you doing?' to John Jones or Sally Smith."

Keeping production lines moving motivated the War Labor Board's formulation of the maintenance-of-membership principle assuring unions that their growth would not be stunted by their willingness to forego their right to strike. Union membership increased at the rate of about a million workers a year between 1941 and 1945. The greatest gains were in the steel, shipbuilding, aircraft, and automotive industries. Unions in the metal trades almost tripled their membership. By 1945 the United Automobile Workers had 1,052,000 members—the largest membership recorded by an American union up to that time.

Under the War Labor Board's "Little Steel" formula wage rates were limited to a maximum of 15% above the level prevailing in January, 1941, but a large number of workers became entitled to fringe benefits such as paid vacations and holidays, shift differentials, and insurance and pension plans.

However, average real weekly earnings in manufacturing remained surprisingly low. They rose from $28.12 in 1941 to a wartime peak of $36.72 in 1944.

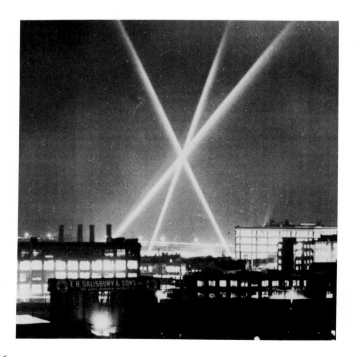

Carpenters and other construction workers almost tripped over each other as they hurried to their jobs on defense projects launched by the government. Below is a scene near Camp Blanding, Florida.

BUSY
SHIPYARDS

Running to and from work absorbed lots of energy at the Bethlehem Fairfield shipyards in Pennsylvania. The picture below was taken during a change of shifts at the Electric Boat Works in Groton, Connecticut.

HOME FRONT MUSCLE

Enthusiastic support of all-out production for victory was evident at rallies organized by the American Federation of Labor and the Congress of Industrial Organizations.

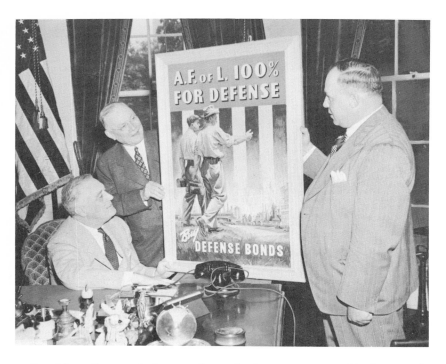

PRESIDENTIAL APPRECIATION

President Roosevelt frequently took time to express his interest in labor's wartime services. He is seen above with AFL president William Green and secretary-treasurer George Meany. Below is a photo taken when merchant seaman were invited to the White House. Balding Joseph Curran, president of the National Maritime Union, is barely visible behind FDR.

Higher wages and stabilized employment were reasons for smiles. Photographer Carl Mydans caught the above faces just as a new shift began. Below is a picture by Ben Shahn, who later attained fame as an artist.

Discriminatory hiring practices gave way substantially in wartime industries as a result of a presidential executive order issued shortly after a protest march on Washington was announced by A. Philip Randolph, leader of the Brotherhood of Sleeping Car Porters. Some unions that had previously refused to admit Negroes relaxed their rules, but prejudice remained a formidable problem.

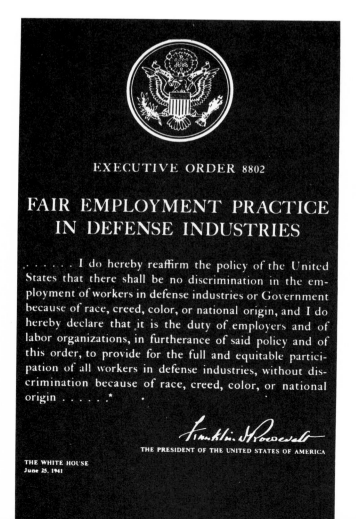

EXECUTIVE ORDER 8802

FAIR EMPLOYMENT PRACTICE IN DEFENSE INDUSTRIES

. . . . I do hereby reaffirm the policy of the United States that there shall be no discrimination in the employment of workers in defense industries or Government because of race, creed, color, or national origin, and I do hereby declare that it is the duty of employers and of labor organizations, in furtherance of said policy and of this order, to provide for the full and equitable participation of all workers in defense industries, without discrimination because of race, creed, color, or national origin . . . . . .*   .

Franklin D Roosevelt
THE PRESIDENT OF THE UNITED STATES OF AMERICA

THE WHITE HOUSE
June 25, 1941

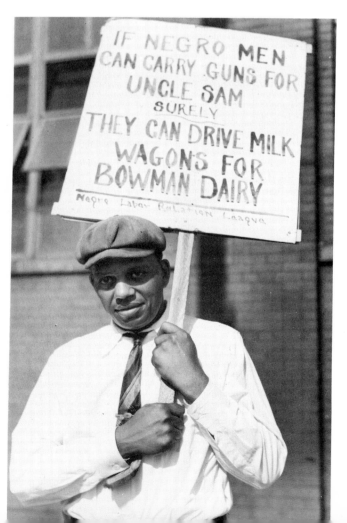

WOMANPOWER

Jobs of many varieties were filled by three million women employed in defense plants, but it was "Rosie the Riveteer" who attained ambiguous fame in songs and cartoons. Another ten million women replaced manpower in non-defense occupations.

They did men's work at the Republic Steel plant in Buffalo.

EMERGENCE OF PHILIP MURRAY

Completely dedicated to the nation's wartime policies, gentle-looking Philip Murray, John L. Lewis' successor as president of the CIO, did his patriotic best to expedite production to the limit of labor's ability.

Almost benign in manner, Murray seemed mild and easy going by comparison with Lewis. In actuality he was a man of hot temper who had learned to control his feelings. Beneath his kindliness was a toughness of spirit and independence of mind that brought him from protege to peer of his predecessor.

Murray was born in Scotland in 1886, the son of a miner. At 10 he went to work in the pits; when he was 16 he and his father—his mother had died years before—came to America and found jobs in the mines near Pittsburgh. When young Phil was 18 he was fired for slugging a check-weighman who was cheating the men; fellow miners not only struck in protest but also elected Murray the head of their local. From then on unionism was his primary interest.

The young Scot's rise in the labor movement was rapid. He became a member of the United Mine Workers executive board at 26 and a district leader at 30. When John L. Lewis was elected president in 1921, he chose Murray for the vice presidency. During the next fifteen years he was at the right hand and almost wholly within the shadow of the nation's flamboyant labor leader. He first emerged into the limelight in 1936, when Lewis placed him in charge of the CIO's

Steel Workers Organizing Committee. The steel companies resisted unionization with all their strength, but Murray developed a highly effective organizing drive that succeeded in signing up a majority of the workers in the major plants—a triumph that stimulated CIO drives in other mass production industries. By May, 1937, Murray was able to announce that SWOC had 325,000 members and contracts with 90 companies. This became the nucleus of the United Steelworkers of America under Murray's presidency.

Following estrangement of relations between President Roosevelt and John L. Lewis (climaxed by the latter's endorsement of Wendell Willkie in 1940) and sharp differences between Lewis and other labor leaders on foreign policy matters, Lewis reluctantly resigned his post as president of the CIO, making way for Murray's election as his successor.

For a while it looked as if Murray's primary function was to serve as surrogate for Lewis but their long friendship was quickly ruptured by their disagreements on wartime policies, amalgamation with the AFL, and other issues. A final break occurred when Lewis took the United Mine Workers out of the CIO.

The Japanese attack on Pearl Harbor convinced Murray that labor should go all-out in its support of the armed forces; Lewis felt that labor could ill afford to sacrifice any of its rights for the sake of a war about which he had misgivings.

On the question of Communist influence in the CIO, Lewis was confident that it could be kept within bounds. Murray had mixed feelings. He was uneasy about the extent to which left-wingers had infiltrated some unions and yet he was loathe to take drastic action against them. "The CIO," he said, "is fundamentally a trade union, but the CIO is fundamentally American. It's not going to be bothered, too much at least, by ideological mumblings of groups that are hell bent upon destroying it. No, it will stand on its record, one of supporting wholeheartedly all of the United States of America."

WARTIME SIDELIGHTS

Top: Philip Murray, Secretary of the Treasury Henry Morgenthau and William Green strip for action at a war bond rally.

Center: A battered piano undergoes crushing strain at the hands of R. J. Thomas, president of the United Automobile Workers, while Sherman Dalrymple, head of the United Rubber Workers, and David McDonald, president of the United Steel Workers, join in an impromptu recital during their tour of European war fronts.

Bottom: Hastily built huts served as temporary field offices near wartime plants. This photo was taken at Childersburg, Alabama.

Sporadic strikes erupted in some defense plants when grievances couldn't be settled through collective bargaining negotiations. At the top is a photograph taken at a North American Aviation plant in June, 1941. Below are scenes outside an aircraft component factory in Bendix, New Jersey.

"You New Dealers, you!" blurted Sewell Avery, head of Montgomery Ward, when he was forcibly removed from the premises because of his refusal to comply with the rulings of the National War Labor Board in 1944. Many employers shared his resentment of governmental power to enforce compliance with labor relations laws but the general consensus was to observe the laws rather than undermine the privileges of private enterprise. Montgomery Ward was run by the Army until the end of the war.

Conscious of their new found political clout, workers were becoming a potent force on local, state, and national levels. If in previous periods of American history they lacked cohesiveness at election time, now they were outspoken power brokers in the democratic process. Below is a photo of President Roosevelt addressing the Teamsters Union convention in 1940; it was on this occasion that he derided Republicans who were trying to make "Fala," his scotch terrier, a serious campaign issue.

President Franklin D. Roosevelt
ADDRESSING THE
FOURTEENTH CONVENTION INTERNATIONAL BROTHERHOOD OF
TEAMSTERS, CHAUFFEURS, STABLEMEN AND HELPERS
OF AMERICA
SEPTEMBER 11, 1940   WASHINGTON, D. C.

POLITICAL MUSCLE POWER

Organized labor was emerging as a major political force. During the 1936 campaign acrimony between the AFL and the CIO was set aside in a massive drive to assure continuation of New Deal policies through President Roosevelt's reelection. Labor's Non-Partisan League, a CIO off-shoot, spearheaded the drive with the help of AFL unions although the AFL executive council withheld its cooperation. The pressure exerted by the League nationally and by the American Labor Party in New York demonstrated that labor had considerable electoral muscle.

In subsequent campaigns the labor vote was to have a decisive influence in industrial states like New York, Pennsylvania, and Michigan. Democratic triumphs during the 1930's and 1940's were substantially due to CIO and AFL support, but while the former was aggressively partisan, the latter held fast to its tradition of rewarding labor's friends (mostly Democrats) and punishing its enemies (mostly Republicans) on an individual basis.

The accompanying illustrations show pamphlets and cartoons disseminated by the CIO's Political Action Committee during the 1940's.

DEMOBILIZATION TROUBLES ESCALATE

Post-war readjustments left many merchant seamen and ex-servicemen jobless despite promises that they would receive preferential reemployment treatment. Many companies shut down temporarily because of reconversion problems; a large number slashed the workweek to forty hours and hundreds of thousands of workers suddenly found themselves with substantial cuts in take-home pay. Below is a photo taken during a strike of packinghouse workers in Kansas City. Leslie Orear is seen addressing a demonstration attended by war veterans who still wore their uniforms. A threat to call out the State Guard angered the men.

Combating post-war inflationary trends placed labor in a difficult position. Constantly rising prices wiped out earlier gains and lowered living standards; this became the basis for higher wage demands that were quickly followed by further price rises. Inflation was also a menace to farmers who found they were being fleeced by wholesalers.

Some unions joined with farmers in selling fruits and vegetables directly to consumers. A few unions marketed canned goods through co-operative arrangements set up for the benefit of members. Wives of workers were encouraged to boycott chain stores that were making huge profits at the expense of consumers.

"To stop inflation is everybody's business," Boris Shishkin, AFL economist, pointed out. "On the stable value of the dollar depends the future worth of our savings, pensions and insurance policies. Much more depends on it: the future stability and growth of our country; even the future of the free world. If inflation is to be stopped, sacrifices are inevitable. But inflation controls will not work unless the anti-inflation program is even-handed. No group of people will be willing to give up things they need when they see others enriching themselves at the same time."

VICTIMS OF
STRIKEBREAKING

Most differences with employers were being settled in executive suites but strike-breaking violence continued to rear its ugly head.

New York's clothing industry ground to a halt when thousands poured into the streets to pay homage to William Lurye, an organizer of the International Ladies Garment Workers who was fatally stabbed during a strike in which employer-hired thugs assaulted union pickets. More than 25,000 persons participated in the funeral cortege.

Fellow packinghouse workers are seen at the side as they accompanied the body of Edward Hucks to his grave. He was shot by a scab during a strike against the Armour Company in 1948.

PICKETING WITH A DIFFERENCE

Breaking sharply with tradition, strikers were using show business techniques to publicize their grievances and demands. Pictures like these, inspired by enterprising press agentry, made it evident that trade unions were keeping up with the times.

Men Who Draw Walt Disney's Animated Cartoons Report Their Own Strike

Disney as his men see him—unhappy because strike is success.

The fellows and girls who draw Mickey Mouse, Donald Duck, and Snow White make less than house painters. Most of them are paid $16 to $20 a week. They formed a union to improve their pay, but, they'll tell you, their boss, Walt Disney, fired many of the leading unionists. So 450 (out of 600) walked out May 28.

They're striking for the same things that steel workers, coal miners, and machinists strike for: more money, shorter hours, and some voice in how their employer shall treat them.

Disney said production was increasing because strike gave him chance to get rid of "deadwood" he hired out of kindheartedness.

Under mask of American Society of Screen Cartoonists, strikers claim is a company union.

Nothing to it, says Walt Owl, through his publicity department.

How a guy feels the first time he pickets. Most strikers were never union members before.

Screen Cartoon Guild takes hard road of organization, leaving alleged company union.

Oh, for the life of a Disney animator, as the public imagines it. Oh, for the life of a Disney animator, as is—without benefit of union protection.

Possibly this reveals the strikers' hopes their numbers will multiply.

The seven dwarfs can whistle at work, but not Disney girls. Discipline is strict.

MICKEY MOUSING

A new variation of strike pressure was applied by members of the Screen Cartoonists Guild who sought higher wages from the Walt Disney studios. Quipped acerbic Dorothy Parker in a telegram to the strikers: "Don't let Mickey Mouse become a rat." Picket lines included dogs, donkeys, and Hollywood actresses. The Guild was an affiliate of the Brotherhood of Painters and Paperhangers.

NATIONWIDE SHUTDOWN STRATEGY

As these pictures suggest, the vast reach of union power after World War II could tie up industries all across the nation. During an unparalleled wave of strikes in 1946 almost every major industry was shut down by strikes lasting from a few days to several months. Below are some of the 120,000 east coast shipyard workers who went on strike in the spring of 1947. Above are trains stalled in Chicago in 1950.

Strife continued to erupt as employers resisted demands for higher wages. In Philadelphia (above) General Electric workers clashed with police seeking to enforce a court injunction prohibiting mass picketing.

In Dayton (below) the Ohio National Guard was called out to break picket lines at the Univis Lens plant; armored tanks were used to disrupt a demonstration near the factory gates.

THE "ABHORRENT" TAFT-HARTLEY RESTRICTIONS

Powerful anti-union sentiment among employers and alarm over postwar strikes contributed to passage in 1947 of the Taft-Hartley Act by a Republican-controlled Congress despite strenuous objections by labor and a bluntly worded veto by President Truman.

Sponsors Senator Robert Taft and Representative Fred Hartley contended that although the National Labor Relations Act had been passed to aid unions in maintaining a balance of rights and responsibilities between workers and employers, the balance had been upset by union practices injurious to management. As a result, they argued, the opportunities for economic progress and the creation of new jobs had been severely hampered. Public opinion polls simultaneously showed that the public at large was apprehensive about the militancy of labor's rank-and-file and the seeming lack of responsibility by its leaders.

Some of the most important collective bargaining rights unions obtained under the New Deal were banned or circumscribed by the Taft-Hartley Act. The closed shop was outlawed and the union shop allowed only if approved by the majority of workers. In addition, the checkoff of union dues, collection of welfare funds, and contract duration provisions were also placed under restrictive regulation.

The concept of striking a "balance" between unions and employers was the basis for the law's prohibition of "unfair labor practices" such as unwillingness to bargain in good faith, secondary boycotts, work stoppages because of jurisdictional disputes, and excessive union initiation fees. Employers as well as workers were permitted to appeal to the National Labor Relations Board for action against unions charged with such practices. Some abuses became subject to penalization by court action and one section of the act (14b) allowed the states to control union membership requirements.

Special rules written into the Taft-Hartley Act were expressly designed to discourage strikes considered injurious to public health or safety. In the case of such conflicts the President was authorized to intervene via boards of inquiry. Moreover, the law sanctioned court injunctions which could postpone work stoppages for several months.

The Taft-Hartley Act also required unions to file with the Labor Department their constitutions, by-laws, and financial statements. In addition it became obligatory for union officers to sign affidavits stating they were not members of any Communist organizations.

Predictably, union opposition to the Taft-Hartley Act was intense. Outright repeal of this "slave labor statute" became a major goal. But even revision of the law was difficult to obtain, partly because of the problem of reconciling the views of those who were fearful of going too far in modifying the measure with the opinions of those who felt that amendments would not satisfy their objections. By 1951, however, practical circumstances brought about general disregard of the requirement that elections be held to validate union-shop agreements. Legislative elimination of the requirement followed.

Some states, particularly in the South, went substantially beyond Taft-Hartley Act restrictions by enacting laws prohibiting not only closed shop contracts but also union-shop agreements, maintenance-of-membership clauses, and related forms of union security. Euphemistically such measures were justified as "right to work" laws, but union officials denounced them as "right to wreck" laws.

COUNTERPOINT

After failure of efforts to secure repeal of the Taft-Hartley Act (passed by a Republican-dominated Congress over a veto by President Truman), AFL and CIO unions concentrated their energies on wiping out Section 14b, which gave the states the right to outlaw union shop contracts.

Labor's support of Truman was a major factor in his unexpected election in 1948, but elimination of objectionable features of the Taft-Hartley Act remained unattainable.

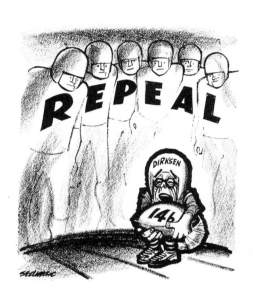

TRUMAN IN TUNE

Some discordant notes occasionally marred President Truman's relations with labor but on the whole the music they played was harmonious. He was not unappreciative of the main source of the support that made spectacular his defeat of Thomas Dewey in 1948. When asked what brought him victory, he remarked: "Labor did it." But when the CIO held its fifteenth convention in November 1952 the election of General Eisenhower demonstrated that labor couldn't do for Adlai Stevenson what it had done for Truman.

The photo at the side was taken at an impromptu concert Truman and James Petrillo, head of the American Federation of Musicians, gave in June 1954. The union presented the ex-President with the piano and honorary lifetime membership.

THE REUTHER STORY

Boyish-looking Walter Reuther, successor of Philip Murray as the head of the CIO, brought to the organization the qualities of a cool but determined fighter for labor's rights, a shrewd negotiator, and an evangelistic social reformer.

The son of a German immigrant who headed the Ohio Valley Trades and Labor Assembly, Reuther was born, appropriately enough, on the eve of Labor Day in 1907. Since there were five children in his family it was necessary for him to drop out of high school and become an apprentice toolmaker. At 19 he landed a job on the 13-hour midnight shift of the Briggs factory in Detroit.

In 1932, in the midst of the Great Depression, he was laid off by Ford because of his union activities. He and his brother Victor decided this was a good time to see the world; they set out on a trip that lasted until 1935 and included a two year stint in a tractor plant in Soviet Russia. When they returned to the U. S., Walter became an organizer for the United Automobile Workers, got elected to the executive board, and helped lead the Detroit and Flint sit-down strikes that culminated in recognition of the UAW. It was during an organizing drive at Ford's River Rouge plant that he and Richard Frankensteen were beaten up by Ford agents in the "Battle of the Overpass."

When war came and the auto industry turned to the manufacture of airplanes and tanks, Reuther became a key figure in the UAW and CIO. His plan for production of "500 planes a day" was widely publicized as an example of the valuable role unions could perform. With the return of peace he led a fight to eliminate Communist infiltration of the UAW and was elected president of the union.

In the course of his rapid rise in the labor movement, Reuther was especially astute as a strike strategist who insisted that industry could afford to raise wages without increasing prices. His "Let's take a look at the books" approach irritated businessmen but impressed the public as a means of making collective bargaining more equitable. A direct result was General Motors' acceptance of a cost-of-living escalator protecting the buying power of the workers' paycheck.

But it was in 1955 that Reuther accomplished his greatest achievement—an agreement by the Ford Motor Company to establish a system of supplemental unemployment benefits providing for payments during lay-off periods. In effect, a guaranteed annual wage was established. By 1967 a Ford worker could collect 95% of his weekly pay for up to a year if he got a layoff slip. General Motors and Chrysler made similar concessions.

In the adjoining photos Reuther is seen with union associates (center) and George Meany, William Green's successor as the head of AFL (bottom).

RACKETEERING
REARS ITS HEAD

Disclosure of racketeering and corruption in some unions gave organized labor in general a black eye it could ill afford.

Revelations by the McClellan Committee — the Senate's "Select Committee on Improper Activities in the Labor or Management Field" headed by Senator John McClellan in the late 1950's—brought to light practices more sordid than labor's severest critics had suspected. While some union officers questioned by the committee dodged behind the Fifth Amendment's protection against self-incrimination, testimony by other witnesses placed on the record damaging evidence of rigged elections, misuse of union funds, kickbacks. There also emerged evidence that some employers preferred to collaborate with racketeers rather than bargain over legitimate trade union demands.

A critic of the McClellan Committee charged that it conducted its hearings "with the soft delicacy of ten brass bands and a steam calliope" but a direct result of its revelations was a massive effort by the AFL-CIO to eliminate racketeering practices.

While waging a drive against mobsters, Joseph Curran (left), president of the National Maritime Union, found himself the target of threats upon his life.

HOFFA
VS. KENNEDY

Heated words passed between stocky Teamster vice president Jimmy Hoffa and youthful Robert F. Kennedy during the McClellan Committee investigation. As chief counsel for the committee, Kennedy subjected Hoffa and president Dave Beck (left) to relentless grilling.

Despite all the unfavorable publicity heaped on Hoffa, he succeeded Beck as head of the Teamsters Union. Under his leadership, the union launched aggressive organization drives among workers in related industries.

FROM HOURLY PAY TO
GUARANTEED ANNUAL WAGES

Espoused by the Steelworkers as a "post-war imperative," the guaranteed minimal annual wage plan was greeted with little enthusiasm by either employers or Fair Dealers. Much to labor's surprise, however, Wendell Willkie, president of the billion-dollar Commonwealth and Southern Corporation, gave the principle of the plan his blessing: "An annual wage to those who work in plants with long seasonal or periodic shutdowns seems fair and necessary . . . Our post-war economy must be built on a high wage level if we hope to furnish a market for the goods of an expanding peace-time production. Our wheels can keep turning only if our workers can keep spending."

By 1955 a firm beachhead was established by the United Auto Workers in Ford and General Motors contracts providing for company contributions to a trust fund supplementing unemployment payments to laid-off workers. About the same time, unions in other industries obtained similar concessions.

(Don Herold's critical cartoon appeared in a YMCA pamphlet prepared for employees of the American Cast Iron Pipe Company.)

TIES WITH WORKERS OF OTHER LANDS

Interest in world affairs, intensified by post-war problems, found expression in the role played by both the AFL and the CIO in the establishment of the International Confederation of Free Trade Unions. Delegates from fifty-one countries representing unions with nearly fifty million members attended the Confederation's first meeting in 1949.

American unions became particularly active in implementation of the Marshall Plan offering war-torn countries rehabilitation aid and helped bolster trade union movements throughout the world.

Paul Hoffman, an administrator of the Marshall Plan, is seen (above) conferring with George Meany, Matthew Woll, and William Green.

GEORGE MEANY TAKES OVER

From the moment burly George Meany became the president of the American Federation of Labor in December, 1952, there wasn't any doubt that he had tight control of the reins of power.

He brooked no interference when Teamster president Daniel Tobin objected to the selection of William Schnitzler as the federation's secretary-treasurer. And when William Hutcheson, head of the Carpenters' Brotherhood, merely hinted he might resign from the AFL executive council because of a jurisdictional controversy, Meany didn't flinch. He accepted Hutcheson's resignation with a whack of the gavel. A much stronger personality than William Green, he has exerted his power without equivocation.

George Meany grew up in a trade union atmosphere. His father headed a large plumber's local in New York — and a large family (ten children). When economic circumstances forced George to leave high school, he became a plumber's apprentice.

Seven years after he earned his journeyman's certificate his local elected him its business agent; subsequently his rise within the AFL was "as steady and sure as the plumbing skills of his old trade." He became successively secretary-treasurer of the New York Building Trades Council (1923), president of the New York State Federation of Labor (1934), and secretary-treasurer of the AFL (1939). The conscientious service he rendered in these posts cleared the way to his selection as William Green's successor.

As a lad of eight, Meany already had a reputation for being "strongwilled and even somewhat rambunctious." Below he is seen with his family shortly before he became the head of the AFL.

556

CREATION OF THE AFL-CIO

Amalgamation of the American Federation of Labor and the Congress of Industrial Organizations on December 5, 1955, marked the end of longstanding antagonisms and the establishment of a united front of 15,000,000 wage earners.

The drive for consolidation of the two federations, previously thwarted many times by unyielding attitudes and problems, was set on course by George Meany and Walter Reuther shortly after they assumed leadership of their respective organizations.

The foundation for unity was laid with the negotiation of a no-raiding pact stipulating that AFL and CIO unions would not recruit members already affiliated with either organization. By February 1955 the basis for merger was spelled out in a constitution approved by conventions of both federations at the end of the year.

AFL president Meany and AFL secretary-treasurer William Schnitzler were elected president and secretary-treasurer of the combined federation.

Primary objectives of the new organization, as set forth in its constitution, included these aims:

• Aid workers in securing improved wages, hours, and working conditions with due regard for the autonomy and integrity of affiliated unions.

• Promote the organization of the unorganized into unions of their own choosing, giving recognition to both craft and industrial unionism.

• Encourage formation of locals, state and local central bodies, and nationals, and affiliation of such organizations with the new federation.

• Encourage all workers without regard to race, creed, or national origin to share in the full benefits of unionism.

• Secure legislation safeguarding and promoting the principle of free collective bargaining.

• Protect and strengthen the nation's democratic institutions.

• Promote the cause of peace and freedom throughout the world.

• Preserve and maintain the integrity of each affiliated union in the organization.

• Encourage the sale and use of union-made goods and union services.

• Protect the labor movement from corrupt influences and the undermining effect of communist groups opposed to the basic principles of democracy.

• Safeguard the democratic character of the labor movement.

• Encourage workers to register and vote and exercise their full rights and responsibilities.

CIO unions constituted the nucleus of an Industrial Department formed to promote the interests and deal with the problems of unions organized on an industrial basis. The department took its place alongside existing AFL departments—building and construction trades, metal trades, union label and service trades, maritime trades, and railroad workers.

557

President Eisenhower helped President Meany lay the cornerstone for the new home of the AFL-CIO, erected only a few hundred feet away from the White House. A united labor movement was a thriving reality when the attractively appointed edifice, built at a cost of $4 million, opened its doors on June 4, 1956. For members of the expanded AFL-CIO executive council (seated below) the new building represented in Meany's words, "a monument to past achievement as well as an instrumentality for future progress."

ZENITH OF POWER: 1955-1972

The merger of the AFL and CIO in 1955 was described by the journalists who reported it to the nation as "the biggest news story in labor history." Indeed it was. The merger constituted a brilliant series of compromises and initiatives. It overcame deep-seated hostilities and jealousies—some personal or political, some organizational or functional. To those who feared the rise of a "monolithic colossus" within the power structure of the nation, the merger was a cause of anxiety. To others, the coming together of all branches of the labor movement into a single organization suggested the time had arrived for bold new efforts at social and economic progress . . . efforts buttressed by the new power of the AFL-CIO.

The preamble of the constitution of the new federation seemed to reflect recognition both of these fears and of these wishes. It talked about the merger as the "expression of the hopes and aspirations of the working people of America," and it pledged the AFL-CIO to a program of militant action on many fronts. But the preamble carefully stated that these objectives of the union federation would be sought "within the framework of our constitutional government and consistent with our institutions and traditions," and it pledged it would "combat resolutely" those who seek to "undermine . . . democratic institutions".

George Meany's closing words to the AFL-CIO's founding convention in December 1955 played upon the same twin theme of militancy and restraint. "This is not going to be any milk toast movement," Meany said. In his view, it would use "every legal means . . . to organize the unorganized," it would be a determined organization: "no little men with loud voices in either political or industrial life are going to turn us aside." Yet, he pointed out, while the convention had reiterated the "traditional objective of the labor movement" to improve the conditions of working people, the AFL-CIO would not seek to achieve this advance "at the expense of our neighbors." Rather, labor would make "our full contribution to the welfare of our neighbors, to the communities in which we live, and to the nation as a whole."

The same theme—that a labor movement of enhanced numbers and presumably increased power must

Above are members of the executive council elected by the first AFL-CIO convention in 1955. Seated, left to right, are Harry Bates, James Petrillo, David Dubinsky, Matthew Woll, secretary-treasurer William Schnitzler, president George Meany, Walter Reuther, George Harrison, David McDonald and James Carey. In the second row are A. Philip Randolph, Maurice Hutcheson, Dave Beck, A.J. Hayes, William Doherty, Charles MacGowan, William McFetridge, A. L. Spradling, Jacob Potofsky, and Willard Townsend. In the back are O. A. Knight, Joseph Beirne, Richard Walsh, L. S. Buckmaster, Herman Winter, Emil Rieve, Joseph Curran and William Birthright.

work with, rather than intimidate, the national community—was stressed by Arthur J. Goldberg, then special counsel to the AFL-CIO, later to become Secretary of Labor in the Kennedy cabinet, a justice of the Supreme Court and ambassador to the United Nations. In his book, "AFL-CIO—Labor United," Goldberg wrote:

"American unions have rapidly emerged from the status of a narrow pressure group into an area of broader interest in the general problems of the nation and the specific community. Where decades ago, union members were apt to be lonely clusters of individuals in an environment almost totally hostile to their organization, labor has succeeded in large degree in throwing off its inferiority complexes and its old suspicion of 'outsiders'. Some observers have talked about the emergence of labor as a new middle class. I am not certain that this characterization is technically correct. But it is true that the members of the AFL and CIO have become first-class citizens where once they were more apt to be regarded as merely the people on the wrong side of the tracks . . . Continued participation in community affairs will strengthen the status of labor in the various localities and the inevitable effect will be the greater prestige and effectiveness for the unions."

Organized labor in the 1970's is big, it has prestige, it has effectiveness—and within its organizational ranks it accommodates sharply defined differences in attitude, structure, ethics and ideology. Whatever its accomplishments in the 15 years after merger, and they have been many and often significant, the record of the AFL-CIO should certainly have assuaged the worries of those who in 1955 saw in the labor merger the creation of a closely-integrated, highly-disciplined power bloc whose existence would place undue stress on the fabric of the American political system. A power bloc, yes; a disproportionately strong juggernaut, no.

By the 1970's, in fact, the role of the trade union and of labor federation had achieved acceptance as a stable aspect of the nation's economic and social structure. American labor has a status broadly comparable to that of the workers' organizations in such countries as Great Britain, Germany and Sweden, where unions had come into existence and gained recognition substantially earlier than in the U. S.

Acceptance of the role of labor is not the same, of course, as acceptance of the ideas or programs of labor. Whether they agree or disagree, however, a legion of policy makers and administrators—in government, in corporations, in politics, in public organizations and in community life—all recognize that the labor presence is a reality: that it must be acknowledged and considered, that its policy position must be considered even if rejected, that its representation must be accept-

ed and accorded proper status, that in innumerable situations the consent of labor is essential to the creation of an effective consensus. There has been considerable progress towards Samuel Gompers' hopes for acceptance of labor as a respectable segment of the community . . . towards the situation in which the unions, in the words and wishes of George Meany, must function and be recognized as a "people's lobby."

In the real world of American public life, of course, few people and few organizations continuously practice all their ideals. A strong case can be made that in working for consumer legislation, or a federal occupational health and safety law, or the non-confirmation of Mr. Haynesworth and Mr. Carswell to the Supreme Court, the AFL-CIO was indeed functioning as a "people's lobby." On the other hand, the disagreements within the labor movement itself lend strength to the suspicion that on some other legislative matters—the building of a supersonic transport, the loan to the nearly bankrupt Lockheed aircraft corporation, the decision whether or not to build a space shuttle, to cite a few examples—the specific interests of a few unions directly involved constituted a strong, perhaps a dominant, factor in the AFL-CIO's decision-making process.

Despite the frequent internal differences over items of legislation within the leadership ranks of the labor movement, the successes in achieving passage of AFL-CIO supported bills, and of defeating those opposed by the unions, must be regarded as one of the major achievements of the 1955 merger. The record, both in the Congress and in the state legislatures, has indicated that the unifying of what were once rival lobbying campaigns by the AFL and CIO separately, has produced many dividends for the workers.

A second notable success has been the development of the operating mechanism of COPE—the AFL-CIO's Committee on Political Education. Functioning as an arm of the federation, and working—or trying to—in close cooperation with the affiliated unions and state bodies, COPE has helped implant in numerous labor organizations a growing sense of the importance to labor of political action. In a surprisingly large number of communities, the unions' COPE operations are more efficient, more practical, more organized than those of the political parties themselves. COPE appears to be ahead of many other organizations in filling the vacuum left by the disappearance in many parts of urban America of the old political machines.

Yet, if it is conceded that labor's influence and effectiveness have increased since 1955, it must be pointed out that the membership growth of the unions must be considered disappointing, whether measured by the optimistic hopes expressed in speeches at the AFL-CIO merger convention or by contemporary stastics relating to the size of the work force. The growth of the population and the work force has not

Assiduous courtship of labor was to count heavily in favor of John F. Kennedy during his spectacular rise from Congressman to President between 1946 and 1960. As chairman of the Senate Subcommittee on Labor and member of the congressional committee that investigated trade union racketeering he won both recognition and respect that stood him in good stead when he became the nation's chief executive. (Below is a photo of JFK delivering a campaign speech in Detroit's Cadillac Square in 1960.)

been accompanied by a corresponding increase in trade union membership. Indeed, a very heavy growth in unionism among government employees—federal, state and local—starting during the Kennedy administration, has offset what might otherwise have been a decline in union strength.

The efforts, supported strongly by the AFL-CIO, to organize farm workers, reflect persistence and determination, but the tiny island of unionism symbolized by Cesar Chavez' United Farm Workers, emphasizes that only a small step has yet been made—an understandable lack of progress in view of the fierce and often violent opposition of agribusiness.

In large part, the absence of growth among the unions is a direct result of a period of intense innovation within the American corporate system both in technology and structure. Complex machines are now performing thousands of industrial tasks that were once performed by men and women. Industries like coal mining, basic steel, automobile and clothing produce far more goods with far fewer people. Other industries—notably electronics and plastics—have exported capital, managerial skill and technology to other countries, where their employees receive lower wages than American workers.

Through recent decades American unions have struggled to keep abreast of the changes in industry and the changes in the work force—a work force in which the blue collar worker, the traditional union member, has declined in number to a minority status.

In the past two decades, for example, graphic arts technology has gone through a more intense series of changes than in all the previous years since Gutenberg invented the press—but unions are still struggling with organizational forms and attitudes created fifty years ago, before this revolution started.

After World War II, the late John L. Lewis decided to cooperate with the mine owners in the introduction of new technology for cutting and extracting coal. The size of the work force plummeted, the wages of the workers remaining on the payroll rose, and the United Mine Workers became in the days after Lewis' death a shrunken caricature of its earlier glory. Does, then, the same fate await other unions, and indeed the AFL-CIO itself, as a result of these continuing changes in the national industrial profile and in the nature of a changing type of work force?

Many unions, perceiving the trends, have moved far beyond their once narrowly defined jurisdictions in the search for members, financial viability and organizational permanence. Thus, the marine engineers association welcomes the air · traffic controllers; the steel union opens its doors to the multi-occupation District 50, which had once been the miscellaneous trades division of the coal mine union. Thus, too, the Service Employees, with strength in building mainte-nance jobs and hospitals, welcomes a union of police officers to its ranks.

The AFL-CIO itself—which its founders envisioned as an all-encompassing organization—has not as yet been able to bring back two of its largest former affiliates: the Teamsters, expelled as "corrupt" during the early days of Jimmy Hoffa reign; or the United Automobile Workers, whose president Walter P. Reuther became increasingly embittered toward the federation during the post-merger years.

Nor has the federation been able to bring into its ranks the many hundreds of thousands of white collar and sub-professional employees who are aligned with organizations like the National Educational Association, the American Nurses Association and other groups which increasingly adapt to their own needs many of the traditional functions of the unions, particularly in the fields of collective bargaining and grievance settlement. The adherence of organizations like these to the AFL-CIO would symbolize the ability of American labor to walk new paths and achieve new patterns of membership affiliation.

The dilemma, and the need, have been clearly expressed by Joseph A. Beirne, who as head of the Communications Workers has had a front row seat from which to observe both the many aspects of the technology revolution that have occurred in the communications industry and the sociological revolution which has brought to his union many persons with a middle class viewpoint—people who, a generation or two ago, might well have recoiled from any contact with 'labor.'

Mr. Beirne sees the unions facing a major challenge: "to rise above structural limitations, bargaining procedures too often obsolescent, and attitudes shaped a generation or more ago. Successful adjustment to change will permit American labor in the years that lie ahead to fulfill its responsibility not only to its members but to the whole nation."

Is American labor capable of committing itself to the kinds of adjustment that so many observers believe will be neccessary during the last three decades of the century? Will the flexibility required to make these adjustments permit a preservation of the traditional values that have given the unions strength and the ability to grow in years past? Can the unions, in finding a niche in the nation's decision-making machinery, preserve the sense of militancy and of humanism that were their notable characteristics in the past?

It is clear that the ability of American labor—essentially, the AFL-CIO—to adapt successfully to the changes that are taking place in the economy and in the political system will measure its potential for survival, growth and service to the nation as a whole. On balance the record offers grounds for cautious optimism in the years ahead. —HENRY C. FLEISHER

News of President Kennedy's tragic death was a stunning blow to workers who felt they had lost "a leader...who gave the nation a new sense of faith in democratic idealism." Below at left is a photo of the President addressing the AFL-CIO convention a few days before his assassination. In the picture at the right Mrs. Kennedy is seen receiving from George Meany a tribute to her husband in which the AFL-CIO pledged to build the world envisioned by New Frontier policies. Attorney General Robert F. Kennedy is at Mrs. Kennedy's side.

Although initially skeptical toward Lyndon B. Johnson when he assumed the Presidency, labor rallied to his support when he laid the groundwork for a revival of Franklin Roosevelt's New Deal through his war on poverty, medicare and medicaid programs, civil rights measures, and improvements in minimum wage and social security benefits.

In the adjoining photos President Johnson is seen addressing New York labor leaders and watching David Dubinsky demonstrate his skill as a garment trade worker.

At the bottom right are four Secretaries of Labor—James Mitchell (1953-59), Frances Perkins (1933-45), Arthur Goldberg (1960-62), and Willard Wirtz (1962-68)—who celebrated the 50th anniversary of the Labor Department in March 1963.

Steady gains were made by labor during the Johnson and Kennedy administrations. Total union membership rose from 16.3 million in 1961 to 17.9 in 1968.

"Huelga!" (Strike!) became the rallying cry for the unionization of agricultural workers under the banner of the United Farm Workers Organizing Committee. Led by Cesar Chavez (center in photo below), the committee's drive promised better conditions and higher wages for countless thousands of men and women who for years had been mistreated by employers and virtually ignored by the labor movement. During the summer of 1972 the committee's organizing efforts were intensified in southern and southwestern states.

Mounting black pressure on both employers and unions made it difficult to disregard the fact that racial discrimination remained a vexing problem of the 1970's despite civil rights laws and presidential executive orders assuring Negroes full equality with Whitey. Employers boasted they were hiring more blacks than ever before but Negro unemployment continued to increase. Labor leaders could brag that 1.5 million blacks were

union members but in some trades discrimination continued to persist.

An effective Negro-labor coalition was in the making at the time of the tragic death of Dr. Martin Luther King, Jr. "Negroes are almost entirely a working people," he declared shortly before his assassination. "Our needs are identical with labor's needs—decent wages, fair working conditions, livable housing, old age security, health and welfare measures, conditions in which families can grow, have education for their children and respect in the community.

"That is why Negroes support labor's demands and fight laws which curb labor. That is why the labor-hater and labor-baiter is virtually always a twin-headed creature spewing anti-Negro epithets from one mouth and anti-labor propaganda from the other mouth . . .

"The two most dynamic and cohesive liberal forces in the country are the labor movement and the Negro freedom movement . . . I look forward confidently to the day when all who work for a living will be one, with no thought to their separateness as Negroes, Jews, Italians or any other distinctions.

"This will be the day when we shall bring into full realization the American dream—a dream yet unfulfilled. A dream of equality of opportunity, of privilege and property widely distributed; a dream of a land where men will not take necessities from the many to give luxuries to the few . . ."

At the side are South Carolina hospital workers celebrating a strike victory in June 1969 .

As the elections of 1972 approached, Nixon's courtship of labor appeared to have borne some fruit but it was unlikely that he would be the beneficiary of the neutral stance taken by the AFL-CIO shortly after the Democratic convention nominated Senator George McGovern for the Presidency. Acting on their own, a substantial number of unions threw their support behind the McGovern ticket in their determination to prevent the reelection of President Nixon and the continuation of his Republican policies.

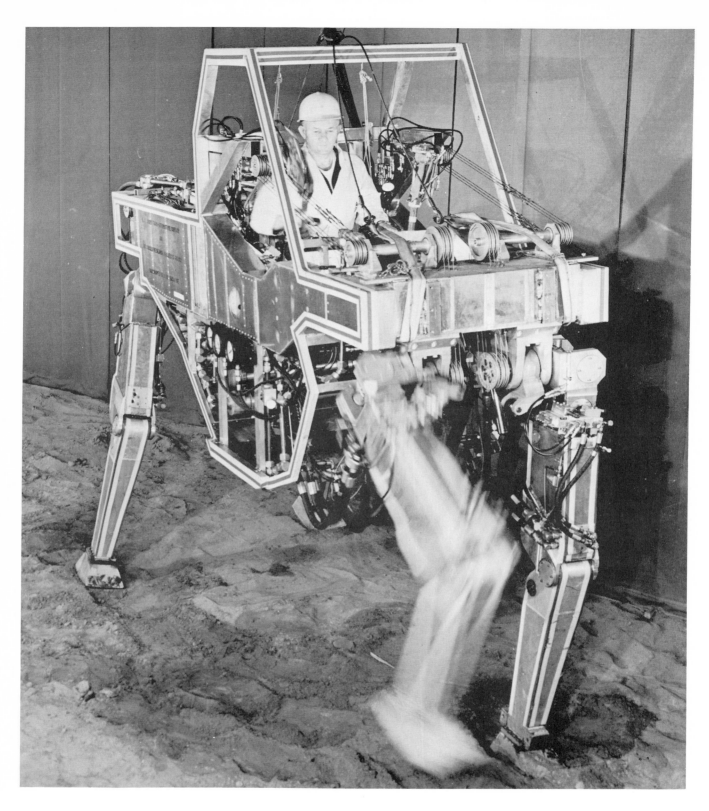

While the economy fumbled its way into the 1970's, technological ingenuity seemed to devour more jobs than it created and a variety of other factors contributed to large scale unemployment. The least trained and least experienced workers were especially hard hit but dramatic changes in major industries were also eliminating the jobs of skilled blue collar workers. Increasingly unions were shifting their bargaining emphasis to employment security and cushions against economic uncertainties. (Above is a General Electric walking machine capable of lifting or pushing aside hundreds of pounds of material.)

CREDITS

ABBREVIATIONS

AAR—Association of American Railroads (Washington, D.C.)

ACW—Amalgamated Clothing Workers (N.Y.C.)

AD—U.S. Department of Agriculture (Washington, D.C.)

AFL—American Federation of Labor and Congress of Industrial Organizations (Washington, D.C.)

AMC—Amalgamated Meat Cutters (Chicago)

AN—Acme Newspictures (N.Y.C.)

ANG—American Newspaper Guild (Washington, D.C.)

AY—Art Young: His Life and Times by Art Young, 1939

BA—Bettman Archives (N.Y.C.)

BB—Brown Brothers (N.Y.C.)

BC—Mill Town by Bill Cahn, 1954

BL—Bancroft Library, University of California (Berkeley)

BM—U.S. Bureau of Mines, Department of Interior (Washington, D.C.)

BSW—Boot and Shoe Workers' Union (Boston)

CAL—California Historical Society (San Francisco)

CHS—Chicago Historical Society

CP—Culver Pictures (N.Y.C.)

CUL—Catholic University Library (Washington, D.C.)

EBA—History of the Last Quarter-Century by E. Benjamin Andrews, 1895

EL—Edith LaFrancis

FDR—Franklin D. Roosevelt Library (Hyde Park, N.Y.)

GEH—George Eastman House (Rochester, N.Y.)

HSP—Historical Society of Pennsylvania (Philadelphia)

HW—Harpers Weekly

IAM—International Association of Machinists (Washington, D.C.)

IBEW—International Brotherhood of Electrical Workers (Washington, D.C.)

IBT—International Brotherhood of Teamsters (Washington, D.C.)

ILGWU — International Ladies Garment Workers Union (N.Y.C.)

INP—International News Photos (N.Y.C.)

IWW—Industrial Workers of the World (Chicago)

JRC—A Documentary History of American Industrial Society edited by John R. Commons, 1910

JU—Judge

LA—Labor Age

LC—Library of Congress (Washington, D.C.)

LD—U.S. Department of Labor (Washington, D.C.)

LIW—Leslie's Illustrated Weekly

LHA—Labor History Archives, Wayne State University (Detroit)

LPA—Labor Press Associates (Washington, D.C.)

MBS—M. B. Schnapper (author's collection)

MHS—Massachusetts Historical Society (Boston)

MLS—Eyes on the World by M. Lincoln Schuster, 1935

MMA—Metropolitan Museum of Art (N.Y.C.)

NA—National Archives (Washington, D.C.)

NLRB—National Labor Relations Board (Washington, D.C.)

NMU—National Maritime Union (N.Y.C.)

NYC—Museum of the City of New York

NYA—New York American

NYHS—New York Historical Society (N.Y.C.)

NYPL—New York Public Library (N.Y.C.)

PA—Pageant of America edited by Ralph H. Gabriel, 1926

PH—Photo-History Magazine

PU—Puck

SHSW—State Historical Society of Wisconsin (Madison)

TL—Tamiment Library of New York University (N.Y.C.)

UAW—United Auto Workers (Detroit)

UBC—United Brotherhood of Carpenters (Washington, D.C.)

UBW—United Brewery Workers (Cincinnati, Ohio)

UMW—United Mine Workers (Washington, D.C.)

UPI—United Press International (N.Y.C.)

USW—United Steelworkers of America (Pittsburgh)

UTW—United Textile Workers (N.Y.C.)

VHS—Virginia Historical Society (Richmond)

VM—Valentine Museum (Richmond, Va.)

WW—Wide World Photos

The following credits refer to illustrations appearing left to right and top to bottom:

7: Hingham, Mass., Historical Society

8: VHS, HSP

9: VHS, NYPL

10: NYPL

11: LC, PA

12: Boston Public Library

13: MHS

14: HSP

15: American Antiquarian Society

16: SI

17: LC

18: Winterthur Museum, NYHS

19: Maryland Historical Society, American Numismatic Society

20: Arch Mercey

21: The Young Mill-Wright by Oliver Evans, 1795

22: Ballou's Pictorial 5-19-1855, HSP

23: MMA, NYHS

24: AFL

25: LD

26: NYHS, LC

27: NYHS

28: Photo-History Magazine 4-1937, PA

29: Columbia U. Library

30: Historical and Philosophical Society of Ohio, SI

31: NYHS

32: NYPL

33-34: NYHS

35: SI

36: Calif. State Library, Floyd Rinhart, GEH, CAL

37: Tenn. State Library

38: SI, NYPL, CAL

39: NMU, Browne's Whaling Cruise by J. Ross Browne (1846), LC

40: NYC, SI

41: BC

42: SI

43: MBS

44: LD, LC

45: NYPL, McCormick Historical Library

46-47: SI

48: LD

49: JRC, MBS

50: MMA

51: LIW 3-17-1860

52: N.Y. Illustrative Zeitung 3-9-1860, LIW 3-17-1860

53: HW 7-25-1868, Nation's Heritage No. 4 1949

54: Labor History, Fall 1960

55: SI

56: NYPL, HW 6-2-1860

57: U. of Va. Library, LC, SI

58: SI

59: NA

60-63: LC

64: HW 9-4-1869, LC

65-66: AAR

67: SI

68: AAR, Eugene V. Debs Foundation

69: AAR

70: HW 4-10-1886

71: Every Saturday 3-18-1871, LC

72: HW, 1877

73-74: SI

75: Marquette Historical Society

76: HW 9-4-1873, NYPL

77: LC, NYPL

78: LIW 10-12-1878, Paterson, N.J., Public Library

79: Harper's Bazaar 4-18-1868

80: NYPL, HW 1-15-1887

83: TL

84: AFL

85: LIW 9-4-1869 and 9-30-1871

86: International Ass'n of Iron Workers, CUL

87: LC

88: LC, LIW 6-29-1872

89: LC, JRC

90: SHSW

91: HW 5-20-1871

92: PU 8-13-1879, HW 3-4-1871

93: NYPL, LC

94: LIW, 3-9-1872

95: LIW 1-21-1874, HW 9-2-1871

96: LIW 12-15-1884, HW 6-26-1869, 3-10-1877

97: LIW 1-6-1872, SHSW, TL

98: LC, N.Y. Telegraph 2-18-1870

99: NYPL, Cooper Union for the Advancement of Science and Art

100: PU 8-7-1878

101: MHS, TL

102: LC, NYPL

103: PU 4-28-1880, LIW 7-27-1887

104: LIW 7-8-1882

105-06: MBS

107: PU 8-21-1878, EBA, LIW 11-20-1880

108: EBA, HW 4-10-1880

109: CAL

110: MBS

111: LIW 5-6-1871, American Heritage 4-1960

112: Pinkerton's National Detective Agency

113: MBS, EBA, The Molly Maguires by Anthony Bimba (1932)

114: LIW 3-25-1871 and 10-25-1884

115: HW 8-11-1877, LIW 8-11-1877

116: LIW 8-4-1877, MBS

117: HW 8-11-1877, LIW 8-4-1877

118: HW 8-18-1877, LIW 8-11-1877 and 8-4-1877

119: LC, Photo-History Magazine 4-1937, LC

120: HW 7-28-1883

121-23: NYC
124: CHS, Brooklyn Public Library
125: SI, LIW 1-28-1888
126: LIW 7-26-1890
127: LIW 11-3-1888, ILGWU
128-29: CUL
130: LC
131: CUL
132-33: LC
134: CUL
135: CUL, HW 3-24-1888
136-37: CUL
139: PU 6-21-1882
140: CUL, PU 3-16-1887
141: LIW 10-16-1886
142: SI
143: The Burlington Strike by C. H. Salmons (1889)
144: LIW 4-17-1886, HW 4-17-1886, LIW 4-17-1886
145: LIW 4-10-1886, 3-20-1886, 4-7-1888
146: Daily Graphic 7-26-1882, Minneapolis Journal 9-13-1902
147-48: LC
149: LIW 3-13-1886, HW 3-13-1886
150: Century Magazine 4-1893, Dynamite: The Story of Class Violence in America by Louis Adamic (1931)
151: HW 5-15-1886, EBA, LIW 5-15-1886
152: Anarchy and Anarchists by Michael Schaack (1887), LIW 5-15-1886
153: LIW 11-12-1887, AY
154: LIW 10-1-1887, 11-5-1887, 11-12-1887, 11-19-1887
155: LIW 1-19-1887
156: PU 5-12-1886
157: JU 11-28-1908, PU 5-19-1886
158: PU 7-21-1886
159: SHSW, PU 3-9-1887
160: PU 5-11-1887 and 1-2-1884
161: N.Y. World 10-30-1884, HW 11-1 and 10-11-1884
162: PU 8-17-1887, JU 8-27-1887
163: LIW 7-21-1888
164: PU 11-17-1886, JU 6-18-1887
165: PU 10-26-1887
166: PU 5-18-1887
167: JU 1886
168: SHSW
169: LC
170: SI
171: LIW 9-16-1882
172: LC, HW 7-1-1882
173: TL, NYC
174: The Labor Problem of Today edited by George E. McNeill (1888)
175: AFL
176: PU 8-25-1886, HW 6-12-1886
177: PU 12-22-1886
178: PU 3-17 and 4-7-1886

179: PU 2-3-1886
180: MBS
181: JU 2-11-1888
182: LD, NYPL, SI, HW 8-15-1868
183: MBS
184: PU 2-25-1891, LC
185: PU 3-6-1901 and 2-8-1896
186: CUL
187: PU 4-13-1887 and 3-23-1887
188: LC, San Francisco Public Library
189: Illinois State Historical Library
190: LC
191: SHSW, NYPL
192: HW 7-16-1892
193-94: LC
195: HW 7-21 and 7-28-1894
196: LC
197: HW 7-14 and 7-21-1894
198: LC
199: HW 3-18-1894
200: HW 9-23-1893 and 1-13-1894
201: HW 5-5 and 1-18-1894
202-04: LC
205: HSW
206: LC
207: MBS, LC
208: Nebraska Historical Society
209: JU 11-10-1900, MBS, LC, HW 9-12-1908
210: JU 1902, PU 8-19-1896
211: PU 8-31-1892
212: CUL, Coin's Financial School, 1896
213: SI, NYPL
214: SI, SHSW
215: PU 5-5-1886
216: SI, JU 11-3-1888
217: PU 1-25-1888, SI
218: SI, JU 7-1-1899
219: MBS
220: MBS, PU 9-28-1892, MBS
221: HW 9-29-1888
222: NYPL, NYA
223: NYA, JU 1907
224: William Ker, John Barrymore
225: MBS, PU 8-1-1883
226: MBS
227: MBS, PU
228: AFL
229: MBS, LD
230: AFL
231: MBS
232: Chicago Times-Herald 11-28-1897
233: MBS
234: UBC, IBT
235: UBC
236: IBEW, UBW
237: U. of Washington Library, GEH, LC
238: LHA, MBS, LHA
239-40: MBS
241: MBS, Oregon Historical Society

242: LHA, CUL, MBS, Washington Star 12-1-1930
243: LHA, LC, CHS
244: MBS
245: NYPL, PU 4-28-1886 and 4-14-1886
246-47: MBS
248: MBS, LA 5-1923, MBS
249-50: MBS
251: PU 10-16-1895, ILGWU, MBS
252: MBS
253: PU 6-12-1895 and 10-13-1897
254: MBS, PU 2-2-1887
255: MBS
256: SI
257: GEH, MBS, LA 8-1927
258: BM
259: LC, MBS
260: UMW, MBS
261: LIW 1-2-1886 and 2-9-1884, HW 6-17-1871, LIW 3-30-1901 and 9-25-1869
262: LC
263: MBS, N.Y. Journal 6-8-1897
264: BM
265: LC
266: BM, SI
267: Hazleton (Pa.) Public Library, MBS
268: LC
269: BB, SI
270: LC
271: CUL, LC
272: UMW
273: LC
274: MBS
275: UMW, MBS, LC
276-78: LC
279: Cartoons Magazine 1913
280-82: LC
283: DA
284: LC
285: LC, UTW
286: CHS, GEH, CHS
287: NYC
288: MBS, LC, MBS
289: MBS
290: GEH, ACW
291: Philadelphia Museum of Art, LD
292: LC, CUL
293: LC
294: AMC, LC
295: ILGWU, BA
296: ACW, BS
297: NYC
298: ACW
299: ACW, ILGWU
300: LC, NYC
301: ACW, LC
302: NYC
303: CP
304: BA, NYC, LC
305: LC
306: EL
307: LC, ACW
308: EL

309: Massillon (Ohio) Museum
310: IAM, LHA
311: U.S. Steel Corp., LC
312: NYPL, HW 9-26-1891, MBS
313: AFL, EL
314: VM, HSW
315: SI
316: IBEW
317: MBS, LA, Ford Motor Co., LA
318: SI, CHS
319: AD, California Redwood Ass'n.
320: University of Oregon Library, Wine Institute
321-22: LC
323: AD
324-25: VM
326: AD
327: AD, AMC, U. of Indiana Library
328: UBW
329: BSW, LC
330: NYC, LD
331: ACW, MBS, CHS
332: ILGWU, ACW
333: United Hat, Cap and Millinery Workers, MBS
334: BSW, MBS
335: HW 9-11-1878 and 6-16-1900, LIW 8-20-1903
336: MBS, HW 6-1-1901
337: PU 3-31-1886, JU 7-18-1903
338: CP, CHS, MBS
339: Square Deal 2-1906, HW 12-1903
340: LIW 9-21-1889
341: Square Deal 5-1906 and 10-1905, HW 7-1903
342: SHSW
343: MBS, JU 1-25-1902
344: MBS
345: Fred Mazzula, LC
346: SHSW, MBS
347: NYC, BL, BB
348: Chicago Tribune, NYC
349: BL, TL, International Socialist Review 12-1908
350: AY
351: SHSW
352: CP
353: ACW
354: ILGWU
355: CHS, ACW
356: ACW
357: ILGWU, ACW, LC
358-59: ILGWU
360: SHSW, LD, ILGWU
361: CHS, LC
362: ACW, ILGWU
363: ILGWU
364: UMW, Fred Mazzula
365: MBS, UMW
366-67: UMW
368: NA
369-70: UMW
371: MBS, U. of Washington Library

THE AMERICAN TWINS.
"United we stand, Divided we fall."

INDEX

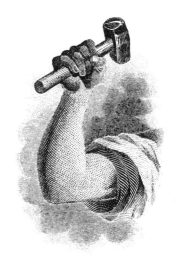

About the Author

M. B. Schnapper, has been a "labor buff" ever since the early 1930's, when he studied labor history and economics under Leo Wolman and Paul Brissenden at Columbia University. His journalistic assignments during the 1930's included coverage of the plight of miners in Kentucky, unemployment demonstrations in New York, the unionization of steel workers in Pittsburgh, and the enactment of New Deal legislation in Washington. Prior to becoming editor of Public Affairs Press in 1938, he served on the staff of President Roosevelt's Committee on Economic Security. He has edited fourteen books on labor subjects and has contributed articles to the *New York Times* magazine section, the *Washington Post, The Nation,* the *Christian Science Monitor,* and other publication'